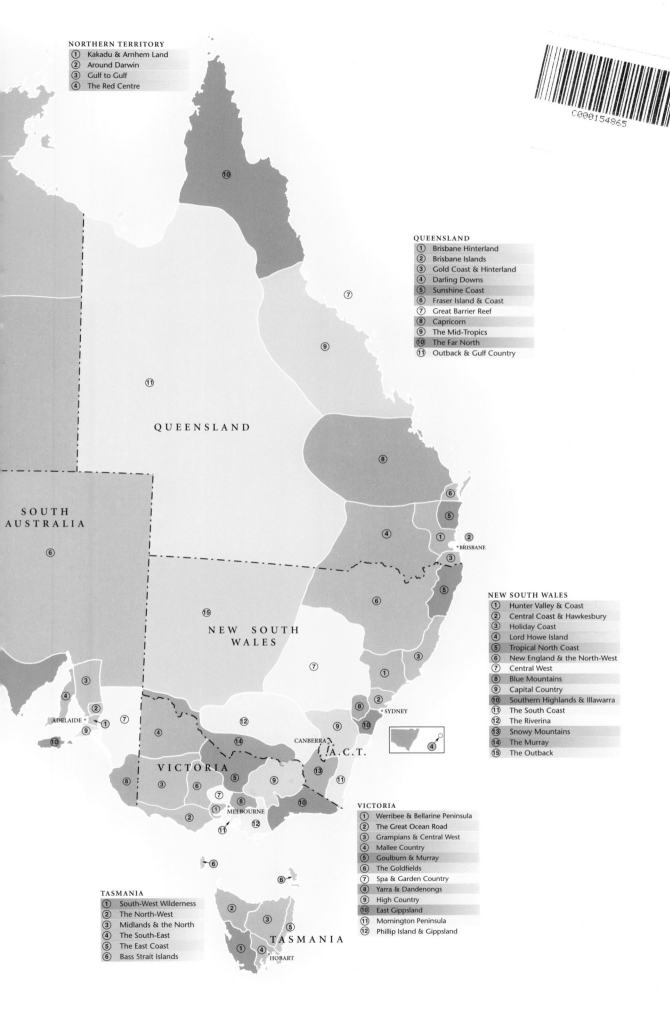

NORTHERN TERRITORY

QUEENSLAND

SOUTH AUSTRALIA

NEW SOUTH WALES

VICTORIA

TASMANIA

BRISBANE

SYDNEY

CANBERRA

A.C.T.

MELBOURNE

ADELAIDE

HOBART

# THE AUSTRALIAN
# TOURING
# COMPANION

EXPLORE AUSTRALIA

# Contents

# JOURNEY THROUGH AUSTRALIA

AUSTRALIA is a small, modern nation in a vast, ancient land. Covering an area the size of Europe, Australia is the world's largest island continent. It is also the oldest, flattest and – with the exception of Antarctica – the driest place on earth. For about 70 000 years the continent was the preserve of around 600 groups collectively known as Aboriginal people. Theirs was the longest continuous occupation in human history. The British settled the east coast in 1788. In the last two hundred years the colonial prison outpost they established has been transformed into a nation of nearly 20 million people.

**FACT FILE**

*Total land area:* 7 692 030 sq km

*Length of coastline including islands:* 59 740 km

*Number of beaches:* 7000

*Longest river:* Murray River – 2520 km

*Highest mountain:* Mount Kosciuszko – 2228 m

*Largest lake:* Lake Eyre – 9500 sq km

*Hottest town:* Marble Bar, WA – av. summer max. 41°C

*Coldest region:* Australian Alps – av. winter min. 5°C

*Wettest place:* Tully, Qld – av. annual median 4048 mm

*Population:* 19 500 000

*Indigenous population:* 427 000

*Population born overseas:* 24 per cent

*Population residing in capital cities:* 60 per cent

### Land of contrast

The vast outback of red earth, vivid skies, weathered mountains and searing heat is unmistakably Australian. This landscape is a source of myth and legend for the first inhabitants and a symbol of the hardships endured by the early white settlers. In contrast, the lushly vegetated east coast, including the island of Tasmania, is a place of rugged peaks, wild rivers, waterfalls and ancient rainforests. Eucalypt forests, wetlands, river plains, snowfields and almost 60 000 kilometres of beaches, coastal cliffs, islands and reefs are other features that contribute to the complex story of the Australian landscape.

### Unique wildlife

Much of the flora and fauna is unique and, like the landscape, extremely varied. The gum is the dominant tree in what is known colloquially as the bush, and boasts five hundred species alone. Our highest profile native animals are marsupials, which include the ever popular koalas and kangaroos. Bar a few distant relatives bearing only the slightest family resemblance, there is nothing else like them on Earth.

### Cities on the coast

The harshness of the interior has kept most of the population near the relatively benign coastline. Most Australians live in cities and towns in the south-east and, to a lesser extent, the south-west of the continent. This preference has created unequal population figures across the six States and two Territories that make up a federated nation. Australia's most populated area, the State of New South Wales, has 6 500 000 residents, while the remote Northern Territory is home to just 192 000.

### Relaxed lifestyle

Many Australians enjoy a way of life that is the envy of the rest of the world. Even the large cities, vital and modern as they are, feel relaxed, easy and overwhelmingly friendly. Accessible beaches and a typically sunny, warm climate have resulted in a lifestyle characterised by outdoor living, barbecues, friends and good health.

# INDIGENOUS AUSTRALIA

Australia's indigenous people have the longest continuous history of any people in the world – between 50 000 and 70 000 years. There are two racially distinct groups: the Aboriginal people, who occupied the mainland and Tasmania, and the Torres Strait Islanders, from the islands off the tip of Cape York. At the time of white settlement the estimated 300 000 Aboriginal people comprised around 600 distinct societies. Today, the history of our indigenous people is central to any understanding of what we are as a nation. Increasingly, Aboriginal tourism, with its associated activities, is the most tangible bridge between Australian indigenous culture and the non-indigenous culture of locals and overseas visitors. Experiences of indigenous culture might include a bush tucker tour, travelling to a rock-art site, attendance at a dance performance or a visit to a cultural centre.

### ◄ TROPICAL NORTH QUEENSLAND

The distinctive art of the East Cape peoples in tropical north Queensland survives in the spectacular rock-art galleries near Laura. Near Cairns is the Tjapukai Aboriginal Cultural Park, an excellent centre featuring performance, demonstrations and art. There are flights from Cairns to the Torres Strait Islands; the best time to visit is July (even-numbered years) for the Torres Strait Cultural Festival. *See also: The Far North p. 125.*

### KAKADU, NT ►

The name Kakadu is derived from Gagudju, one of the three traditional owners and now managers of this World Heritage Area. The area – one of the most intensely populated before white settlement – has over 5000 rock-art sites, the largest collection in the world. There are numerous ways to explore the magnificent Aboriginal heritage of this area: start at the Bowali Visitor Centre, with its many historic displays and general tour information. *See also: Kakadu & Arnhem Land p. 100.*

### TASMANIA'S ABORIGINAL PEOPLE

Tasmania's indigenous population, known as Palawa, migrated to the island about 35 000 years ago. On the eve of white settlement their population of over 4000 was divided between nine groups. White settlers drove the Palawa from their hunting grounds by use of violence and the spread of disease. The Black War, as it became known, culminated in the 1830s with the colonial government rounding up the 130 remaining survivors and banishing them to Flinders Island (see *Bass Strait Islands* p. 141). Many of Tasmania's traditional sites, from middens to rock art, lie in protected areas and are not easily accessible. The rich repository of sites in the Tasmanian wilderness played a significant part in the area's World Heritage listing. Kutikina Cave, with evidence of 20 000 years of occupation, can be reached via a rafting tour of the Franklin River.

## ▼ THE OUTBACK, NSW

Lake Mungo is Australia's most significant archaeological site. Burial sites, cooking hearths and campfires, preserved in lunar-like dunes, provide evidence of a period of human occupation dating back 60 000 years. Cultural tours operate from Mildura. Superb rock art is to be found at Mount Grenfell Historic Site (near Cobar), home of the Ngiyampaa, and in Mutawintji National Park, Wiljali country, where the traditional owners conduct regular tours of some of the more than 300 sites. *See also: The Outback p. 37.*

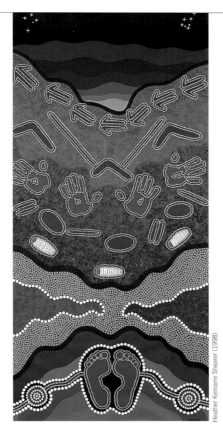

Heather Kemarre Shearer (1998)

## ▲ ADELAIDE, SA

Adelaide is home to two major centres dealing with Aboriginal culture. The Aboriginal-owned and-operated Tandanya houses a permanent collection of art, hosts contemporary art exhibitions and stages performance events. The South Australian Museum is home to the largest collection of Aboriginal cultural materials in the world. These items are presented in a series of sensitive and provocative displays in the new Aboriginal Cultures Gallery. *See also: Adelaide p. 67.*

## ◀ RED CENTRE, NT

The World Heritage Uluru–Kata Tjuta National Park is the traditional land of the Anangu, who help manage tours to art sites and other places of cultural and spiritual significance. To the north, in Alice Springs, which is Arrernte country, are a number of galleries and centres including the award-winning Aboriginal Art and Cultural Centre. Alice is also the base for tours to the surrounding country. *See also: The Red Centre p. 104.*

## FLINDERS RANGES, SA

ese ancient hills are home to the dnyamathanha – meaning 'hills people', collective term for a number of traditional nguage groups. Highlights of this lturally rich and spiritually significant ea include the Yourambulla Caves, here there are rock shelters with charcoal awings and ochre paintings. A number sites surround the stunning visual ntrepiece of Wilpena Pound ('Wilpena' erives from an Adnyamathanha word eaning 'cupped hands' or 'bent fingers'). *e also: Flinders Ranges & Outback p. 74.*

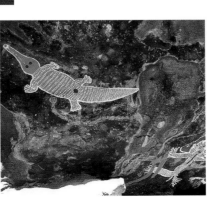

## TIME LINE: ABORIGINAL AUSTRALIA

**70 000–50 000 BC**  *The first indigenous people cross from Indonesia to the New Guinea–Australia landmass*

**35 000 BC**  *Aboriginal people reach Tasmania*

**10 000 BC**  *Rising sea levels after the last Ice Age isolate Aboriginal people in Australia from Asia, and those in Tasmania from the mainland*

**6000 BC**  *Distinct tribes and clans occupy the entire continent; economies adapt to different environments; religious beliefs and oral traditions derived from the Dreamtime indicate complex social organisation; extensive rock art appears*

**1770**  *The Tharawal of the Botany Bay region make contact with Captain Cook*

**1778**  *The Eora are displaced by the establishment of a penal colony at Sydney Cove*

**1789**  *A smallpox epidemic kills about half the Aboriginal population living in the vicinity of Sydney's penal colony*

**1838**  *Twelve whites massacre 28 Aboriginal people at Myall Creek*

**1876**  *Truganini, believed to be the last full-blooded Tasmanian Aboriginal person, dies*

**1860–1900**  *Protection Boards established across Australia; most Aboriginal people living on missions or government reserves*

**1901**  *The Commonwealth Constitution does not allow Federal parliament to legislate for Aboriginal people to be counted in the census*

**1910**  *Legislation in New South Wales increases government powers to remove Aboriginal children from their parents; similar provisions enacted in other States*

**1967**  *In a referendum, Australians vote with a 90 per cent majority to count Aboriginal people in the census*

**1971**  *Neville Bonner, the first Aboriginal parliamentarian, is elected to the Senate*

**1972**  *Aboriginal people erect a Tent Embassy outside Parliament House, Canberra, marking a new era of political activism*

**1992**  *In a decision known as Mabo, the High Court rejects the notion of terra nullius ('land belonging to no one') and affirms that Aboriginal people were in possession of the land before 1788*

**1996**  *In the Wik case, the High Court holds that pastoral leases granted by the Queensland Government did not extinguish native title*

**1997**  Bringing Them Home, *the report of a government inquiry into the Stolen Generation, is tabled in Federal parliament. The Howard government refuses to make a formal apology but the spirit of Reconciliation is embraced by many Australians.*

## ◀ THE KIMBERLEY, WA

The Kimberley retains a large Aboriginal population – at least 50 per cent of the total Kimberley population. This remote area has one of the country's most important collections of rock art, of which there are two main types: the Bradshaw and the more recent Wandjina. Tours of rock-art sites are available from some of the big stations in the area, and a variety of cultural tours operate from the region's community and cultural centres. *See also: The Kimberley p. 92.*

# NEW ARRIVALS

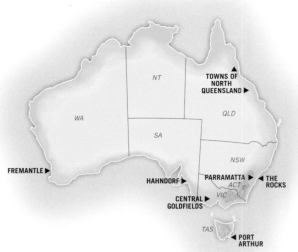

Since the arrival of the First Fleet in 1788, the pace of development in Australia has been rapid and far-reaching. While not all our historic heritage has been preserved, what remains offers a substantial, if not comprehensive, interpretation of the unique and often remarkable events of Australian history. Convict settlements tell the story of the grim and unpromising early years; isolated townships provide evidence of courageous attempts to tame a harsh environment; and ornate Victorian architecture boasts of the greatest gold rush in history. A new appreciation of this unique heritage has resulted in the restoration of many historic sites over the past couple of decades, with locations now popular with a large number of visitors.

### ▲ THE ROCKS, NSW

The Rocks marks the site of the first European settlement in Australia and is probably the country's most intact historic precinct. A mix of early buildings – bond stores, maritime warehouses, churches, pubs, low-slung cottages and wharves – is crowded across the peninsula at the heart of Sydney's CBD. *See also: Sydney p. 17.*

### HAHNDORF, SA ▶

This charming village forms an important part of one of the great stories of Australian history – immigration. Hahndorf was settled in the 1830s by Australia's first significant non-British immigrant group – German Lutheran peasants fleeing religious persecution. Today much of their culture is preserved through buildings, produce shops, restaurants and festivals. The nearby Barossa Valley also has a significant German heritage. *See also: Adelaide Hills p. 69.*

### PORT ARTHUR, TAS. ▶

There is no other site in the world like Port Arthur. Built in the early 1800s by convicts as a prison for convicts, it is our most graphic reminder of why and how modern Australia came into being. The site comprises a clutch of sandstone buildings – a penitentiary, hospital, asylum and church among them – set along the dramatic coast of the Tasman Peninsula. *See also: The South-East p. 138.*

**▲ FREMANTLE, WA**
Fremantle is one of the world's best-preserved 19th-century ports and serves as a fascinating reminder of the significance of maritime history in an island nation. Established in 1829, Fremantle contains a range of buildings that includes public offices, warehouses, shipping-company headquarters, shopfronts and houses, many now open to the public as museums and galleries. *See also: Perth p. 82.*

**▼ PARRAMATTA, NSW**
Now an outer suburb of Sydney, Parramatta was originally preferred over Sydney Harbour by European settlers and officials, not least because of its proximity to farmland and distance from the convict population. Parramatta preserves important fragments of the earliest colonial years, including the country's oldest buildings – Elizabeth Farm, home to pastoralists John and Elizabeth Macarthur, and the first Government House. Both are open to the public. *See also: Sydney p. 18.*

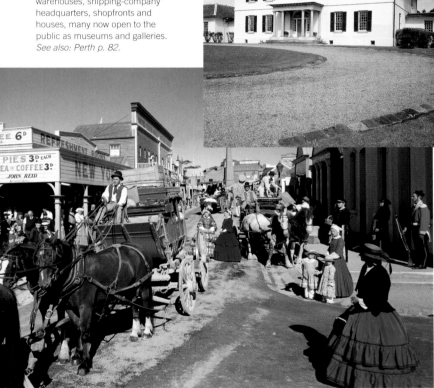

**▲ CENTRAL GOLDFIELDS, VIC.**
Many areas in Australia experienced a gold rush in the second half of the 19th century, but nowhere were the yields as great and the effects as dramatic as in Victoria. The legacy is a series of towns – particularly Ballarat and Bendigo – boasting significant concentrations of rural Victorian-era architecture. Less conspicuous but also significant are the sites marking the history of the Chinese in Australia. *See also: The Goldfields p. 54.*

**◀ TOWNS OF NORTH QUEENSLAND**
Among others, the remote towns of Cooktown, Townsville, Charters Towers and Ravenswood are places where Australian themes of isolation, hardship and adaptation had their origins. Settled for a variety of reasons – to service farming communities or the gold rush, or as ports – they preserve significant recollections of the 19th century. Of particular interest are the architectural adaptations designed to cope with extreme environmental conditions. *See also: The Mid-Tropics p. 124 and The Far North p. 125.*

## SINCE EUROPEAN DISCOVERY

*1606* The Duyfken, a Dutch ship, explores the western coast of Cape York Peninsula

*1616* Dirk Hartog on the Eendracht lands on an island off the Western Australian coast

*1770* James Cook takes possession of the east coast of New Holland for the British Crown

*1788* The First Fleet establishes a British penal colony at Botany Bay

*1803* Matthew Flinders completes the first circumnavigation of Australia and establishes it as a continent

*1803* A British settlement is established on the River Derwent in Van Diemen's Land

*1813* Wentworth, Blaxland and Lawson find a path across the Blue Mountains

*1824* The Moreton Bay Penal Settlement is established near what will become Brisbane

*1829* Western Australia is founded by British emigrants

*1835* John Batman 'buys' the site of Melbourne from the Kulin people

*1836* South Australia is proclaimed a British colony

*1840* The British Government abolishes convict transportation to New South Wales after more than 84 000 convicts have arrived

*1851* Gold is discovered in New South Wales and Victoria

*1901* The six Australian colonies federate to form the Commonwealth of Australia

*1908* Land known as Canberra, at the foothills of the Australian Alps, is chosen as the site of the national capital

*1914–18* World War I: Australia fights against Germany with the loss of almost 62 000 Australian lives

*1929* The Great Depression, triggered by the Wall Street crash, spreads to Australia

*1939–45* World War II: Australia fights in Europe, Asia and the Pacific, with the loss of more than 39 000 Australian lives

*1951* A referendum to outlaw the Communist Party of Australia is narrowly defeated

*1966* The government begins dismantling restrictive immigration legislation known as the 'White Australia' policy

*1988* Australia celebrates 200 years of European settlement

# NATURAL WONDERS

A ustralia is renowned for the beauty and diversity of its natural environment. As well as the vast tracts of desert that one would expect in the earth's oldest, driest and flattest continent, it is a place of lush forests, wild rivers, ancient mountains, dramatic alpine peaks, glacial lakes and a magnificent coastline. Two sites, the stunning Great Barrier Reef and the massive monolith of Uluru – both among the most recognised natural features in the world – have contributed greatly to the development of Australia as a major nature-travel destination. Other places, such as the remote wilds of Tasmania and the vast expanse of The Kimberley, are valued for their lonely beauty and remarkably unspoiled condition.

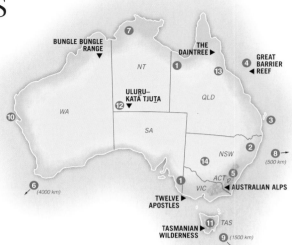

### ▲ THE DAINTREE, QLD

Part of the Wet Tropics World Heritage Area, the Daintree is popular place for exploring the dense and tangled primeval forests of tropical north Queensland. Phenomenally diverse and spectacularly beautiful, the forests are home to some of the world's most ancient plant species, as well as some of Australia's most brilliant birds and butterflies. *See also: The Far North p. 125.*

### ▼ AUSTRALIAN ALPS, NSW & VIC.

Few people realise that Australia has an alpine area more extensive that the snowfields of Austria and Switzerland combined. Straddling the Great Dividing Range, the Alps area is preserved in a series of connecting national parks. A landscape of glacial lakes, mighty rivers and rugged peaks make this one of the world's most spectacular alpine areas. *See also: Snowy Mountains p. 34 and The High Country p. 58.*

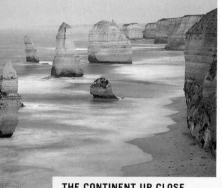

### ◀ TWELVE APOSTLES, VIC.

These massive limestone obelisks were once part of the original cliff-line, but have since become 'stranded' under the constant pressure of sea and wind erosion. Surrounded by swirling waves, and capturing the ever-changing coastal light, the Twelve Apostles are regarded as one of Australia's great scenic experiences. *See also: The Great Ocean Road p. 49.*

### ▲ BUNGLE BUNGLE RANGE, WA

These black-and-orange-striped, weathered mounds, which rise up out of the remote plains of The Kimberley in north-west Australia, were created 350 million years ago, and contain sedimentary layers said to be 1600 million years old. Palm-lined gorges and clear pools of water intersect the ancient domes. Travel into the area is by 4WD or scenic flight. *See also: The Kimberley p. 92.*

### THE CONTINENT UP CLOSE

The character of the Australian landscape dates back 290 million years to a time when the continent was submerged under a huge ice cap. Since then, the deep valleys and high mountains of a glaciated landscape have been eroded away to a fairly uniform flatness (with some exceptions, spectacular for their shape – the Bungle Bungles and Uluru among them). The loss of high mountains brought a gradual increase in aridity. The formation of the rain clouds slowed and vast tracts of desert began to appear where lush forests had once stood. Today approximately 80 per cent of the continent is arid. There would probably be more arid land except for a dramatic geological episode 80 million years ago – the upthrust of the Great Dividing Range. This feature, stretching from north to south on the east of the continent, is where Australia's tallest peaks, grand forests and most significant rivers are found.

◀ **TASMANIAN WILDERNESS**
Covering nearly 20 percent of the total area of the island State, the Tasmanian wilderness is one of only three temperate wildernesses remaining in the Southern Hemisphere. It encompasses Australia's longest caves, ancient rocks, remote wild rivers, some of the world's oldest trees, and the stunning glaciated landscape of Cradle Mountain–Lake St Clair. *See also: South-West Wilderness p. 135 and The North-West p. 136.*

▲ **GREAT BARRIER REEF, QLD**
The world's largest reef is an enduring symbol of the rarity and beauty of Australia's natural environment. Stretching for 2000 km along the coast of Queensland, this maze of coral reefs and cays supports an astonishing diversity of life, from 1500 species of fish to sea mammals, turtles, sea grasses and molluscs. Brilliant colours, forms and textures have made these underwater landscapes one of the world's great diving destinations. *See also: Great Barrier Reef p. 119.*

◀ **ULURU–KATA TJUTA, NT**
These notable rock formations sit above an otherwise flat desert plain at the geographic heart of the continent. Uluru, with a height of 348 m and a base circumference of 9.4 km, is the largest monolith in the world. Neighbouring Kata Tjuta comprises 36 steep-sided domes that are possibly the eroded remains of a monolith many times the size of Uluru. *See also: The Red Centre p. 104.*

## FOCUS ON WORLD HERITAGE

**❶ *Australian Fossil Mammal Sites (Naracoorte & Riversleigh)***
Two sites that have yielded 20 million-year-old fossils of extinct Australian species. See also: The South-East p. 76 and Outback & Gulf Country p. 128.

**❷ *Central Eastern Rainforest Reserves of Australia***
Large discontinuous patches of subtropical, warm temperate and Antarctic beech cool temperate rainforest. See also: Holiday Coast p. 23, Tropical North Coast p. 25, New England & the North-West p. 26 and Gold Coast & Hinterland p. 114.

**❸ *Fraser Island***
World's largest sand island, with complex dune system, freshwater dune lakes and rainforest. See also: Fraser Island & Coast p. 118.

**❹ *Great Barrier Reef***
World's largest reef, with the most diverse reef fauna. See also: Great Barrier Reef p. 119.

**❺ *Greater Blue Mountains Area***
A deeply incised plateau with dramatic cliffs and valleys and eucalypt forests. See also: Central Coast & Hawkesbury p. 22 and Blue Mountains p. 28.

**❻ *Heard and McDonald Islands***
An active volcano (on Heard), glacial landscapes and rare sub-Antarctic flora and fauna.

**❼ *Kakadu National Park***
Myriad natural environments and the world's oldest, most extensive rock art. See also: Kakadu & Arnhem Land p. 100.

**❽ *Lord Howe Island***
Home to a wealth of flora and fauna species, many unique to this remote volcanic island. See also: Lord Howe Island p. 24.

**❾ *Macquarie Island***
An island composed of oceanic crust and mantle rocks, home to 850 000 penguin pairs.

**❿ *Shark Bay***
Large population of sea mammals, and 3.5 billion-year-old stromatolites representing the oldest life on earth. See also: Outback Coast & Mid-West p. 91.

**⓫ *Tasmanian Wilderness***
Forest, rivers, caves, glacial lakes, and 40 Aboriginal sites pointing to at least 30 000 years' occupation. See also: South-West Wilderness p. 135, The North-West p. 136 and Midlands & the North p. 137.

**⓬ *Uluru–Kata Tjuta National Park***
Massive rock formations in the desert, with numerous Aboriginal sites. See also: The Red Centre p. 104.

**⓭ *Wet Tropics of Queensland***
Ancient rainforests containing an almost complete evolutionary record of Earth's plant life. See also: The Mid-Tropics p. 124 and The Far North p. 125.

**⓮ *Willandra Lakes***
Haunting landscape of ancient lunettes, and site of excavations that showed an Aboriginal presence dating back 60 000 years. See also: The Outback p. 37.

# MAGNIFICENT COASTLINE

The outback may be the place of Australian myth and legend, but most Australians choose to live – and holiday – within reach of a beach. The superb scenery of almost 60 000 kilometres of coastline, which takes in the country's hundreds of offshore islands, ranges from the sultry mangrove inlets of the far north to the white sweeping sands of the Indian Ocean coast and the rugged cliffs and legendary surf of the continent's south. Going to the beach in Australia can mean an afternoon of bodysurfing in the suburbs; a sojourn in a international tropical resort; time out in a reclusive fishing community; a drive along dramatic clifftops; or an exploration of one of several coastal World Heritage areas of great beauty and environmental significance.

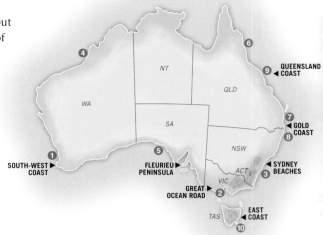

▲ **GREAT OCEAN ROAD, VIC.**
Australia's most scenic coastal road links the many towns and attractions of this popular holiday region. The diverse attractions include top surfing breaks and their attendant communities, thickly forested mountains, family beaches, restaurants to suit everyone, wildlife-watching and some remarkable historic maritime sites. *See also: The Great Ocean Road p. 49.*

▲ **SOUTH-WEST COAST, WA**
This wild and rugged coastline stretches from Cape Naturaliste to Cape Leeuwin, where the Indian and Southern oceans meet. There are a couple of small holiday villages and the popular hinterland winegrowing area of Margaret River, but most of the coast, with its cliffs, limestone caves, sand dunes and forests, is untouched by development and preserved within the Leeuwin–Naturaliste National Park. The area is renowned for its world-class surfing breaks. *See also: The South-West p. 86.*

▲ **GOLD COAST, QLD**
Australia's largest and best-known international resort is centred on an outstanding subtropical coastline, legendary for its 35 beautiful beaches, great surf and year-round sunshine. Once a sleepy holiday backwater, the area is now a major urban centre offering everything from 18-hole golf to designer shopping, deep-sea fishing, fine dining and major theme park attractions. *See also: Gold Coast & Hinterland p. 114.*

## COAST SAFETY

Swim between the flags on patrolled beaches; on unpatrolled beaches, take a walk and enjoy the scenery. Most beaches in popular areas, particularly near towns, are patrolled in the high season and some are patrolled year round. Surfers should always check conditions with locals before taking to the water, as should anglers. Between October and May the extremely dangerous box stinger inhabits the coastal waters of Queensland and other parts of northern Australia; beachgoers are advised not to enter the water during this period. Sharks are common in Australian waters and warnings should be heeded. In northern Australia saltwater crocodiles are found in the sea, estuaries and tidal rivers, and on land at the water's edge, and are extremely dangerous. Do not enter the water or remain at the water's edge in known crocodile areas and, if unsure, check with the locals. Avoid the hot Australian sun and the damage it can do. Don't sunbake in the middle of the day, wear a hat at all times, and apply sunblock every two hours.

**◄ EAST COAST, TAS.**
One of Australia's most relaxed, old-fashioned and least hurried coastal regions, the East Coast is a haven of tiny fishing villages, bushland, farmland and pristine beaches. Highlights include the history and scenic beauty of Maria Island, superb underwater scenery near Bicheno, and the magnificent Freycinet Peninsula in the national park. *See also: The East Coast p. 140.*

**▲ FLEURIEU PENINSULA, SA**
Just an hour or two from Adelaide, this is South Australia's premier coastal retreat. On the east coast lie surf beaches, conservation parks and the busy resort town of Victor Harbour; on the west, the calmer blue waters of Gulf St Vincent, a string of pretty, low-key holiday villages and some stunning coastal scenery. Nudging the coast are some spectacular rural landscapes, incorporating one of Australia's top wine and food districts. *See also: Fleurieu Peninsula p. 77.*

**▲ QUEENSLAND COAST**
The hundreds of beautiful islands that crowd the Queensland coast include the islands near Brisbane; the outstanding World Heritage-listed Fraser Island; and about 1000 Great Barrier Reef islands (of which 22 offer accommodation). There is an island to suit everyone's idea of a holiday in paradise, be it a lonely campsite beneath a palm, an environmental escape, a fishing, water-skiing and diving adventure, or a week by the pool with a book. *See also: Brisbane Islands p. 113, Fraser Island & Coast p. 118 and Great Barrier Reef p. 119.*

**SYDNEY BEACHES, NSW ►**
Sydney's surf beaches are the envy of many a metropolis. Flanking the city to the north and south, generous in length and width and admirably patrolled for most of the year, they provide an easy escape from the bustle of city life for thousands of residents and holiday-makers alike. The jewel in the crown is the world-famous Bondi – a cultural institution as much as a patch of sand and surf. *See also: Sydney p. 18.*

## TOP BEACHES

**❶ The Basin beaches, Rottnest Island, WA**
On the island's north side, reef-protected beaches offer a safe haven for holidaying families. See also: Rottnest Island p. 84.

**❷ Bells Beach, Torquay, Vic.**
Australia's top surfing destination and site of the legendary Bells Beach Classic each Easter. See also: The Great Ocean Road p. 49.

**❸ Booderee National Park beaches, Jervis Bay, NSW**
A series of near-deserted beaches, surrounded by native bush and boasting what is claimed to be the whitest sand in the world. See also: The South Coast p. 32.

**❹ Cable Beach, Broome, WA**
A luxurious sweep of white sand fronting turquoise waters and forming the scenic centrepiece of Australia's most remote and exotic resort town. See also: The Kimberley p. 92.

**❺ Cactus Beach, Penong, SA**
The three famous surfing breaks of this remote destination are strictly for surfers with frontier spirit and the skill to match. See also: Eyre Peninsula & Nullarbor p. 73.

**❻ Four Mile Beach, Port Douglas, Qld**
A beach so beautiful that it helped turn a sleepy seaside village into an international resort. See also: The Far North p. 125.

**❼ Noosa National Park beaches, Qld**
A subtropical wonderland of peaceful, pandanus-fringed coves providing a retreat from the otherwise busy Sunshine Coast. See also: Sunshine Coast p. 117.

**❽ Watego Beach, Byron Bay, NSW**
Tune in and drop out at this popular north-facing surf beach in one of Australia's less conventional towns. See also: Tropical North Coast p. 25.

**❾ Whitehaven, Whitsunday Island, Qld**
A paradise on an uninhabited island: 7 km long, protected by national park – and pristine. See also: Great Barrier Reef p. 119.

**❿ Wineglass Bay, Freycinet Peninsula, Tas.**
Bushland in national park opens up to this magnificently sculpted, crescent-shaped beach. See also: The East Coast p. 140.

# WILD AUSTRALIA

Australia has some of the world's most distinctive plants and animals. Pouched mammals, prehistoric reptiles, majestic gums and brilliant desert flowers are just a sample of the country's many strange and beautiful living things. Around a quarter of overseas visitors to the country rate the wildlife as a major attraction and at least a couple of our more famous creatures – kangaroos and koalas in particular – are regarded as national icons. Beyond the fascination of individual species, Australia offers a series of exceptionally well-preserved natural environments, from marine waters to deserts and rainforests, where animals and plants can be seen in their natural settings and as part of the complex communities to which they belong.

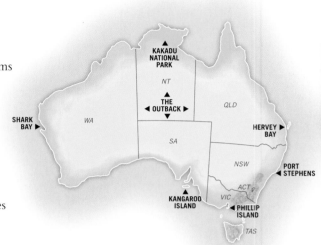

### ▼ SHARK BAY, WA
This World Heritage wonderland is best known for its bottlenose dolphins, which glide into the shallow waters of Monkey Mia and approach entranced visitors. Other highlights of this extraordinary area include the 230 bird species and a population of about 10 000 dugongs – the largest in the world. *See also: Outback Coast & Mid-West p. 91.*

### ▲ THE OUTBACK
Although referred to as the continent's 'Dead Heart', the vast areas of arid land at the centre of Australia support prolific and varied life including 2000 plant species and the highest concentration of reptiles in the world. Among its mammal species is the mighty red, the largest member of the kangaroo family with the male reaching two metres in height.

## ISOLATION AND EVOLUTION
For 50 million years, wild Australia developed in isolation. The result is a unique set of plants and animals. Marsupials, represented by 180 species on this continent, are uncommon elsewhere. Likewise, the curious monotreme (an exclusive club with only platypuses and echidnas as members) is found nowhere else except New Guinea. When it comes to plants, only 15 per cent of our 28 000 indigenous species are found beyond Australia's shores. Aridity and poor soil have aided difference, with many species developing special characteristics to cope with harsh conditions. These adaptations have led to enormous biodiversity. Western Australia has about 11 000 wildflower species, giving the State one of the world's richest floras, while the rainforests of the east coast are among the most biologically complex places on Earth.

## ▲ KAKADU NATIONAL PARK, NT

This large World Heritage-listed park is one of Australia's most biologically diverse and prolific regions. Around 1600 plant species thrive in Kakadu; they represent most of the native habitats of northern Australia. The wildlife is no less impressive and includes 280 bird species (one third of all Australian species), 123 reptile species, and 52 freshwater fish species. *See also: Kakadu & Arnhem Land p. 100.*

### ▼ KANGAROO ISLAND, SA

Isolation from the mainland has helped Australia's third largest island maintain an unusual concentration of wildlife. Highlights include a large colony of sea lions at Seal Bay; about 600 New Zealand fur seals at Cape du Couedic; 240 bird species; plenty of kangaroos, wallabies and possums; and koalas and platypuses. *See also: Kangaroo Island p. 78.*

### ◄ PORT STEPHENS, NSW

One of the largest koala colonies in Australia is to be found in the wild here at Tilligerry Habitat. Probably the country's best known native animal, these short, tailless marsupials are usually inactive for 20 hours a day and normally feed only on eucalypts. The waters of Port Stephens are home to around 160 bottlenose dolphins and serve as a thoroughfare for migrating humpback whales, which appear seasonally. *See also: Hunter Valley & Coast p. 20.*

### ◄ HERVEY BAY, QLD

Between August and October each year up to 400 humpback whales visit Hervey Bay, the whale-watching capital of Australia. It is believed that they pause here for rest and recreation on their 12 000-km journey between their breeding grounds in the Pacific Ocean and their feeding grounds in the Antarctic. Whale-watching cruises operate in the bay. *See also: Fraser Island & Coast p. 118.*

### ▲ PHILLIP ISLAND, VIC.

The little (fairy) penguins of Phillip Island are Victoria's best-known wildlife attraction. Each evening visitors can watch scores of these small creatures, measuring about 33 cm, returning to their sand burrows after a day of sea-fishing. Other island features include the koalas at the Koala Conservation Centre and the resident seals, which can be seen on a cruise to Seal Rocks or via satellite transmission at the Seal Rocks Sea Life Centre. *See also: Phillip Island & Gippsland p. 62.*

## FLORAL EMBLEMS

**Commonwealth of Australia**

golden wattle
(*Acacia pycnantha*)

**New South Wales**

waratah
(*Telopea speciosissima*)

**Australian Capital Territory**

royal bluebell
(*Wahlenbergia gloriosa*)

**Victoria**

common heath
(*Epacris impressa*)

**South Australia**

Sturt's desert pea
(*Swainsona formosa*)

**Western Australia**

red and green kangaroo paw
(*Anigozanthos manglesii*)

**Northern Territory**

Sturt's desert rose
(*Gossypium sturtianum*)

**Queensland**

Cooktown orchid
(*Dendrobium phalaenopsis*)

**Tasmania**

Tasmanian blue gum (*Eucalyptus globulus*)

# ADVENTURE HOLIDAYS

When it comes to adventure holidays and outdoor activities, Australia is a destination without peer. The continent's diverse and well-preserved environment of remote bush, snowfields, rugged cliffs, wild rivers, extensive coastline and underwater reefs is a mecca for the world's walkers, skiers, climbers, rafters, anglers and divers – and for all the first-time or would-be adventurers needing guidance. Many of these activities are offered within the boundaries of national parks and other conservation areas. Australia's regulated and well-organised tourism industry means that there are plenty of experienced operators offering training, tours, charters and equipment.

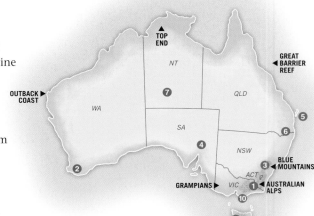

## ◀ GREAT BARRIER REEF, QLD

Novices and experienced divers alike come from around the world to test their skills in what is the most challenging and fascinating diving environment on earth. From Bundaberg to Cooktown, the facilities are extensive. The reef's islands, particularly the Whitsundays, are also known for their superb sailing opportunities. Most popular is bareboating, which involves hiring a fully equipped, easy-to-sail yacht (without a crew) for at least several days' touring. *See also: Great Barrier Reef p. 119.*

## AUSTRALIAN ALPS, NSW & VIC. ▶

This region, incorporating the ski slopes of Victoria and New South Wales, is the hallowed ground of winter sports enthusiasts including downhill and cross-country skiers. Less well known is the range of adventure activities available during the summer months; these include walking, caving, horseriding and whitewater rafting. *See also: Snowy Mountains p. 34 and The High Country p. 58.*

## ◀ TOP END, NT

The remote and sparsely populated tropical north attracts adventurers with a frontier spirit. Activities include barramundi fishing in the tidal rivers of the west coast or the crystal clear rivers of the east; deep-sea fishing via Darwin or the Gove Peninsula; canoeing in the gorges of Nitmiluk National Park; and 4WD expeditions in Litchfield National Park. *See also: Around Darwin p. 102, Gulf to Gulf p. 103 and Kakadu & Arnhem Land p. 100.*

## SAFETY AND ENVIRONMENT

Adventure activities may involve risk that can prove fatal if participants are ill prepared. For the more hazardous sports, such as rock-climbing, cross-country skiing, sportfishing and diving, training with a professional operator is recommended, and even experienced participants should consider joining a tour or charter. Local visitor information centres and activity-based clubs can make recommendations. For bushwalking, a few rules stand fast. Always tell someone where you are going and when you expect to be back. For walks in national parks, get ranger advice about which walks suit your fitness. Always carry water – no matter how short the walk – and wear sturdy shoes and a hat. Observe fire warnings and fire bans. Walks of more than a day should be attempted only with a tour group or by experienced walkers. The flipside to many adventure activities in Australia is their potential for causing environmental damage. Participants can do their bit by observing the following: take only photographs (not flora, fauna or other matter) and stay on designated tracks.

### ▲ OUTBACK COAST, WA

Way off the beaten track, this remote coastal area has a range of adventure attractions that make the long journey worthwhile. The Ningaloo Reef, second only in scale and interest to the Great Barrier Reef, offers superb diving (where possibilities include swimming with whale sharks) and is also emerging as a popular sea-kayaking destination. Further south, Kalbarri National Park has 80 km of deep gorges for canoeing, as well as good walking tracks and top-class fishing off the coast. *See also: Outback Coast & Mid-West p. 91.*

### ▲ SOUTHERN RIVERS, TAS.

The wild rivers of the island State offer world-class whitewater rafting. The best known and probably most challenging run is the remote Franklin River in the depths of the south-west's World Heritage wilderness, where operators run tours of up to 12 days. Beginners should consider a one- or two-day tour of the gentler waters of the Picton River, to the south-east. *See also: The South-East p. 138 and South-West Wilderness p. 135.*

### ◀ GRAMPIANS, VIC.

Mount Arapiles, just to the west of the Grampians proper, is regarded as Australia's best rock-climbing venue. It has 3000 climbing routes across its surface, attracting enthusiasts from around the world. Rock-climbing, abseiling and bushwalking take place throughout the Grampians, as well as a range of other activities including ballooning via the town of Stawell. *See also: Grampians & Central West p. 50.*

## TOP TRACKS

**❶ Australian Alps Walking Track, ACT, NSW & Vic.**
*A 680-km track, usually completed in sections, taking in rivers, peaks and valleys.* See also: Snowy Mountains p. 34 and The High Country p. 58.

**❷ Bibbulmun Track, WA**
*A walk that traverses WA's spectacular south-west – 963 km from Kalamunda to Albany.* See also: Darling Range & Swan Valley p. 85, The South-West p. 86 and Great Southern p. 87.

**❸ Blue Mountains, NSW**
*Anything from an hour's stroll to a week-long trek, through some of Australia's most accessible bush.* See also: Blue Mountains p. 28.

**❹ Flinders Ranges, SA**
*A range of walks weaves across the ridges, gorges and river valleys of this ancient landscape.* See also: Flinders Ranges & Outback p. 74.

**❺ Fraser Island, Qld**
*Take a four-day, 76-km walk through this World Heritage island's sand-dune lake system.* See also: Fraser Island & Coast p. 118.

**❻ Lamington National Park, Qld**
*Around 160 km of walking tracks through primordial subtropical forests.* See also: Gold Coast & Hinterland p. 114.

**❼ Larapinta Trail, NT**
*A 220-km walking track along gorges, chasms, pools and arid habitats of the West MacDonnell Ranges.* See also: The Red Centre p. 104.

**❽ Overland Track, Tas.**
*Australia's best-known, spectacular long walk – 7 days from Cradle Mountain to Lake St Clair.* See also: The North-West p. 136.

**❾ South Coast Track, Tas.**
*A challenging 10-day hike that explores Tasmania's uninhabited south coast.* See also: South-West Wilderness p. 135.

**❿ Wilsons Promontory, Vic.**
*Pristine beaches and bush along 150 km of tracks in one of Australia's loveliest coastal parks.* See also: Phillip Island & Gippsland p. 62.

### ◀ BLUE MOUNTAINS, NSW

The dense bush, misty valleys, deep canyons and rugged cliffs of this World Heritage Area make it a natural adventure playground for mountaineering enthusiasts. Rock-climbing, abseiling and canyoning are all on offer and the attendant facilities are excellent. Horseriding in the Megalong Valley is a gentler choice of activity, while the bushwalking throughout the mountain area is some of the best in the country. *See also: Blue Mountains p. 28.*

# NEW SOUTH WALES

New South Wales, the first colony, dominated the early years of European settlement in Australia. The Premier State, as it styles itself, has a third of Australia's population (approximately 6 500 000 people), a bigger economy than any other State, and Australia's largest and most widely recognised city, Sydney.

## Something for everyone

The 1000-km New South Wales coastline offers surfing beaches, and inlets, harbours, lakes and estuaries for fishing and boating. Inland, a steep escarpment rises to a succession of mountains and plateaus. The snowfields of the Australian Alps, rising to 2228 m at Mount Kosciuszko, attract skiers during winter. The high country gives way to the western slopes, a well-watered region of grasslands supporting cattle, sheep and wheat, and to the dry western plains that cover nearly two-thirds of the State.

The climate is mainly temperate; only the north-west experiences extreme summer heat. On the coast, summers are warm and humid and winters pleasantly cool and generally dry. Winter frosts are widespread inland but only the Australian Alps receive regular snowfalls.

## Economic backbone

New South Wales accounts for one-third of Australia's manufacturing, with the Port Kembla steel works providing the backbone of heavy industry. Vast black coal deposits near Gunnedah and Narrabri, and in the Hunter Valley and South Coast, contribute three-quarters of the State's income from mining. The rural economy rests on wheat and other cereals, wool, cattle and cotton.

Tourism has grown rapidly. New South Wales is Australia's most visited State, with about 7 800 000 domestic and 2 280 000 international visitors each year. Many of these visits are for business, reflecting Sydney's growing importance in the globalised economy.

## An ancient past

About 40 000 Aboriginal people lived in the area of New South Wales before white settlement. Evidence of Aboriginal occupation is everywhere: shell middens on the coast, canoe trees on the riverbanks, and numerous rock-art galleries. The discovery of a 60 000-year-old human skeleton at Lake Mungo in the dry west has forced a revision of the human history of the continent. Today about 100 000 Aboriginal and Torres Strait Islander people call the State home.

## Nation or gaol?

Captain Cook claimed the eastern half of New Holland for the British Crown in 1770. Seventeen years later, eleven ships carrying 1487 people – 759 of them convicts – sailed from England to establish a penal colony in New South Wales. Captain Arthur Phillip, commander of the First Fleet, selected the site on Sydney Harbour known today as Circular Quay. In all, 72 326 male and 12 083 female convicts arrived from the United Kingdom. Transportation ceased in 1850 after the British government decided that New South Wales was more valuable as a destination for poor British emigrants, whose passages would be paid from the sale of colonial land.

## Squatters and settlers

The colony struggled for thirty years until wool provided an export income. After 1813, squatters occupied the vast grasslands west of the Blue Mountains. Many Aboriginal people, deprived of their traditional hunting grounds, died from malnutrition, European diseases and at the hands of the white settlers. The most notorious massacre was at Myall Creek, near Glen Innes, in 1838 when white stockmen shot twenty-eight Aboriginal men, women and children and burned their bodies.

The discovery of gold north of Bathurst in 1851 brought many immigrants to New South Wales, including thousands of Chinese. In the second half of the 19th century, New South Wales lived off the sheep's back. Victoria, by encouraging industry through tariff protection, supplanted its mother colony – for a time – as the manufacturing and commercial centre of Australia.

## Politics and power

Democracy was born in Australia with the election of twenty-four members in the thirty-six-seat New South Wales Legislative Council in 1843. Squatters dominated the first decade of the representative government but, after the advent of the fully elected Legislative Assembly in 1856, their influence declined. Universal male suffrage and the secret ballot followed two years later; women did not get the vote until 1902. The left-wing Labor Party has dominated in this State just as the conservative Liberal Party has been the party of power in Victoria.

## Into the 21st century

Since New South Wales federated with the other five States to form the Commonwealth of Australia, the State has grown rapidly except during the depression years of the 1930s. Industrialisation and the mechanisation of farming have seen a population shift to the cities since the 1920s.

Landmarks over the last fifty years have included the Snowy Mountains Scheme in the 1950s, the opening of the Sydney Opera House in 1973, the Bicentennial celebrations of 1988, the recent opening of Fox Studios Australia in Sydney to produce big-budget, high-tech films for international distribution, and the staging of the 2000 Olympic Games.

Yet the State's greatest achievement has been the expansion of its national parks. Many pristine beaches and waterways, foreshore bushland on Sydney Harbour, coastal rainforests, the wetlands and marshes of the western slopes and the austere and dramatically beautiful desert landscapes of the far west are now protected for the enjoyment of residents and visitors alike.

Historic building in the old mining town of Silverton, near Broken Hill

For more information on New South Wales, see Tourist Bureaus, opposite page 236.

# SYDNEY

With a population of 4 million and over 2 million international visitors per year, Sydney is widely regarded as one of the world's most beautiful cities. It is Australia's largest city and boasts great restaurants, theatre, superb architecture, cultural diversity and interesting historic sites. All this, set within a landscape of sweeping surf beaches, bushland, soaring cliffs and the glittering waters of Sydney Harbour, makes this city an irresistible destination and rewarding to explore.

## VISITOR INFORMATION

**Sydney Visitor Centre The Rocks**
106 George St (02) 9255 1788

**Sydney Visitor Centre Darling Harbour**
Palm Grove (02) 9281 0788

**Circular Quay Information Kiosk**
Cnr Alfred and Pitt sts

**Martin Place Information Kiosk**
Cnr Elizabeth St and Martin Pl.

**Town Hall Information Kiosk**
George St

**Manly Visitor Information Centre**
Manly Wharf Forecourt
(02) 9977 1088

## CITY CENTRE

See map on page 208.

**Art Gallery of New South Wales**
208 H7
One of the most comprehensive collections in the country, including the largest permanent collection of Aboriginal art in the world.

**Australian Museum** 208 F9
Australia's oldest; housing natural history displays and one of the world's best indigenous exhibitions.

**Australian National Maritime Museum** 208 B8
The maritime adventures of an island continent, from the seagoing ways of the Aboriginal people to today's beach culture.

**Cadmans Cottage** 208 E4
The oldest existing residence in Australia, built in 1816; also the NPWS Information Centre.

**Chinese Garden** 208 C10
Lakes, waterfalls, pavilions and rare exotic species.

**Customs House** 208 F5
An 1885 Classical Revival building, home to a display of contemporary and indigenous art and culture.

**Darling Harbour** 208 B10
Leisure precinct containing some of the city's major cultural and entertainment institutions.

**Government House** 208 G4
Set within the lush surrounds of the Royal Botanic Gardens; the magnificent state rooms, with period furnishings, may be seen on guided tours.

**Hyde Park Barracks Museum** 208 F8
Fine example of Georgian Colonial architecture, completed in 1819; contains a fascinating museum of social and architectural history; opposite is Hyde Park, home to some interesting civic memorials.

**Justice and Police Museum** 208 F5
Displays the history of crime and punishment in Sydney.

**Museum of Sydney** 208 F5
A thought-provoking survey of what has made Sydney the city it is.

**Oxford Street** 208 H12
Heartland of gay Sydney.

**Powerhouse Museum** 208 B11
Former power station that now houses fascinating scientific, social and technological displays.

**The Rocks** 208 E4
Historic waterside area with weekend market, galleries, cafes and craft shops.

**Royal Botanic Gardens** 208 H6
On the site of Sydney's first farm, these magnificent gardens contain some 17 000 native and exotic species.

**State Library of New South Wales** 208 F6
Includes the Mitchell Library, and its priceless collection of Australiana.

**Sydney Aquarium** 208 C8
An amazing array of sea life swims through underwater tunnels; also a living replica of the Great Barrier Reef.

**Sydney Harbour Bridge** 208 E2
The second longest single-span bridge in the world. The south-east Pylon Lookout contains the Harbour Bridge Exhibition and a viewing platform; there is a three-hour guided climb to the top.

**Sydney Observatory** 208 D4
Features night viewing and an astronomy museum.

**Sydney Opera House** 208 G3
An architectural giant of the 20th century; guided tours are available.

**Sydney Tower** 208 E8
The highest observation deck in the Southern Hemisphere, for a bird's eye view of the city.

**Victoria Barracks** 208 I13
Considered one of the best examples of Imperial military architecture in the world.

## TOP EVENTS

**Sydney Festival** (Jan.)
Arts, culture and summer fun

**Gay and Lesbian Mardi Gras** (Feb.)
Sydney's biggest party

**Archibald Prize Exhibition** (Mar.–Apr.)
National portrait prize – and the best gossip in Sydney

**Australian Fashion Week** (May)
The latest in Australian and international delights

**Sydney Film Festival** (June)
A winter retreat for film lovers

**City to Surf** (July)
Challenging road-race taking in Heartbreak Hill

**Australian International Motor Show** (Nov.)
Latest and futuristic models in a 10-day showcasing

## GETTING AROUND

Travelling through Sydney can be a daunting thought for those from out of town. The traffic is dense, the peak 'hour' lasts for several hours and some of the traffic lanes are narrow. However, with some planning, Sydney is not a difficult city to negotiate. Carefully choose a main through-route and then navigate using the route signs. Main routes are generally clearly signposted. If you are travelling in a motorhome or towing a van it is easier to keep to the centre lane and flow with the traffic. Avoid left-hand lanes wherever possible as these regularly end with little warning. Keep an eye on the lane width as they do vary and try not to wander from your lane. The South Western Motorway (Route 5), the Western Motorway (Route 4), the Eastern Distributor (Route 1) and the Hills Motorway (Route 2) are all toll roads with attended toll gates. Beware of using parking meters as they are very expensive. All the major attractions within the city centre can be reached easily on foot. However, the red Explorer Buses do circuits of the city attractions, and the blue buses cover the bay and beaches. For the outlying attractions and the harbourside eastern suburbs, take a ferry ride and enjoy the harbour experience.

**Airport shuttle bus**
Airport Express 13 15 00

**Motoring organisation**
NRMA 13 21 32

**Public transport**
Bus, Train and Ferry Information Line 13 15 00

**Bus tours and speciality trips**
Explorer Buses red (city sights), blue (Bondi and eastern suburbs), yellow (airport) 13 15 00

**Metro Monorail & Light Rail**
(02) 8584 5288

**Taxis**
ABC Taxis 13 25 22, Legion Cabs 13 14 51, Manly Cabs 13 16 68, Premier Cabs 13 10 17

**Water Taxis**
Water Taxis Combined (02) 9555 8888

**Cruises**
Bounty Cruises (02) 9247 1789, Captain Cook Cruises (02) 9206 1111, Matilda Cruises (02) 9264 7377, Blue Line Cruises (02) 8296 7296

## SUBURBS AND SURROUNDS

See map on page 19.

**Bicentennial Park** 19 E8
Covering 60 ha of dryland and 40 ha of conservation wetlands.

**Bondi Beach** 19 I9
Excellent for swimming and strolling.

**Centennial Park** 19 H9
Beautiful 220 ha of woodlands, lakes, trails and gardens.

**Elizabeth Bay House** 19 H8
Built in 1839, this spectacular property is fully furnished as a museum charting the life of the upper classes in 19th-century Sydney.

**Elizabeth Farm** 19 C7
Incorporates the oldest European building in Australia (1793); once the home of the Macarthurs, wool industry pioneers.

**Ferry Trip to Watsons Bay** 19 I7
The foreshore of the eastern suburbs on display; a popular picnic destination.

**Homebush Bay** 19 E7
Focus of the Sydney 2000 Olympic Games.

**Ku-ring-gai Chase National Park** 19 G1
A magnificent stretch of bush set around the glittering waters of the Hawkesbury River; fishing, bushwalking and river cruises are popular.

**Manly** 19 I6
Old-fashioned, seaside holiday village; its beach is one of Sydney's best.

**North Head** 19 I7
The best coastal views in Sydney.

**Old Government House** 19 C7
Australia's oldest public building, with the country's best collection of Colonial furniture.

**Old Quarantine Station** 19 I7
Used to house afflicted convicts, settlers and interned immigrants from 1832 to 1984; take an evening ghost tour and enjoy the billy tea and damper afterwards.

**Royal National Park** 19 D13
A landscape of sandstone outcrops, woodland, rainforest, cliffs and beaches; walk, fish or camp.

**Sydney Tramway Museum** 19 D13
The largest collection of trams in the Southern Hemisphere; runs novelty tram trips.

**Taronga Zoo** 19 H7
First opened in 1916, of particular interest is the Free Flight Birdshow in an open amphitheatre.

**University of Sydney** 19 G9
Australia's oldest university, famed for its ivy-covered 19th-century buildings and beautiful landscaping.

**Vaucluse House** 19 I8
Once the home of Blue Mountains explorer W. C. Wentworth, the house is fully furnished, with a beautiful 19th-century landscaped garden.

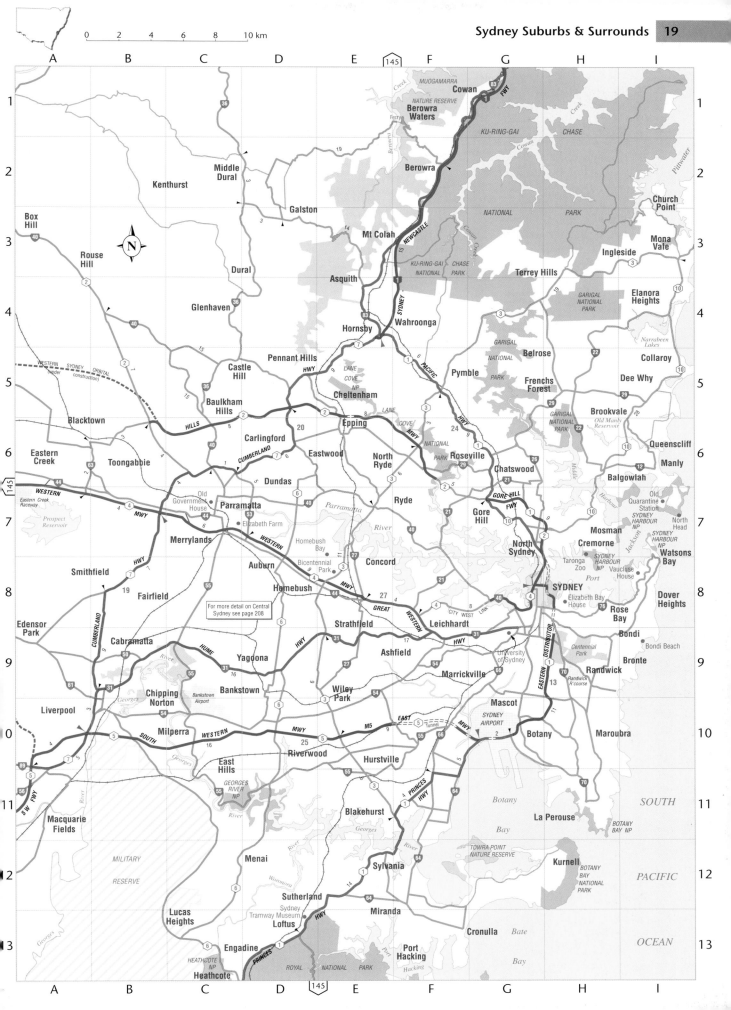

# HUNTER VALLEY & COAST

The Hunter is one of Australia's top wine-producing regions, but this is only a small part of its charm for visitors. Rich alluvial plains, historic towns, horse-breeding properties and tree-lined country avenues create one of the State's most attractive rural landscapes. In the north-east, the region is bound by the high cliffs and rainforest wilderness of Barrington Tops National Park. Over on the coast is Lake Macquarie, a saltwater paradise for boaters and anglers, while to its north lies Newcastle, Australia's second oldest city and major port and industrial centre. Further north again, past the 32-km stretch of Stockton Beach, is Port Stephens, a vast semi-enclosed body of water populated by dolphins and ringed by the white volcanic sands of near-perfect beaches.

## EXPERIENCE IT!

❶ **Trek** the 4-hour-return Rocky Crossing Walk through subtropical rainforest in Barrington Tops National Park

❷ **Dine** at Chez Pok in Peppers Guest House (at Pokolbin), one of the Hunter's many fine restaurants

❸ **Shop** for antiques, crafts and curios at heritage-listed Morpeth, Australia's oldest river port

❹ **Take** a tour to see Aboriginal hand stencils at Wollombi

❺ **Fish** the fresh waters of Lake Glenbawn near Scone

## VISITOR INFORMATION

Hunter Valley (Cessnock):
(02) 4990 4477

Newcastle: (02) 4974 2999

Port Stephens (Nelson Bay):
(02) 4981 1579; 1800 808 900

www.winecountry.com.au

### CLIMATE CESSNOCK

|  | J | F | M | A | M | J | J | A | S | O | N | D |
|---|---|---|---|---|---|---|---|---|---|---|---|---|
| Max. °C | 31 | 31 | 29 | 26 | 21 | 19 | 18 | 19 | 23 | 25 | 29 | 30 |
| Min. °C | 17 | 17 | 16 | 12 | 7 | 7 | 4 | 6 | 9 | 12 | 14 | 16 |
| Rain mm | 80 | 84 | 79 | 64 | 59 | 59 | 45 | 41 | 43 | 57 | 60 | 76 |
| Raindays | 8 | 8 | 8 | 7 | 6 | 7 | 6 | 6 | 6 | 7 | 7 | 8 |

## FOCUS ON

### Top Wines

The Tyrrell family pioneered the wine industry in the Pokolbin district late in the 1850s. The McWilliams and the Draytons soon followed. Premium wines made from shiraz and semillon grapes grown on the lower Hunter's alluvial red soils are unique. A Hunter shiraz is dusty, mellow and soft on the palate. A Hunter semillon, Australia's most distinctive white, is bone-dry with a suggestion of citrus; try Tyrrells Vat 1 Semillon. In good years, Hunter chardonnay ranks with Australia's best; Tyrrells Vat 47 Chardonnay is notable. McWilliam's Mount Pleasant Elizabeth (semillon) and Philip (shiraz) are aged for 5 years before release and offer a relatively inexpensive introduction to the delights of Hunter reds and whites. McWilliam's more expensive Rosehill Shiraz provides a consistent example of a top-quality Hunter red. The Allandale and Capercaillie estates offer splendid chardonnay and semillon and very accessible shiraz. For a tiny winery producing superlative shiraz and chardonnay, look in on Thalgara.

### Upper Hunter

This striking landscape of alluvial plains and rugged mountains supports 7 wineries, including the large estates of Rosemount and Arrowfield. The area just to the north, around Scone, is one of the world's largest thoroughbred horse breeding centres, and boasts some spectacular rural scenery.

### Lower Hunter

The Lower Hunter is Australia's oldest and best known winegrowing district. Around 3000 ha of vines and over 60 wineries are set across rolling hills against the backdrop of the Broken Back Range. A day's tour should start at the wine and information centre in Cessnock. Excellent food and accommodation are available throughout the region.

### Lake Macquarie

This is a magnificent saltwater expanse, four times the size of Sydney Harbour, offering every kind of water sport from angling to skiing, swimming, diving, sailing or kayaking. Don't miss Dobell House at Wangi Wangi (Sundays only), former home of prominent Australian painter William Dobell.

**Barrington Tops National Park**
Situated on one of the highest points of the Great Dividing Range (1600 m), Barrington Tops is the most southerly of the State's World Heritage Rainforest Reserves. Rugged basalt cliffs, cool-temperate and subtropical rainforests, gorges, waterfalls and a touch of light snow in winter make this stunning landscape a popular spot with walkers, campers and climbers.

**Maitland**
Situated on the Hunter River, Maitland was established in the 1820s to service the European settlers who cultivated the rich alluvial plains of the surrounding district. In the early 20th century, it boomed with the discovery of rich coal seams in the valley. Today it remains an elegant, prosperous-looking centre with intact streetscapes and a wealth of heritage buildings.

**TOP EVENTS**

| | |
|---|---|
| **Feb.** | Vintage Festival (Lower Hunter) |
| **Mar.** | Beaumont Street Jazz and Arts Festival (Newcastle) |
| **Apr.** | Heritage Afloat (Lake Macquarie) |
| **Apr.** | Harvest Festival (Cessnock) |
| **Apr.** | Heritage Month (Maitland) |
| **May** | Lovedale Long Lunch (Lovedale, near Cessnock) |
| **May** | Jazz Festival (Morpeth) |
| **Aug./Sept.** | Cathedral Flower Festival (Newcastle) |
| **Sept.** | Garden Ramble (Maitland) |
| **Sept.** | Folk Festival (Wollombi) |
| **Oct.** | Jazz in the Vines (Cessnock) |
| **Oct.** | Opera in the Vineyards (Cessnock) |
| **Oct.** | Mattara Festival (Newcastle) |
| **Oct.** | Festival of Wine and Roses (Singleton) |
| **Dec.** | King Street Fair (Newcastle) |

*For more detail see map 145.*

Map labels: N, 0 20 km, Hunter River, SCONE, Lake Glenbawn ⑤, BARRINGTON TOPS NATIONAL PARK ①, MERRIWA, UPPER HUNTER WINE REGION, MUSWELLBROOK, DENMAN, Hunter, WOLLEMI NATIONAL PARK, SINGLETON, River, MAITLAND ②, MORPETH, Port Stephens, NELSON BAY, Stockton Beach, RAYMOND TERRACE, NEWCASTLE, POKOLBIN, CESSNOCK, LOWER HUNTER WINE REGION ③, YENGO NP, WOLLOMBI ④, WANGI WANGI, Lake Macquarie

**Port Stephens**
Port Stephens, reached via the township of Nelson Bay, is a haven of calm blue waters and sandy beaches, offering excellent boating, fishing and swimming. It is also something of a wildlife haven: about 160 bottlenose dolphins have permanent residence here, migrating whales can be seen in season from a cruise of Stockton Sand Dunes, and koalas can be spotted near Tilligerry Habitat.

**Newcastle**
Australia's second oldest city was founded as a penal colony in 1804. Newcastle rises up the surrounding hills from a spectacular surf coastline, its buildings a pleasant chaos of architectural styles from different historical periods. The city boasts a range of attractions including good restaurants, a premier regional gallery and many historic sites.

# CENTRAL COAST & HAWKESBURY

Within an hour of Sydney, visitors will discover a vast and largely unexplored wilderness, Australia's most historic farming district, the glittering waters and sandstone cliffs of one of the country's most popular national parks and a great sweep of magnificent coastline supporting lively holiday settlements. Explore these places as day trips from the city, or take a couple of days, book into a B&B, a caravan park or luxury resort, and discover the charms and diversity of Sydney's favourite weekend retreats.

## TOP EVENTS

**Jan.**  Entertainment on Waterfront Stage (The Entrance)

**May**  Bridge to Bridge Powerboat Classic (Windsor)

**June/ July**  Food, Wine and Chocolate Festivals (Terrigal)

**Mar.**  Central Coast Chilli Festival (Erina, near Terrigal)

**Sept.**  Hawkesbury District Orchid Spring Show (Richmond)

**Oct.– Nov.**  Fruits of the Hawkesbury Festival (Windsor, Richmond)

**Nov.**  Oyster and Wine Festival (Woy Woy)

**Dec.**  Tuggerah Lakes Mardi Gras Festival (The Entrance)

## EXPERIENCE IT!

**①** *Explore* Old Sydney Town and the Australian Reptile Park, both west of Gosford

**②** *Visit* the Bulgandry Aboriginal Engraving site in Brisbane Water National Park

**③** *Take* a drive through the bountiful fruit-growing district of the Yarramalong Valley

## VISITOR INFORMATION

Terrigal: (02) 4385 4430; 1300 130 708
www.cctourism.com.au

Windsor: (02) 4577 2310
www.hawkesburyvalley.com

## FOCUS ON

### Fishing

Fishing is one of the area's great attractions. There are plenty of boat ramps and boat-hire outlets and no shortage of local bait and tackle suppliers. The trouble-free waters of the Hawkesbury are good for bream, luderick, mulloway and flathead, with bass in the upper reaches. Bream and whiting are a possibility for anglers in the calm stretches of Brisbane Water and Tuggerah Lake. On the coast, beach fishing yields bream, tailor and mulloway. There are excellent rock platforms, particularly around Terrigal (and including The Skillion), where anglers try for some of the big ocean fish, including tuna and kingfish.

### Macquarie towns

In 1810 Governor Macquarie established a number of towns on the high ground of the fertile river plains north-west of Sydney. The area preserves some of Australia's oldest buildings and sites. Windsor's St Matthew's Church (pictured) is the oldest Anglican church in Australia, built in 1817. Even older is the surrounding cemetery. It contains graves dating back to 1810, some belonging to pioneers who arrived on the First Fleet.

### Wollemi National Park

This 500 000-ha wilderness includes areas still unmapped. The 1994 discovery of a new tree species in a rainforest gully was compared with finding a living dinosaur. Take the 1-km walk to the Glow Worm Tunnel, or visit the Colo River west of Wisemans Ferry, where there are walks, canoeing and camping.

### CLIMATE GOSFORD

|  | J | F | M | A | M | J | J | A | S | O | N | D |
|---|---|---|---|---|---|---|---|---|---|---|---|---|
| Max. °C | 27 | 27 | 26 | 24 | 20 | 18 | 17 | 19 | 21 | 24 | 25 | 27 |
| Min. °C | 16 | 17 | 15 | 12 | 8 | 6 | 4 | 5 | 7 | 11 | 13 | 15 |
| Rain mm | 139 | 148 | 150 | 136 | 119 | 128 | 79 | 76 | 69 | 83 | 92 | 102 |
| Raindays | 11 | 11 | 11 | 11 | 9 | 10 | 8 | 8 | 8 | 9 | 10 | 10 |

### Central Coast

This holiday region contains a number of coastal communities fronting surf beaches and calm-water salt lakes. Choose cosmopolitan Terrigal, the family-friendly pace of The Entrance or the exclusivity of Pearl Beach near Woy Woy. National parks in the area provide a peaceful alternative to the busy beach scene.

*For more detail see map 105.*

### Ku-ring-gai Chase National Park

This 15 000-ha bush, river and sandstone landscape forms a scenic border on the northern edge of Sydney's suburbs. Attractions includes diverse flora (about 1000 species including the spectacular waratah), walks, views, access to the Hawkesbury River and engravings of the Guringgai people on the Basin Trail at West Head.

### Lower Hawkesbury

The mouth of the Hawkesbury River opens up into a dazzling network of calm bush-lined waterways, which provide the perfect setting for a houseboat holiday or a day of boating and angling. Hop aboard Australia's last river postal run: the Riverboat Postman departs from Brooklyn at 9.30 a.m. on weekdays.

# HOLIDAY COAST

This is classic Australian holiday territory: miles of perfect beaches; friendly seaside towns, both big and small; pristine areas of wilderness offering refuge from the holiday bustle; and a near-perfect subtropical climate. Choose between the tranquillity of a small fishing settlement – Seal Rocks, for example – and the resort-town excitement of somewhere like Coffs Harbour. As you would expect, the accommodation choices in the area are substantial, ranging from camping in the rainforests of the local national parks to well-serviced caravan parks, guesthouses and luxury resorts.

## TOP EVENTS

**Jan.** Golden Lure Tournament (Port Macquarie)

**Easter** Arts and Crafts Exhibition (Dorrigo)

**Easter** Aquatic Festival (Taree)

**June** Non-Conventional Homes Eco Tour and Envirofair (Taree)

**Aug.** Jazz Festival (Bellingen)

**Sept.** Country Music Festival (Kempsey)

**Oct.** Global Carnival (Bellingen)

**Oct.** Food and Wine Fiesta (Coffs Harbour)

**Oct.** Oyster Festival (Forster)

## EXPERIENCE IT!

**1** *Scuba-dive* at Broughton Island, 2 km offshore in Myall Lakes National Park

**2** *Dine* on oysters and watch the trawlers at Tuncurry's Wallis Lake Fishermen's Co-op

**3** *See* rare coastal rainforest at Sea Acres Rainforest Centre, south of Port Macquarie

## VISITOR INFORMATION

Coffs Harbour: (02) 6652 1522; 1300 369 070

Port Macquarie: (02) 6583 1293; 1800 025 935
www.portmacquarieinfo.com.au

## FOCUS ON

### Beaches

The popularity of this area has everything to do with the quality of the beaches. Most towns are flanked by kilometres of perfect coast, which means a choice between a stretch of sand with a lively social scene, or one that offers seclusion. Elizabeth Beach (near Forster) is calm, seasonally patrolled and popular with families. Solitude seekers and nature lovers should explore the bays and coves protected by Crowdy Bay National Park. Further north, top spots include Crescent Head (popular with surfers, particularly long-board riders), South West Rocks, the beaches of Hat Head National Park and those around Coffs Harbour.

**CLIMATE** **PORT MACQUARIE**

|  | J | F | M | A | M | J | J | A | S | O | N | D |
|---|---|---|---|---|---|---|---|---|---|---|---|---|
| **Max. °C** | 26 | 26 | 25 | 23 | 21 | 18 | 18 | 19 | 20 | 22 | 23 | 25 |
| **Min. °C** | 18 | 18 | 17 | 14 | 11 | 8 | 7 | 8 | 10 | 13 | 15 | 17 |
| **Rain mm** | 156 | 177 | 175 | 169 | 146 | 133 | 98 | 84 | 83 | 96 | 101 | 127 |
| **Raindays** | 13 | 13 | 14 | 13 | 11 | 10 | 9 | 9 | 9 | 11 | 11 | 11 |

### Dorrigo National Park

World Heritage-listed, this park preserves rugged escarpment country and the prehistoric growth of the country's most accessible temperate rainforest area. There are excellent walking tracks, lookouts and picnic areas, and opportunities to see lyrebirds and brush turkeys. The popular Skywalk is an elevated walkway through the dense canopy of rainforest.

*For more detail see maps 145 & 147.*

For more detail see maps 145 & 147.

### Bellingen

This inland township is situated on the Bellinger River in the rich dairy lands that were the setting for Peter Carey's *Oscar and Lucinda*. It offers charming 19th-century rural streetscapes, as well as a New Age character colourfully expressed in the art and craft stores, markets and cosy cafes.

### Coffs Harbour

During the holiday season, the population of Coffs swells from about 22 000 to 100 000. Attractions include the Big Banana, marking one of the area's largest industries; the Pet Porpoise Pool, which features trained sea mammals; seasonal whale-watching; and Muttonbird Island for its large seasonal colony of short-tailed shearwaters (muttonbirds).

### Myall Lakes

The 'Murmuring Myalls' are 10 000 ha of connected lakes separated from the coast by a long line of windswept dunes. Hire a houseboat and explore the calm waters, or drop in for angling, windsurfing or canoeing. There are some spectacular beaches and lookouts along the adjoining coast.

### Ocean Drive

The 48-km Tourist Drive 10 between Kew and Port Macquarie offers golden beaches, rolling surf, rugged cliffs and tranquil coastal lakes. Take in the views from North Brother Mountain (pictured) in tiny Dooragan National Park and look for dolphins off the magnificent, 16-km-long Lighthouse Beach.

# LORD HOWE ISLAND

The Lord Howe Group of Islands lies in subtropical waters about 500 km off the northern New South Wales coast. Listed as a World Heritage site, these volcanic remnants have great natural value and beauty, with sandy beaches, coral reefs, imposing forest-covered mountains and some of the rarest flora and fauna on earth. Fly from Sydney, Brisbane or Port Macquarie for wildlife-watching, walking, surfing, cruising, diving and relaxing in one of Australia's most unspoilt holiday environments. The narrow crescent-shaped main island is 11 km long and has a strict tourist capacity of 400, so book well in advance to avoid disappointment.

## TOP EVENTS

**Feb.**   Discovery Day Celebrations

**Oct.–**  Gosford to Lord Howe Island
**Nov.**   Yacht Race

**Nov.**   Lord Howe Island Golf Open

## EXPERIENCE IT!

❶ **Fish** or surf at Blinky Beach

❷ **Tee** off at one of the world's most scenic golf courses at the base of Mount Lidgbird

❸ **Enjoy** knockout views of The Lagoon along with fine food at the White Gallinule restaurant

### Admiralty Islands
About 2 km offshore, travel north by scenic cruise past this group of eight rocky outcrops, a well-known breeding ground for large colonies of seabirds. Sooty terns (pictured) nest here in spring.

## VISITOR INFORMATION
Lord Howe Island Visitor Centre
(02) 6563 2114

## FOCUS ON

### World Heritage features
The Lord Howe Group of Islands comprises a series of 7-million-year-old volcanic formations. Because of its isolation and the absence of humans until recently, Lord Howe has a significant natural history. Fifty-seven of the islands' 180 flowering plants and 54 fern species are not found elsewhere. At settlement (1834) there were 15 species of land birds, 14 of which were unique. Six species survive. Hundreds of thousands of seabirds roost on the islands. These include the world's largest colony of red-tailed tropic birds, as well as sooty terns, brown noddies, several shearwater species and the world's only providence petrel breeding colony.

### CLIMATE

|  | J | F | M | A | M | J | J | A | S | O | N | D |
|---|---|---|---|---|---|---|---|---|---|---|---|---|
| **Max. °C** | 25 | 26 | 25 | 23 | 21 | 19 | 19 | 19 | 20 | 21 | 22 | 24 |
| **Min. °C** | 20 | 20 | 20 | 18 | 16 | 14 | 13 | 13 | 14 | 15 | 17 | 19 |
| **Rain mm** | 108 | 114 | 122 | 149 | 160 | 177 | 178 | 141 | 135 | 127 | 116 | 117 |
| **Raindays** | 11 | 13 | 15 | 18 | 21 | 22 | 23 | 21 | 17 | 14 | 12 | 12 |

### The Lagoon
A reef supporting many of the area's 98 coral species encloses the crystal waters of this 6-km-long lagoon on the western side of the main island. Spend the day sunbaking and swimming at Old Settlement Beach or go snorkelling at Escotts Hole, about 1 km out. Glass-bottomed boat and snorkelling tours are available.

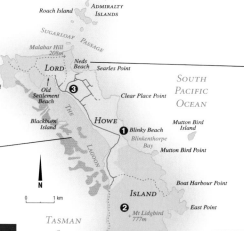

*Roach Island* · ADMIRALTY ISLANDS

SUGARLOAF PASSAGE

*Fishy Point*   Malabar Hill 208m
   Neds Beach
LORD   Searles Point
*North Head*   Old Settlement Beach   ❸   Clear Place Point   SOUTH PACIFIC OCEAN
*Blackburn Island*   HOWE   ❶ Blinky Beach   Mutton Bird Island
   Blinkenthorpe Bay
   Mutton Bird Point
THE LAGOON

N   0   1 km

ISLAND   Boat Harbour Point

TASMAN SEA   ❷ Mt Lidgbird 777m   East Point

Red Point

LORD HOWE ISLAND PERMANENT PARK PRESERVE NATURE RESERVE

Mt Gower 875m
*South Head*   King Point
*Gower Island*

Lord Howe Island   25 km   Balls Pyramid

Observatory Rock
Wheatsheaf Islet   Balls Pyramid

### Neds Beach
Lush forests of kentia and banyan trees, two of the main island's most prolific and distinctive species, fringe this beautiful surf beach. Hand-feed the tropical fish, swim, surf the break, snorkel or take a 45-minute walk up Malabar Hill on the northern headland for superb island views.

### Mount Gower
This 875-m mountain is the main island's highest point. Take a 9-hour guided walk to the summit through the island's endemic plants and areas of stunted rainforest – a fairytale world of gnarled trees, orchids and moss-covered basalt outcrops. Mists permitting, the view from the summit is spectacular.

### Balls Pyramid
An extraordinary cathedral-shaped rocky island rising 551 m out of the sea 25 km south-east of the main island. Once nearly 6 km wide, this island's width has been eroded to only 400 m. The Pyramid is a major breeding ground for seabirds and can be seen by air charter or boat cruise. Deep-sea fishing in the vicinity is excellent.

# TROPICAL NORTH COAST

Exquisite beaches, wide rivers, World Heritage forests and an alternative lifestyle culture are some of the features of this tropical paradise in the far north-east of the State. Popular activities include fishing, whitewater rafting, diving and surfing. Market shopping, festivals, scenic drives, excellent local restaurants and accommodation offering everything from rainforest retreats to beachfront B&Bs are attractions for the more sedentary traveller. The region is a magnet for visitors world-wide but avoids the trappings of most large-scale popular resorts. It remains non-commercial, culturally interesting as well as environmentally 'tuned in'.

## TOP EVENTS

**Jan.** East Coast Sculpture Show (Thursday Plantation, near Ballina)

**Easter** East Coast Blues Festival (Byron Bay)

**May** Mardi Grass Festival (Nimbin)

**July** Grafton Cup

**Aug.** Tweed Valley Banana Festival and Harvest Week (Murwillumbah)

**Sept.** Rainforest Week (Tweed Heads)

**Oct.** Bounty Festival (Ballina)

**Oct.– Nov.** Jacaranda Festival (Grafton)

**Oct.** Seafood Expo (Yamba)

## EXPERIENCE IT!

❶ **Dive** with turtles in the warm waters of Julian Rocks Aquatic Reserve, near Byron Bay

❷ **Visit** Tropical Fruit World, north of Murwillumbah, to see 500 varieties of tropical fruit

❸ **Take** the Tweed Range Scenic Drive (via Nimbin or Murwillumbah) for a 60-km tour of the Border Ranges World Heritage forests

## VISITOR INFORMATION

Byron Bay: (02) 6685 8050
Grafton: (02) 6642 4677
www.tropicalnsw.com.au

## FOCUS ON

### Alternative lifestyle

This once sleepy dairy-farming and fishing district was colonised by alternative lifestyle enthusiasts some thirty years ago. The beautiful Byron Bay is known as the Cosmic Capital of Australia. Along with the town's new affluence you'll find health food outlets, alternative remedies and a colourful procession of residents, including refugee celebrities. Nimbin, the site of the 1973 counter-culture event, the Aquarius Festival, is still a place to 'drop in and drop out'. Organic food, markets, mudbrick buildings and murals are signature features. Other centres with an element of alternative style are The Channon (near Nimbin), Mullumbimby, Murwillumbah and Lismore.

### Mount Warning National Park
The summit of Mount Warning is the first place in Australia to be lit by the sun in the morning. A bushwalking track leads up from the car park through pockets of subtropical and warm-temperate rainforest. The park, along with other north coast and hinterland reserves, is a World Heritage area, classified as part of the Central Eastern Rainforest Reserves.

### CLIMATE BYRON BAY

| | J | F | M | A | M | J | J | A | S | O | N | D |
|---|---|---|---|---|---|---|---|---|---|---|---|---|
| **Max. °C** | 27 | 27 | 26 | 25 | 22 | 20 | 19 | 20 | 22 | 23 | 25 | 26 |
| **Min. °C** | 21 | 21 | 20 | 17 | 15 | 12 | 12 | 13 | 14 | 16 | 18 | 20 |
| **Rain mm** | 169 | 191 | 214 | 179 | 191 | 161 | 102 | 95 | 67 | 106 | 118 | 148 |
| **Raindays** | 14 | 16 | 17 | 15 | 14 | 12 | 10 | 9 | 9 | 11 | 12 | 13 |

### Holiday coast
The bustling riverside settlement of Tweed Heads is great for active families while laid-back Byron Bay is perfect for surfers, singles and sophisticates. Camping and caravan facilities make Ballina and Evans Head appeal to those on a budget, while Iluka and Yamba draw visitors with a bent for angling, surfing and an old-fashioned holiday style.

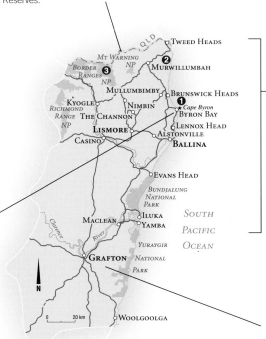

### Cape Byron
Cape Byron is the continent's most easterly point. Its dominant position makes it an excellent place to watch the 2000–3000 humpback whales which travel north along this coastline from late June or early July before heading south again in September. At the tip of the headland is the Cape Byron Lighthouse, said to be the most powerful in Australia.

For more detail see map 147.

### Grafton
This picturesque rural town, with a number of 19th-century buildings, is best known for its beautiful civic landscaping, particularly the mature jacaranda trees with their vivid purple springtime blossom. Located on the Clarence River, Grafton is also a busy centre for water sports, particularly whitewater rafting and canoeing.

# NEW ENGLAND & THE NORTH-WEST

The New England district is some 200 km inland and approximately 1000 m above sea level. Chilly winters, golden autumns, heritage buildings and intensively farmed stretches of land contrast with the tropical coastal scenery of the nearby north coast. New England, however, also has superb tracts of native rainforest, including World Heritage-listed areas. To the west the country flattens out into plains with the occasional dramatic outcrop. Here you'll find historic towns in farmland, and the first red reaches of the outback. The region is also known for its fossicking opportunities – for everything from blue sapphires to rare black opals.

## TOP EVENTS

**Jan.** Country Music Festival (Tamworth)

**Jan.** Great Inland Fishing Festival (Inverell)

**Mar.** Autumn Festival (Armidale)

**Apr.** Oracles of the Bush (bush poetry, Tenterfield)

**May** Australian Celtic Festival (Glen Innes)

**Oct.** Sapphire City Floral Festival (Inverell)

**Oct.** Federation Festival (Tenterfield)

**Oct.** Spring Wine Festival (Tenterfield)

**Nov.** Golden Grain and Cotton Festival (Moree)

## EXPERIENCE IT!

**❶ Drive** to the summit of Mt Kaputar for views of one-tenth of NSW

**❷ Take** a Woollool Woollool Aboriginal Cultural Tour from Tenterfield to see the Bald Rock monolith

**❸ Fish**, swim, water-ski, sail or picnic at Copeton Dam

## VISITOR INFORMATION

Armidale: (02) 6772 4655;
1800 627 736
www.new-england.org/armidale

Tamworth: (02) 6755 4300
www.nnsw.com.au

## FOCUS ON

### Fossicking

The New England district is a fossicker's paradise. Quartz, jasper, serpentine and crystal are common finds, while sapphires, diamonds and gold present more of a challenge. Fossickers Way is a well-signposted tourist route that introduces visitors to the district, beginning at Nundle and travelling north as far as Glen Innes. The route passes through a number of towns including Inverell, the world's largest producer of sapphires. In the far west of the district, Lightning Ridge is well known as a source of the rare black opal. There are designated fossicking areas here, as well as underground mine tours.

### Tenterfield

Visit the School of the Arts building, where in 1889 politician Henry Parkes advocated federation, earning the town the descriptor 'Birthplace of our Nation'. Or find Tenterfield Saddler, the shop that inspired singer and composer Peter Allen to write the song of the same name. Other attractions include magnificent autumn foliage and excellent heritage buildings.

| CLIMATE **ARMIDALE** | | | | | | | | | | | | |
|---|---|---|---|---|---|---|---|---|---|---|---|---|
| | J | F | M | A | M | J | J | A | S | O | N | D |
| **Max. °C** | 27 | 26 | 24 | 21 | 17 | 14 | 13 | 14 | 18 | 21 | 24 | 26 |
| **Min. °C** | 14 | 14 | 12 | 8 | 4 | 2 | 0 | 2 | 4 | 7 | 10 | 12 |
| **Rain mm** | 103 | 86 | 67 | 46 | 44 | 58 | 49 | 49 | 52 | 68 | 80 | 88 |
| **Raindays** | 10 | 10 | 10 | 8 | 8 | 10 | 9 | 9 | 8 | 9 | 9 | 10 |

### New England National Park

Part of the World Heritage-listed Central Eastern Rainforest Reserves, this 71 000-ha park contains three distinct environments: subtropical rainforest, subalpine landscape and temperate forest. Much of the park is wilderness, for experienced walkers only; however, there are easy walks to the lookouts on the north-western (Armidale) side.

*Map showing QUEENSLAND, LIGHTNING RIDGE, MOREE, WARIALDA, BALD ROCK NP, BOONOO BOONOO NP, TENTERFIELD, WASHPOOL NP, GIBRALTAR RANGE NP, GLEN INNES, INVERELL, Copeton Dam, BINGARA, WALGETT, WEE WAA, MOUNT KAPUTAR NP, NARRABRI, BARRABA, GUYRA, ARMIDALE, NEW ENGLAND NP, URALLA, MANILLA, GUNNEDAH, WALCHA, OXLEY WILD RIVERS NP, TAMWORTH, NUNDLE, MURRURUNDI. Gwydir River. 0–50 km scale.*

For more detail see map 146–7.

### Tamworth

Australia's Country Music Capital hosts the huge Australian Country Music Festival each January. Other attractions include the 12-m high Golden Guitar (home of the Country Music Gallery of Stars, where you'll find wax replicas of favourite country artists), Country Music Hands of Fame (artists' handprints) and some superb heritage buildings.

### Armidale

Armidale, at the heart of New England, is a sophisticated university and cathedral town, with over 30 National Trust-listed buildings in gracious tree-lined streets. Visit the Aboriginal Cultural Centre and Keeping Place and the New England Regional Art Museum. The latter holds the multi-million dollar Hinton Collection, Australia's most significant provincial art holding.

### Wollomombi Falls

Located in the Oxley Wild Rivers National Park, the stunning 220-m-high Wollomombi Falls are among the highest falls in the country. Other attractions of the park include camping, walks and superb escarpment scenery.

# CENTRAL WEST

This land of open spaces straddles the western slopes of the Great Dividing Range and the expanse of the Western Plains. Cotton crops, vineyards, cattle and sheep draw on the rich volcanic soil and dominate the landscape, but nature exerts its presence often and, in the case of the strange formations of the Warrumbungles, with great spectacle. The history of the district is varied and well preserved, and appears most notably in the wonderful 19th-century goldmining settlements. Modern attractions include the Western Plains Zoo, and two major space observatories built to take advantage of the region's endless stretch of clear sky.

## TOP EVENTS

| | |
|---|---|
| **Feb.–Mar.** | *Banjo Paterson Festival (Orange)* |
| **Easter** | *Orana Country Music Festival (Dubbo)* |
| **Apr.** | *Marti's Balloon Fiesta (Canowindra)* |
| **Aug.** | *Jazz Festival (Dubbo)* |
| **Sept.** | *Wine Festival (Mudgee)* |
| **Oct.** | *Festival of the Stars (Coonabarabran)* |
| **Oct.** | *Sakura Matsuri (Cherry Blossom Festival, Cowra)* |
| **Oct.** | *Country Music Spectacular (Parkes)* |
| **Nov.** | *Bathurst FAI 1000 Car Race* |

## EXPERIENCE IT!

❶ **Visit** *Siding Springs Observatory, west of Coonabarabran, home to Australia's largest telescope*

❷ **Go** *birdwatching at the 20 000-ha wetlands of Macquarie Marshes Nature Reserve*

❸ **Tour** *the Wellington Caves and see one of the world's largest stalagmites*

## VISITOR INFORMATION

Bathurst: (02) 6332 1444; 1800 681 000
www.bathurstnsw.gov.au

Dubbo: (02) 6884 1422; 1800 674 443
www.dubbotourism.com.au

## FOCUS ON

### Mudgee and Gulgong wines

German settler Adam Roth planted vines at Mudgee in the 1850s. Thirteen wineries had been established by 1890 but just three survived the depression later in the decade. The red wine boom of the 1960s saw many new vineyards planted. The Mudgee and Gulgong area has 23 wineries offering tastings, and over 100 vineyards where plantings exceed 4000 ha. Warm summers favour the production of full-bodied shiraz and chardonnay that cellar well over four to five years (longer for shiraz from top vintages). Try Huntington's shiraz; the organic, preservative-free wines of Botobolar; Craigmoor's chardonnay; or the cabernet sauvignon from Thistle Hill.

### CLIMATE DUBBO

| | J | F | M | A | M | J | J | A | S | O | N | D |
|---|---|---|---|---|---|---|---|---|---|---|---|---|
| **Max. °C** | 33 | 32 | 29 | 25 | 20 | 16 | 15 | 17 | 21 | 25 | 29 | 32 |
| **Min. °C** | 18 | 18 | 15 | 11 | 7 | 4 | 3 | 4 | 6 | 10 | 13 | 16 |
| **Rain mm** | 61 | 54 | 49 | 45 | 48 | 49 | 45 | 45 | 44 | 49 | 51 | 50 |
| **Raindays** | 6 | 5 | 5 | 5 | 6 | 8 | 8 | 8 | 7 | 7 | 6 | 6 |

## Warrumbungle National Park

The Warrumbungles are extraordinary rock formations created by ancient volcanic activity. Best known is The Breadknife (pictured) which juts savagely out of the surrounding bushland. The surrounding 21 000-ha national park marks the area where the flora and fauna of the Western Plains merge with those of the Great Dividing Range.

## Western Plains Zoo

Five km from Dubbo, this excellent open range zoo covers 300 ha and is home to around 1400 animals representing 130 species. A series of environments recreate the natural habitats of the world's continents. Visitors can use their own car, hire a bicycle or use walking trails to all areas.

*For more detail see maps 144, 146, 149 & 151.*

## Hill End

This small town remains largely unchanged since the 1870s gold boom. From the 1950s onwards, prominent Australian artists, most notably Russell Drysdale, were attracted by the aesthetic qualities of the town and surrounding landscape. The post office (pictured) is typical of Hill End's many historic buildings.

## Cowra

In 1944, during World War II, 1000 Japanese soldiers tried to escape Cowra's POW camp, resulting in the death of 235 soldiers. The Japanese cemetery and a magnificent Japanese garden commemorate that history; they are linked by a 5-km avenue of cherry trees. These days Cowra is known for its gourmet produce and developing premium wine production.

## Bathurst

This is Australia's oldest inland settlement. Founded 1815, Bathurst is noted for its Colonial and Victorian architecture, including Miss Traill's House (c.1845), open to the public. Also of interest is Ben Chifley's Cottage (home of the wartime prime minister), the excellent regional art gallery and Mount Panorama, venue for the Bathurst 1000.

# BLUE MOUNTAINS

The misty, bush-clad cliffs and valleys of the Blue Mountains are the eroded remains of a giant plateau that rose up out of a river delta 80 million years ago. Occupied for at least 20 000 years by Aboriginal peoples, the mountains proved an impenetrable barrier until 1813 to the European settlers of Sydney seeking westward expansion. These days the area provides an accessible and spectacularly beautiful nature retreat for the city's residents, with bushwalking, adventure sports, gourmet retreats and cool-climate gardens among the many attractions.

## TOP EVENTS

**Feb.** Blue Mountains Festival of Folk, Roots and Blues (Katoomba)

**Mar.** Blue Mountains Herb Fest (Medlow Bath)

**Apr.** Autumn Gardens Festival (Mt Wilson)

**May** Songs of the Wind Festival (throughout region)

**June** Winter Magic Festival (Katoomba)

**June– Aug.** Yulefest (throughout region)

**Sept.– Nov.** Spring Gardens Festival (throughout region)

**Oct.** Village Fair (Leura)

**Nov.** Rhododendron Festival (Blackheath)

## EXPERIENCE IT!

**❶ Go** canyoning in the Grand Canyon, south-east of Blackheath

**❷ Book** a weekend at Cleopatra, a French-style gourmet retreat in Blackheath

**❸ Descend** the Giant Stairway into the Jamison Valley, south of Katoomba

## VISITOR INFORMATION

Blue Mountains Visitor Information Centre Echo Point Rd, Katoomba and Glenbrook: 1300 653 408 www.bluemountainstourism.org.au

## FOCUS ON

### Gardens

Volcanic soil and cool-climate conditions have made the Blue Mountains one of the best known gardening regions in Australia. Visit Everglades near Leura, a 6-ha classically designed garden that melds with the surrounding bush. Mount Wilson is a tiny village of grand estates, nearly all with large historic gardens of formal lawns, cool-climate plantings, woodlands and huge European trees; many properties are open to the public. Mount Tomah Botanic Garden is the cool-climate annexe of Sydney's Botanic Garden. Here, specialist displays in terraces bring together thousands of worldwide rare species, including the Wollemi Pine, discovered 1994 in Wollemi National Park.

### Grose Valley

A visit to the National Parks and Heritage Centre on Govetts Leap Road is a must for visitors who are keen to explore the network of trails overlooking and leading into the Grose Valley. The escarpment in this area east of Blackheath is particularly dramatic and the views are breathtaking.

### CLIMATE KATOOMBA

|  | J | F | M | A | M | J | J | A | S | O | N | D |
|---|---|---|---|---|---|---|---|---|---|---|---|---|
| **Max. °C** | 23 | 22 | 20 | 17 | 13 | 10 | 9 | 11 | 14 | 17 | 20 | 22 |
| **Min. °C** | 13 | 13 | 11 | 9 | 6 | 4 | 2 | 3 | 5 | 8 | 10 | 12 |
| **Rain mm** | 160 | 170 | 169 | 126 | 103 | 123 | 89 | 81 | 74 | 93 | 103 | 125 |
| **Raindays** | 13 | 12 | 13 | 10 | 9 | 9 | 9 | 9 | 9 | 10 | 11 | 12 |

*For more detail see maps 104–5.*

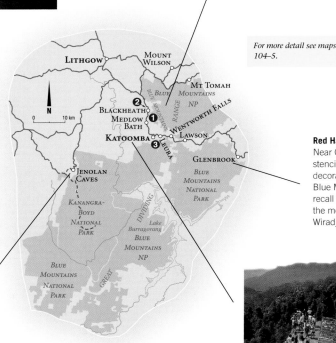

### Red Hands Cave

Near Glenbrook, Aboriginal red-ochre hand stencils, between 500 and 1600 years old, decorate the walls of the Red Hands Cave in Blue Mountains National Park. The stencils recall the presence of the first inhabitants of the mountains, the people of the Dharug, Wiradjuri and Gandangara tribes.

### Jenolan Caves

Formed 400 million years ago in a belt of limestone, this is one of the most extensive and complex underground limestone cave systems in the world. Of the 300 or so 'rooms', 9 are open to the public – by tour only.

### Three Sisters and Echo Point

This feature has been carved by millions of years of erosion, although Aboriginal legend has it that the rock was formed when a father turned his daughters to stone to protect them from an evil figure. Nearby, visitors can ride into or across the Jamison Valley aboard the Scenic Railway or Scenic Skyway.

# CAPITAL COUNTRY

This is a rich agricultural region, radiating out from the northern borders of the Australian Capital Territory. Set along the tableland of the Great Dividing Range, it is characterised by a landscape of undulating hills, golden plains and rocky outcrops. It is best known for its history of European settlement which, dating back to the 1820s, is recorded in the heritage architecture of the district's towns. Other attractions include boutique-style, cool-climate wineries and some beautiful areas of native landscape, which have survived early clearing and settlement. Most attractions are within an easy daytrip from Canberra.

## TOP EVENTS

*Feb.*  Australian Blues Music Festival (Goulburn)

*Feb.*  Hilltops Flavours of the Harvest Festival (Young)

*Mar.*  Country Weekend (Crookwell)

*Mar.*  Weekend of Heritage (Goulburn)

*Apr.*  Heritage Festival (Braidwood)

*Oct.*  Days of Wine and Roses (throughout district)

*Oct.*  Lilac City Festival (Goulburn)

*Nov.*  Music at the Creek (Braidwood)

*Nov.–Dec.*  National Cherry Festival (Young)

## EXPERIENCE IT!

❶ *Explore the dramatic Bungonia Gorge, in Bungonia State Reserve Area*

❷ *Go back in time at the Bywong Goldmining Town, a re-creation of an early mining settlement, north-west of Bungendore*

❸ *Pick cherries in season in the orchards of Young*

## VISITOR INFORMATION

Canberra: (02) 6205 0044
www.canberratourism.com.au
Goulburn: (02) 4823 4492;
1800 353 646

## FOCUS ON

### History

The first inhabitants of the area were the Ngaunawal, whose ancestors, archaeological evidence from Lake George suggests, may have arrived anywhere from 75 000 to 120 000 years ago. Europeans sighted the district in the late 1790s and the Goulburn plains were named in 1818. Settlers arrived between the 1820s and the 1850s, first attracted by the rich grazing land and later by the discovery of gold. Today a number of towns, including Yass, Young, Gunning, Bungendore and Braidwood, retain significant collections of heritage buildings and charming streetscapes. The district as whole provides an evocative glimpse of 19th-century life in rural Australia.

### Yass

In 1821 the explorer Hamilton Hume declared the Yass district a place where 'sheep would thrive uncommonly well'. Hume's home, Cooma Cottage (pictured), built in 1835, is now open to the public. The town retains a strong 19th-century flavour, thanks to its intact shopfronts and early public buildings.

### Capital wineries

The region's cool, dry climate has proved a bonus for local winegrowing. A number of small vineyards, most offering sales, are located on the north and north-east borders of the ACT. Look out for Murrumbateman Winery, Lark Hill and Brindabella Hills Winery.

### CLIMATE GOULBURN

|  | J | F | M | A | M | J | J | A | S | O | N | D |
|---|---|---|---|---|---|---|---|---|---|---|---|---|
| Max. °C | 27 | 26 | 24 | 20 | 16 | 12 | 11 | 13 | 16 | 19 | 22 | 26 |
| Min. °C | 13 | 13 | 11 | 8 | 5 | 2 | 1 | 2 | 5 | 7 | 9 | 12 |
| Rain mm | 63 | 52 | 57 | 57 | 53 | 49 | 45 | 59 | 52 | 58 | 67 | 57 |
| Raindays | 10 | 9 | 9 | 9 | 11 | 11 | 12 | 12 | 11 | 12 | 12 | 9 |

### Brindabella National Park

The lush Brindabella Range, the setting for stories by novelist Miles Franklin, provides a magnificent backdrop to the cleared hills and plains of the surrounding district. Four-wheel-drive access is recommended for this park. Camping, bushwalking and birdwatching are popular activities.

### Namadgi National Park

Namadgi takes in much of the Brindabella Range, covering almost half the ACT. It offers significant Aboriginal rock art and a harsh but beautiful environment of mountains, valleys and bush. Camping, bushwalking and scenic touring are available. Access is along the Monaro Highway via Canberra.

*For more detail see maps 144, 152 & 153.*

### Goulburn

Established 1833, this town displays elaborate 19th-century architecture, a legacy of early wool-growing wealth. Goulburn boasts two cathedrals and a regional art gallery. On the town's outskirts, The Big Merino (pictured) sells wool products.

### Braidwood

Braidwood is a beautifully preserved 19th-century town. Its elegant Georgian buildings recall early agricultural settlement while ornate Victorian structures mark the town's goldmining boom. Today, art and craft, antiques, cafes and its reputation as a setting for films help underpin the local economy.

# SOUTHERN HIGHLANDS & ILLAWARRA

This region combines European-style rural scenery with a fine stretch of typically Australian coastline. The highlands, within the Great Dividing Range, is an area of Colonial sandstone buildings, traditional gardens, quaint villages and excellent B&Bs and guesthouses catering to the steady stream of visitors who, for well over a century, have been arriving from Sydney to seek the peace and clean air of a hillside retreat. Towards the coast, the rural landscape drops away into escarpments, woodland, rainforest and waterfalls, while on the coastal plains the scene is one of dairy farms, river valleys, surf beaches and rugged sea cliffs. Proximity to Sydney and the variety of landscapes makes this a first-rate touring region. Travel inland to the highlands, spend a night or two, and then work your way east for a return trip via the coast.

## EXPERIENCE IT!

❶ *Fish*, swim, surf or stroll pristine shores at Seven Mile Beach National Park

❷ *Explore* the Wombeyan Caves (via Mittagong), one of the most extensive and complex cave systems in Australia

❸ *Sail* or windsurf the waters of the giant coastal lagoon of Lake Illawarra

❹ *Take* a drive up Mount Gibraltar, near Bowral, for splendid views across the Highlands and beyond

❺ *Scuba-dive* or snorkel at Bass Point, Shellharbour

## VISITOR INFORMATION

Wollongong: 1800 240 737
www.tourismwollongong.com

Southern Highlands
Visitor Information Centre
Mittagong: (02) 4871 2888;
1300 657 559
www.highlandsnsw.com.au

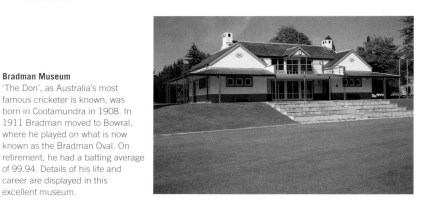

### Bradman Museum
'The Don', as Australia's most famous cricketer is known, was born in Cootamundra in 1908. In 1911 Bradman moved to Bowral, where he played on what is now known as the Bradman Oval. On retirement, he had a batting average of 99.94. Details of his life and career are displayed in this excellent museum.

### CLIMATE BOWRAL

|         | J | F | M | A | M | J | J | A | S | O | N | D |
|---------|----|----|-----|----|----|----|----|----|----|----|-----|----|
| Max. °C | 25 | 25 | 23 | 20 | 16 | 13 | 12 | 13 | 16 | 19 | 21 | 24 |
| Min. °C | 13 | 13 | 11 | 7 | 4 | 2 | 1 | 2 | 4 | 7 | 9 | 11 |
| Rain mm | 88 | 80 | 110 | 88 | 77 | 84 | 45 | 63 | 57 | 84 | 100 | 73 |
| Raindays | 14 | 13 | 13 | 11 | 12 | 11 | 10 | 10 | 11 | 13 | 13 | 12 |

## FOCUS ON

### Towns of the Highlands
Bowral, with its historic streetscapes, restaurants and cafes, B&Bs and guesthouses and superb gardens, is the centre of the Southern Highlands holiday region. Historic Berrima, once the commercial heart of the district, now serves as a timepiece of Colonial Georgian Australia. Nearby Mittagong boasts lovely gardens, as well as good cafes and interesting shopfront architecture. Sutton Forest and Moss Vale are pretty towns with an air of the English countryside, while Bundanoon, further south, is known for its excellent guesthouses, health resort and views across Morton National Park. Away from the main tourist route are Robertson and Burrawang, peaceful settlements steeped in 19th-century history. Don't miss Ranelagh House in Robertson, designed in 1924 to resemble an English manor. The rolling hills of this district were the backdrop for the Australian film *Babe* (1996). To the south is Berry (established 1822), set in the dairy country of the Shoalhaven River district, and boasting charming heritage buildings, galleries, antique shops and guesthouses.

### Berrima
Established in the 1830s, Berrima is Australia's best-preserved Georgian settlement. Architectural highlights include the gaol (1839) and Berrima Courthouse (1838), pictured here. A self-guide historical walking tour is available. Look out for Berkelouw's Book Barn, which has around 200 000 second-hand books.

### Morton National Park
This vast tract of wilderness is best explored via the 14 designated walking tracks leading from the township of Bundanoon, including a night walk to Glow Worm Glen. Sandstone cliffs, wooded valleys, waterfalls and the winding tributaries of the Shoalhaven River are among the natural attractions.

**Gardens of the highlands**

The highlands are known for their traditional English-style gardens. In Bowral, the historic Corbett Gardens and the gardens of the Grand Mecure Hotel come alive at tulip time in spring. During September and October the many established private gardens of the region, mostly around Mittagong and Bowral, open their gates for vibrant springtime displays.

**Royal National Park**

The Royal, designated in 1879, was Australia's first national park. Features include Aboriginal rock engravings, beaches and waterholes, pockets of rainforest set amid stretches of woodland and heath, and some the State's most spectacular coastal scenery, seen from rugged sandstone cliffs. Camping, walks, cycling and picnic facilities are available.

For more detail see maps 144–5.

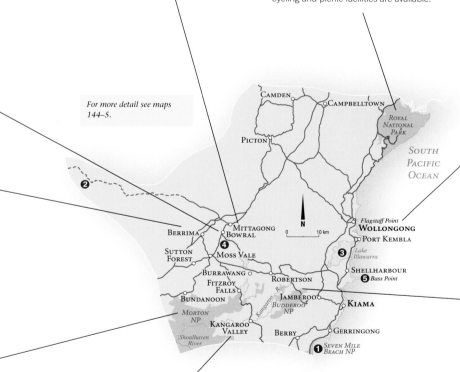

**Wollongong**

Wollongong, an Aboriginal word for 'sound of the sea', is a major regional city set along a stretch of coast that includes 17 surf beaches. Visit the city's boat harbour, fish co-op and restaurants on Flagstaff Point; drive north through the old coal mines for coastal views; and to the south, see Nan Tien Temple, the largest Buddhist temple in the Southern Hemisphere.

**Minnamurra Falls**

The Minnamurra Falls, in Budderoo National Park, is one of several groups of falls formed by the massive sandstone escarpment that defines the edge of the Southern Highlands. Nearby is the Minnamurra Rainforest Centre, which incorporates a raised walkway leading into pockets of dense temperate and subtropical rainforest.

**Kangaroo Valley**

This valley, known for its stunning combination of rural and native scenery, is best explored from the scenic route (via Nowra Road) leading down from the highlands to the coast. Attractions include the historic townships of Kangaroo Valley and Berry, Hamden Bridge, which crosses the Kangaroo River, and the 80-m-high Fitzroy Falls (pictured).

# THE SOUTH COAST

This long, beautiful stretch of sandy beaches, rivers, lakes, fishing villages, rolling hills, rugged escarpments and native forests has proved remarkably resilient to the excesses of coastal development. Whaling and wholesale logging have come and gone and sustainable tourism and dairying are the mainstays. Because the climate is cooler here, summer is the peak period. Even then the area has a laid-back feel. Weekend trips from Canberra are common, but visitors from Sydney or Melbourne usually stay for at least a week, to take full advantage of all the national parks and the surfing, fishing, walking and touring opportunities.

## TOP EVENTS

| | |
|---|---|
| **Jan.** | Blue Water Fishing Classic (Bermagui) |
| **Mar.** | Seaside Fair (Bermagui) |
| **Easter** | Tilba Festival (Central Tilba) |
| **Easter** | Blessing of the Fleet (Ulladulla) |
| **Aug.** | Festival of Food and Wine by the Sea (Ulladulla) |
| **Oct.** | Whale Festival (Eden) |
| **Oct.** | Country Music Festival (Merimbula) |
| **Oct.** | Jazz Festival (Moruya) |
| **Oct.** | Great Southern Blues Festival (Narooma) |

## EXPERIENCE IT!

❶ **Board** a charter and go deep-sea fishing offshore from Bermagui

❷ **Go** surfing at Tathra Beach and visit the historic Tathra Wharf

❸ **Eat** fresh Clyde River oysters on the waterfront at Batemans Bay

## VISITOR INFORMATION

Batemans Bay: (02) 4472 6900; 1800 802 528
Eden: (02) 6496 1953; 1800 633 012
Nowra: (02) 4421 0778; 1800 024 261
www.southcoast.net.au

## FOCUS ON

### Aboriginal culture

Before European colonisation, the Yuin occupied the area from Jervis Bay to Twofold Bay, sustained by the produce of coast and rivers. Today the area remains steeped in Yuin history. At Wallaga Lake the Umbarra Cultural Centre offers tours, including one to the summit of Mount Dromedary (Gulaga), where, according to legend, the great creation spirit, Daramulun, ascended to the sky. Booderee National Park, within Jervis Bay Territory, is once again Yuin land after the successful 1995 land claim. Jointly managed by the Wreck Bay Aboriginal Community and Parks Australia, Booderee has numerous middens and significant sites, and an art and craft centre. The Murramarang Aboriginal Area, near Bawley Point, has a self-guide interpretive walk.

### CLIMATE MERIMBULA

| | J | F | M | A | M | J | J | A | S | O | N | D |
|---|---|---|---|---|---|---|---|---|---|---|---|---|
| **Max. °C** | 24 | 25 | 23 | 21 | 19 | 16 | 16 | 17 | 18 | 20 | 21 | 23 |
| **Min. °C** | 15 | 15 | 14 | 11 | 8 | 6 | 4 | 5 | 7 | 9 | 12 | 14 |
| **Rain mm** | 80 | 71 | 95 | 71 | 70 | 64 | 37 | 45 | 52 | 77 | 85 | 65 |
| **Raindays** | 10 | 9 | 10 | 9 | 10 | 9 | 7 | 9 | 10 | 11 | 12 | 11 |

### Central Tilba

This tiny National Trust village, in a spectacular mountain landscape, is a showpiece for late-19th-century rural architecture. It contains 25 timber structures of special interest, most of them built in the 1890s. Once a goldmining centre, the town now caters for tourists, with cafes, galleries and art and craft shops.

### Jervis Bay

Part of this area is within Jervis Bay Territory and includes the national capital's seaport. The bay, in part bordered by NSW Jervis Bay National Park, is known for its dramatic underwater landscapes and its dolphins; diving and dolphin cruises are available. Nearby Booderee National Park protects important Aboriginal sites as well as beautiful beaches and bush.

### Montague Island

Montague Island, half an hour's boat ride from Narooma, is a wildlife paradise, with populations of 8000 pairs of little (fairy) penguins, 600 Australian fur seals, and various species of seabirds. It is also an excellent place to spot migrating humpbacks (September–November). Contact the national parks office in Narooma for tour details.

*For more detail see map 152.*

### Eden

From the 1820s until the 1930s, this town served the huge whaling industry of these southern waters. Today Eden is a major whale-watching destination, particularly for humpbacks (October–November). Don't miss the Killer Whale Museum. Nearby are the beautiful Ben Boyd National Park (pictured) and historic Boydtown.

### Mimosa Rocks National Park

The area covered by this national park is a traditional home of the Yuin. The park crosses a landscape of beaches, sea caves, cliffs, forests and wetlands. There are several secluded campsites, and swimming, walking, diving, fishing and birdwatching are among the activities on offer.

# THE RIVERINA

The Riverina stretches across the flat, fertile plains of south central New South Wales. It is one of Australia's richest agricultural regions, watered by the Murrumbidgee River through a vast irrigation system. The spacious landscape, brilliantly clear skies and warm weather make touring the district a special pleasure. The towns of the region are busy, prosperous places, some bearing a strong Southern European character as a result of almost a century of settlement by immigrant farmers. Good restaurant and cafes, heritage buildings and excellent accommodation are to be found.

## TOP EVENTS

**Jan.** *Australian Surf Carnival (Hay)*

**Feb.** *Tumbafest (food and wine, Tumbarumba)*

**Mar.** *John O'Brien Bush Festival (Narrandera)*

**Easter** *SunRice Festival (even-numbered years, Leeton)*

**June** *Taste of Riverina (alternates Griffith/Wagga)*

**Aug.** *Wattle Time (Cootamundra)*

**Sept.** *Jazz Festival (Wagga Wagga)*

**Apr.– May** *Festival of the Falling Leaf (Tumut)*

**Nov.** *Dog on the Tuckerbox Festival; Snake Gully Cup (Gundagai)*

## EXPERIENCE IT!

❶ **Visit** the Dog on the Tuckerbox, five miles from Gundagai (8 km north)

❷ **Fish** for trout in the mountain streams around Tumut

❸ **Go** four-wheel driving across the Riverina outback, west of Hay

## VISITOR INFORMATION

Wagga Wagga: (02) 6926 9621; 1800 648 144

www.riverinatourism.com.au

## FOCUS ON

### Regional produce

The region produces rice, citrus and stone fruit, grapes, poultry and vegetables in massive quantities, as well as gourmet products. It is Australia's biggest producer of rice; visit the Sunrice Country Visitors Centre in Leeton. For fruit products, tour the Berri Juice Factory at Leeton, the Catania Fruit Salad Farm at Hanwood (near Griffith) and the Fruits of Batlow Packing Complex at Batlow (known for its apples). In Leeton, Mick's Bake House makes excellent breads, while the Riverina Cheese Factory sells its produce at the Fresh Fruit Market. In Wagga, drop in to Tavenders Gourmet Produce for local lines.

### CLIMATE TEMORA

|        | J  | F  | M  | A  | M  | J  | J  | A  | S  | O  | N  | D  |
|--------|----|----|----|----|----|----|----|----|----|----|----|----|
| Max. °C | 31 | 31 | 28 | 22 | 18 | 14 | 13 | 15 | 18 | 22 | 26 | 30 |
| Min. °C | 16 | 16 | 13 | 9  | 6  | 3  | 2  | 3  | 5  | 8  | 11 | 14 |
| Rain mm | 50 | 37 | 42 | 44 | 46 | 42 | 47 | 46 | 42 | 54 | 46 | 41 |
| Raindays | 6 | 5 | 5 | 6 | 9 | 10 | 13 | 12 | 9 | 9 | 7 | 6 |

### Griffith

The main township of the Riverina, Griffith was developed in response to the introduction of irrigation and was designed by Walter Burley Griffin, architect of Canberra. It is the centre for food and wine production in the region, and has good restaurants and cafes.

### Riverina wineries

The Riverina is responsible for 60 per cent of grapes grown in New South Wales. There are 14 wineries in the district, mostly around Griffith, including the De Bortoli, Miranda and McWilliams wineries. This region is best known for its rich botrytised semillon.

### Hay

Hay lies at the centre of a huge stretch of semi-arid grazing country known as the Hay Plains (pictured). The town was established in 1859 and boasts an interesting collection of late 19th-century heritage buildings, including Bishop's Lodge (1888, in South Hay), a classic Australian homestead surrounded by a superb garden.

*For more detail see maps 150–1 & 152.*

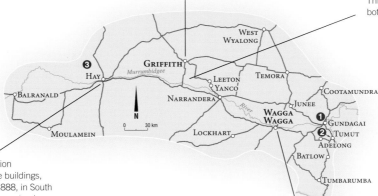

### Wagga Wagga

Wagga, on the banks of the Murrumbidgee, is the State's largest inland city and a major centre for commerce, agriculture and education. Visit the two local wineries (one of which is a leading viticulture teaching facility), the Botanic Gardens, and the Regional Art Gallery, home of the National Art Glass Collection. River walks and cruises are popular activities.

# SNOWY MOUNTAINS

Alpine New South Wales stretches from ACT to the border of Victoria along the spine of the Great Dividing Range. Kosciuszko National Park lies at the heart of the region, protecting the continent's highest mountain, its only glacial lakes, some of its rarest native species, and the headwaters of legendary rivers. Nestled within the folds of the landscape's peaks and valleys are a collection of world-class ski resorts that attract hundreds of thousands of skiers from across Australia and around the world each winter. In spring and summer a brilliant sweep of wildflowers cover the fields, mountain streams run full with melting snow, and tribes of bushwalkers, campers, anglers, scenic drivers and horseback and mountain-bike riders arrive to savour the warm-weather delights of this diverse and spectacular 'roof' of Australia.

## CLIMATE THREDBO

|  | J | F | M | A | M | J | J | A | S | O | N | D |
|---|---|---|---|---|---|---|---|---|---|---|---|---|
| Max. °C | 21 | 21 | 18 | 14 | 10 | 6 | 5 | 6 | 10 | 13 | 16 | 19 |
| Min. °C | 7 | 7 | 5 | 2 | –1 | –3 | –4 | –2 | –1 | 1 | 3 | 5 |
| Rain mm | 116 | 84 | 113 | 119 | 172 | 160 | 161 | 186 | 208 | 207 | 159 | 119 |
| Raindays | 11 | 10 | 11 | 12 | 15 | 16 | 16 | 17 | 18 | 16 | 15 | 12 |

## FOCUS ON

### Ski resorts

The Snowy Mountain resorts are well equipped in terms of lessons, lifts, ski hire, transport, food, accommodation and entertainment. All ski resorts are in Kosciuszko National Park and most are 90–100 km south of Cooma. Perisher, Smiggin Holes, Mount Blue Cow and Guthega are collectively known as Perisher Blue Ski Resort, the largest in Australia, with 50 lifts and a variety of slopes. A good range of accommodation is available at Perisher and Smiggin Holes, but overnight parking is limited (many leave their cars at Bullocks Flat). Accommodation is limited at Guthega and not available at Blue Cow. Thredbo, the main village, has excellent skiing and tourist facilities. Charlotte Pass, 8 km from the Mount Kosciuszko summit, is Australia's highest settlement and provides access to some of the region's highest and most spectacular runs. In the north of the park, Mount Selwyn is a good place for families and beginners, and is one of the main centres for cross-country skiing.

## EXPERIENCE IT!

1. **Go** whitewater rafting on the headwaters of the Murray near Khancoban
2. **Re-live** the adventures of legendary mountain horsemen on a horseriding tour via Adaminaby
3. **Take** a 24-km-return walk from Charlotte Pass (via Jindabyne) along Australia's highest walking track, past the glacial Blue Lake
4. **Tour** the historic sites of Cooma on the self-guide Lambie Town Walk
5. **Visit** the Gaden Trout Hatchery near Jindabyne

## VISITOR INFORMATION

Snowy Region Visitor Information Centre
Jindabyne: (02) 6450 5600;
1800 636 525
www.snowymountains.com.au

### Snowy River

This once mighty river was damned and diverted for the Snowy Mountains Scheme. Some 100 000 men from 30 countries worked for 25 years on the largest engineering project of its kind in Australia. Drop in at the Snowy Mountains Authority Information Centre in Cooma, or visit the power stations near Khancoban.

### Alpine Way

Stretching 111 km from Jindabyne to Khancoban, this spectacular route traverses the national park, winding around the Thredbo slopes, passing through Dead Horse Gap and crossing the valley of the Murray headwaters. The route is best driven during spring and summer, although the winter scenery is superb.

### Mount Kosciuszko

This is Australia's highest mountain, 2228 m above sea level. Explorer Paul Edmond de Strzelecki named the mountain in 1840 for the Polish patriot Tadeusz Kosciuszko. From Thredbo, the summit is easily reached via the Crackenback chairlift (operating all year), with a 12-km-return walk through wildflowers in spring and summer.

### Thredbo

This charming alpine village with its peaked European-style lodges makes for an unusual sight in the Australian landscape. Packed and brimming with life during winter, it has year-round facilities and is also popular in the summer months with bushwalkers, wildflower enthusiasts, anglers and mountain-bike riders.

## Yarrangobilly Caves

Located at the park's northern end, these caves with their underground pools, frozen waterfalls and weird web of limestone formations are said to be the most lavishly decorated in the country. Five out of 70 caves are open to the public. A naturally formed thermal pool offers year-round swimming.

## Kosciuszko National Park

The State's largest park, declared 1967, takes in 690 000 ha of peaks, valleys, glacial lakes, woodlands and fields. The park protects many rare and unusual species, including the distinctive snow gum, the only native tree that can survive above 1800 m, and the pygmy possum (pictured), which lives above altitudes of 1400 m.

### TOP EVENTS

| | |
|---|---|
| **Jan.** | *Blues Festival (Thredbo)* |
| **Mar.** | *Tour de Snowy – women's cycling (throughout region)* |
| **Mar.** | *Strzelecki Polish Festival (Jindabyne)* |
| **Mar.** | *Global Music Festival (Thredbo)* |
| **Easter** | *Fair (Berridale)* |
| **May** | *Legends of Jazz (Thredbo)* |
| **Sept.** | *Shout About Trout (Jindabyne)* |
| **Sept.** | *Xtreme Winter Games (Perisher Blue)* |
| **Oct.** | *Coomafest (Cooma)* |
| **Oct.** | *Spring Festival (Khancoban)* |
| **Nov.** | *Snowy Mountains Trout Festival (throughout region)* |
| **Dec.** | *Monaro Wool Week (Cooma)* |
| **Dec.** | *Man from Snowy River Rodeo (Jindabyne)* |

*For more detail see map 152.*

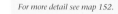

## Lake Jindabyne

Created as part of the Snowy Mountain Scheme, this huge mountain lake, along with nearby Lake Eucumbene, has a reputation as one of the best inland fishing destinations in the State, particularly for trout fishing. Sailing, windsurfing and water-skiing are popular in summer.

## Skitube

This European-style alpine train provides transport for skiers during winter and the chance for a scenic tour in summer. It leaves Bullocks Flat some 20 km south-east of Jindabyne, crosses the Thredbo River, climbs through stands of massive mountain ash, then disappears underground to link Perisher resort and the Mount Blue Cow ski area (pictured).

# THE MURRAY

The Murray, Australia's most important river, runs for 2750 km from the peaks of the Snowy Mountains across three States. It was a great natural resource for the indigenous peoples, who settled the area in greater numbers than anywhere else on the continent. European settlers used the river as a major trade route and a centre for agricultural activity. More recently, the Murray has developed its leisure credentials, thanks to magnificent river red gum scenery and quiet sandy beaches (perfect for water sports), as well as a variety of introduced attractions ranging from excellent golf courses to vineyards and river cruises.

## TOP EVENTS

*Jan.* New Year's Day Power Boat Racing (Mulwala)

*Jan.* Federation Festival (Corowa)

*Feb.* Vintage Engine Rally (Barham)

*Feb.* Riverboats, Food, Jazz and Wine (Echuca–Moama)

*Easter* Jazz Festival (Deniliquin)

*July* Winter Breakaway Festival (Corowa)

*Sept.– Oct.* Play on the Plains Festival (Deniliquin)

*Oct.* Food and Wine Festival (Albury)

*Nov.* Festival of the Bogong Moth (Albury)

## EXPERIENCE IT!

**❶ Hire** a houseboat or catch a paddle-steamer from the old river port settlement of Echuca (Vic.), the twin town of Moama

**❷ Swim** at one of the 25 river beaches at Tocumwal

**❸ Take** a river cruise at Wentworth

## VISITOR INFORMATION

Albury: (02) 6041 3875; 1800 800 743

## FOCUS ON

### Golf

These days golf rivals agriculture as the activity for which the region is best known. Alongside the great stretches of cultivated land lie emerald-green fairways, most offering superb riverside scenery and excellent accommodation and club facilities, along with great golfing. The 36-hole Cobram-Barooga course is one of the district's best, as is Albury's Thurgoona Country Club, regularly rated among Australia's top 100 courses. There is a testing 27-hole course at Corowa, and a fine 18-hole course at the township of Howlong. Another favourite is the picturesque Tocumwal course, where kangaroos are on hand as spectators.

### CLIMATE ALBURY

|         | J  | F  | M  | A  | M  | J  | J  | A  | S  | O  | N  | D  |
|---------|----|----|----|----|----|----|----|----|----|----|----|----|
| Max.°C  | 31 | 31 | 28 | 23 | 16 | 13 | 12 | 14 | 17 | 21 | 25 | 28 |
| Min. °C | 14 | 15 | 12 | 8  | 5  | 3  | 2  | 4  | 5  | 8  | 10 | 13 |
| Rain mm | 23 | 26 | 36 | 46 | 72 | 59 | 83 | 85 | 73 | 73 | 39 | 67 |
| Raindays| 5  | 4  | 6  | 7  | 11 | 12 | 15 | 14 | 11 | 10 | 7  | 8  |

### Deniliquin

Deniliquin, just to the north of the Murray, lies at the centre of one of the largest irrigation areas in the State. It is known for its massive rice export mill and its merino sheep studs, and is set amid a fine landscape of rural and river scenery.

### Corowa

Corowa is the quintessential Australian river town with wide streets, turn-of-the-century architecture and an attractive riverside golf course. Federation got a jump-start here in 1893 at the Corowa Federation Conference, now commemorated in the Federation Museum. In 1889 Tom Roberts completed his iconographic work, Shearing of the Rams, at a sheep station nearby.

*For more detail see map 150–1.*

### Lake Mulwala

The damming of the Yarrawonga Weir in 1939 created this 6000-ha artificial lake, around which the town of Mulwala has grown. The lake has become well known as a premier water sports destination, offering yachting, water-skiing, sailboarding, swimming, canoeing and fishing.

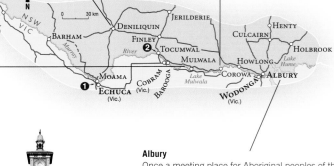

### Albury

Once a meeting place for Aboriginal peoples of the area, Albury today is a large regional centre, familiar to motorists who travel the busy Sydney-to-Melbourne Hume Highway. Attractions include interesting heritage buildings including the railway station (pictured), a large regional art gallery and good restaurants. Lake Hume, one of Australia's biggest artificial lakes, is enormously popular for water sports.

# THE OUTBACK

This vast, arid, sparsely populated landscape covers a good two-thirds of the country's most urbanised State. Mining and sheep farming, the main activities of human endeavour, keep life firmly rooted in a frontier past although such contemporary touches as the occasional film crew or espresso cafe are evident. One radical change has been the creation of a series of national parks over several decades. These parks preserve the region's stunning beauty, its natural heritage and its rich indigenous history. Conditions can be difficult out here.

## TOP EVENTS

**Mar.** Outback and All That Jazz (Broken Hill)

**Mar./ Apr.** St Patricks Race Day (Broken Hill)

**July** Tibooburra Festival

**Aug.** Festival of the Miner's Ghost (Cobar)

**Aug.** Burke and Wills Fishing Challenge (Menindee)

**Sept.** Mateship Festival (Bourke)

**Sept.– Oct.** Darling River Surfboat Classic (Brewarrina)

**Oct.** Rodeo (Bourke)

**Oct.** Country Music Festival (Broken Hill)

## EXPERIENCE IT!

❶ **Go** yachting, fishing, swimming, or camp, at lakes near Menindee

❷ **Fossick** for opals in the dugout town of White Cliffs

❸ **Explore** Willandra, once the west's best known sheep station, now part of Willandra National Park (via Hillston)

## VISITOR INFORMATION

Broken Hill: (08) 8087 6077
Bourke: (02) 6872 2280
www.outbacknsw.org.au

## FOCUS ON

### Willandra Lakes World Heritage Area

Willandra Lakes, covering 240 000 ha in the State's far west, comprises dry Pleistocene lakes formed over two million years ago. Fringed by huge dunes, the lakes bear evidence of major stages in the earth's evolution. Archaeological evidence also points to continuous Aboriginal occupation for about 50 000 years when the lakes were full and teeming with wildlife. The lakes dried around 12 000 years ago, but Aborigines continued to use the area. Human skeletons excavated there are believed to be about 60 000 years old. Mungo National Park covers 10 per cent of the area; the remainder is under pastoral lease.

| CLIMATE BROKEN HILL | | | | | | | | | | | | |
|---|---|---|---|---|---|---|---|---|---|---|---|---|
| | J | F | M | A | M | J | J | A | S | O | N | D |
| Max. °C | 32 | 32 | 29 | 24 | 19 | 16 | 15 | 17 | 20 | 24 | 28 | 30 |
| Min. °C | 19 | 18 | 16 | 12 | 9 | 7 | 6 | 7 | 9 | 12 | 14 | 17 |
| Rain mm | 23 | 23 | 19 | 18 | 22 | 23 | 17 | 20 | 20 | 25 | 19 | 20 |
| Raindays | 3 | 3 | 3 | 3 | 4 | 5 | 5 | 5 | 4 | 4 | 3 | 3 |

*For more detail see maps 148–9 & 150–1.*

### Bourke

'If you know Bourke you know Australia', said Henry Lawson. Situated on the Darling River, the town began in the 1850s as a paddleboat destination. Later a service centre for a vast sheep-grazing area, Bourke has become synonymous with the outback. The town's colourful past is recalled in its heritage sites.

### Sturt National Park

Occupying 310 000 ha of Corner Country – the point where three States meet – Sturt offers varied landscapes of hill, rock and plain, congregations of native birds and animals, and wonderful wildflowers after rain. Camping is available; check in at the park centre, and take advantage of their tours.

### Mutawintji National Park

Driving and walking allows visitors to enjoy sandstone cliffs, river red gums, gorges, rock pools and desert plains in this superb landscape. A program of tours and other activities provides a memorable insight into this area's Aboriginal heritage, which includes some of the State's best Aboriginal rock art.

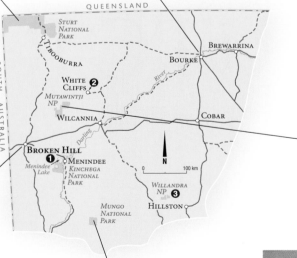

### Broken Hill

Broken Hill was established in the 1880s to service the mining of massive deposits of silver, lead and zinc in the Barrier Ranges. With its historic buildings, 20 or so art galleries and a constant stream of filmmakers and artists, it is an oasis of civilisation in a surreally sparse landscape.

### Mungo National Park

Mungo is the focal point of Willandra Lakes World Heritage area. A 60-km signposted drive covers a large area, including remarkable sculptured dunes, The Walls of China. Aboriginal tours are run from Mildura (Victoria); further activities are available at the park headquarters, where non-campers can stay in former shearers' quarters.

### Meeting place

The site of the capital was first occupied by two groups of Aboriginal people, the Ngunnawal and the Ngario. The large campsites found along the banks of the Molonglo indicate a substantial Aboriginal population in the area. In 1820 Charles Throsby Smith was the first European to explore the area. Four years later, Joshua Moore took up 1000 acres (400 hectares) on the banks of the Molonglo River, a tributary of the Murrumbidgee River. He named his property Canberry, an Aboriginal word meaning 'meeting place'.

### A capital plan

In 1912 Walter Burley Griffin and Marion Mahony Griffin, American architects from Chicago, won an international competition for the design of the capital city. The plan incorporated vistas: boulevards lined with trees and monumental buildings; spacious parks; and residential and commercial areas extending to the hills beyond. Canberra to this day is one of only a few completely planned cities in the world.

# AUSTRALIAN CAPITAL TERRITORY

The Australian Capital Territory, occupying 2400 square kilometres, lies in the valley of the Molonglo River and at the foothills of the Great Dividing Range. Canberra, capital of Australia and seat of Federal Government, is a model metropolis.

Growth was slow in the capital in the 1930s and 1940s. Many Federal Government departments and their public servants remained in Melbourne or Sydney. By the 1950s the population had struggled to reach 25 000. But after the filling of Lake Burley Griffin in 1965, grand buildings were constructed along its shore: the National Library (1968), the High Court (1980), the National Gallery (1982) and the new Parliament House (1988). Office blocks appeared and government departments and their personnel transferred – often reluctantly – to the new capital.

Today the residents of the ACT enjoy the highest standard of living of any Australian State or Territory. As well as a gracious environment, Canberra offers amenities and facilities far beyond those of any other similar-sized city in the world.

For more information on the Australian Capital Territory, see Tourist Bureaus, opposite page 236.

# CANBERRA

Canberra, the capital of Australia, is a planned city set graciously on the shores of Lake Burley Griffin. The cultural and political life of the country is on show here. This small city, with a population of only 310000, claims some of the nation's most significant institutions, including a magnificent art gallery and one of the best war museums in the world. Grand public buildings and monuments complement the order and beauty of the city's original design.

## CITY CENTRE
See map on page 209.

**Australian War Memorial** 209 H4
Probably the world's largest war museum with an estimated four million items; also on site is the Bradbury Aircraft Hall and Anzac Hall, housing large relics.

**Blundell's Cottage** 209 F7
Built in 1858, this cottage re-creates the struggle of the labouring classes in those early farming years.

**National Capital Exhibition** 209 D6
See exhibits on the history and development of the city and take in the views of the parliamentary precinct.

**National Gallery of Australia** 209 F9
A brilliant overview of Australian art, including an extensive Aboriginal collection.

**National Library of Australia** 209 D8
This grand neo-classical structure contains over six million books, including the diaries of Captain Cook's *Endeavour* voyages.

**National Museum of Australia** 209 B7
Housing an extraordinary collection of Aboriginal artefacts and bark paintings, the museum also features displays and gardens that document our history from European settlement.

**Old Parliament House** 209 D9
Wander through for a fascinating recollection of the events and intrigues of Australian political life; the National Portrait Gallery is also housed here.

**Parliament House** 209 C11
Take a free tour of Canberra's centrepiece, with more than 4500 rooms and 3000 artworks, and watch the politicians at work.

**Questacon – The National Science and Technology Centre** 209 D8
Fascinating hands-on displays and experiments within five galleries.

**ScreenSound Australia** 209 B4
Dedicated to the preservation of Australia's film and sound archive, the museum has regularly updated displays and a 1930s cinema.

**VISITOR INFORMATION**
**Canberra Visitors Centre**
330 Northbourne Ave, Dickson
(02) 6205 0044, 1300 554 114
www.canberratourism.com.au

**TOP EVENTS**

**Summernats Car Festival** (Jan.)
A major meeting of street-machine enthusiasts

**Royal Canberra Show** (Feb.)
Rural displays, fireworks and a grand parade

**National Multicultural Festival Canberra** (Feb.)
Capital arts and culture

**Australian Science Festival** (Aug.)
Science and technology at their interactive best

**Floriade** (Sept.–Oct.)
One of the country's best botanic events

## SUBURBS AND SURROUNDS

See map on page 41.

### Australian Institute of Sport 41 F3

Tour the complex where the top athletes train.

### Australian National Botanic Gardens 41 F4

The largest collection of native plant species in the country; also includes a rainforest gully and an Aboriginal plant-use walk.

### Calthorpes' House 41 F6

A 1927 house in Spanish Mission style containing original furnishings and providing a glimpse of middle-class domestic life in the fledgling capital.

### Canberra Deep Space Communications Complex 41 C8

Assisting NASA with its deep-space tracking, this impressive complex has an excellent museum and display area with astronaut suits and space food.

### GETTING AROUND

Canberra is a city with a very high rate of car usage and it is easy to see why: wide roads cater for bus-only public transport that can be variable at off-peak times. For a convenient way to get around the main attractions, catch a double-decker City Sightseeing bus departing from the Melbourne Building. The road infrastructure is probably the best in Australia and visitors will find that they can cover long distances in a short time. Clean air, wide streets and plenty of parkland make Canberra a great place to explore on foot or by bicycle. A boat cruise of Lake Burley Griffin is an essential visitor experience; tours depart from the Southern Cross Yacht Club at Lotus Bay.

**Motoring organisation**
NRMA 13 21 32

**Public transport**
ACTION Buses 13 17 10

**Taxis**
Canberra Cabs 13 22 27

**Lake cruises**
Canberra Steam Boat Cruises 0419 418 846, Lakeside Boat Hiring and Charters 0418 828 357, Southern Cross Cruises (02) 6273 1784

### Cockington Green 41 F2

A miniature re-creation of an English rural village.

### Cuppacumbalong Craft Centre 41 E11

Near the town of Tharwa on the Murrumbidgee River, this old homestead and its beautiful 19th-century gardens have become the showroom for quality works by Canberra's craftspeople.

### Federation Square and Ginninderra Village 41 F2

The Square boasts excellent speciality shops and a walk-in aviary; opposite, Ginninderra Village has craft studios and art galleries housed in historic buildings.

### Fyshwick Markets 41 H5

The city's fresh produce markets with fruit and vegetables sold at very reasonable prices.

### Lanyon Homestead 41 F11

One of Australia's most beautiful 19th-century homesteads; one section of this restored 1850s farmhouse now houses the Sidney Nolan Gallery.

### Mount Ainslie Lookout 41 G4

Drive to the lookout for fabulous views of the city and surrounding mountain ranges.

### Mount Stromlo Observatory 41 D5

Houses a huge telescope that charts the night skies; visitors can tour the facility and learn about the wonders of the galaxy.

### Namadgi National Park 41 C12

A stretch of alpine wilderness with fabulous bushwalks; it has a visitor information centre near Tharwa.

### National Aquarium and Wildlife Park 41 E5

Featuring an amazing collection of freshwater fish and a wildlife sanctuary where all the Australian favourites are on display.

### Royal Australian Mint 41 F5

Producing around two million coins each day, visitors can view the production process here and learn about the history of money minting.

### Telstra Tower Lookout 41 F4

Also known as Black Mountain Tower, it gives superb views of Canberra and surrounds.

### Tidbinbilla Nature Reserve 41 A9

This 5500-ha area of bushland is a refuge for many species of native wildlife; there are walking tracks, picnic spots and a cafe.

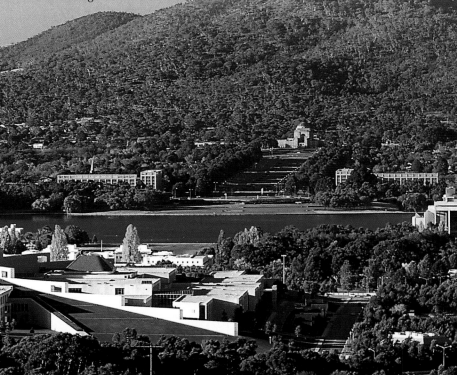

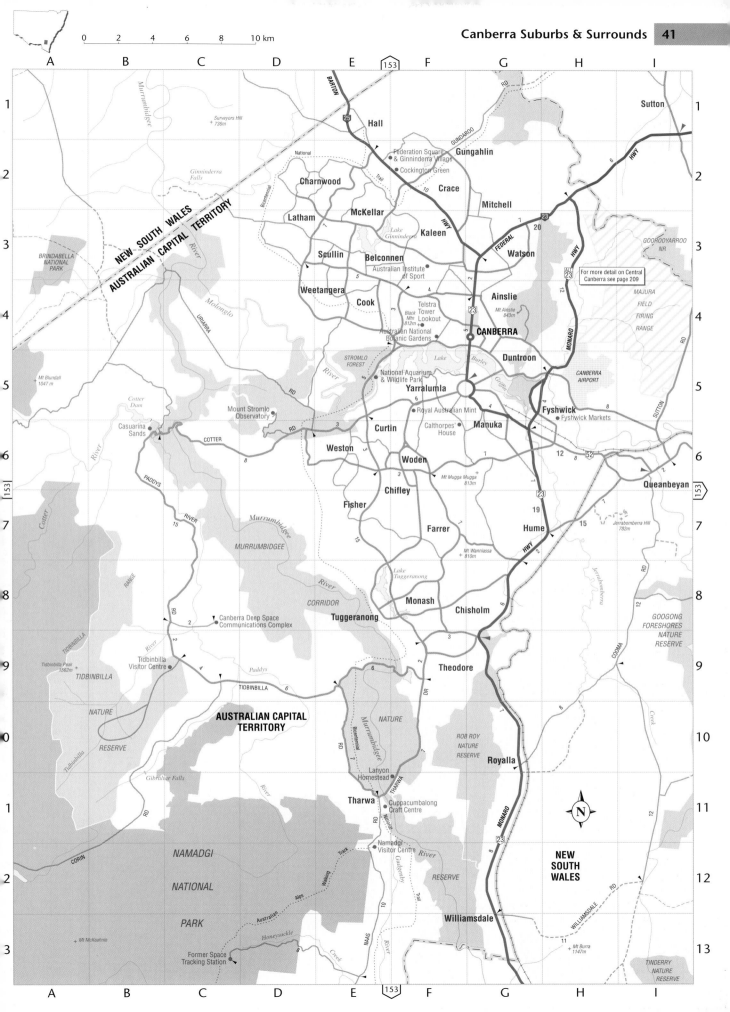

# VICTORIA

Victoria is Australia's second smallest State with an area of 227 420 square kilometres, just 3 per cent of the continent's total landmass. It has, however, a remarkably diverse landscape, industry, culture and population.

### Small State, rich resources

Eastern Victoria is dominated by the Great Dividing Range. Heavy rainfalls provide winter snow for the ski resorts and water for the rivers flowing inland. The Murray River, rising in the high country, flows north-west through farming and grazing country to the semi-arid plains of the Mallee. The Goulburn River passes through central Victoria before joining the Murray. Irrigation schemes on the banks of these two rivers support orchards and grape-growing.

The semi-arid Mallee country of north-west Victoria supports wheat and sheep. South of the majestic granite Grampians, the golden-brown Wimmera landscape gives way to the rich wool country of the Western District. Victoria's wild south-west coast is known for its shipwrecks and dramatic sea-stranded sandstone formations, most notably the Twelve Apostles.

Gippsland, in eastern Victoria, supports dairying in the lush foothills of the high country. The vast brown coal deposits of central Gippsland generate electricity to power Victorian industry. The stunning beaches, inlets, lakes and lagoons of the coast are renowned for commercial fishing and summer tourism.

## A bad deal

The Koories, as the Aboriginal people of south-east Australia are collectively known, arrived at least 40 000 years before the Europeans. As many as 50 000, organised into over 30 different dialect groups, enjoyed a more sedentary lifestyle than groups in the drier regions of the continent. Different groups established complex fishing economies, quarried and traded stone for weapons and tools and, in the Grampians, created extraordinary galleries of rock art.

In May 1835, John Batman crossed Bass Strait from Van Diemen's Land in search of grazing land and, with blankets and tomahawks, 'bought' 243 000 hectares of land around Port Phillip from the tribes of the Kulin, the nation of people who lived in much of central Victoria.

## Third time lucky

Before the arrival of Batman, the British government made two attempts to settle the Port Phillip district in a bid to stop other European powers occupying the south-east corner of the continent. Both attempts at settlement failed because of poor soil and lack of water.

A superintendent administered the Port Phillip District, originally part of New South Wales, from 1839 to 1851. A campaign for separation from New South Wales culminated in the creation of the colony of Victoria on 1 July 1851. Victoria became a separate State at the time of Federation, in 1901.

## Gold!

Gold was discovered just weeks after Victoria became a separate colony. Capital and immigrants poured in from around the world. Australia experienced its first and only civil insurrection as miners joined the Eureka Rebellion in 1854 to protest against the inequities of the goldfields licensing system. Violence against Chinese miners and the subsequent restriction of Chinese immigration were among the era's less glorious events.

Wool from the Western District added to Victoria's wealth and, as gold petered out, investors turned to manufacturing, commerce and real estate. By 1880 Melbourne had become the financial and commercial centre of the colonies, as well as a showcase for the ornate, monumental architecture of the period. The golden age ended in the 1890s when rising interest rates and British

bank failures stemmed the flow of money to Victoria. Falling prices for wool and other commodities, industrial unrest and the collapse of the building industry ushered in a decade of depression.

## Changing the stock

Victoria's population throughout its establishment years was drawn overwhelmingly from Anglo-Celtic stock. This changed after World War II as thousands of Italians, Greeks and other displaced Europeans (as well as many British) poured into the State as part of an Australia-wide immigration program.

Coolart Homestead (1895) on the Mornington Peninsula

The next thirty years would see the immigrant base swell with arrivals from Turkey, Lebanon, South America and Asia. Today, one in four Victorians was born overseas and the population can claim the heritage of 100 different nations. Cultural diversity has become one of the State's defining features, not only in Melbourne, with its prominent Greek, Italian, Spanish, Vietnamese and Turkish neighbourhoods, but in country areas as well. Immigrants have laid out their orchards, market gardens, olive groves and vineyards alongside the traditional wheatfields and sheep and cattle properties of the Anglo-Celts. Many Victorians prominent in science, education, the arts, business, the media, politics and sport are of post-war immigrant origin.

## The pursuit of leisure

Along with multiculturalism and conservative politics (conservative governments have ruled Victoria for 82 years out of 100) the State is known for its cultural and leisure activities. Melbourne stages Australia's biggest writers' festival, one of the world's top comedy festivals and the Australian Open, one of the four Grand Slam tennis tournaments. The State has 332 museums and galleries and around 21 per cent of Victorians visit a gallery each year. Victorians also love their sport and about 35 per cent of the population attends at least one Australian Rules football game each year. Known as the Garden State for many years, Victoria today attracts over 40 per cent of its population to its peerless public gardens, a legacy of the State's early wealth.

For more information on Victoria, see Tourist Bureaus, opposite page 236.

# MELBOURNE

Described as the world's most livable city, Melbourne is a vibrant and multicultural metropolis offering great restaurants, excellent shopping and world-class sporting venues. It also boasts stunning new buildings, tree-lined boulevards and magnificent public gardens. Situated at the head of Port Phillip and centred on the north bank of the Yarra River, the city has a population of about 3.4 million. Visitors will find there is always something happening in Melbourne, whether it be a lively festival or a sporting event.

**VISITOR INFORMATION**

**Melbourne Visitor Information Centre**
Melbourne Town Hall
Cnr Swanston and
Little Collins sts (03) 9658 9658

**Information kiosks**
Flinders Street Station and
Bourke Street Mall

**Victorian Tourism Information Service**
13 28 42
www.melbourne.vic.gov.au
www.visitvictoria.com

## CITY CENTRE

See map on page 210.

**The Block Arcade** 210 D7
The oldest arcade in Australia, with a mosaic floor, glass and iron-lace roof and stylish shops, including tearooms.

**Chinatown** 210 E6
Packed with fascinating restaurants, shops and a fine museum.

**Crown Entertainment Complex** 210 C10
Something for everyone – shop, wine and dine or have a flutter at the casino.

**Federation Square** 210 E8
Shops, restaurants, the National Gallery of Victoria and the Australian Centre for the Moving Image.

**Fitzroy Gardens** 210 H6
Beautiful gardens with Captain Cook's Cottage, the Fairy Tree and Model Tudor Village.

**Ian Potter Centre: National Gallery of Victoria** 210 E8
A fine collection of Australian and international masterpieces at the new Federation Square site.

**Koorie Heritage Centre** 210 F5
An insight into Victorian Aboriginal cultural life.

**Melbourne Aquarium** 210 C9
The magic of marine life – over 270 species from the Southern Ocean and inland waterways.

**Melbourne Central** 210 D6
Huge retail complex featuring a 20-storey glass cone that encloses a historic shot tower.

**Melbourne Cricket Ground (MCG)** 210 I9
The hallowed venue for AFL and national and international cricket; also contains the Australian Gallery of Sport, an Olympic Museum and a Melbourne Cricket Club Museum.

**Melbourne Museum** 210 F3
A superb introduction to Melbourne and Australia.

**Old Melbourne Gaol** 210 E5
Contains chillingly macabre exhibits, including the gallows where Ned Kelly swung.

**Queen Victoria Market** 210 B4
A large range of fresh fish, meat, fruit, vegetables and delicatessen lines along with clothing and general merchandise are on offer at this Melbourne landmark; open Tuesdays and Thursdays to Sundays.

**Rialto Towers**
**Observation Deck** 210 C8
Stunning 360-degree views of the city from Australia's tallest building.

**Royal Botanic Gardens** 210 I12
Melbourne's showpiece and considered to be among the best in the world.

**Southgate** 210 E9
Riverside promenade with restaurants, shops, wine bars and outdoor eating areas, along with fabulous sculptures.

**St Patrick's Cathedral** 210 G5
Massive 19th-century bluestone building, and one of the world's best examples of Gothic Revival architecture.

**State Library of Victoria** 210 D5
Begun in 1854 and completed in 1913, the library holds more than one million books.

**Victoria Police Museum** 210 A10
Houses memorabilia from some of Victoria's most famous criminal cases, including Ned Kelly's armour.

**Victorian Arts Centre** 210 E9
Contains three theatres, the Performing Arts Museum and the George Adams Gallery.

### TOP EVENTS

**The Australian Open** (Jan.)
Grand Slam tennis excitement

**The Australian Formula One Grand Prix** (Mar.)
The fastest fun around

**Moomba Festival** (Mar.)
The idea of Moomba is just to enjoy yourself

**Melbourne Food and Wine Festival** (Mar.)
Taste the best of the world's food and wine

**Melbourne International Comedy Festival** (Apr.)
International and local laughs

**AFL Grand Final** (Sept.)
Heroes of the footy field battle it out

**Royal Melbourne Show** (Sept.)
The country comes to the city

**Melbourne Festival** (Oct.)
Celebrating the city's heart and soul, with art, dance, opera and theatre

**Spring Racing Carnival** (Oct.–Nov.)
Includes the Melbourne Cup

## GETTING AROUND

The city centre is easy to explore, with its wide streets laid out in a grid system. Parking in the centre consists of mainly short-term parking meters and undercover carparks, which at peak times can be difficult to find or expensive. Outside the centre there is usually no problem finding a parking spot.

Public transport is excellent, particularly the tram system. There are free City Circle trams around the perimeter of the central grid, in both directions. Normal tram services criss-cross the city on their way to the suburbs. The main terminus for the suburban train lines is Flinders Street Station. Trains from here go round an underground loop that can be used instead of the City Circle tram to explore Melbourne. Buses cover major routes that are not reached by trams or trains.

A good way to explore the city is on the City Wanderer (summer only) or the City Explorer, the former extending as far as the Westgate Bridge and Williamstown. Both buses operate daily. The Yarra River has a variety of tour boats, including water taxis and ferries. Many are moored at Southgate or Princes Bridge, and destinations include Williamstown, St Kilda and the bay.

**Airport shuttle bus**
Skybus (03) 9335 3066

**CityLink**
A toll road linking the Tullamarine, West Gate and Monash freeways. There are no toll booths. Travellers can buy an e-TAG or a Day Pass, or pay by credit card afterwards, within 24 hours of making a journey. Prices vary and motorhomes and commercial vehicles, including utilities, cost more. There is no additional fee for towing a caravan. Call 13 26 29

**Motoring organisation**
RACV 13 19 55

**Public transport**
Trams, including free City Circle trams, suburban trains and buses 13 16 38

**Tourist Bus**
City Explorer, City Wanderer (03) 9563 9788

**Taxis**
Bay City Cabs Combined 13 22 27, Embassy 13 17 55, Northern Suburban 13 11 19, Silver Top 13 10 08, West Suburban (03) 9689 1144

**Yarra River boat trips**
Melbourne River Cruises (03) 9629 7233, Southbank Cruises (03) 9645 9944, Williamstown Bay and River Cruises (03) 9682 9555, Penguin Waters Cruises (03) 9386 2986

## SUBURBS AND SURROUNDS

See map on page 47.

**Dandenong Ranges** 47 H7
Scenic hills and native rainforests only 50 km from the city; extensive gardens, galleries, and craft shops for leisurely browsing.

**Gulf Station** 47 H5
Oldest working farm in the Yarra Valley, first occupied in the 1850s, with old slab-timber farmhouse, stables, barns, animals and early farm implements and machinery.

**Healesville Sanctuary** 47 I5
The 32-ha wildlife sanctuary is world-renowned, with over 200 animal and bird species.

**Melbourne Cemetery** 47 C7
Dating back to the 1850s; explore Melbourne's history on a guided tour.

**Melbourne Zoo** 47 C7
An essential stop for animal lovers; see the magnificent butterfly house and walk the 'people cage' through the lions' enclosure.

**Montsalvat** 47 E6
An artists' colony established in the 1930s, featuring Medieval-style buildings and with residents' artworks and crafts for sale; a popular jazz festival is held each January.

**Museum of Modern Art at Heide** 47 D6
Set in the tranquil parklands of Bulleen, one of Australia's most renowned art spaces, housing a collection of the great Australian modernists and new artists.

**Organ Pipes National Park** 47 A5
An 85-ha park named after its unusual 20-m wall of basalt columns; they were formed over one million years ago from lava flow from local volcanoes.

**Puffing Billy Railway** 47 H9
Old-fashioned steam train with open carriages and restaurant car that travels 25 km through forest from Belgrave to Gembrook and back again.

**Rippon Lea** 47 D8
National Trust Romanesque mansion with 5 ha of beautiful English-style landscaped gardens and resident peacocks.

**Scienceworks** 47 B8
Exciting interactive science and technology museum, with new Planetarium, and Australia's first plane and car on display.

**St Kilda** 47 C8
Lively beachside suburb that hosts an art and craft market on the Esplanade every Sunday; Acland Street is famous for its continental cake shops.

**Studley Park Boathouse** 47 D7
Hire a boat or just sit by the Yarra and enjoy the Devonshire teas and bush atmosphere.

**William Ricketts Sanctuary** 47 G8
William Ricketts lived and worked at this beautiful mountain-side sanctuary until his death at 94 years of age; his sculptures, scattered here through the forest, were inspired by Aboriginal people and their affinity with nature.

**Williamstown** 47 B8
Take a ferry from St Kilda to Melbourne's oldest suburb, a former maritime village with quaint pubs, churches and cottages.

**Yarra Valley** 47 I6
Good scenery, excellent wineries, fine food outlets, historic gardens and ancient forest.

# WERRIBEE & BELLARINE PENINSULA

The Bellarine Peninsula lies at the western entrance to Port Phillip, connected by car ferry to the Mornington Peninsula. Geelong, at the base of the peninsula, is a large regional city with strong links to the great days of the wool industry. Beyond Geelong are resort towns that offer surfing, swimming, sailing, scuba-diving, golf, tennis and bushland walks. Visitors can dine opulently in Queenscliff or take in the sea air from a caravan at Point Lonsdale. Wine buffs will be delighted with the pinot noirs and chardonnays offered for tasting at the wineries on the peninsula and around Geelong.

## TOP EVENTS

| | |
|---|---|
| **Jan.** | *Waterfront Festival (Geelong)* |
| **Feb.** | *Australian International Air Show (Avalon Airfield, near Geelong, odd-numbered years)* |
| **Feb.–Mar.** | *Spray Farm Winery Summer Concert Series (near Drysdale)* |
| **Mar.** | *Highland Gathering (Geelong)* |
| **Apr.** | *Alternative Farmvision (Geelong)* |
| **June** | *National Celtic Folk Festival (Geelong)* |
| **Sept.** | *Momenta Arts (Geelong)* |
| **Oct.** | *Racing Carnival (horseracing, Geelong)* |
| **Nov.** | *Music Festival (Queenscliff)* |

## EXPERIENCE IT!

**❶ See** native birds in wetland and grassland at Serendip Sanctuary, north of Lara

**❷ Enjoy** the promenade at Geelong's Eastern Beach and swim in the restored 1930s sea baths

**❸ Play** at Barwon Heads Golf Club, one of Victoria's top three public courses

## VISITOR INFORMATION

Geelong: (03) 5222 2900; 1800 620 888
Queenscliff: (03) 5258 4843

## FOCUS ON

### Holiday havens

Just an hour or so from Melbourne, this district is enormously popular with Melburnians for a weekend away. Queenscliff offers luxurious accommodation and fine dining; the Maritime Centre displays the region's historic relationship with the sea. The tiny historic town of Point Lonsdale has great views of the turbulent entrance to Port Phillip. Ocean Grove, the peninsula's biggest town, is popular with retirees, surfers and scuba divers. A bridge across the estuary leads to Barwon Heads, setting for the television series *SeaChange*. This is a small town with an excellent surfing beach and good accommodation and restaurants.

### The You Yangs

These granite tors rising suddenly from the Werribee Plain are visible from Melbourne's bayside suburbs. There is a fairly easy 3.2-km-return walk from the car park to the top of Flinders Peak (347 m). The view on a clear day extends to Mount Macedon, Geelong and Melbourne's tall buildings.

*For more detail see maps 224 & 227.*

### CLIMATE GEELONG

| | J | F | M | A | M | J | J | A | S | O | N | D |
|---|---|---|---|---|---|---|---|---|---|---|---|---|
| **Max. °C** | 25 | 26 | 24 | 20 | 17 | 14 | 14 | 15 | 17 | 19 | 21 | 24 |
| **Min. °C** | 14 | 14 | 13 | 10 | 8 | 6 | 5 | 6 | 7 | 8 | 10 | 12 |
| **Rain mm** | 44 | 38 | 35 | 39 | 47 | 43 | 42 | 47 | 53 | 63 | 52 | 48 |
| **Raindays** | 8 | 6 | 9 | 12 | 14 | 16 | 16 | 17 | 16 | 15 | 13 | 10 |

### Geelong

The National Wool Museum records the development of Victoria's second city as a port for the wealthy wool industry of the Western District. Geelong has over 100 National Trust-classified buildings and a lively waterfront where attractions include delightful bollards – colourful, oversized figures representing local personalities.

### Werribee Park

The Chirnside family built a 60-roomed Italianate mansion here in the 1870s. It survives as a museum, grandly furnished to recreate the lifestyle of a wealthy family in Victoria's boom years. Other attractions are the Victoria State Rose Garden, and Victoria's Open Range Zoo, home to many exotic animal species.

### Bellarine wineries

The vineyards planted around Geelong in the 1850s were uprooted during the 1870s phylloxera outbreak. The industry was revitalised in the 1960s. There are now some 20 wineries, with a number offering sales. Scotchmans Hill has views to the coast and a growing reputation for its pinot noir and chardonnay.

*(Map showing You Yangs Regional Park, Werribee, Lara, Geelong, Drysdale, Bellarine Peninsula, Ocean Grove, Barwon Heads, Point Lonsdale, Queenscliff, Sorrento, Port Phillip, Mornington Peninsula)*

### Queenscliff's historic hotels

Queenscliff was established as a fishing village in the 1850s and today has attractive historic buildings and a picturesque waterfront. It is known for its grand Victorian-era hotels, namely Mietta's Queenscliff (pictured), Vue Grand and Ozone. With their highly regarded restaurants and sense of luxury, they offer a great weekend away.

# THE GREAT OCEAN ROAD

The south-west coast of Victoria is one of Australia's great scenic destinations. The Great Ocean Road, the region's main touring route, weaves a breathtaking course across a coastal landscape of rugged cliffs and unique geological formations, quiet bays and wild surf beaches, rainforests and waterfalls. En route is a string of charming holiday towns, with many attractions, including heritage sites and wildlife. Inland, the geological theme continues in the craters and lakes of the region's volcanic landscape. The accommodation choices throughout the region include everything from gourmet retreats to B&Bs, hillside cabins and remote camping spots.

## TOP EVENTS

**Jan.**   *Pier to Pub Swim; Mountain to Surf Footrace (Lorne)*

**Feb.**   *Food and Wine Festival (Heywood, near Portland)*

**Mar.**   *Folk Festival (Port Fairy)*

**Easter** *Bells Beach Surfing Classic (Torquay)*

**Apr.**   *Country Music Festival (Colac)*

**May**    *Racing Carnival (horseracing, Warrnambool)*

**July**   *Fun 4 Kids (children's festival, Warrnambool)*

**Sept.**  *Angair Wildflower Festival (Anglesea)*

**Dec.**   *Falls Festival (Lorne)*

## EXPERIENCE IT!

❶ **Spot** *southern right whales at Logans Beach, Warrnambool (June to September)*

❷ **Walk** *the Alan Marshall Memorial Walking Track to the summit of Mt Noorat, near Terang*

❸ **Take** *a boat trip at Cape Bridgewater to see Australian fur seals at play*

## VISITOR INFORMATION

Lorne: (03) 5289 1152
Warrnambool: (03) 5564 7837
www.greatoceanrd.org.au

## FOCUS ON

### Maritime history

There are about 160 wrecks along the vital though treacherous south-west coast shipping route. Victoria's Historic Shipwreck Trail, between Moonlight Head (in Port Campbell National Park) and Port Fairy, marks 25 sites with plaques telling the history of the wrecks. Not to be missed is the evocative *Loch Ard* site, near Port Campbell. Maritime history is preserved in the superb streetscape of Port Fairy, an 1830s whaling port, and in the 200 heritage buildings of Portland, Victoria's first settlement. At Flagstaff Hill Maritime Museum in Warrnambool you'll find a completely rebuilt 19th-century maritime village, and a collection of seafaring treasures.

### CLIMATE WARRNAMBOOL

|          | J  | F  | M  | A  | M  | J  | J  | A  | S  | O  | N  | D  |
|----------|----|----|----|----|----|----|----|----|----|----|----|----|
| Max. °C  | 24 | 23 | 22 | 20 | 17 | 15 | 14 | 15 | 16 | 18 | 20 | 22 |
| Min. °C  | 13 | 14 | 13 | 11 | 9  | 7  | 6  | 7  | 8  | 9  | 10 | 12 |
| Rain mm  | 33 | 34 | 48 | 60 | 78 | 77 | 88 | 86 | 74 | 67 | 55 | 44 |
| Raindays | 8  | 8  | 10 | 13 | 17 | 17 | 20 | 19 | 17 | 15 | 13 | 11 |

### Mount Eccles National Park

Mount Eccles is at the far edge of the 20 000-year-old volcanic landscape that extends west from Melbourne. Geological features of the park include a complex cave system, scoria cones and a large lake (suitable for swimming), enclosed within three volcanic craters. There are excellent walking trails and camping is available.

*For more detail see maps 156–7.*

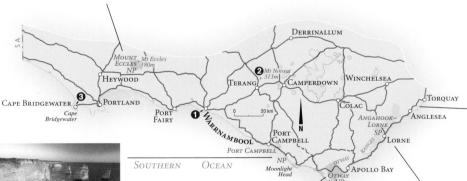

**Surf coast**
Torquay is Victoria's premier surfing town. This is where young surfers start out and old surfers settle down, where surfing is business as well as fun. Factory outlets offer great bargains on surf gear and the local Surfworld Surfing Museum celebrates the wonders of the wave. Bells and Jan Juc beaches are just around the corner.

**The Twelve Apostles**
These spectacular sandstone stacks were part of the original cliffs until wind and water carved them into their present shape and left them stranded in wild surf off the shoreline. Preserved within Port Campbell National Park, they are one of Australia's most photographed sights and the region's signature attraction.

**The Otways**
Ancient southern temperate rainforest is preserved in the hills and gullies of this magical landscape. Follow a rainforest boardwalk at Maits Rest in Otway National Park, drive along the 20-km scenic Turtons Track, north-east of Apollo Bay, and visit historic Cape Otway Lighthouse.

**Lorne**
This popular resort village is the inner city of the south-west coast: it has excellent cafes and restaurants and a lively summertime crowd. As well, it offers good beaches and surfing opportunities. Nearby, in Angahook–Lorne State Park (pictured), beautiful forests and waterfalls provide time out for walkers and nature lovers.

# GRAMPIANS & CENTRAL WEST

Victoria's central west is a mix of ancient mountains, semi-arid plains and classic farming landscapes. In the south, the rugged 400 million-year-old blue-grey shapes of the Grampians rise from the cleared plains, a dense and awe-inspiring environment of forests, fern gullies, soaring cliffs, waterfalls, creeks, lakes and swampland. In the many rock shelters of the area, details of pre-European Aboriginal life are impressively recorded. Anglo-Celtic settlement has made its mark with the hundred of thousands of hectares of wheat crops and sheep paddocks that dominate what is Australia's richest farming country, while the proliferation of olive groves and vineyards signal a more Mediterranean landscape. In the north, the timeless pink-tinged salt lakes and claypans mark the limits of agricultural expansion and a return to a native landscape.

## CLIMATE STAWELL

|  | J | F | M | A | M | J | J | A | S | O | N | D |
|---|---|---|---|---|---|---|---|---|---|---|---|---|
| Max. °C | 28 | 28 | 25 | 20 | 16 | 13 | 12 | 14 | 16 | 19 | 22 | 26 |
| Min. °C | 13 | 13 | 12 | 9 | 7 | 4 | 4 | 5 | 6 | 8 | 9 | 11 |
| Rain mm | 37 | 28 | 37 | 46 | 63 | 46 | 67 | 63 | 60 | 61 | 40 | 28 |
| Raindays | 6 | 4 | 7 | 9 | 12 | 14 | 18 | 17 | 13 | 11 | 9 | 7 |

## FOCUS ON

### Aboriginal culture in the Grampians

The Djab Wurrung and Jardwadjali peoples shared the territory they called Gariwerd, for at least 5000 years before European settlement, though some evidence points to 30 000 years of habitation. The Brambuk Aboriginal Cultural Centre at Halls Gap, run by five Koorie communities, is an excellent first stop for information about the region's heritage. There is a ceremonial ground for cultural demonstrations, including performances of Koorie dance and music, while traditional bush tucker is served in the cafe. There are 100 recorded rock-art sites in the region, representing more than 80 per cent of all sites found in Victoria. A Brambuk-guided tour of some of the sites (most are in Grampians National Park) is probably the most rewarding way to experience the meaning and nature of the art. Notable 'shelter' sites include: Gulgurn Manja, featuring over 190 kangaroo, emu and handprint motifs; and Ngamadidj, a site consisting of 16 figures painted with white clay. Bunjil's Rock Shelter is just outside the park.

## TOP EVENTS

**Jan.** Champagne Picnic Races (Great Western, near Ararat)

**Feb.** Grampians Jazz Festival (Halls Gap)

**Feb.** Country Muster (Penshurst, near Hamilton)

**Mar.** Jailhouse Rock Festival (Ararat)

**Mar.** Vintage Car Rally (Casterton)

**Easter** Easter Gift (professional foot race, Stawell)

**Easter** Y-Fest (wide-ranging festival, Warracknabeal)

**Apr.** Wimmera German Fest (Dimboola)

**May** Grampians Gourmet Weekend (Halls Gap)

**July** Kelpie Working Dog Auction (Casterton)

**Sept.** Cymbidium Orchid Festival (Ararat)

**Oct.** Golden Gateway Festival (Ararat)

**Oct.** Southern Grampians Open Gardens (Cavendish, near Hamilton)

**Oct.** Spring Garden Festival (Horsham)

**Nov.** Kannamaroo Rock 'n' Roll Festival (Horsham)

### Grampians day drive

From Halls Gap, drive to Boroka Lookout, Reed Lookout and Mackenzie Falls (pictured). Pause for lunch at Zumsteins, an historic site, picnic area and home to a large kangaroo population. Return to Halls Gap via Silverband Falls and through the stringybark forests and tree ferns at Delleys Dell.

## VISITOR INFORMATION

Halls Gap: (03) 5356 4616

Hamilton: (03) 5572 3746; 1800 807 056

Horsham: (03) 5382 1832; 1800 633 218

www.grampians.org.au

### Mount Arapiles

Mount Arapiles, part of the Mount Arapiles–Tooan State Park, is regarded as Australia's best rock-climbing venue. It attracts interstate and international enthusiasts with its 2000 rock-climbing routes marked out across 365 m of sandstone cliffs. Courses and tours are available.

### Halls Gap

Halls Gap, 24 km south-west of Stawell and surrounded by Grampians National Park, is the gateway to the central Grampians. This little village is connected to a network of scenic drives and walking tracks into the mountains. The area attracts bushwalkers, campers, abseilers and, between August and October, wildflower enthusiasts.

### Byaduk Caves

These caves, located in Mt Napier State Park, are part of a giant 24-km flow, and evidence of the volcanic activity that shaped the region's landscape. The caves, one of which is open, are a wonderland of ropey lava, columns, stalactites and stalagmites. A map of permitted areas is essential (available from Hamilton's information centre).

For more detail see maps
156–7 & 158–9.

## EXPERIENCE IT!

❶ **Take** *a dawn balloon flight from Stawell over the Grampians*

❷ **Visit** *the Historical Centre and the North Western Agricultural Machinery Museum at Warracknabeal, to get a picture of pioneering life*

❸ **Swim** *in summer at Lake Bellfield, just south of Halls Gap*

❹ **Choose** *one of the short walks through the eastern part of Little Desert National Park, near Nhill*

❺ **Drive** *to the top of One Tree Hill at Ararat for a 360° view of the region*

**The wheat belt**
The plains of the Wimmera yield huge crops of wheat, barley and canola. Towns of interest include historic Warracknabeal and Jeparit, birthplace of Australia's longest-serving prime minister, Sir Robert Menzies. Dimboola and Nhill provide access to the sandhills, floodplains and wildflower displays of Little Desert National Park.

**The olive groves of Laharum**
Mount Zero Olives at Laharum, 30 km south of Horsham, is the largest olive plantation in the Southern Hemisphere (55 000 trees on 730 ha). The first trees were planted in 1943, after WW II had stopped olive oil imports. Buy oil, vinegar and lentils, and stay overnight.

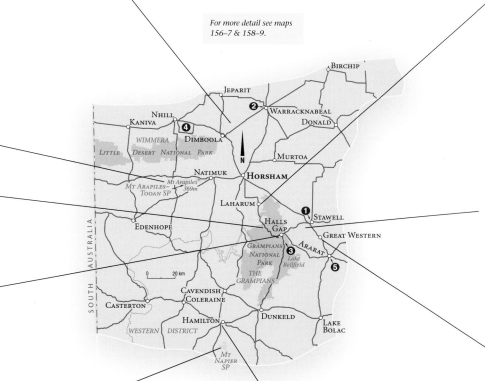

**Bunjil's Rock Shelter**
Depicted in a hillside alcove east of the Grampians is Bunjil, the Great Ancestor Spirit of the Dreaming, who created the people, the land, customs and law. In the Grampians area it is the only art site where more than one colour is used and a known figure is represented. Approach from the Western Highway, near Stawell.

**Hamilton**
Hamilton is the commercial hub of the wool-rich Western District. Gracious houses and churches on its tree-lined streets testify to over a century of prosperity. The town boasts botanic gardens (pictured) and an excellent gallery. Close to town are historic homesteads in magnificent gardens; these properties are generally open in spring.

**Wines of Great Western**
Grapevines were first planted at Seppelt's Great Western vineyards in 1865. Seppelt Winery is best known for its red and white sparkling wines, cellared in 1.6 km of National Trust-classified tunnels dug by miners late in the 19th century. Other wineries in the area include Best's and Garden Gully.

# MALLEE COUNTRY

The Murray River is the lifeblood of the semi-arid mallee country of north-west Victoria. After several attempts, Australia's first large-scale irrigation scheme was established in Mildura by two Canadian brothers, the Chaffeys, around 1900. Since then, water from the Murray has allowed the cultivation of citrus fruit, olives, avocados and grapes and the development of the major riverside settlements of Mildura and Swan Hill. Despite intensive farming, vast spaces of mallee and semi-arid country intercut by lakes and rivers is preserved in accessible national parks and reserves.

## TOP EVENTS

**Mar.**  Arts Festival (Mildura)

**Mar.**  Redgum Festival (Swan Hill)

**July**  International Balloon Fiesta (Mildura)

**July**  Italian Festa (Swan Hill)

**Aug.**  Great Australian Vanilla Slice Triumph (Ouyen)

**Sept.**  Country Music Festival (Mildura)

**Sept.**  Big Lizzie Festival of Vintage Tractors (Mildura)

**Oct.**  Mallee Wildflower Festival (Ouyen)

**Nov.**  Sunraysia Jazz and Wine Festival (Mildura)

## EXPERIENCE IT!

**❶ Board** a paddle-boat in Swan Hill to see where Major Mitchell named the town for the region's black swans

**❷ Photograph** the Pink Lakes from a walking trail in Murray–Sunset National Park

**❸ Dine** at Stefano's in Mildura, home to television chef Stefano di Pieri

**VISITOR INFORMATION**
Mildura: (03) 5021 4424; 1800 039 043
Swan Hill: (03) 5032 3033; 1800 625 373
www.murrayoutback.org.au

## FOCUS ON

### Murray and mallee wildlife

Despite the degree of settlement, the region has abundant wildlife. Most notable is the birdlife: spoonbills, herons, eagles, mallee fowl, harriers and kites are to be found in parks and on roadsides and riverbanks. Hattah–Kulkyne National Park protects around 200 bird species as well as the red kangaroo, comparatively rare in Victoria. The Murray–Sunset National Park – true desert country in parts – includes riverine plains. It supports an array of native fauna, including mallee fowl and the rare black-eared miner. Wyperfeld National Park is a wildlife haven: follow the Brambruk Nature Trail for kangaroos and the prolific birdlife.

### Mildura

With its museums and galleries, excellent dining and surrounding wineries and orchards, Mildura is like a colourful Mediterranean oasis. Go to the zoo, visit Rio Vista museum (pictured), once home of William Chaffey, or book a day tour, with indigenous guides, to Mungo National Park in NSW (see The Outback in New South Wales, p. 37).

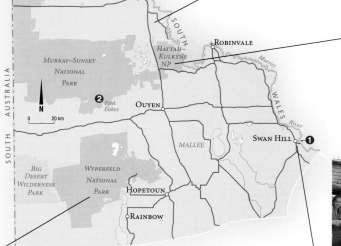

| CLIMATE **MILDURA** | | | | | | | | | | | | |
|---|---|---|---|---|---|---|---|---|---|---|---|---|
| | J | F | M | A | M | J | J | A | S | O | N | D |
| Max. °C | 32 | 31 | 28 | 23 | 19 | 16 | 15 | 17 | 20 | 24 | 27 | 30 |
| Min. °C | 17 | 16 | 14 | 10 | 8 | 5 | 4 | 5 | 7 | 10 | 12 | 15 |
| Rain mm | 22 | 22 | 19 | 20 | 27 | 23 | 27 | 27 | 29 | 32 | 25 | 22 |
| Raindays | 4 | 3 | 4 | 7 | 8 | 10 | 9 | 8 | 7 | 6 | 4 |

### River district wines

The winegrowing areas of Mildura and Swan Hill have long been the Australian industry's heartland, producing 37 per cent of the total output – most for the bulk market, although prestige production is rising. The dozen or so wineries include the large Lindemans Karadoc.

### Hattah–Kulkyne National Park

This magnificent park covers 48 000 ha of low scrub and native pine. A network of creeks and lakes is fed by overflow from the Murray. The larger lakes abound in birdlife and are perfect for canoeing.

### Wyperfeld National Park

A park of brilliant sunsets, huge open spaces and spring wildflowers, Wyperfeld is explored via walks from Wonga Campground and Interpretative Display Centre, 50 km west of Hopetoun. The park is home to the endangered mallee fowl (pictured), a turkey-size bird that makes nesting mounds up to 5 m across.

*For more detail see maps 158 & 160–1.*

### Swan Hill Pioneer Settlement

This 7-ha park offers a lively experience of river port life in early Australia. The re-creation features aspects of local Aboriginal culture as well as the production and sale of 19th-century goods by staff in period dress. Ride on yesteryear's transport, or book for the popular Sound and Light Tour.

# GOULBURN & MURRAY

The Goulburn River is the backbone of Victoria's central northern region. Rising in the Yarra Ranges, the Goulburn runs north into the Murray River near Echuca (an Aboriginal word meaning 'meeting of the waters'). Victoria's richest farming country is north of Nagambie in the Goulburn Valley. The canneries of Shepparton, the region's hub, process much of the harvest grown on irrigated land. In the central reaches of the Murray are attractions of great historical interest, particularly the paddle-steamers at Echuca. As well, there are ecologically significant wetlands with ancient river gums, and opportunities for freshwater fishing.

## TOP EVENTS

**Jan.** Peaches and Cream Festival (Cobram, odd-numbered years)

**Feb.** Aquatic Festival (Cohuna)

**Feb.** Riverboats, Food, Jazz, and Wine Festival (Echuca)

**Feb.** Southern 80 Ski Race (Torrumbarry Weir to Echuca)

**Mar.** Goulburn Valley Vintage Festival (Nagambie)

**Apr.** Barmah Muster (Barmah State Forest, near Echuca)

**June** Steam, Horse and Vintage Car Rally (Echuca)

**Oct.** Port of Echuca Steam Heritage Festival

**Nov.** Sun Country Dolls, Bears and Collectibles Show (Cobram)

## EXPERIENCE IT!

**❶ Take** time in Yarrawonga at the Tudor House Clock Museum's display of hundreds of timepieces

**❷ Cruise** the Murray aboard a paddle-steamer from the Port of Echuca

**❸ Head** for Australia's largest cactus collection, the 2-ha Cactus Country, at Strathmerton

## VISITOR INFORMATION

Echuca: (03) 5480 7555; 1800 677 679
www.echucamoama.com

Shepparton: (03) 5831 4400;
1800 808 839

## FOCUS ON

### Food and wine

Irrigation has transformed the once dusty Goulburn Valley into the fruit bowl of Victoria. Orchards, market gardens and farms supply the canneries in Shepparton, which are among the largest in the Southern Hemisphere. The valley is dotted with outlets for venison, poultry, smoked trout, berries, organic vegetables, honey, jams, preserves, fruit juices, mustards, pickles, vinegar and liquored truffles. The region's nine wineries make reliable reds and distinctive whites. Near Nagambie, Mitchelton Wines is known for marsannes and rieslings grown on sandy, riverine soils. At nearby Avenel, Plunkett Wines make long-finishing chardonnay from grapes grown high in the Strathbogie Ranges.

## Barmah State Park and State Forest

These adjacent areas form the State's biggest river red gum forest. Ulupna Island and Barmah Lake have camping facilities, walks and beach access; bush camping is permitted elsewhere. A 60-km scenic drive takes in sites of historical interest. The Dharnya Centre interprets the culture of the Yorta Yorta people.

*For more detail see maps 159 & 162–3.*

## CLIMATE ECHUCA

|          | J  | F  | M  | A  | M  | J  | J  | A  | S  | O  | N  | D  |
|----------|----|----|----|----|----|----|----|----|----|----|----|----|
| Max. °C  | 31 | 31 | 27 | 22 | 18 | 14 | 13 | 15 | 18 | 22 | 26 | 29 |
| Min. °C  | 15 | 15 | 13 | 9  | 7  | 5  | 4  | 5  | 6  | 9  | 11 | 14 |
| Rain mm  | 27 | 27 | 32 | 33 | 42 | 43 | 41 | 43 | 40 | 43 | 32 | 29 |
| Raindays | 4  | 4  | 5  | 6  | 9  | 10 | 11 | 11 | 10 | 9  | 6  | 5  |

## Cobram

This lovely fruit-growing town is surrounded by peach, nectarine, pear and orange orchards. The town also offers access to a number of wide sandy beaches on the Murray, perfect for swimming, fishing, picnicking and water sports. Camping facilities are available, and across the river in NSW is the renowned 36-hole Cobram–Barooga Golf Club.

## Port of Echuca

The historic port of Echuca with its impressive red-gum wharf recalls the second half of the 19th century, when the Murray carried wool and other goods from farms and stations. A number of beautifully restored paddle-steamers are moored here.

## Chateau Tahbilk

Chateau Tahbilk (1860) was established on the sandy loam of the Goulburn River south of Nagambie. One of Australia's most beautiful wine properties, it has a National Trust-classified cellar which, with other buildings, is a working example of early Australian winegrowing. Chateau Tahbilk produces top quality wines and has won over 1000 awards.

## Tatura

Internment camps were set up around this small farming town during WW II for German POWs and Australians thought to be German sympathisers. Tatura's museum (open weekends and public holidays) has relevant photographs and memorabilia, and a German cemetery is adjacent to the town cemetery.

# THE GOLDFIELDS

The Goldfields region of Central Victoria is the historic jewel of rural Australia. The discovery of gold near Ballarat in 1851 transformed a sleepy farming district into a rowdy, anarchic, cosmopolitan and fantastically wealthy goldmining frontier as immigrants from all over the world poured in to try their luck. Development took place on a massive scale between the 1850s and 1890s. Today the area preserves an intense concentration of Victorian architecture, in both the grand public buildings, parks and gardens of Ballarat and Bendigo and the more modest but charming streetscapes of smaller towns such as Castlemaine, Creswick, Clunes, Maldon and St Arnaud. The region's many galleries, museums, working mines and interpretative centres recall all the drama and detail of the goldfields history, while stylish B&Bs, hotels, restaurants and cafes supply visitors with modern comforts.

## CLIMATE BENDIGO

|  | J | F | M | A | M | J | J | A | S | O | N | D |
|---|---|---|---|---|---|---|---|---|---|---|---|---|
| Max. °C | 29 | 29 | 25 | 21 | 16 | 13 | 12 | 14 | 16 | 20 | 24 | 26 |
| Min. °C | 14 | 15 | 13 | 9 | 7 | 4 | 3 | 5 | 6 | 8 | 11 | 13 |
| Rain mm | 34 | 32 | 36 | 41 | 55 | 60 | 56 | 58 | 54 | 53 | 38 | 33 |
| Raindays | 5 | 4 | 5 | 7 | 10 | 12 | 13 | 13 | 11 | 10 | 7 | 6 |

## FOCUS ON

### Gold-rush history

Sovereign Hill in Ballarat is one of the country's best historic theme parks. It offers a complete recreation of life on the 1850s goldfields. The nearby Gold Museum, part of the Sovereign Hill complex, features displays of gold nuggets and coins and changing exhibits on the history of gold. The Eureka Stockade Centre, also in Ballarat, offers interpretative displays on Australia's only armed insurrection, which took place in 1854. See the original Eureka Flag at the Ballarat Fine Art Gallery, which also houses historic collections of Australian and gold-rush art. In Eureka Street is the tiny Montrose Cottage (1856), an ex-miner's house furnished in the style of the period; here a moving museum display recalls the lives and contribution of women in the gold-rush era. In Bendigo, the Central Deborah Gold Mine offers tours 80m down a 410-m-deep reef mine and excellent displays on goldmining techniques.

## TOP EVENTS

| | |
|---|---|
| *Jan.* | *Organs of the Ballarat Goldfields* |
| *Jan.* | *Highland Gathering (Maryborough)* |
| *Feb.* | *Gold King Festival (Buninyong, near Ballarat)* |
| *Mar.* | *Begonia Festival (Ballarat)* |
| *Easter* | *Fair (Bendigo, features Chinese dragon)* |
| *Easter* | *Fair (Maldon)* |
| *Apr.* | *Pyrenees Vignerons' Gourmet Food and Wine Race Meeting (Avoca)* |
| *Apr.* | *State Festival (Castlemaine, odd-numbered years)* |
| *Apr.* | *Food, Wine and Jazz Festival (Smeaton, near Creswick)* |
| *July* | *Winter Festival (Ballarat)* |
| *Aug.–Sept.* | *Golden Wattle Festival (Maryborough)* |
| *Aug.–Nov.* | *Royal South Street Eisteddfod (Ballarat)* |
| *Oct.* | *Vintage Car Hill Climb (Maldon)* |
| *Nov.* | *Festival of Gardens (Castlemaine, odd-numbered years)* |
| *Dec.* | *Tram Spectacular (Bendigo)* |

## VISITOR INFORMATION

Ballarat: (03) 5320 5741; 1800 648 450

Bendigo: (03) 5444 4445; 1800 813 153

www.goldfields.org.au

### Backblocks of the goldfields

Some of the quieter towns are tucked away in a rural pocket north-west of Bendigo. In Dunolly, where 126 nuggets were found in the town itself, see replicas at the Goldfields Historic and Arts Society. St Arnaud boasts the beautiful Queen Mary Gardens and a number of old pubs and verandah-fronted shops. There are eucalyptus distilleries at Inglewood and Wedderburn.

### Maryborough Old Railway Station

Mark Twain described this as 'a railway station with a town attached'. Grand for the size of the town, this former railway station houses a tourist complex that includes an antique emporium, a woodworking shop, and a restaurant and cafe.

### Maldon

The 1860s streets of Maldon are shaded by European trees and lined with old buildings of local stone. Declared a Notable Town by the National Trust, Maldon has historic B&Bs and a tourist steam railway. Take in the view from the Anzac Hill lookout.

### Sovereign Hill

One of Victoria's top tourist attractions, Ballarat's Sovereign Hill is a living museum. Blacksmiths, bakers, innkeepers and storekeepers in period dress ply their trades amid the tents while miners pan for gold. In the evenings, 'Blood on the Southern Cross', a sound and light re-enactment of the Eureka Rebellion, is played out across the town streets.

**Whipstick State Park**

This 2300-ha park, 21 km north of Bendigo, conserves distinctive whipstick mallee forest and protects abundant birdlife. There are picnic areas, walking tracks and designated gold-fossicking areas.

**EXPERIENCE IT!**

❶ *Book* a weekend's indulgence at the Warrenmang Vineyard Resort, north-west of Avoca in the Pyrenees wine district

❷ *Enjoy* the begonias in March at Ballarat's historic Botanic Gardens on the shores of Lake Wendouree

❸ *Learn* more about Australia's often maligned native dog at the Dingo Farm near Castlemaine

❹ *See* potters in action at the long-established Bendigo Pottery

❺ *Ride* a camel at Sedgwick's Camel Farm, south-east of Bendigo (weekends; weekdays by appointment)

**Bendigo's Chinese sites**

The restored Joss House (pictured), on the city's northern outskirts, and the Golden Dragon Museum in Bridge Street are reminders of the substantial presence of Chinese on the goldfields. The museum has an excellent display of Chinese regalia. A ceremonial archway leads to the Garden of Joy, built 1996 to represent the Chinese landscape in miniature.

**Pall Mall, Bendigo**

The tree-lined French-style boulevard of Pall Mall is probably country Australia's most impressive street, with many of its buildings dating back to the gold rush. Don't miss the grand Shamrock Hotel, opened 1897. City heritage tours are available aboard Vintage Trams.

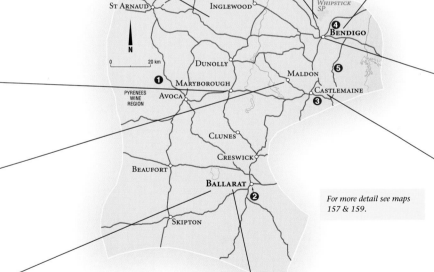

For more detail see maps 157 & 159.

**Castlemaine**

This historic goldmining town has a community of painters, potters, instrument makers and other craftspeople. The original market building (1862), with its classical Roman facade, now houses visitor information and a gold-diggings interpretive centre. Don't miss the 1860s Buda Historic Home, with its heritage-listed garden.

**Ballarat's gardens and gallery**

A large part of Ballarat's visual charm is its beautiful parks and gardens with begonias, the city's floral emblem, a common theme. Australia's oldest and largest provincial gallery is in Ballarat's elegant Lydiard Street. Paintings by Tom Roberts, Sir Sidney Nolan, Russell Drysdale and Fred Williams feature, as well as more contemporary works and exhibitions.

# SPA & GARDEN COUNTRY

Ancient volcanic eruptions, lava flows and erosion have formed a stunning mountain landscape rising out of the coastal plains to the north-west of Melbourne. Gold and timber attracted the first European settlers to the district. Soon afterwards, Melbourne's elite arrived to take the health-giving waters at the mineral springs in the area and to establish their grand, European-style country gardens on the basalt-rich soil. Today the district retains the air of a 19th-century hills retreat, with historic spa towns, mansions, gardens, galleries, craft shops, forest walks and drives, and gracious guesthouses and B&Bs.

## TOP EVENTS

**Jan.**  Picnic Races
(Hanging Rock, near Mount Macedon)

**Jan.**  Lavandula Harvest Festival
(Shepherds Flat, near Hepburn Springs)

**Feb.**  Country Music Festival (Kyneton)

**May**  Hepburn Swiss-Italian Festival
(Daylesford)

**July**  Fine Food and Wine Fayre
(Glenlyon, near Daylesford)

**Sept.**  Daffodil and Arts Festival (Kyneton)

**Oct.**  Macedon Ranges Budburst Wine Festival
(throughout wine district)

**Dec.**  Highland Gathering (Daylesford)

**Dec.**  Five Mile Creek Festival (Woodend)

## EXPERIENCE IT!

❶ **Visit** one of the region's wineries to taste chardonnay, riesling or pinot noir; brochures available from Woodend.

❷ **Dine** at the award-winning Lake House in Daylesford

❸ **Shop** for cool-climate plants at the nurseries of Macedon

## VISITOR INFORMATION

Daylesford: (03) 5348 1339
Woodend: (03) 5427 2033

## FOCUS ON

### Country gardens

Gardens flourish in the volcanic soil and cool, moist climate of the spa country. There are botanic gardens in Daylesford and Malmsbury. Around the village of Mount Macedon classic mountainside gardens surround large houses; check with visitor information for their spring and autumn open days. Cope-Williams Vineyard at Romsey is well known for its English-style garden and cricket green, while at Blackwood the beautiful Garden of St Erth offers 2 ha of exotic and native species (closed Wed. and Thurs.). For something special, visit the Lavandula Lavender Farm near Hepburn Springs, where the lavender crop sits well beside cottage-style plantings.

### CLIMATE KYNETON

|  | J | F | M | A | M | J | J | A | S | O | N | D |
|---|---|---|---|---|---|---|---|---|---|---|---|---|
| Max. °C | 27 | 27 | 24 | 18 | 14 | 11 | 10 | 12 | 15 | 18 | 22 | 25 |
| Min. °C | 10 | 10 | 8 | 6 | 4 | 2 | 2 | 2 | 3 | 5 | 7 | 9 |
| Rain mm | 37 | 39 | 47 | 54 | 75 | 90 | 82 | 84 | 74 | 69 | 52 | 50 |
| Raindays | 5 | 5 | 6 | 9 | 12 | 15 | 16 | 16 | 13 | 11 | 9 | 7 |

### Daylesford and Hepburn Springs

The spa complex at Hepburn Springs offers heated spas, flotation tanks, saunas and massages. The adjacent town of Daylesford is an attractive weekend destination with galleries, antique shops, heritage buildings and B&Bs. Worth a visit is the Convent Gallery (pictured), a 19th-century former convent that houses notable local artwork, sculpture and jewellery.

*For more detail see maps 154, 157 & 159.*

### Hanging Rock

This impressive rock formation, north of the village of Mount Macedon, was created by the erosion of solidified lava. The spot was inspiration for Joan Lindsay's novel *Picnic at Hanging Rock* and a setting for the subsequent film. Walking tracks lead up to a superb view, with glimpses of koalas along the way.

### Wombat Forest Drive

Start this 65-km-return forest drive (gravel and sealed road) at Blackwood. The waters of Lyonville Mineral Springs, in a glade on the Loddon River, are rich in potassium and calcium. Trentham Falls (pictured) is an ideal spot for a picnic.

### Lerderderg Gorge and State Park

The Lerderderg River has cut a deep gorge through sandstone and slate in this 13 400 ha park. Rugged treed ridges enclose much of the river. Also a feature are quiet forest pools and wetland. Explore on foot, or take a scenic drive via O'Briens Road (turn off south of Blackwood).

### Organ Pipes National Park

Lava flows created a 20-m wall of basalt columns in a gorge in this 121-ha park near Sunbury. The 'organ pipes' can be seen from the carpark, or close up via an easy walking trail. A regeneration program is gradually bringing this once denuded area back to its native state.

# YARRA & DANDENONGS

Wineries, fine-food outlets, historic gardens, ancient forests, snowfields and excellent activities for children are some of the diverse attractions that make this region so popular with daytrippers and weekenders alike. The scenic Yarra Valley, about an hour's drive from Melbourne, is one of Australia's best producers of cool-climate wines. The Dandenong Ranges, east of the city, offer an intoxicating mix of native mountainside forests and remarkable European-style gardens. Between the two areas, some of the State's most magnificent forests and a series of charming villages form a gateway to Victoria's beautiful alpine country.

## TOP EVENTS

| | |
|---|---|
| *Jan.* | *Upper Yarra Draughthorse Festival (Warburton)* |
| *Feb.* | *Coldstream Country and Western Festival (Healesville)* |
| *Mar.* | *Grape Grazing Festival (throughout Yarra Valley wine district)* |
| *Apr.* | *Great Train Race (Emerald)* |
| *Apr.* | *Musica Viva Yarra Valley Festival (at Domain Chandon, near Yarra Glen)* |
| *July* | *Winterfest (Warburton)* |
| *Aug.–Nov.* | *Rhododendron Festival (Olinda)* |
| *Sept.–Oct.* | *Tesselaar's Tulip Festival (Silvan, near Olinda)* |
| *Nov.* | *Gateway Festival (Healesville)* |

## EXPERIENCE IT!

❶ *Enjoy fine Italian fare at the De Bortoli estate, north of Yarra Glen*

❷ *Follow the Yarra Valley Regional Food Trail for berries, trout, chocolates and cheese (brochure at Healesville's information centre)*

❸ *See winter snow on Mount Donna Buang, near Warburton*

## VISITOR INFORMATION

Healesville: (03) 5962 2600
Dandenong Ranges Tourism
Upper Ferntree Gully: (03) 9758 7522
www.yarrarangestourism.com

## FOCUS ON

### Tours of the forest

This area has some of the State's best forest scenery. Bushwalkers, horseriders and cyclists can travel the 38-km Warburton Rail Trail starting in Lilydale. The Beeches, via Marysville, is a 5-km stroll through forests of ancient beech and mountain ash. The less energetic can take a forest drive through or around the Yarra Ranges National Park: the Black Spur (between Healesville and Marysville); Acheron Way (from Warburton to Marysville); or Lady Talbot Drive (from Marysville and return). For something special, visit Mount Donna Buang Rainforest Gallery (9 km from Warburton), which includes a viewing platform and rainforest walkway.

### CLIMATE HEALESVILLE

| | J | F | M | A | M | J | J | A | S | O | N | D |
|---|---|---|---|---|---|---|---|---|---|---|---|---|
| Max. °C | 26 | 26 | 24 | 19 | 16 | 12 | 12 | 14 | 16 | 19 | 22 | 24 |
| Min. °C | 11 | 12 | 11 | 9 | 7 | 4 | 4 | 5 | 6 | 8 | 9 | 11 |
| Rain mm | 58 | 68 | 64 | 91 | 96 | 82 | 87 | 98 | 94 | 106 | 93 | 86 |
| Raindays | 7 | 7 | 8 | 11 | 14 | 14 | 16 | 17 | 15 | 14 | 12 | 10 |

### Gardens of the Dandenongs

Mountain ash forests and fern gullies frame the historic cool-climate gardens of one of Australia's best-known gardening regions. Many of the private gardens are open daily. Non-private gardens include the National Rhododendron Gardens and the R. J. Hamer Forest Arboretum (both near Olinda), the William Ricketts Sanctuary (Mount Dandenong) and the Alfred Nicholas Memorial Gardens (Sherbrooke); small fees may apply.

### Yarra Valley wineries

The 30 or so wineries of this charming district produce high-quality chardonnay, cabernet sauvignon and pinot noir. Visit Domain Chandon, built by French champagne makers Moet et Chandon; the magnificent tasting-room offers fine views of the vine-covered plains and hilly backdrop. Early-morning balloon flights provide another perspective.

### Marysville and Lake Mountain

This beautiful sub-alpine village with its excellent cafes and art and crafts outlets is the centre for forest walks and provides access to the magnificent Steavenson Falls. Lake Mountain, 19 km east, is a popular tobogganing and cross-country skiing resort in winter.

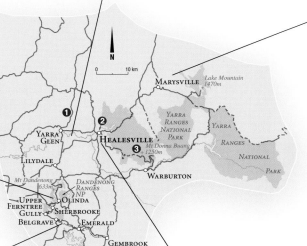

*For more detail see map 154.*

### Puffing Billy steam train

In the early 1900s four railways were established to develop rural areas near Melbourne; only the Puffing Billy line survives. Now one of the State's top attractions, the little train with its open carriages and restaurant car travels 25 km through the tree ferns, from Belgrave to Gembrook and back again.

### Healesville Sanctuary

Spread across 32 ha of bushland, this world-renowned native animal sanctuary has over 200 animal and bird species, many in natural habitats. Special features include talks by keepers, a nocturnal viewing area, bird of prey displays and the platypus exhibit.

# THE HIGH COUNTRY

The Victorian Alps is a continuation of the Great Dividing Range, which runs along Australia's east coast. Mount Hotham and Falls Creek, both on the Bogong High Plains, offer some of the State's most challenging skiing. Fast-flowing trout streams originate in these mountains and feed into the upper reaches of the Murray River. The foothills to the north-west of the High Country are used for farming and grazing. In this area there are several old goldfield towns (for example Beechworth) of great charm and historical interest. Lake Eildon, Victoria's largest constructed lake, stores water flowing west from the near-wilderness of Alpine National Park. The Hume Highway traverses the plains west of the Strathbogie Ranges, passing towns raided by the Kelly gang in the 1870s. Just west of Wodonga, grapes from the hot, alluvial flats on the south side of the Murray are made into the widely known fortified wines of Rutherglen.

## FOCUS ON

### Ski country

Victoria's ski resorts are within easy distance of Melbourne. The main resort mountains and their distances from Melbourne are Mount Buller (221 km via Mansfield), Mount Buffalo (331 km via Myrtleford), Mount Hotham (363 km via Bright) and Falls Creek (367 km via Mount Beauty). The ski season starts officially on the Queen's Birthday weekend early in June and ends on the first weekend in October. Snowsport conditions, however, depend on the weather. All resorts offer protected runs for beginners and cross-country skiing. Mount Hotham, known as the 'powder snow capital' of Australia, has the most challenging runs for experienced downhill skiers and snowboarders. Life in the high country does not stop when the snow melts. The adventurous can try mountain bike riding, tandem paragliding, abseiling or caving. Mountain lakes and streams offer trout fishing, swimming, sailing and canoeing. Trails across the mountains, ablaze with wildflowers in summer, can be explored on horseback or foot. The less energetic can just breathe the crystalline air and gaze across hazy blue ridges.

## TOP EVENTS

**Mar.** Man from Snowy River Festival (Corryong)

**Mar.** Harvest Festival (Mansfield)

**Mar.** Tobacco, Hops and Timber Festival (Myrtleford)

**Mar.** Tastes of Rutherglen (district wineries)

**Easter** Golden Horseshoes Festival (Beechworth)

**Apr.** Music Muster (Mount Beauty)

**Apr.** Autumn Festival (Bright)

**June** Winery Walkabout (Rutherglen wineries)

**July** Winter Wonderland Festival (Bright)

**Aug.** International Kangaroo Hoppet (cross-country ski race, Falls Creek)

**Sept.** Wine Show (Rutherglen)

**Oct.** Alpine Spring Festival (Bright)

**Oct.** Great Alpine Bike Ride (Myrtleford to Bright)

**Nov.** Gang Gang Mountain Bike Festival (Mount Beauty)

**Nov.** Brown Brothers Wine and Food Weekend (Milawa)

**Nov.** Wangaratta Festival of Jazz

**Dec.** Golden Spurs Rodeo (Myrtleford)

## VISITOR INFORMATION

Albury–Wodonga: (02) 6041 3875; 1800 800 743

Bright: (03) 5755 2275; 1800 500 117

Wangaratta: (02) 5721 5711; 1800 801 065

### CLIMATE HOTHAM HEIGHTS

|  | J | F | M | A | M | J | J | A | S | O | N | D |
|---|---|---|---|---|---|---|---|---|---|---|---|---|
| Max. °C | 18 | 19 | 15 | 10 | 6 | 3 | 1 | 3 | 5 | 9 | 13 | 15 |
| Min. °C | 8 | 9 | 7 | 4 | 1 | −2 | −4 | −2 | −1 | 1 | 4 | 5 |
| Rain mm | 88 | 59 | 121 | 154 | 195 | 175 | 266 | 256 | 210 | 179 | 168 | 172 |
| Raindays | 10 | 7 | 12 | 12 | 15 | 16 | 19 | 19 | 17 | 15 | 15 | 14 |

**Historic Beechworth**
The National Trust has classified over 30 buildings, some built of honey-coloured granite, in what is now one of Australia's best-preserved gold rush towns. Dine in a stately former bank, visit the powder magazine, and wander through an evocative cemetery (pictured) for Chinese goldminers who never returned to their ancestral land.

**Kelly country**
A giant effigy of Ned Kelly (pictured) greets visitors to Glenrowan. After killing three local policemen in 1878, the Kelly gang hid for two years in the Warby Range (near Wangaratta), raiding nearby towns. Ned was captured in 1880 after a shootout in Siege Street, Glenrowan, and was later hanged. Visit the Ned Kelly Memorial Museum and Homestead in Gladstone Street.

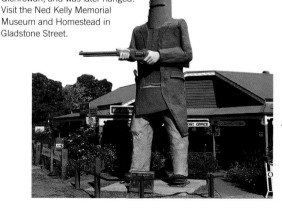

**Lake Eildon**
Created by damming the Goulburn River in the 1950s, this lake, with six times the capacity of Sydney Harbour, is popular with water sports enthusiasts, anglers and houseboat holidaymakers. The surrounding Lake Eildon National Park offers bushwalking, camping, and 4WD tracks through the foothills of the Victorian Alps.

## EXPERIENCE IT!

❶ **Go** *abseiling, rock-climbing, kayaking or bushwalking with experts in the wilderness of Alpine National Park*

❷ **Indulge** *in a weekend of fine dining at Howqua Dale Gourmet Retreat near Howqua*

❸ **Ride** *the high country on horseback, via the mountain town of Corryong*

❹ **Visit** *the childhood home of novelist Henry Handel Richardson and see a remarkable grapevine at historic Chiltern*

❺ **Shop** *for gourmet cheese at Milawa and taste excellent fortified wines nearby*

### Wines of Rutherglen

Vines on alluvial flats in a shallow loop of the Murray River produce some of the world's great fortified wines. The region is known for tokays and muscats, big reds and, more recently, lighter reds such as gamay. There are over a dozen wineries near Rutherglen; look out for All Saints (with a National Trust-classified building), Pfeiffer, Chambers and Campbells.

### The Upper Murray

The Murray River rises in rugged alpine country in north-east Victoria on the border of New South Wales. The swift mountain streams that feed the Murray are a paradise for trout fishermen. The river and its rapids can be negotiated by canoe on half-day, weekend or four-day adventure tours. The heavily timbered Burrowa–Pine Mountain National Park, which has waterfalls, lyrebirds, wallabies and wombats, will challenge most bushwalkers. Access is via the town of Corryong.

### The Great Alpine Road

This road travels some 307 km (a 5-hour journey) through the high country and beyond. Beginning in Wangaratta, it traverses the hop fields and walnut groves around Myrtleford and Bright. It climbs into the Alps, passing through the vast 645 000-ha Alpine National Park including one of Victoria's favourite downhill skiing areas, Mount Hotham, and descends through rugged gorge country to Bairnsdale and the East Gippsland lakes.

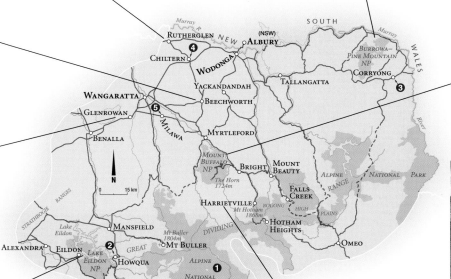

*For more detail see maps 163 & 164.*

### Mount Buffalo National Park

This 31 000-ha national park is the State's oldest, declared in 1898. A plateau of boulders and tors includes The Horn (pictured), the highest point, for great views at sunrise. Walking tracks are set among streams, waterfalls, and snow gum and mountain ash forest. There is summer camping, swimming and canoeing at Lake Catani. In winter, the Mount Buffalo ski area is popular with families.

# EAST GIPPSLAND

Australia's largest system of inland waterways, the remote splendour of Ninety Mile Beach, and scenic foothills of the high country are the natural features that make East Gippsland one of Victoria's top holiday destinations. These diverse landscapes offer extraordinary touring opportunities. Other recreational activities include fishing, sailing, swimming, surfing and, in the foothills, whitewater rafting, abseiling and caving. Accommodation can be had in caravan parks, motels, B&Bs and on houseboats, or in the camping grounds of the beautiful coastal and mountain national parks.

## TOP EVENTS

| | |
|---|---|
| **Jan.** | *Lakes Summer Festival (Lakes Entrance)* |
| **Feb.** | *Bruthen Blues Bash (near Bairnsdale)* |
| **Feb.** | *Jazz Festival (Paynesville)* |
| **Mar.** | *Marlay Point–Paynesville Overnight Yacht Race (from Marlay Point, near Sale)* |
| **Easter** | *Rodeo (Buchan)* |
| **Easter** | *Festival of the Great Southern Ocean (Mallacoota)* |
| **Apr.** | *Australian Line Dancing Championships (Bairnsdale)* |
| **June** | *Gippsland Wool and Fibre Fair (Bairnsdale)* |
| **Oct.** | *International Festival of the Lakes (Lakes Entrance)* |

## EXPERIENCE IT!

❶ **Swim** in the rock pools of the Mitchell River Gorge, in Mitchell River National Park

❷ **Stay** at the remote Point Hicks Lightstation in Croajingolong National Park

❸ **Tour** the Royal and Fairy caves in Buchan Caves Reserve

## VISITOR INFORMATION

Lakes Entrance: (03) 5155 1966; 1800 637 060

Orbost: (03) 5154 2424; 1800 637 060

www.lakesandwilderness.com.au

## FOCUS ON

### Fishing

Fishing is a huge drawcard in East Gippsland. Fish for trout in the mountain streams and rivers – such as the Delegate River – or head for the coast. The lakes, rivers and inlets around Paynesville, Marlo, Bemm River and Mallacoota are great for bream, trevally and flathead. Boat angling is the best choice here, although land-based angling will yield results. Ninety Mile Beach and the remote beaches of The Lakes National Park provide some of the best surf fishing in the State, with salmon, tailor and flathead among the prospects.

### CLIMATE LAKES ENTRANCE

| | J | F | M | A | M | J | J | A | S | O | N | D |
|---|---|---|---|---|---|---|---|---|---|---|---|---|
| **Max. °C** | 24 | 24 | 22 | 20 | 17 | 15 | 15 | 16 | 17 | 19 | 20 | 22 |
| **Min. °C** | 14 | 15 | 13 | 11 | 8 | 6 | 5 | 6 | 7 | 9 | 11 | 13 |
| **Rain mm** | 57 | 35 | 55 | 61 | 79 | 65 | 55 | 57 | 57 | 61 | 73 | 74 |
| **Raindays** | 8 | 7 | 10 | 10 | 12 | 13 | 12 | 14 | 13 | 13 | 13 | 11 |

### Snowy River National Park

The much-celebrated Snowy River begins as a trickle near Mt Kosciuszko and passes through wild limestone gorge and forest country before reaching a coastal lagoon. McKillops Bridge (via Buchan) is a beautiful area with camping and barbecue facilities, swimming spots and some good short walks.

*For more detail see maps 155 & 164–5.*

### Bataluk Cultural Trail

This driving tour starts at the visitor centre in Sale and links sites significant to the Gunai (Kurani) people, who travelled the area for at least 18 000 years before European settlement. Features include Buchan Caves (pictured), and the legend-rich Den of Nargun (a cave) in Mitchell River National Park.

### Mallacoota

Surrounded by the remote ocean beaches, estuarine waterways and unspoilt bush of Croajingolong National Park, this old-fashioned resort offers one of the best fishing, walking, boating, swimming and nature-watching holidays in Victoria. The town hosts a popular arts festival at Easter.

### Large lakes and a long beach

Gippsland Lakes, a vast natural resort, is contained on the coastal side by a strip of sand and channels and the remote Ninety Mile Beach. At the system's centre, the water-bound Lakes National Park offers birdwatching, walking, swimming and camping. Access is via boat from Paynesville or road and foot from Loch Sport.

### Lakes Entrance

Lakes Entrance (pictured), at the head of the Lakes, is a great base for fishing and boating and offers accommodation at all levels. For a holiday afloat, book a self-drive cruiser from nearby Metung. There are several wineries in the area. Wyanga Park Winery offers a lakes cruise from town to its cellar door and restaurant.

# MORNINGTON PENINSULA

This broad peninsula separating Port Phillip and Western Port has a long history as a summer retreat for Melburnians. It offers a clutch of well-serviced seaside towns with access to three seafronts: the sheltered 'front' beaches of Port Phillip, the wild 'back' beaches on Bass Strait, and the relatively unpopulated surf beaches of Western Port. During winter, holidaymakers turn their attention to the region's scenic countryside and its impressive collection of cool-climate vineyards and gourmet food producers. In any season, popular activities are walking, fishing, golfing (a choice of 20 courses), and grazing at the many restaurants, pubs and cafes.

## TOP EVENTS

**Jan.**  Swim Classic (Portsea)

**Jan.**  Sail Melbourne (coastal towns throughout region)

**Mar.**  Maize Maze Festival (Arthurs Seat, near Dromana)

**Mar.**  Pinot Week (throughout wine district)

**Mar.**  Cool Climate Wine Show (Red Hill)

**Mar.**  Street Festival (Sorrento)

**June**  Queen's Birthday Wine Weekend (throughout wine district)

**Oct.**  Mornington Food and Wine Festival (throughout wine district)

**Nov.**  Film Festival (Rosebud)

## EXPERIENCE IT!

**①** **Shop** till you drop at the popular community market at Red Hill (first Sat. of month, Sept.–May)

**②** **Canter** on the sands or take an equine winery tour with Gunnamatta Trail Rides, via Rye

**③** **Visit** McCrae Homestead, the cottage home of 19th-century artist Georgiana McCrae, at McCrae

### VISITOR INFORMATION

Mornington Peninsula Visitor Centre
Dromana: (03) 5987 3078;
1800 804 009

### FOCUS ON

#### Wineries

The grape came relatively late to the Mornington Peninsula: the longest surviving vineyard, Elgee Park, north of Merricks, was established early in the 1970s. Viticulture exploded during the 1980 and 1990s; now there are nearly 40 wineries on the Mornington Peninsula, most clustered around Red Hill. The vineyards are in a cool climate, tend to be small and set in postcard landscapes, concentrate on the classic varieties of pinot noir and chardonnay, and produce fairly expensive wines. Stonier's Winery, Tucks Ridge and Main Ridge Estate are a few of the names to look out for.

| CLIMATE MORNINGTON | | | | | | | | | | | | |
|---|---|---|---|---|---|---|---|---|---|---|---|---|
| | J | F | M | A | M | J | J | A | S | O | N | D |
| Max. °C | 25 | 25 | 23 | 19 | 16 | 14 | 13 | 14 | 16 | 18 | 20 | 23 |
| Min. °C | 13 | 14 | 13 | 11 | 9 | 7 | 7 | 7 | 8 | 10 | 11 | 12 |
| Rain mm | 46 | 43 | 50 | 62 | 71 | 71 | 69 | 71 | 72 | 70 | 60 | 55 |
| Raindays | 7 | 7 | 8 | 11 | 14 | 15 | 15 | 15 | 14 | 13 | 11 | 8 |

#### French Island

Half this sparsely inhabited island, a 15-min ferry ride from Stony Point, is national park. It supports 600 indigenous plant species, a large koala population and 234 bird species. There is no car access: explore by foot, hire a bicycle or book a tour. Camping and guesthouse accommodation is available.

### Sorrento sojourns

The Queenscliff–Sorrento car ferry crosses Port Phillip several times a day, offering visitors a tour of the two quite distinct peninsulas – Bellarine and Mornington – without a long drive by land. Dolphin cruises, some of which offer a swim with Port Phillip's bottlenose population, operate in summer.

### Portsea

Near the north-west tip of the peninsula, this village has been long favoured by Melbourne's wealthy. It has large houses, some of which have their own private boathouses (pictured), elegant hotels, comfortable motels and B&Bs, good dining and a legendary pub. Further west, don't miss Fort Nepean, once an important defence site, and London Bridge, a rock formation off Portsea Surf Beach.

*For more detail see map 154.*

### Mornington Peninsula National Park

This park extends along the south coast of the peninsula where the Bass Strait surf pounds windswept beaches and headlands. A 32-km walking track runs from Portsea Surf Beach right along the coast to Cape Schanck, with its historic lighthouse (1858), at the peninsula's southern tip.

### Arthurs Seat

Just inland from Dromana off the Nepean Highway, in a state park of the same name, Arthurs Seat offers superb views back over Melbourne and the bay. The 300-m summit is reached by chairlift. Nearby is Arthurs Seat Maze, which features a series of themed gardens and mazes including the largest Maize Maze in the Southern Hemisphere.

# PHILLIP ISLAND & GIPPSLAND

This is an area as diverse as it is beautiful. Along the coast, wild beaches and calm inlets give way to historic fishing, mining and farming towns, and spectacular stretches of bushland, much of it protected by national park. Wildlife thrives, most famously in the penguin and seal colonies of Phillip Island. Inland, the forested ridge country of the Strzelecki Ranges meets the central Gippsland plain where Australia's largest deposits of brown coal are mined to fuel the power stations that generate most of Victoria's electricity. Throughout much of the district, well-watered fields and rolling hills support one of Australia's biggest dairy industries and burgeoning wine and gourmet food production. In the north, gentle foothills rise to the high country of the Great Dividing Range, offering skiing in winter and walking tracks through grasslands and alpine flowers in summer.

## TOP EVENTS

| | |
|---|---|
| *Jan.* | *King of the Mountain Woodchop (Erica, near Walhalla)* |
| *Jan.* | *South Gippsland Food and Wine Festival (Leongatha)* |
| *Feb.–Mar.* | *Music in the Park (Traralgon)* |
| *Mar.* | *Jazz Festival (Inverloch)* |
| *Mar.* | *Potato Festival (Koo-wee-rup)* |
| *Mar.* | *Jazz Festival (Moe)* |
| *Mar.* | *Blue Rock Classic (cross-country horse race, Moe)* |
| *Mar.* | *Fishing Contest (Port Albert)* |
| *Easter* | *Coal Skip Fill (Wonthaggi)* |
| *Easter* | *Tarra Festival (Yarram)* |
| *Apr.* | *World Superbike Championships (Phillip Island)* |
| *Sept.* | *Daffodil and Floral Festival (Leongatha)* |
| *Oct.* | *Grand Prix Motorcycle Race (Phillip Island)* |
| *Nov.* | *Seabank Fishing Competition (Yarram)* |

## VISITOR INFORMATION

Phillip Island (Newhaven):
(03) 5956 7447; 1300 366 422

Traralgon: (03) 5174 3199;
1800 621 409

South Gippsland Visitor
Information Centre
Korumburra: (03) 5655 2233;
1800 630 704

www.phillipisland.net.au

### Gourmet Deli Trail

Tour for trout, venison, fine cheeses, baked goods, berries, potatoes, herbs and wine on the Gourmet Deli Trail. The extensive area covered includes the towns of Warragul, Foster and Wonthaggi and annotated maps are available from information centres. There are a dozen or so cool-climate wineries; try Bass Phillip's pinot noir at Leongatha.

## CLIMATE LEONGATHA

| | J | F | M | A | M | J | J | A | S | O | N | D |
|---|---|---|---|---|---|---|---|---|---|---|---|---|
| Max. °C | 25 | 25 | 23 | 19 | 16 | 14 | 13 | 14 | 16 | 19 | 21 | 23 |
| Min. °C | 12 | 12 | 11 | 9 | 7 | 5 | 5 | 5 | 7 | 8 | 9 | 11 |
| Rain mm | 59 | 61 | 71 | 88 | 85 | 95 | 83 | 95 | 88 | 96 | 81 | 68 |
| Raindays | 10 | 9 | 11 | 15 | 17 | 18 | 18 | 20 | 17 | 16 | 14 | 11 |

## FOCUS ON

### Phillip Island wildlife

The Penguin Parade on Summerland Beach in Phillip Island Nature Park is a major international tourist attraction. Just after sunset, little (fairy) penguins, the world's smallest at 33 cm tall, come home to their burrows in the sand dunes after a day in the sea. To protect the penguins, visitors are restricted to designated viewing areas and no cameras are allowed. Bookings are essential during peak holiday periods. The Visitor Centre also offers a simulated underwater tour showing the penguins foraging for food and avoiding predators. Seal Rocks, 2 km offshore, is home to thousands of sunbaking, sea-frolicking seals. These creatures can be viewed up close from aboard a seal-watching cruise boat, or on a visit to the Seal Rocks Sea Life Centre near The Nobbies, where real-time images of the seals are relayed onto giant screens. Another popular resident species on the island is the koala. Visit the Koala Conservation Centre and take a walking tour across the park's network of raised walkways.

### The Grand Ridge Road

Join The Grand Ridge Road (Tourist Route 93) at tiny Seaview. This mostly gravel road travels 132 km along the spine of the Strzelecki Ranges, offering spectacular views. The drive passes Tarra–Bulga National Park (pictured), where ash, myrtle beech, sassafras, and tree ferns form an exquisite 'cathedral', full of birdsong.

### Phillip Island

Although best known for its little (fairy) penguins (pictured), Phillip Island has other impressive attractions. The main town, Cowes, has sheltered beaches, safe for swimming and water sports. Visitors can walk around the island's highest point, Cape Woolamai, visit an historic home on Churchill Island (road access), or attend the Grand Prix Motorcycle Race (each October).

## EXPERIENCE IT!

**❶ Tour** *the State Coal Mine at Wonthaggi with an old-time miner as a guide*

**❷ Take** *a 3-hour tourist train ride along an historic Gippsland route, beginning at Leongatha*

**❸ Fish** *at Anderson Inlet near Inverloch, one of the State's best fishing spots*

**❹ Spend** *a day at Korumburra's Coal Creek Heritage Village, a re-creation of a 19th-century coalmining town*

**❺ Stop** *to smell the roses in spring at the Rose Garden, Commercial Road, Morwell*

### Baw Baw National Park

The Aboriginal word for echo gives the name to this alpine park. In the highest part of the park, Mount Baw Baw (via Moe) has ski facilities and is seldom crowded. The eastern section (via Erica and Walhalla) is popular in summer with walkers, wildflower enthusiasts and campers.

### Walhalla

Tourist Route 91, from Moe or Traralgon, leads to the perfectly preserved former goldmining town of Walhalla, situated in a steep, narrow valley. Historic buildings of gold-boom days include the post office, old bakery, museum and Windsor House (pictured). Take the signposted town walk, or a 45-min ride on the Walhalla Goldfields Railway (weekends and holidays), or inspect the Long Tunnel Mine (open most days).

*For more detail see maps 154–5.*

### The power track

At the centre of the Latrobe Valley lies one of the world's largest brown coal deposits. The PowerWorks museum at Morwell explains the processes that supply 85 per cent of Victoria's electricity. Tours of the open mines and power stations operate daily from the museum.

### Wilsons Promontory

The Prom is a remote and beautiful landscape supporting diverse native flora and fauna in a near wilderness. The 30-km scenic access road ends at Tidal River, where there are cabins and camping facilities. Access to 150 km of walking tracks across bays and bush is from Tidal River and other points along the road.

### Port Albert

This quaint fishing village, near the ruins of an 1840s port, sits on a narrow spit of land beside sheltered waters. About 40 old buildings survive. The town is a major centre for fishing, with plentiful snapper, whiting, flathead, bream and trevally in the shallow waters offshore.

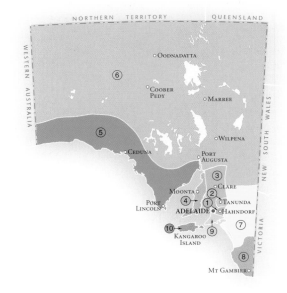

# SOUTH AUSTRALIA

A cosmopolitan culture, an unhurried pace of life, festivals of unparalleled quality, ancient landscapes of almost mythical beauty and the clear skies – these factors, combined with ease of travel and comparatively low prices, make South Australia an exceptional touring and holiday destination.

## From desert to sea

South Australia is the driest State in the world's second driest continent. It lies mid-way across the continent's south end and is just under a million square kilometres in area.

The 3700-kilometre coastline offers diverse scenery, from seaside cliffs edging the Nullarbor Plain to the blue-green shallows of Gulf St Vincent, the wetlands and sandhills of The Coorong, and the bush-fringed wild beaches of Kangaroo Island.

South Australia's most spectacular mountain range, the Flinders Ranges, extends north-east from the head of Spencer Gulf. The beauty of this eroded landscape is equalled only by its geological significance as one of the oldest landscapes on earth.

The range country gives way to vast salt lakes. Lake Eyre, the largest, is 15 metres below sea level and is dry for most of the time. A vast sand and gibber desert extends north and west of the great salt lakes to the borders of Western Australia and the Northern Territory. Much of this area receives less than 150 millimetres of rain annually.

Most of the State's agricultural activity, including its huge wine industry, is located along the fertile plains and hills of the south-east corner of the State, where the Murray River's South Australian journey begins and ends.

## Living on the land

Aboriginal people have inhabited the land known today as South Australia for at least 40 000 years. Anthropologists estimate the Aboriginal population at the time of European settlement at about 15 000, divided into 50 or so groups. The Aboriginal peoples were nomadic hunters and gatherers but their material culture varied with their geographical habitat. In the arid western desert, very small groups moved constantly between waterholes, hunting wildlife. The groups living in the central lakes district benefited from the great north–south trading route that ran the length of the continent, while the peoples of the more temperate and the coastal regions hunted game, fished, gathered wild fruit and nuts and made reed baskets.

## Whaleboat down the Murray

Europeans first sighted the South Australian coast in 1627 when a Dutch ship, the *Gulden Zeepaard* (Golden Seahorse), sailed into the Great Australian Bight while on a voyage to the East Indies. Abel Tasman then mapped part of the coast, and Flinders and Baudin made separate surveys in 1802. Charles Sturt made an overland journey to South Australia in 1829–30 by sailing a whaleboat down the Murray River.

## Under the gum tree

Early in the 1830s the South Australian Land Company was formed to establish a colony in South Australia. The objective was to create 'a virtuous and enlightened society'; an agrarian paradise funded by land sales and populated by free settlers rather than convicts. The British Government passed the South Australian Act in 1834, authorising the colony. In November 1836 Surveyor-General Colonel Light surveyed the site of Adelaide in preparation for his famously elegant plan for the city. In a ceremony conducted under a gum tree at Glenelg in December, Governor Hindmarsh proclaimed South Australia a colony.

Representative government arrived in South Australia in 1851 with the establishment of a Legislative Council; responsible government was established in 1856 with a Legislative Assembly. South Australia became an Australian State, with Federation in 1901.

## New ideas

South Australia, with its history of enlightened democracy, has been described as a laboratory for new social and political ideas. Australia's first significant non-British immigrant group found its home in South Australia: a group of 517 German immigrants, most of them Lutheran peasants fleeing religious persecution, arrived in 1838 and began laying down roots and traditions still evident in South Australian life and society today. South Australian women were given the right to vote and stand for Parliament in 1896. Australia's first Aboriginal governor, Sir Douglas Nicholls, was appointed in 1976 and Australia's first female governor, Dame Roma Mitchell, was appointed in 1991. In the 1970s, South Australia's reputation as a leader in social change and policy skyrocketed with the election of Don Dunstan as premier (1970–79). A self-confessed rebel, Dunstan oversaw radical changes in such areas as consumer protection, the environment, Aboriginal land rights and homosexual law.

## Land of plenty

South Australia today has a population of 1 500 000. The State that the first settlers imagined as a paradise for land-holders and farmers is now heavily urbanised, with about 70 per cent of the population living in Adelaide. Discoveries of rich mineral deposits from the 1840s onwards shifted the economic focus away from agricultural self-sufficiency to mining and export activities. With this, the importance of the major towns and the capital increased. Nevertheless, the agrarian spirit lives on. South Australia, despite its low rainfall and its focus on heavy industry and mining, remains a place of produce. It boasts fine vineyards, orchards, olive and almond groves, shimmering wheat fields and abundantly stocked coastal waters.

German-style house built in Hahndorf in the 1840s

For more information on South Australia, see Tourist Bureaus, opposite page 236.

# ADELAIDE

Adelaide is set on the wide curves of the River Torrens between the Mount Lofty Ranges and Gulf St Vincent. It is the only major metropolis in the world where the city's centre is completely encircled by parkland. It has a population of almost 1.1 million, but remains a friendly and open place. The city offers visitors a well-preserved history, the warmth and light of the South Australian outdoors and excellent wining and dining.

## GETTING AROUND

Adelaide's city centre is compact and easily negotiated on foot. The Explorer Tram offers visitors the chance to tour the city's attractions at a leisurely pace and with the benefit of a recorded commentary. A fleet of Popeye motor launches cruise the River Torrens and also provide an ideal means of transport to the Adelaide Zoo. The historic Glenelg tram is the most famous of Adelaide's tourist rides. It departs Victoria Square regularly for a return trip to Adelaide's premier seaside suburb. Car travel is recommended for touring some of the further-flung regions; the roads are excellent and, provided you have a road map, navigation should not be a problem.

**Airport shuttle bus**
Transit Regency Coaches
(08) 8381 5311

**Motoring organisation**
RAA (08) 8202 4600

**Public transport**
Passenger Transport Information Hotline
(08) 8210 1000

**Taxis**
Suburban Transport Services 13 10 08,
United Yellow Cabs 12 22 27

**River Torrens cruises**
Popeye Motor Launches
(08) 8295 4747

**Port Adelaide cruises**
Port Adelaide River Cruises
(08) 8341 1194

**Bicycle hire**
Contact Bicycle SA for operators
(08) 8232 2644

## VISITOR INFORMATION

**South Australian Visitor and Travel Centre**
1 King William Street
(08) 8303 2033
freecall 1300 655 276
www.visit.adelaide.on.net

## TOP EVENTS

**Schützenfest** (Jan.)
Celebration of South Australia's German heritage

**Adelaide Festival of the Arts and Adelaide Fringe Festival** (Feb.–Mar., even-numbered years)
Highly regarded international festivals

**Glendi Festival** (Mar.)
Greek culture, food, song and dance

**500 in Adelaide** (Apr.)
V8 supercar race on a modified Grand Prix circuit

**Tasting Australia** (Oct., odd-numbered years)
Sample the latest innovations in food and wine

## CITY CENTRE

See map on page 211.

**Adelaide Casino** 211 E8
Located in a beautifully restored railway station.

**Adelaide Festival Centre** 211 E7
One of the best performance venues in the world, with various exhibitions scattered throughout the centre.

**Art Gallery of South Australia** 211 F8
A superb overview of Australian art from the 18th century on.

**Botanic Gardens** 211 G7
Join a free tour of these beautiful, formal 16-ha gardens on the edge of the CBD.

**Central Market** 211 D10
Bustling market with some of the best and cheapest local produce in the country.

**Edmund Wright House** 211 E8
Historic house that displays travelling exhibitions from the National Museum of Australia; also the home of the State History Centre.

**Light's Vision** 211 D6
On Montefiore Hill, bronze statue of Colonel Light, the first surveyor-general of the city.

**Migration Museum** 211 E7
Housed in the former Destitute Asylum; features exhibits charting migrants' lives before, during and after their arrival.

**Museum of Classical Archaeology** 211 F8
Within the grounds of the University of Adelaide, this museum houses objects that date back to the third millennium BC.

**Rundle Mall** 211 E8
The major shopping precinct and a vibrant, cosmopolitan cafe strip.

**St Peter's Cathedral** 211 E6
One of Australia's finest cathedrals, built in 1869 in the Gothic Revival style.

**South Australian Museum** 211 F8
Features the world's largest collection of anthropological Aboriginal artefacts and a range from the Pacific Islands and Egypt.

**Tandanya – National Aboriginal Cultural Institute** 211 G9
Houses displays of Aboriginal culture, art, artefacts and a performance space for dance and theatre.

**Treasury Building** 211 E9
Dating back to 1839; now a museum charting the fascinating history of exploration and surveying in South Australia.

## SUBURBS AND SURROUNDS

See map on page 68.

**Adelaide Hills** 68 F4
Historic villages, gardens, museums and vineyards sit among bushland and European-style farmland.

**Belair National Park** 68 D5
The State's oldest national park, established in 1891; includes the impressive gardens of the governor's old summer residence.

**Cleland Wildlife Park** 68 E4
Excellent park housing native marsupials and aviaries; night-time walks available.

**Glenelg** 68 B5
Board a tram to this seaside resort with its old-world feel; the amusement centre Magic Mountain is nearby.

**McLaren Vale wine region** 68 C8
Set among rolling acres of almond and olive groves, these 53 wineries form one of the country's top wine-producing regions.

**South Australian Maritime Museum** 68 C2
Re-creations of 19th-century dock life and the immigrant experience, including replicas of parts of old sailing boats.

**Victor Harbor** 68 D13
Popular holiday resort located on the Fleurieu Peninsula; includes a horse-drawn tram, heritage sites, penguins, dolphins and whales.

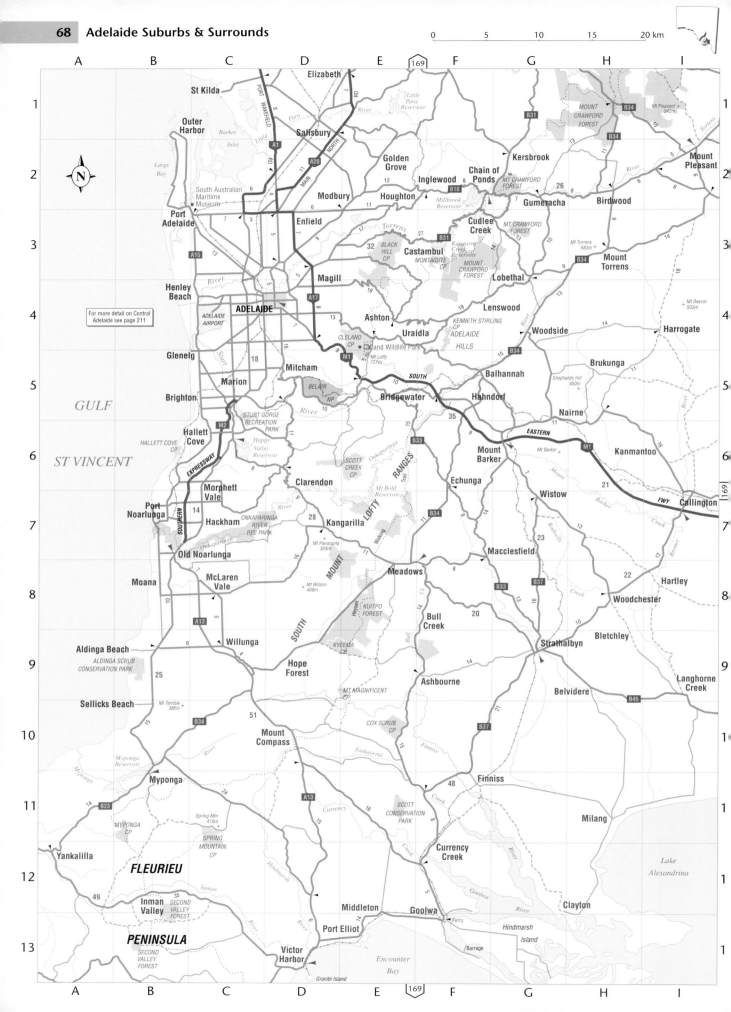

# ADELAIDE HILLS

This magnificent landscape of hills and valleys rises in the east above the coastal plains of Adelaide. It is well known for its interesting mix of Australian bushland and European-style farmland, as well as its historic villages, gardens, museums, galleries, vineyards, lookouts and native fauna. The city, only 20 minutes away, is a suitable base for those who wish to take a few days to tour the district. Alternatively, book into a local B&B or guesthouse and get the full rustic experience of this scenic pocket of South Australia.

## TOP EVENTS

| | |
|---|---|
| *Mar.* | Adelaide Hills Harvest Festival |
| *Easter* | Oakbank Easter Racing Carnival |
| *Apr.* | Mount Lofty Spring Bulb Festival (Stirling) |
| *May* | Autumn Leaves Festival (Aldgate) |
| *Sept.* | Bay to Birdwood Run (vintage vehicles, even-numbered years) |
| *Sept.* | Hills Affare (wine and food, Stirling) |
| *Oct.* | Heysen Festival (Hahndorf) |
| *Nov.* | Rock and Roll Rendezvous (Birdwood) |
| *Nov.* | Great Train Race (Mount Barker) |

## EXPERIENCE IT!

❶ *Board* the steam train at Mount Barker for a trip to Victor Harbor

❷ *Journey* back in time along the guided trail at the Jupiter Creek Gold Fields near Echunga

❸ *Climb* the biggest rocking-horse in the world at The Toy Factory, Gumeracha

### Birdwood National Motor Museum
The largest museum of its kind in the Southern Hemisphere, this museum has over 300 vintage exhibits tracing the history of motoring.

### Mount Lofty Lookout
Spectacular views of Adelaide and the Hills may be enjoyed from the lookout at the 727-metre summit of Mount Lofty. Drop into the information centre to plan your day and enjoy 'food with a view' in the adjacent restaurant and cafe.

### Cleland Wildlife Park
Within Cleland Conservation Park, this excellent wildlife park features a large collection of everybody's favourite marsupials, as well as aviaries and nocturnal walks. Combine your visit with a picnic in the adjacent Mount Lofty Botanic Gardens.

## VISITOR INFORMATION
Adelaide Hills Visitors Centre
Hahndorf: (08) 8388 1185
www.visitadelaidehills.com.au

## FOCUS ON
### Food and wine
The Adelaide Hills is becoming increasingly well known for its excellent regional produce and as a touring destination for those with gourmet expectations. Best experiences include a visit to Petaluma's Bridgewater Mill for tastings and sales of Petaluma wines, or lunch at the restaurant attached. In Hahndorf you can sample German-style produce at Hahndorf's Smallgoods, taste wine and cheese at Hillstowe Wines and buy berry produce at Beerenberg Strawberry Farm. Mount Barker's gourmet outlets include Brezel Bakehouse and Springs Smoked Seafoods, while near Birdwood you can buy German breads at the Lobethal Bakery, visit the Netherhill Strawberry Farm and taste the grapes at Chain of Ponds Wines.

### CLIMATE MOUNT BARKER

| | J | F | M | A | M | J | J | A | S | O | N | D |
|---|---|---|---|---|---|---|---|---|---|---|---|---|
| **Max. °C** | 27 | 27 | 25 | 20 | 16 | 14 | 13 | 14 | 16 | 19 | 22 | 25 |
| **Min. °C** | 12 | 12 | 10 | 8 | 7 | 5 | 4 | 5 | 6 | 7 | 9 | 10 |
| **Rain mm** | 26 | 26 | 31 | 59 | 89 | 100 | 106 | 102 | 86 | 68 | 40 | 34 |
| **Raindays** | 6 | 5 | 7 | 11 | 15 | 16 | 17 | 18 | 15 | 13 | 9 | 7 |

*For more detail see map 169.*

### Hahndorf
This distinctive town was settled in the 1830s by Prussian refugees. Its heritage is preserved in classic buildings and German-style shops, museums and cafes. Visit The Cedars, former home of artist Hans Heysen, and see local artworks in the splendid Hahndorf Academy.

### Belair National Park
South Australia's oldest national park, established in 1891, offers a natural landscape of eucalypt forests and brilliant flowering native species. Garden lovers will enjoy a stroll through the gardens of the governor's old summer residence (pictured), which dates back to 1859.

# BAROSSA VALLEY

The Barossa is Australia's best known wine-producing area. Along with nearby Eden Valley, it offers a landscape of vine-covered hills dotted with historic villages, stone cottages, and the grand buildings of old wine estates. It is also a place of rich culture. These traditions are based on a 150-year history of German settlement and can be seen in every aspect of life, from the spires of the Lutheran churches to the local German breads and pastries. Only an hour from Adelaide, and boasting some of the best restaurants and accommodation of any regional area, the Barossa is a popular weekend destination.

## TOP EVENTS

| | |
|---|---|
| **Feb.** | Barossa Under the Stars (Tanunda) |
| **Feb.** | Oompah Festival (Tanunda) |
| **Mar.** | Tanunda Show and Essenfest (Tanunda) |
| **Apr.** | Barossa Vintage Festival (throughout region, odd-numbered years) |
| **May** | Barossa Balloon Regatta (Nuriootpa) |
| **Sept.** | Spring into the Barossa (throughout region) |
| **Oct.** | Barossa International Music Festival (throughout region) |
| **Oct.** | Brass Band Contest (Tanunda) |

## EXPERIENCE IT!

**❶ Take** a tour of the historic Lutheran churches of Tanunda

**❷ Travel** Menglers Hill Road Scenic Drive between Angaston and Tanunda to appreciate the rustic charms of the region

**❸ Dine** at Vintners Bar and Grill in Angaston, one of the many excellent restaurants

## VISITOR INFORMATION

Barossa Wine and Visitor Centre
Tanunda: (08) 8563 0600
www.barossa-region.org

## FOCUS ON

### Gourmet tradition

Whereas many parts of Australia have developed gourmet credentials over the last decade or so, the Barossa has a culinary heritage that goes back 150 years. German-style baking is a highlight: try the Lyndoch Bakery, or the Apex Bakery in Tanunda, established 70 years ago. Old-fashioned ice-cream is made and served at Tanunda's Nice Ice and in Angaston you'll find the shopfront for Australia's biggest processor of dried fruit – Angus Park Fruit Company. Maggie Beer's Farm Shop at Nuriootpa sells the products that have made her name, while Angaston Gourmet Foods is a great place for all the region's best products.

### CLIMATE NURIOOTPA

| | J | F | M | A | M | J | J | A | S | O | N | D |
|---|---|---|---|---|---|---|---|---|---|---|---|---|
| **Max. °C** | 29 | 29 | 26 | 21 | 17 | 14 | 13 | 14 | 17 | 20 | 24 | 26 |
| **Min. °C** | 14 | 14 | 12 | 9 | 7 | 5 | 4 | 5 | 6 | 8 | 10 | 12 |
| **Rain mm** | 19 | 19 | 22 | 38 | 55 | 56 | 66 | 64 | 60 | 49 | 29 | 24 |
| **Raindays** | 5 | 4 | 5 | 8 | 12 | 13 | 16 | 16 | 13 | 11 | 8 | 6 |

### Barossa wineries

The Barossa is one of the oldest and largest wine areas in Australia and is best known for its riesling and shiraz. The biennial Barossa Vintage Festival (pictured) is a time of great activity and colour.

### Seppeltsfield

Seppelts estate, established in the 1850s, is one of the grandest in the country. Elegant bluestone buildings are surrounded by superb gardens and an avenue of date palms. Don't miss the hilltop mausoleum built in the style of a Doric temple. Tours available.

### Kaiser Stuhl Conservation Park

This rugged mountainside park offers a view of what the Barossa would have looked like before European settlement. A couple of excellent walking trails allow visitors to explore the varied terrain as well as offering a glimpse of local wildlife.

*For more detail see maps 167 & 169.*

### Gawler

This heritage-listed town was a 19th-century market centre for the rural area north of Adelaide. It preserves magnificent buildings, from mansions to 1840s cottages, and is admired for its original design, which features civic squares, wide streets and reserves.

### Eden Valley wineries

This elevated wine-growing area is regarded as a distinct region. A small number of wineries are open for tastings. In Springton, find the Herbig Tree, a giant red gum that was temporary home to a German family in the 1850s.

# CLARE VALLEY & THE MID-NORTH

The Mid-North was settled in the 1840s as a major coppermining and agricultural district. The area is renowned for its scenic beauty – old stone cottages and a spread of rolling hills and vineyards. The wineries of the Clare Valley are the prime regional attraction, followed by the coppermining sites preserved in the area – said to be among the most important historic industrial sites in Australia. These attractions, plus galleries, antique and craft stores, and B&Bs and restaurants, make this peaceful region a great choice for a daytrip or a weekend away.

## TOP EVENTS

*Mar.*  Twilight Jazz Affair (Burra)
*Easter*  Easter Races (Clare)
*Apr.*  Picnic Races (Burra)
*Apr.*  Spanish Festival (Clare)
*May*  Antique Fair (Burra)
*May*  Gourmet Weekend (Clare)
*Aug.*  Balaklava Cup (horseracing, Balaklava)
*Oct.*  Spring Garden Festival (Clare)

## EXPERIENCE IT!

❶ **Buy** local gourmet produce, including olive oil, from Clare retailers

❷ **Picnic** at Burra Gorge, 27 kilometres south-east of Burra

❸ **Cycle** or walk the Riesling Trail, a scenic 27-kilometre path following the old railway line between Clare and Auburn

## VISITOR INFORMATION

Clare: (08) 8842 2131
Burra: (08) 8892 2154
www.classiccountry.org.au

## FOCUS ON

### History

Historically, this is one of the most interesting and well-preserved areas of rural South Australia. In 1839 Edward Eyre explored the Clare Valley and his favourable reports led quickly to pastoral settlement. Places of interest include historic buildings in many towns, particularly in Clare and Mintaro streetscapes. North-west of Clare is Bungaree, a Merino sheep station established 1841. Copper was discovered in the region in 1842 and soon vast mines and major settlements were established. Mining history is preserved in Burra and Kapunda; in both places you'll find accommodation and numerous sites that recall the mining boom of the mid to late 19th century.

### CLIMATE CLARE

|        | J | F | M | A | M | J | J | A | S | O | N | D |
|--------|---|---|---|---|---|---|---|---|---|---|---|---|
| Max. °C | 30 | 29 | 27 | 22 | 17 | 14 | 13 | 15 | 18 | 21 | 25 | 27 |
| Min. °C | 13 | 13 | 12 | 8 | 6 | 4 | 3 | 4 | 5 | 7 | 10 | 12 |
| Rain mm | 25 | 24 | 25 | 47 | 73 | 80 | 82 | 80 | 73 | 57 | 37 | 29 |
| Raindays | 4 | 4 | 5 | 8 | 12 | 14 | 15 | 15 | 13 | 11 | 7 | 6 |

*For more detail see maps 169 & 171.*

### Clare Valley wineries

This winegrowing district extends for 35 kilometres across the fertile valley. Although the climate is generally Mediterranean, many Clare Valley wines have cool-climate characteristics. The region is known for quality, and its rieslings are widely regarded as among the best in Australia. There are about 30 wineries, ranging from big names to charming boutique-style establishments.

### Sevenhill

Austrian Jesuit priests established Clare's first winery here in the early 1850s to ensure a steady supply of altar wine. There have been seven Jesuit winemakers since then, and the range now includes good table wine. Next to the cellars, St Aloysius Church (completed 1875) is worth a visit.

### Burra

Located in the sparse landscape of the Bald Hills Range, this former coppermining centre is a mid-19th-century timepiece. It comprises public buildings, shops, miners' cottages, miners' dugouts and the open-cut mine (pictured). Museums chart the area's history, and mine site tours are available. Many cottages have been converted to visitor accommodation.

### Mintaro

Mintaro is an almost intact 19th-century South Australian village with attractive stone buildings, many of them incorporating the region's unique slate. Mintaro General Store (pictured) is typical of local heritage charm. South-east is Martindale Hall, an 1879 mansion used for the film *Picnic at Hanging Rock* (1975) and now open as a hotel.

# YORKE PENINSULA

Yorke Peninsula, only an hour and a half from Adelaide, is a popular holiday destination. Flanked by the mostly calm waters of Gulf St Vincent on one side and Spencer Gulf on the other, it is known for its great range of seaside activities including fishing, diving and surfing, and for its spectacular coastal scenery. The area was put on the map in the late 1850s by the discovery of rich copper-ore deposits. Many of the now peaceful resort towns along the coast were once busy ports. Today the area is one of the world's richest barley- and wheat-growing regions.

## TOP EVENTS

**Jan.** Festival of the Crab (Port Germein)

**Easter** Bowling Carnival (Kadina)

**Apr.** Prawnfest (odd-numbered years, Wallaroo)

**May** Mine Shafters B&S Ball (Kadina and Wallaroo)

**May** Kernewek Lowender (odd-numbered years, Kadina, Moonta and Wallaroo)

**Sept.** Blessing of the Fleet (Port Pirie)

**Oct.** Gala Day (Edithburgh)

**Oct.** Yorke Surfing Classic (Innes National Park)

**Oct.** Festival of Country Music (Port Pirie)

## EXPERIENCE IT!

**1** **Go** diving and follow the Wardang Island Maritime Heritage Trail to eight shipwrecks

**2** **Travel** the countryside in a fully self-contained Gipsy Wagon from Brentwood

**3** **Visit** State-heritage Moonta Mines and see a miner's cottage, a museum and a mine railway

## VISITOR INFORMATION

Harvest Corner Information Centre
Minlaton: (08) 8853 2600
www.yorkepeninsula.com.au

## FOCUS ON

### Fishing

Yorke Peninsula is one of the State's top fishing destinations, with jetties at Wallaroo, Moonta Bay, Edithburgh, Stansbury and Port Victoria. The rocky points and sandy coves of the region also provide excellent opportunities for land-based anglers. Snapper, squid, tommy ruff, garfish and whiting are among the more commonly caught species. Reef-fishing is also popular. Browns Beach, on the western side of Innes National Park, is renowned for its big hauls of salmon. Near Goose Island, just north of Wardang Island on the west coast, are two reefs that offer excellent boat-fishing for a variety of species.

### Port Victoria

This town was once the main port of call for the clippers and windjammers that transported grain to the Northern Hemisphere, a history recorded in the local Maritime Museum. Port Victoria is now a resort town, offering access to swimming beaches and to Wardang Island, a popular diving spot with an underwater heritage trail featuring eight wrecks.

| CLIMATE KADINA | | | | | | | | | | | | |
|---|---|---|---|---|---|---|---|---|---|---|---|---|
| | J | F | M | A | M | J | J | A | S | O | N | D |
| Max. °C | 30 | 30 | 28 | 23 | 19 | 16 | 15 | 17 | 19 | 23 | 26 | 28 |
| Min. °C | 16 | 16 | 14 | 11 | 9 | 7 | 6 | 7 | 8 | 10 | 12 | 14 |
| Rain mm | 15 | 18 | 19 | 33 | 46 | 51 | 49 | 45 | 39 | 33 | 22 | 18 |
| Raindays | 3 | 3 | 4 | 6 | 10 | 11 | 13 | 13 | 10 | 8 | 5 | 4 |

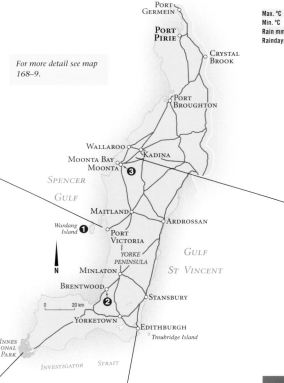

For more detail see map 168–9.

### Little Cornwall

This is a collective name for Wallaroo, Moonta and Kadina and refers to the Cornish immigrants who arrived in the early 1860s to mine the substantial copper deposits of the region. The towns preserve some historic architecture – the legacy of early wealth – as well as having museums and festivals that recall the rich local history.

### Innes National Park

At the southern tip of the peninsula, Innes National Park protects salt lakes, low mallee scrub, wildflowers, sandy beaches and rugged cliffs. Browns Beach and Pondalowie Bay are popular for surfing, diving and fishing. A 1904 shipwreck can be glimpsed on Ethel Beach, and the interesting remains of Inneston mining town (pictured) are on the eastern side of the park.

### Edithburgh

The town's jetty was once the site of a large shipping operation, when thousands of tonnes of salt were harvested from the nearby lakes and exported. Edithburgh is now a popular resort town. Attractions include a tidal pool for safe swimming, good diving locations and access to Troubridge Island, home to populations of little (fairy) penguins, black-faced shags and crested terns.

# EYRE PENINSULA & NULLARBOR

This region offers vast distances and spectacular scenery. It stretches 1000 kilometres from the large town of Whyalla to the remote border of Western Australia, taking in the calm waters of Spencer Gulf and the wild Southern Ocean in the Great Australian Bight. Fishing and surfing spots here are among the best in the world. Wildlife, wildflowers, coastal scrub and low hills dominate the eastern reaches; in the west, vast treeless plains and the spectacular sea cliffs of the Nullarbor Plain take over. Travel in the cooler months to avoid extreme heat and take precautions when crossing the Nullarbor.

## TOP EVENTS

**Jan.** Tunarama Festival (Port Lincoln)

**Feb.** Lincoln Week Yachting Regatta (Port Lincoln)

**Apr.** Australian Amateur Snapper Fishing Championship (Whyalla)

**Apr.** World Championship Kalamazoo Classic (Cummins)

**Apr.** Cup Race Meeting (Streaky Bay)

**Aug.** Agricultural Show (Whyalla)

**Sept.** Agricultural Show (Ceduna)

**Oct.** Oyster-Fest (Ceduna)

**Nov.** Camel Cup Races (Streaky Bay)

## EXPERIENCE IT!

❶ **Fish** from a charter around the Sir Joseph Banks Group of Islands, via Tumby Bay

❷ **Swim** with sea-lions and dolphins at Baird Bay, near Streaky Bay

❸ **Visit** Australia's largest permanently land-locked ship at the Whyalla Maritime Museum

## VISITOR INFORMATION

Port Lincoln: (08) 8683 3544
Ceduna: 1800 639 413
www.epta.com.au

## FOCUS ON

### Wildlife

This sparsely settled district remains a wildlife haven. White-bellied sea eagles, ospreys, pied and sooty oystercatchers and silver and Pacific gulls are just some of the birds found on the coastline. Sir Joseph Banks Group of Islands, via Tumby Bay, is Australia's largest breeding ground for Cape Barren geese; other creatures in this marine conservation park are New Zealand fur seals, sea-lions and dolphins. Point Labatt, near Streaky Bay, is home to Australia's only resident mainland colony of sea-lions, while Head of Bight offers the ultimate wildlife experience – a view of southern right whales in their breeding grounds (June to October).

### Nullarbor Plain

The Nullarbor, Latin for 'treeless', is a plain of 250 000 square kilometres, resting on a massive area of limestone riddled with underground caves. Along the coast a long line of sheer-faced cliffs drop suddenly into the wild waters of the Great Australian Bight. Between June and October a popular activity is whale-watching, from cliffs 300 kilometres west of Ceduna.

**CLIMATE PORT LINCOLN**

|          | J  | F  | M  | A  | M  | J  | J  | A  | S  | O  | N  | D  |
|----------|----|----|----|----|----|----|----|----|----|----|----|----|
| Max. °C  | 25 | 25 | 24 | 22 | 19 | 17 | 16 | 17 | 18 | 20 | 22 | 24 |
| Min. °C  | 15 | 16 | 15 | 13 | 11 | 9  | 8  | 8  | 9  | 11 | 12 | 14 |
| Rain mm  | 13 | 15 | 20 | 37 | 57 | 75 | 79 | 69 | 50 | 35 | 22 | 19 |
| Raindays | 4  | 4  | 5  | 10 | 14 | 16 | 18 | 17 | 14 | 11 | 7  | 6  |

### Spencer Gulf coast

Here calm waters serve peaceful holiday villages, as well as the northerly regional centre of Whyalla. At Port Lincoln in the south, the huge natural harbour is home to Australia's foremost tuna fleet. Beaches, boat hire, museums, golf, walks and drives are all on offer, but the biggest drawcard is fishing – jetty angling or game-fishing – in some of the best grounds in Australia.

*For more detail see maps 168 & 176–7.*

NULLARBOR PLAIN
W A
NULLARBOR NP
Head of Bight
GREAT AUSTRALIAN BIGHT
PENONG
CEDUNA
N
0   60 km
STREAKY BAY
BAIRD BAY
Point Labatt ❷
ELLISTON
WUDINNA
KIMBA
❸ WHYALLA
COWELL
CUMMINS
Spencer Gulf
TUMBY BAY ❶ Sir Joseph Banks Group
COFFIN BAY
COFFIN BAY NP
PORT LINCOLN
SIR JOSEPH BANKS GROUP CP

### Surf coast

Renowned surf beaches nestle in along this remote coastline, mainly between Ceduna and the tiny settlement of Penong 73 kilometres away. The best known beach is Cactus, just south of Penong, which boasts three world-famous surfing breaks.

**Note:** Sharks have been known to frequent these waters – seek local advice.

### Coffin Bay National Park

This park protects a pristine coastal wilderness of exposed cliffs, small coves and beaches and abundant wildlife. Bush camping, surfing, wildflower-viewing (in spring), walking and fishing are all popular activities. Many of the vehicle tracks are four-wheel-drive only, but for conventional vehicles there is a popular scenic tour called the Yangie Trail, beginning at Coffin Bay township.

# FLINDERS RANGES & OUTBACK

This vast, varied region, covering about 70 per cent of the State, offers spectacular scenery and abundant flora and fauna. While many attractions are easily reached along well-maintained roads, other spots are remote and require special preparations and, in some cases, a four-wheel drive vehicle. Always check weather conditions ahead. Camping and caravanning holidays are very popular in these parts, a fact reflected by the high quality of many facilities. Fees are charged for entry to national parks; a pass should be bought in advance for the desert parks in the north. Conditions apply to travel in Aboriginal lands.

## TOP EVENTS

*Easter* Opal Festival (Coober Pedy)

*Apr.* Antique and Craft Fair (Port Augusta)

*May* Race Meeting and Gymkhana (Oodnadatta)

*June* Glendi Festival (Greek culture, Coober Pedy)

*July* Australian Camel Cup (Marree)

*Aug.* Races (Innamincka)

*Sept.* Art Exhibition (Hawker)

*Sept.* Opal Festival (Andamooka)

## EXPERIENCE IT!

❶ **Take** a Ridgetop Tour via Arkaroola for a taste of the ancient world of the Flinders Ranges

❷ **Admire** desert flora at Port Augusta's Australian Arid Lands Botanic Gardens

❸ **Visit** Kanyaka Homestead Historic Site, south of Hawker

## VISITOR INFORMATION

Wadlata Outback Centre
Port Augusta: (08) 8641 0793
www.flinders.outback.on.net

## FOCUS ON

### Ancient landforms

Traces of the first life on earth, marine animal fossils, have been found in the Flinders Ranges. There are numerous places to experience the geological and scenic wonders of these ancient peaks and valleys. In the south around Wilpena, attractions include the Great Wall of China (a massive limestone ridge) and Bunyeroo and Brachina gorges, where an interpretative walk retraces 1000 million years of fossil history. In the north, in and around the Gammon Ranges National Park, visit the Bararrana, Wearing, Mount Chambers, Big Moro, Italowie and Weetootla gorges, and the Bolla Bollana and Nooldoonooldoona waterholes.

### CLIMATE HAWKER

|          | J  | F  | M  | A  | M  | J  | J  | A  | S  | O  | N  | D  |
|----------|----|----|----|----|----|----|----|----|----|----|----|----|
| Max. °C  | 34 | 33 | 30 | 25 | 20 | 16 | 16 | 18 | 21 | 26 | 29 | 32 |
| Min. °C  | 17 | 18 | 15 | 11 | 7  | 5  | 4  | 4  | 7  | 10 | 13 | 16 |
| Rain mm  | 20 | 21 | 17 | 20 | 31 | 39 | 35 | 33 | 28 | 24 | 22 | 21 |
| Raindays | 3  | 2  | 2  | 3  | 5  | 7  | 7  | 7  | 6  | 5  | 4  | 3  |

### Coober Pedy

This town is famous for its opal production (70 per cent of world's supply), and for buildings constructed underground to protect residents against extreme temperatures. Visit the museums and mines, try your hand at prospecting, and shop for opals.

### Lake Eyre

Australia's largest salt lake, in Lake Eyre National Park, is also the continent's lowest lying land at 15 metres below sea level. A few times each century the dry lake fills and hundreds of thousands of birds flock to the area to feed and breed.

### Innamincka and Cooper Creek

Near Innamincka is the part of Cooper Creek where the Burke and Wills expedition ended in tragedy. Memorials include the Dig Tree, across the Queensland border. The nearby Coongie Lakes form a remarkable wetland in the midst of gibber plains.

### Yourambulla Caves

One of several Aboriginal rock-art sites in the Flinders Ranges, these caves are reached via a 15-minute walk off the road south of Hawker. The images are characterised by the use of black and yellow pigment rather than the common red ochre.

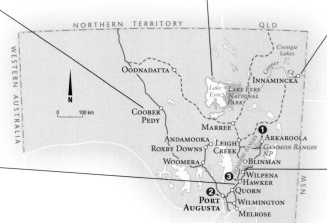

*For more detail see maps 170–1, 172–3 & 174–5.*

### Wildflowers of the ranges

In spring, rainfall permitting, native flowers carpet the semi-arid landscape of the Flinders Ranges. Stunning displays can be seen throughout the region, including around the popular Wilpena Pound in Flinders Ranges National Park. Favourites include Sturt's nightshade, silver tails, yellow buttons and the brilliant Sturt's desert pea (pictured).

# THE MURRAY

The Murray River runs through South Australia for 650 kilometres. It crosses a variety of landscapes that include rugged cliff-lined river valleys, mallee scrub, red gum forests, lagoons, orchards and vineyards. The river empties into massive Lake Alexandrina on the coast and feeds the wondrous Coorong wetlands. Its rich history of trade and agriculture has been preserved in the many river towns along the way. As South Australia's only river of significance, it provides a welcome focus in a State known for its aridity. Over the years the Murray has become a popular alternative to a seaside destination.

## TOP EVENTS

| | |
|---|---|
| **Jan.** | *Apex Fisherama (Loxton)* |
| **Feb.** | *Mardi Gras (Loxton)* |
| **Mar.** | *Rotary Food Fair (Waikerie)* |
| **Mar.** | *Riverland Run, Rally and Rock (Renmark)* |
| **May** | *Riverland Rock 'n' Roll Festival (Waikerie)* |
| **June** | *SA Country Music Festival (Barmera)* |
| **Oct.** | *Rose Festival  (Renmark)* |
| **Nov.** | *Steam Rally Festival (Murray Bridge)* |
| **Nov.– Dec.** | *Loxton Lights Up (Christmas lights)* |

## EXPERIENCE IT!

**❶ Visit** *the Monarto Zoological Park at Murray Bridge*

**❷ Captain** *your own houseboat for a few days of river sightseeing*

**❸ Discover** *the rich Aboriginal history of the Coorong at the museum at Camp Coorong*

## VISITOR INFORMATION

Murray Bridge Information Centre:
(08) 8539 1142
Riverland Information Centres
Berri, Loxton, Renmark: 1300 657 625

## FOCUS ON

### Paddle-steamers

Paddle-steamers were first used in South Australia when the *Mary Ann* was launched at Mannum in 1853. Carrying goods and passengers, they were vital in the development of the all-important trade route that ran from the mouth of the river into New South Wales and Victoria. Two of the original boats, the PS *Mayflower* and the PS *Marion*, operate as day-cruisers, departing from Morgan and Mannum respectively. Longer tours are available on the PS *River Murray Princess* – the largest paddleboat ever built in the Southern Hemisphere – and the *Proud Mary*, which specialises in nature tours.

### Morgan

Morgan's days as a busy river port may be over, but a rich heritage of sites and buildings preserve something of the excitement of river trading in the late 19th century. Look out for the wharves (built in 1877), the customs house and courthouse. For an insight into the history of these buildings drop in to the Port of Morgan Historical Museum in the old railway buildings.

### Riverland produce

The Riverland is the fruit bowl of South Australia, producing over 90 per cent of the State's citrus, stone fruit and nuts. Winegrowing is also a feature: tastings and sales are available at half-a-dozen estates, including Angoves near Renmark and Banrock Station Wine and Wetland centre at Kingston-on-Murray.

### CLIMATE RENMARK

| | J | F | M | A | M | J | J | A | S | O | N | D |
|---|---|---|---|---|---|---|---|---|---|---|---|---|
| **Max. °C** | 32 | 32 | 29 | 24 | 20 | 17 | 16 | 18 | 21 | 25 | 28 | 30 |
| **Min. °C** | 17 | 17 | 14 | 11 | 8 | 6 | 5 | 6 | 8 | 11 | 13 | 15 |
| **Rain mm** | 16 | 19 | 14 | 18 | 25 | 25 | 23 | 25 | 28 | 28 | 21 | 18 |
| **Raindays** | 3 | 3 | 3 | 4 | 6 | 8 | 8 | 8 | 7 | 6 | 4 | 4 |

### Camping and watersports

From Murray Bridge to Renmark there are caravan parks and camping grounds with river frontage and access to a wide range of watersports, including canoeing, fishing and swimming. The Murray River National Park provides a couple of quiet spots at the north-east end of the river for those who like their recreation in a park setting.

### The Coorong

The Coorong, a shallow lagoon in Coorong National Park, is one of Australia's significant wetland areas. It stretches 135 kilometres along the coast, separated from the Southern Ocean by the dunes of Younghusband Peninsula. Apart from its spectacular scenery, The Coorong is best known for its abundant birdlife, with over 240 species recorded. Popular activities include fishing, camping and walking.

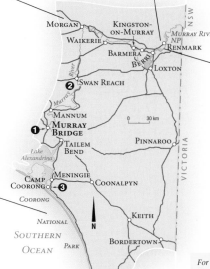

*For more detail see maps 166 & 169.*

# THE SOUTH-EAST

Beginning 300 kilometres to the east of Adelaide and stretching across to the Victorian border along the Princes Highway, the South-East is a major holiday centre. It is best known for its coastline of historic fishing villages and stunning beach scenery, and for the prestigious wineries of the Coonawarra district. Other attractions include the World Heritage-listed Naracoorte Caves and the large regional centre of Mount Gambier set in pine forests on the edge of an ancient volcano. The district makes for a great long weekend away or an ideal place to break the journey between Melbourne and Adelaide.

## TOP EVENTS

| | |
|---|---|
| **Jan.** | Cape Jaffa Seafood and Wine Festival |
| **Jan.** | Fishing Contest; Lobster Festival (Kingston S.E.) |
| **Jan.** | Bayside Festival (Port MacDonnell) |
| **Jan.** | Vigneron Cup (Penola) |
| **Feb.** | Country Music Festival (Mount Gambier) |
| **May** | Arts Festival (Penola) |
| **May** | Generations in Jazz (Mount Gambier) |
| **Nov.** | Cabernet Celebrations (Coonawarra) |
| **Nov.** | Spring Village Fair and Blessing of the Fleet (Robe) |

## EXPERIENCE IT!

**1** **Go** birdwatching at Bool Lagoon Game Reserve, one of the region's largest wetlands

**2** **Walk** the massive dunes of Canunda National Park

**3** **Visit** the Mary MacKillop Interpretative Centre at Penola to learn about this unusual pioneer

## VISITOR INFORMATION

Lady Nelson Visitor and Discovery Centre
Mount Gambier: (08) 8724 9750
www.seol.net.au/tse

## FOCUS ON

### Seaside towns

The South-East includes some of the State's most scenic coast, where golden beaches frame the blue-green waters of the Southern Ocean. Quiet resort towns, such as Robe, offer good swimming, surfing and fishing. Nearby lies Kingston S.E., a major lobster port (look out for the unusual lighthouse and the Big Lobster), and Cape Jaffa, site of wrecks well known to divers. Further south is Beachport, settled as a whaling station in the 1830s. The town's long jetty is a popular fishing spot. Port MacDonnell, near the Victorian border, boasts the State's largest lobster fleet.

### CLIMATE MOUNT GAMBIER

| | J | F | M | A | M | J | J | A | S | O | N | D |
|---|---|---|---|---|---|---|---|---|---|---|---|---|
| **Max. °C** | 24 | 25 | 23 | 20 | 17 | 14 | 14 | 15 | 16 | 19 | 21 | 23 |
| **Min. °C** | 12 | 12 | 11 | 9 | 8 | 6 | 5 | 6 | 7 | 8 | 9 | 11 |
| **Rain mm** | 32 | 29 | 36 | 63 | 84 | 97 | 107 | 100 | 77 | 63 | 46 | 41 |
| **Raindays** | 7 | 7 | 9 | 13 | 17 | 18 | 20 | 20 | 17 | 15 | 11 | 9 |

### Robe

Settled in the 1840s, Robe is one of South Australia's oldest and best-preserved towns. It boasts a fine collection of stone cottages, shops, public buildings and hotels, many of them National Trust-classified. Set around Guichen Bay at the heart of spectacular coastal landscape, Robe combines a quaint fishing village atmosphere with excellent facilities for holidaymakers.

*For more detail see map 166.*

### Naracoorte Caves

Along with Queensland's Riversleigh Fossil Field, this is one of Australia's most significant cave systems, a fact reflected by its World Heritage listing. There are 60 known caves, several of which are open to the public. At the excellent Wonambi Fossil Centre, displays show how fossils found in the caves have played a key role in charting the continent's evolutionary history.

### Coonawarra

Coonawarra is Australia's most valuable piece of wine real estate. Just 12 kilometres long and 2 kilometres wide, its soil is rich terra rossa, which produces wine of the highest quality. The region's cabernet sauvignon, in particular, is outstanding. Established names include Wynns, Mildara, Petaluma and Rouge Homme. Over 20 wineries offer cellar-door sales and tastings.

### Mount Gambier

This major regional centre is near the State border, roughly half way between Adelaide and Melbourne. It is set on the slopes of an extinct volcano near the intensely coloured Blue Lake. There are a number of caves in the area, including the Engelbrecht Caves (popular with divers) and the Umpherston Sinkhole.

# FLEURIEU PENINSULA

This peninsula is one of South Australia's most popular and accessible holiday destinations. It is known for its wineries, magnificent coastline, scenic landscapes and gourmet produce. Some of the Fleurieu's rural villages date back 160 years. Many of the attractions are only an hour or so from Adelaide and visitors can schedule day tours using the city as a base. Travellers heading for the Victor Harbor district, on the far side of the peninsula, might consider booking a night or two of accommodation to take account of longer distances.

## TOP EVENTS

| | |
|---|---|
| Jan. | Granite Island Regatta (Victor Harbor) |
| Jan. | Milang to Goolwa Freshwater Sailing Classic |
| May | Vintage Affair (Langhorne Creek) |
| June | Sea and Vines Festival (McLaren Vale) |
| June | Whale Season Launch (Victor Harbor) |
| July | Almond Blossom Festival (Willunga) |
| Aug. | Collectors, Hobbies and Antique Fair (Strathalbyn) |
| Oct. | Wine Bushing Festival (McLaren Vale) |
| Oct. | Folk and Music Festival (Victor Harbor) |

## EXPERIENCE IT!

❶ *Lunch* amid the vines at the Salopian Inn, McLaren Vale

❷ *Cruise* from the river port of Goolwa to the mouth of the Murray

❸ *Ride* the horse-drawn tram from the township of Victor Harbor to Granite Island, to see fairy penguins

## VISITOR INFORMATION

McLaren Vale and Fleurieu Visitor Centre
McLaren Vale: (08) 8323 9944
Victor Harbor: (08) 8552 5738
www.fleurieu.com.au/tourism

## FOCUS ON

### Wine districts

The McLaren Vale winegrowing district, just 45 minutes from Adelaide, has 53 wineries offering tastings, set against a landscape of weathered hills and rolling acres of almond and olive groves. With a viticultural history dating back to 1838, the region is highly regarded, particularly for its full-bodied reds and notably its shiraz. It supports a wide range of wineries from boutique outfits to some of the big players. In the highly productive Langhorne Creek area a few wineries offer tastings, although many of the grapes grown here are used by wineries in other regions around the country.

### McLaren Vale

This is the heart of the winegrowing region. Several wineries are near the town's centre, as are the olive and almond groves, where visitors can buy local produce. Maps are available at the visitor information centre in the main street.

**CLIMATE VICTOR HARBOR**

| | J | F | M | A | M | J | J | A | S | O | N | D |
|---|---|---|---|---|---|---|---|---|---|---|---|---|
| Max. °C | 24 | 24 | 23 | 21 | 19 | 16 | 15 | 16 | 18 | 20 | 22 | 23 |
| Min. °C | 16 | 16 | 15 | 12 | 10 | 8 | 8 | 8 | 9 | 11 | 12 | 14 |
| Rain mm | 22 | 20 | 23 | 43 | 62 | 71 | 74 | 67 | 55 | 46 | 28 | 23 |
| Raindays | 4 | 4 | 6 | 10 | 14 | 15 | 16 | 16 | 14 | 11 | 8 | 6 |

### Strathalbyn

Picturesque Strathalbyn was settled in 1839 by Scottish immigrants and is a heritage town. The thirty or so listed buildings are fine examples of the State's 19th-century rural architecture. Shop here for antiques, bric-a-brac and arts and crafts.

*For more detail see map 169.*

### Gulf St Vincent coast

Enjoy the scenery at Second Valley and Cape Jervis or go snorkelling at Port Noarlunga. Bathe at one of a number of family beaches, or wine and dine on superb local produce at the Star of Greece at Port Willunga.

### Victor Harbor

Located on the Southern Ocean side of the peninsula, historic Victor Harbor has long been a popular holiday resort. Attractions include the horse-drawn tram, heritage sites, penguins, dolphins, whales and the bush trails in wilderness parks west of town.

### Mount Compass Gourmet Trail

Mount Compass is the centre of gourmet food production in this region, with trout, berry, deer, pheasant and marron farms open for viewing and sales. Pick up a touring map from the visitor information centre in McLaren Vale.

# KANGAROO ISLAND

Australia's third largest island is located in the remote Southern Ocean, 16 kilometres off the tip of the Fleurieu Peninsula. Its most popular attraction is a large local population of native creatures who live undisturbed in pristine natural habitats. Other attractions include coastal scenery, maritime history and a range of fine regional foods. The island is reached by vehicular ferry from Cape Jervis or by plane from Adelaide. Daytrips are popular, but there is plenty of accommodation for those who wish to stay longer.

## TOP EVENTS

**Feb.** Racing Carnival (Kingscote)

**Feb.** Street Fair (Kingscote)

**Easter** Easter Fair (Parndana)

**Easter** Easter Art Exhibition (Penneshaw)

**Oct.** Agricultural Show (Kingscote)

**Nov.** Floraison (Flowering of the Vineyards, Emu Bay)

## EXPERIENCE IT!

❶ **Taste** the island's gourmet produce by visiting producers located inland from Kingscote

❷ **Swim** safely at the tidal pool at Emu Bay or the rock pool at Stokes Bay

❸ **Canoe** the waters or walk the bush tracks of Antechamber Bay

## VISITOR INFORMATION

Kangaroo Island Visitor Information Centre
Penneshaw: (08) 8553 1185
www.tourkangarooisland.com.au

## FOCUS ON

### Wildlife-Watching

As a result of its isolation from the mainland, Kangaroo Island has one of Australia's most impressive concentrations of wildlife still in its native habitat. Seal Bay is home to a colony of sea lions, while at Cape du Couedic in Flinders Chase National Park, there is a 600-strong colony of New Zealand fur seals. This national park is also the best place to see such land animals as kangaroos, tammar wallabies, brushtail possums and the occasional koala or platypus. Little (fairy) penguins can be seen on tours operating from Kingscote or Penneshaw. There is a large and varied bird population (240 species) across the island, with Murray Lagoon (en route to Seal Bay) particularly good for waterbirds.

### CLIMATE KINGSCOTE

|         | J  | F  | M  | A  | M  | J  | J  | A  | S  | O  | N  | D  |
|---------|----|----|----|----|----|----|----|----|----|----|----|----|
| Max. °C | 25 | 24 | 23 | 21 | 18 | 16 | 15 | 15 | 17 | 19 | 21 | 23 |
| Min. °C | 15 | 16 | 14 | 13 | 11 | 9  | 8  | 8  | 9  | 10 | 12 | 14 |
| Rain mm | 15 | 17 | 18 | 37 | 60 | 72 | 78 | 65 | 46 | 36 | 23 | 19 |
| Raindays| 3  | 3  | 5  | 9  | 13 | 15 | 18 | 16 | 13 | 10 | 6  | 5  |

*For more detail see maps 168–9.*

### Cape Borda Lighthouse

The unusually shaped lighthouse, built in 1858, was converted to automatic operation in 1989. Guided tours are conducted regularly and accommodation is available in the old lighthouse keeper's residence.

### Kingscote

The island's largest town and the site of the South Australia's first settlement (1836). Attractions include a nearby colony of little (fairy) penguins, Hope Cottage Folk Museum (an 1850s historic house), the State's oldest cemetery and a very good fishing jetty.

### Flinders Chase National Park

This park is known for its wonderfully varied springtime wildflowers, its wildlife (including a New Zealand fur seal colony at Cape du Couedic), and its unusual geological formations, most notably Admirals Arch and Remarkable Rocks (pictured). There are walking trails and camping is available at designated sites. Accommodation is available in the former keeper's residence at Cape du Couedic.

### Seal Bay Conservation Park

Some 500 Australian sea lions can be seen feeding their young and resting between fishing expeditions at this popular beachside wildlife colony. See the creatures from a boardwalk, or up close on a ranger-guided tour.

# WESTERN AUSTRALIA

Western Australia, the nation's largest State, covers an area of 2 529 000 square kilometres. This is one third of the total area of the continent, yet its population of 1 805 400 (just 10 per cent of the national total) is concentrated around the capital city of Perth.

In geographical terms, Western Australia is the country's most remote State: Perth is considerably closer to Singapore than it is to the cities of Australia's eastern seaboard.

## Ancient landscapes

Western Australia occupies the world's most ancient landscape. In the far north lies The Kimberley, a remote, mythic land of strangely worn mountains, rock formations and gorges. To the south the majestic Hamersley Range, rich in iron ore deposits, rises from red plains. Around Perth, river valleys, escarpments, vineyards and forests border the outer suburbs. In the south-west, giant jarrah and karri forests cover much of the landscape, while to the south-east, the treeless Nullarbor Plain lies across the world's largest limestone slab.

Trackless deserts and arid plains separate Western Australia from the rest of the continent. This natural border has created a zone of biological isolation that has produced unique native flora; some 75 per cent of the 11 000 or so species found in Western Australia are found nowhere else in the world.

The 12 500-kilometre coastline starts in the Timor Sea, stretches out along the Indian Ocean, and sweeps east to meet the Southern Ocean. Its far north section is one of the most remote coastal areas in the world. Around the tropical resort town of Broome are long sandy, beautiful beaches. Further south is the World Heritage-listed Shark Bay, with its prolific population of dolphins, dugongs and turtles and its strange stromatolites. The entire coast provides opportunities for every kind of water recreation.

## Early history

The first inhabitants of what is now called Western Australia were Aboriginal peoples of many different language groups who domiciled according to the availability of resources. They occupied four distinct geographical and cultural zones and had a total population of between 40 000 and 80 000. The earliest confirmed archaeological site, a camp on the Swan River, dates back 39 500 years. Unconfirmed estimates of The Kimberley's rock art, however, suggest a human presence as far back as 80 000 years.

Dutch seafarers made many sightings of the west coast of Australia after 1616, invariably describing the land as sterile, forbidding and inhospitable. The British sent a small party of soldiers and convicts to King George Sound in 1826 to discourage French interest. When Captain James Stirling had convinced the British government that the country of the Swan River was not inferior to the plains of Lombardy, Captain Fremantle claimed Western Australia for the British Crown on 2 May 1829.

The colony was not as lush and fertile as Stirling had believed. Most of the new settlers soon ran out of money and the colony struggled for the next sixty years. Wool provided much-needed income as the settlers occupied the grasslands to the north and east. Between 1850 and 1868 the British sent out 9718 convicts for public works.

## Politics of isolation

Western Australia remained a Crown colony for longer than the other Australian colonies. Representative government arrived in 1890 with a Legislative Assembly and, three years later, an elected Legislative Council. Since the 1920s, government has been shared fairly evenly between Labor and the Coalition. The present Labor government was elected in 2001.

Western Australia joined the Commonwealth at Federation in 1901. For years many Western Australians remained unconvinced, in 1933 voting by 2:1 to secede. However, the House of Commons ruled that secession could not be demanded by a State. The threat of Japanese invasion in 1942 silenced most of the secessionists.

## Wealth and wonder

The great gold discoveries around Coolgardie and Kalgoorlie in the 1890s attracted immigrants and capital, transforming Western Australia from a remote pastoral backwater into one of the world's great producers of gold, iron ore, nickel, diamonds, mineral sands and natural gas.

Despite the urbanisation of its population, Western Australia has always relied on primary industry, principally wheat, sheep, beef and, controversially, hardwood from the great southern forests. Tourism is the latest industry to thrive on the State's natural resources. Each year, more visitors experience the unspoilt beauty, compelling vastness and ancient mysteries of this landscape.

## Modern exploration

Travellers to the south of the State can enjoy the temperate Mediterranean-style climate year-round. Those planning to visit the tropical north should go during the dry season (May to October), while outback adventurers should avoid the summer.

In most parts of the State, long distances separate towns. Travellers intending to explore remote areas should familiarise themselves with prevailing conditions, ensure that their vehicles are roadworthy and carry adequate supplies of water, food and petrol.

The Exchange Hotel, one of 92 hotels in Kalgoorlie's heyday

For more information on Western Australia, see Tourist Bureaus, opposite page 236.

# PERTH

With an almost Mediterranean climate and a magnificent coastal river setting, Perth is ideal for an outdoor lifestyle. Visitors will find clean surf beaches, tranquil forests and well-kept parklands – all within easy reach of the city centre. Perth is a cosmopolitan city with a population of almost 1.4 million. The Swan River winds through the suburbs, widening to lake-size near the city centre, where the serene blue hills of the Darling Range form a distant backdrop.

## CITY CENTRE

See map on page 212.

**Art Gallery of Western Australia** 212 E5
Houses a fine collection of Australian and international works.

**Ferry trip** 212 D7
From the Barrack Street Jetty, past the exclusive waterside suburbs to Fremantle, South Perth and the Swan Valley wine region.

**Kings Park** 212 A7
A 404-ha bushland reserve with landscaped gardens, walkways, lakes, a war memorial and good views of the city.

**Northbridge** 212 C4
Lively arts precinct including the Perth Cultural Centre, the Art Gallery of Western Australia and the Perth Institute of Contemporary Arts; colourful weekend art and craft markets in the Cultural Centre Mall.

**Old Mill** 212 A9
Picturesque 1838 white-washed windmill; now houses an interesting collection of early colonial artefacts.

**Perth Institute of Contemporary Arts (PICA)** 212 D5
Sample the latest in visual and performance art.

**Perth Mint** 212 F7
Houses the world's largest collection of natural gold specimens; lift a gold bar and watch a gold pourer at work.

**Perth Zoo** 212 C12
Set in a magnificent garden; includes a butterfly house and Australian animal exhibits.

**Queens Gardens** 212 H7
Site of a 19th-century brickworks; now ornamental lily ponds and garden beds.

**WACA Oval** 212 I7
Famous venue for national and international cricket and Australian Rules Football matches; tours of the ground and museum run Tuesdays at 10 a.m.

**Western Australian Museum** 212 E4
Comprehensive collection including two of Perth's oldest buildings: the original Perth Gaol (1856) and an 1860s cottage.

**VISITOR INFORMATION**

**Western Australian Visitors Centre**
Cnr Forrest Pl. and Wellington St
(08) 9483 1111
freecall 1300 361 351
www.westernaustralia.net
www.perthwa.com

**Fremantle Tourist Bureau**
Fremantle Town Hall
Cnr William and Adelaide sts
(08) 9431 7878

**TOP EVENTS**

**Hopman Cup** (Jan.)
Prestigious international tennis event

**Perth International Arts Festival** (Jan.–Feb.)
Exciting program with great diversity

**Kings Park Wildflower Festival** (Sept.)
Australia's premier native plant and wildflower exhibition

**Rally Australia** (Nov.)
Four days of action-packed, world-class motor sport

## SUBURBS AND SURROUNDS

See the map on page 83.

**Canning Vale Sunday
Markets** 83 F13
Western Australia's biggest
undercover marketplace.

**Claremont Museum** 83 B9
The former Freshwater Bay School,
built in 1862 by convicts; now houses
an interesting social history display.

**Darling Range** (to east of map)
Approximately 80 000 ha of
escarpment and jarrah forest in the
Hills Forest area.

**Fremantle Arts Centre and History
Museum** 83 B12
A striking Gothic building, once a
female lunatic asylum; now offers
contemporary art exhibitions,
Fremantle history displays, a ghost
walk and a garden area with cafe.

**Fremantle Prison** 83 A12
Convict-built from limestone
quarried on site in the 1850s; huge,
forbidding and full of history.

**Lake Monger** 83 D7
See Western Australia's famous black
swans and other waterbirds.

**Ocean beaches** 83 A3
Beautiful Indian Ocean beaches for
swimming or relaxing; stop off at
Sorrento Quay where you will find a
marine retail village and a world-class
oceanarium, Underwater World.

**Subiaco** 83 D8
A popular shopping, cafe and market
area in one of Perth's oldest suburbs;
art and craft stalls in a restored
warehouse close to the station run
from Thursday to Sunday.

**Swan Brewery** 83 G12
Tours available of this state-of-the-art
brewery renowned for its Swan and
Emu beers.

**Swan Valley** 83 I5
A premier wine-producing district
ideal for touring, with historic
attractions such as the town of
Guildford, and Woodbridge House in
West Midland.

**University of Western
Australia** 83 D9
Landscaped gardens and
Mediterranean-style buildings;
contains the Brendt Museum of
Anthropology and the Lawrence
Wilson Art Gallery.

**Western Australian Maritime
Museum** 83 A12
Displays include an excellent
reconstruction of the 1629 Dutch
wreck *Batavia*.

### GETTING AROUND
The city centre is compact and easy to
explore. A free, regular bus service
known as the CAT (Central Area Transit)
System operates around central Perth.
You can also travel free on Transperth
buses and trains within the Free Transit
Zone in the city centre. Transperth
produces a handy tourist guide and map
that shows the Free Transit Zone.

A good way to discover the city is on the
Perth Tram Co. tours, which operate
daily. These replicas of the city's first
trams extend east to Burswood
International Resort Casino and west to
the University of Western Australia. You
can break your journey at any point. On
weekdays Fremantle Tram Tours
operates a 'tram' tour (the vehicle
is actually a bus) around the streets of
historic Subiaco and out to Lake Monger.

**Airport shuttle bus**
Airport City Shuttle Service
(08) 9475 2999

**Motoring organisation**
RAC 13 11 11

**Public transport**
Transperth 13 62 13

**Tram tours**
Perth Tram Company (08) 9322 2006,
Fremantle Tram Tours (08) 9339 8719

**Swan River boat cruises**
Captain Cook (08) 9325 3341,
Boat Torque Cruises (08) 9221 5844

**Taxis**
Black and White Taxis 13 10 08,
Swan Taxis 13 13 30

**Bicycle hire**
Bikewest (08) 9216 8000

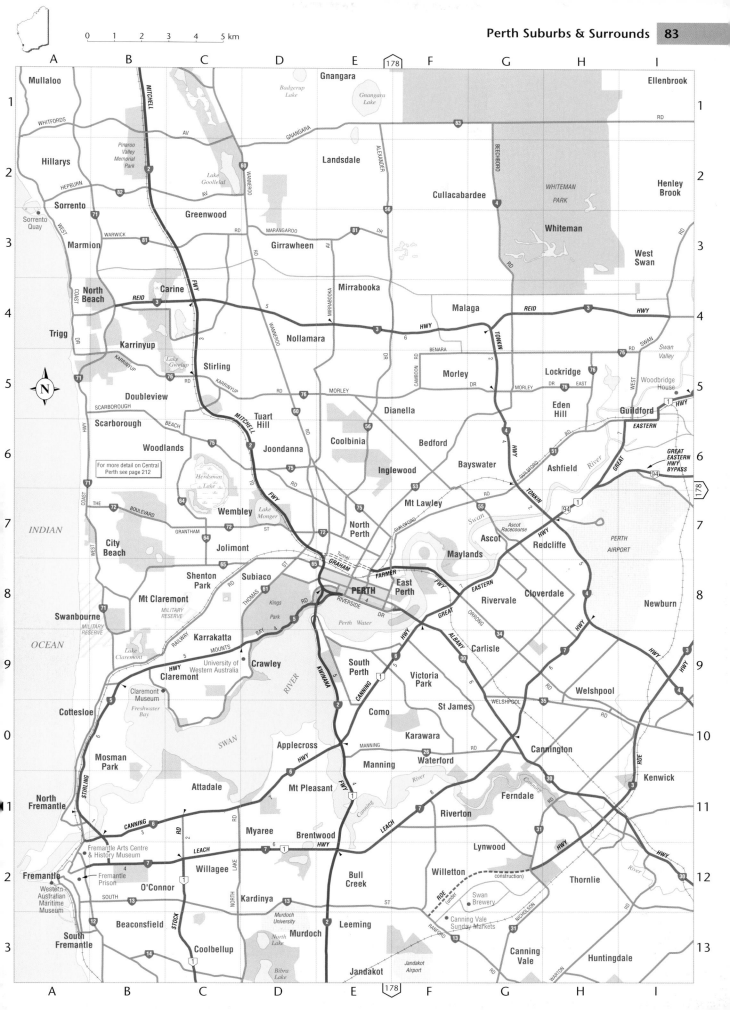

# ROTTNEST ISLAND

In 1696 Dutch explorer Willem de Vlamingh declared Rottnest Island a 'terrestrial paradise', although he named it Rotte-nest (Rats' nest) for the rat-like beasts he encountered. The island, 11 km long and 5 km wide, lies in azure waters 18 km west of Perth. Although about half a million people visit annually it remains unspoiled, with sandy coves and bays, interesting flora and fauna, and land and underwater heritage sites. Daytrips are popular, as are longer stays in the low-key accommodation on offer. Ferries and an air taxi service operate from the mainland. No private cars are permitted; explore the island by foot, bike, bus or train.

## TOP EVENTS

| | |
|---|---|
| *Jan.– Mar.* | *Rottnest Island Celebrates Summer* |
| *Feb.* | *Rottnest Island Channel Swim* |
| *Oct.* | *Marathon and Fun Run* |
| *Nov.* | *Surf Assault* |
| *Dec.* | *Rottnest Swim Thru* |

## EXPERIENCE IT!

❶ **Fish** the recreational waters of Rottnest for species such as flathead, tailor, moon wrasse, marlin and tuna

❷ **Watch** for humpback whales off Cape Vlamingh in the winter months

❸ **Enjoy** a late-afternoon drink in the beer garden at the Rottnest Hotel

## VISITOR INFORMATION

Rottnest Island
Visitor Information Centre
Settlement: (08) 9372 9752
www.rottnest.wa.gov.au

## FOCUS ON

### Island heritage

Known as Wadjemup to the Nyungar people, Rottnest was unoccupied when Europeans arrived, although there is evidence of occupation around 7000 years ago, when the island was linked to the mainland. Europeans settled on the island in 1831. From 1838 to 1903 it was used as a prison for Aboriginal people. During WW I it became an internment camp and in 1917 it was declared an A-class reserve. Many heritage sites are well preserved and Rottnest has an early streetscape, Settlement's Vincent Way. Other interesting sites are the prison buildings of Settlement, Rottnest Lighthouse (1859) at Wadjemup Hill and Oliver Hill Gun Battery (1930s).

### The Basin

An outer reef surrounds Rottnest, protecting the clear waters and creating calm conditions for family swimming. The Basin provides one of a number of beautiful sandy beaches on the eastern end of the island. It is within easy walking distance of the Settlement area, and has basic facilities.

### Underwater heritage

Heritage-listed wrecks around Rottnest include the *City of York*, wrecked in 1899 after the captain failed to identify a lighthouse flare correctly and set course for the rocks. Waterproof maps of the island's 15 sites are available. Scuba and snorkelling tours are popular, as are tours aboard the glass-bottomed *Underwater Explorer*.

### CLIMATE

|  | J | F | M | A | M | J | J | A | S | O | N | D |
|---|---|---|---|---|---|---|---|---|---|---|---|---|
| Max. °C | 26 | 27 | 25 | 23 | 20 | 18 | 17 | 17 | 18 | 20 | 22 | 24 |
| Min. °C | 18 | 19 | 18 | 16 | 14 | 13 | 12 | 12 | 12 | 13 | 15 | 17 |
| Rain mm | 7 | 13 | 14 | 37 | 106 | 156 | 149 | 104 | 61 | 39 | 17 | 10 |
| Raindays | 2 | 2 | 4 | 8 | 15 | 18 | 20 | 18 | 14 | 11 | 6 | 3 |

### West End

The 'West End' of Rottnest can be reached on an 11-km bike ride along a sealed road, or on a bus tour. There are stunning ocean views from Cape Vlamingh and a 1-km heritage trail that affords sightings of wedge-tailed shearwaters, fairy terns, quokkas and bottle-nosed dolphins.

*Map of Rottnest Island showing North Point, Charlotte Point, The Basin, Bathurst Point, Thomson Bay, Settlement, Indian Ocean, Rocky Bay, Wadjemup Hill, Oliver Hill, South Point, Strickland Bay, Salmon Bay, Porpoise Bay, Salmon Point, Parker Point, Cape Vlamingh (West End)*

### Quokka country

The quokka is a native marsupial found primarily on Rottnest. It is nocturnal, furry and grows to hare size. There are about 10 000 quokkas on the island. Find the interpretive signs about 1 km south of Settlement (heading towards Kingstown Barracks) and good viewing spots around the salt lakes.

### Rottnest Museum

Built by Aboriginal prisoners in 1857 as the island granary, this heritage building now houses a series of fascinating displays charting the cultural, environmental and maritime history of the island.

# DARLING RANGE & SWAN VALLEY

Barely half an hour from the centre of Perth are two distinct country landscapes, perfect for scenic touring, picnicking, walking and wildflower-watching. To the north-east is the wine district of Swan Valley, offering cellar-door tastings, restaurants and cafes, galleries, native landscapes including Walyunga National Park (a good spot for wildflowers), and charming B&B accommodation. Directly east is the Darling Range incorporating the Hills Forest (an 80 000-ha stretch of unique Western Australian jarrah forest), where visitors can choose from national parks, historic towns, lakes and weirs, scenic drives with spectacular views, and a superb botanic garden.

## TOP EVENTS

| | |
|---|---|
| Apr. | Mundaring Hills Festival (Mundaring) |
| Aug. | Avon Descent (along Avon/Swan River) |
| Oct. | Spring in the Valley (wine festival, throughout Swan Valley) |
| Nov. | Arts Festival (Darlington, near Mundaring) |

## EXPERIENCE IT!

❶ **Travel** the one-way Zig Zag Scenic Drive for views and wildflowers, via Kalamunda

❷ **Picnic** in Walyunga National Park and enjoy wildflowers in spring

❸ **See** the Lesmurdie Brook drop 50 m over Darling Escarpment, in Lesmurdie Falls National Park

*For more detail see map 178.*

## VISITOR INFORMATION

Mundaring Tourist Association
Mundaring: (08) 9295 0202
Swan Valley Tourist Information Centre
Guildford: (08) 9279 9859

www.mundaringtourism.com.au

## FOCUS ON

### Heritage sites

In historic Guildford you can enjoy two heritage sites. Pause at the Rose and Crown Hotel (1841), the oldest trading hotel in the State. If you time your visit for Sunday afternoon you can roam among yesteryear's farm tools, fashions and household items at the Old Courthouse, Gaol and Museum. At nearby West Midland and overlooking the Swan River is the National Trust's Woodbridge House (1855), a fine example of Victorian architecture. Just south of Upper Swan, in a charming setting on the western bank of the river, is the State's oldest church, the 1830s All Saints Church.

**CLIMATE GUILDFORD**

| | J | F | M | A | M | J | J | A | S | O | N | D |
|---|---|---|---|---|---|---|---|---|---|---|---|---|
| Max. °C | 32 | 32 | 30 | 27 | 22 | 19 | 18 | 19 | 21 | 23 | 27 | 30 |
| Min. °C | 17 | 17 | 15 | 13 | 10 | 8 | 7 | 8 | 9 | 10 | 13 | 15 |
| Rain mm | 8 | 10 | 17 | 43 | 122 | 177 | 172 | 139 | 86 | 56 | 20 | 13 |
| Raindays | 2 | 2 | 4 | 7 | 14 | 17 | 19 | 17 | 14 | 11 | 6 | 4 |

### Whiteman Park
This recreation park offers Australian experiences that include bushwalking, camel-riding, whip-cracking and sheep-shearing. Bush music and Aboriginal cultural displays are offered on regular Australiana theme days, and visitors can tour the native landscape of the park aboard a vintage tram or horse-drawn cart.

### John Forrest National Park
Located in the Hills Forest area, John Forrest was declared a national park in 1947. A drive through the park has vantage points with heart-stopping views across Perth and the coastal plain. A popular walk is the Heritage Trail on the western edge, past waterfalls and an old rail tunnel.

### Swan Valley wineries
There are nearly 30 wineries in the Valley, with some of Australia's finest vineyards in West Swan Road. The climate favours full-bodied whites; labels you will come across include Houghton (pictured), Evans and Tate, and Sandalford. For a treat that offers scenery as well as wine-tasting, take the Swan River wineries cruise.

### Araluen Botanic Park
Tall forest trees (jarrah, eucalypt and marri) frame the rock pools, waterfalls and European-style terraces of these beautiful 59-ha gardens. Established in the 1930s by the Young Australia League, the gardens have picturesque walking trails, picnic and barbecue areas and, in spring, magnificent tulip displays.

### Mundaring Weir
The rolling lawns and bushclad surrounds of the weir reserve make it ideal for picnics. Drop into the C. Y. O'Connor Museum (named for the man who met the challenge of supplying water to the goldfields) and the Hills Forest Activity Centre, where visitors can sign up for activities including bushcraft.

# THE SOUTH-WEST

Western Australia's south-west corner, with a climate comfortable enough to allow year-round visits, is about three-and-a-half hours' drive from Perth. Mandurah, at the beginning of a stretch of low, sandy inlets and lakes, is the first of a number of seaside resorts. The rocky Limestone Coast beyond Cape Naturaliste, broken by good surf beaches, ends at Cape Leeuwin where the Indian and Southern oceans meet. The State's premier winegrowing region, at Margaret River, is a few kilometres inland. The old-growth jarrah and karri forests on the low plateau 30 km from the coast are one of the south-west's unique features.

## TOP EVENTS

**Jan.**   Summerfest (Busselton)

**Feb.**   Amberley Semillon and Seafood Weekend (Amberley Estate, near Yallingup)

**Feb.**   Crab Festival (Mandurah)

**Feb.–**   Leeuwin Estate Concert
**Mar.**   (Leeuwin Estate, near Margaret River)

**Mar.**   Margaret River Masters (surfing competition, Margaret River)

**June**   15 000 Motocross (Manjimup)

**Aug.**   Tulip Festival (Balingup, near Donnybrook)

**Nov.**   Wine Festival (Australind, even-numbered years)

**Nov.**   Spring Festival (Rockingham)

## EXPERIENCE IT!

**❶ Climb** the spiral ladder to the top of the 61-m karri Gloucester Tree in Gloucester National Park

**❷ Cruise** to see dolphins in Koombana Bay at Bunbury

**❸ Visit** the restored 1859 homestead Wonnerup House, 10 km east of Busselton

## VISITOR INFORMATION

Mandurah: (08) 9550 3999
Margaret River: (08) 9757 2911
www.margaretriverwa.com

## FOCUS ON

### Old-growth forests

Western Australia's only forests are in the cool, well-watered south-west. Jarrah, a beautifully grained, deep-red hardwood, flourishes between Dwellingup and Collie. Forests of karri, one of the world's tallest trees, reaching 90 m in a hundred years, are found in the wetter areas, from Manjimup to Walpole. Pemberton is the focus of a struggle over logging between the timber industry and conservationists that has become a State and Federal political issue. Dwellingup's Forest Heritage Centre shows both sides of the controversy and features the forest (at treetop level, from the Canopy Walk) and the furniture made from forest timbers, in the workshops below.

### CLIMATE BUSSELTON

|          | J  | F  | M  | A  | M   | J   | J   | A   | S   | O  | N  | D  |
|----------|----|----|----|----|-----|-----|-----|-----|-----|----|----|----|
| Max. °C  | 29 | 28 | 26 | 23 | 19  | 17  | 16  | 17  | 18  | 20 | 24 | 27 |
| Min. °C  | 14 | 14 | 13 | 11 | 9   | 8   | 8   | 8   | 9   | 11 | 13 |    |
| Rain mm  | 10 | 11 | 22 | 42 | 118 | 175 | 167 | 117 | 75  | 52 | 24 | 13 |
| Raindays | 3  | 2  | 4  | 8  | 15  | 19  | 22  | 19  | 16  | 13 | 7  | 4  |

*For more detail see map 178.*

### Peel Coast

The coastal towns south of Rockingham offer swimming, boating, fishing and crabbing. The Yalgorup National Park protects ten coastal lakes, with views over ocean and dunes at high points. From Preston Beach, a walking track crosses tuart and peppermint woodlands to Lake Pollard, where black swans gather from October to March.

### Limestone Coast

Protected by the Leeuwin–Naturaliste National Park, the Limestone Coast offers a splendid stretch of rocky headlands, wild beaches and limestone caves. Walking, surfing at Yallingup beach, scuba-diving, and whale-watching and salmon fishing from September to December, are other attractions.

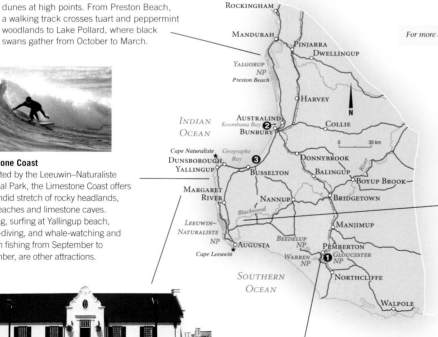

### Blackwood Valley

The Blackwood River meanders for 500 km through wheat-belt plains and forested valleys to its broad estuary at Augusta. Secluded spots along the river between Nannup and Alexandra Bridge offer tranquil camping, fishing, swimming and canoeing. The Sheoak Walk is a 1-hour loop through the forest close to Nannup.

### Margaret River wine styles

The region's reputation for premium wines rests principally on cabernet sauvignon and chardonnay grown on grey-brown, gravelly-sandy soils. Try the cabernet from Vasse Felix, Moss Wood and Cullen and the chardonnays from Leeuwin Estate, Voyager Estate (pictured) and Ashbrook.

### Pemberton

At tiny Pemberton you can take the tramway (pictured) through the heart of the great karri and marri forests, and visit the virgin forests in Warren and Beedelup national parks. You can also sample the marron – freshwater cray – grown in local hatcheries, and tour the 28 or so wineries.

# GREAT SOUTHERN

The Great Southern region begins at Katanning and Kojonup, small towns at the southern extremity of the wheat belt. The road south crosses sheep country, with views of the jagged peaks of the blue and purple Stirling Range. A stop at Mount Barker offers a chance to taste the intensely floral rieslings grown in the region's burgeoning winegrowing area. Albany, on panoramic King George Sound, is the centre of the region. This comfortable, historic town, with its range of accommodation and restaurants, is the ideal base for exploring the rugged coast east to Bremer Bay and west to the surfing beaches near the secluded riverside town of Denmark.

## TOP EVENTS

**Mar.** Wine Summer Festival (Porongurup, near Mount Barker)

**Easter** Brave New Works (new performance art, Denmark)

**Aug.** Prophet Mohammad's Birthday (Katanning)

**Aug.** Strauss Festival (Albany)

**Sept.** Country and Wildflower Festival (Kojonup)

**Oct.** Great Southern Wine Festival (Albany)

**Oct.** Wildflower Weekend (Porongurup, near Mount Barker)

**Nov.** Art Show (Cranbrook)

**Dec.** Vintage Blues Festival (Albany)

## EXPERIENCE IT!

❶ **Surf** the mighty Southern Ocean at Denmark's Ocean Beach

❷ **See** southern right whales with their newborn calves around Bremer Bay, from August to November

❸ **Eat** at The Old Farm (the State's oldest farm), Strawberry Hill, 2 km west of Albany's centre

## VISITOR INFORMATION

Albany: (08) 9841 1088; 1800 644 088
www.albanytourist.com.au

## FOCUS ON

### Albany heritage

Albany, the oldest white settlement in Western Australia, was officially founded on 21 January 1827 by a party of 21 soldiers and 23 convicts who had arrived on the *Amity* a month earlier. Albany's magnificent harbour, commanding the sea lanes between Europe and Asia and eastern Australia, became a whaling station and later a coaling port for steamships. Museums now occupy three historic buildings, and a full-size replica of the *Amity* stands next to one, the Residency Museum. Stirling Terrace has some evocative Victorian shopfronts while Princess Royal Fortress on Mount Adelaide has restored buildings, gun emplacements and fine views.

### CLIMATE ALBANY

|  | J | F | M | A | M | J | J | A | S | O | N | D |
|---|---|---|---|---|---|---|---|---|---|---|---|---|
| Max. °C | 25 | 25 | 24 | 22 | 19 | 17 | 16 | 16 | 17 | 19 | 21 | 24 |
| Min. °C | 14 | 14 | 13 | 12 | 10 | 8 | 8 | 7 | 8 | 9 | 11 | 12 |
| Rain mm | 27 | 24 | 28 | 63 | 102 | 103 | 124 | 106 | 82 | 78 | 48 | 25 |
| Raindays | 8 | 9 | 11 | 14 | 18 | 19 | 21 | 21 | 18 | 15 | 13 | 10 |

### Frontier and flowers

The Old Military Barracks in Kojonup, now a museum, was built in 1845 to protect travel on the road between Perth and Albany. Gardens are also a feature of the town with many residents taking part in the Australian Open Garden Scheme. The surrounding countryside is lush with wildflowers in spring.

*For more detail see map 178 & 180.*

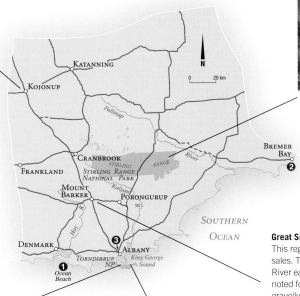

### Torndirrup National Park

The Southern Ocean has sculpted The Blowholes, The Gap, and Natural Bridge in this park just 15 minutes from Albany on a sealed road. Granite outcrops and cliffs alternate with dunes, and sandy heath supports peppermint, banksia and karri. Whales can be seen from the cliffs from August to November.

### Stirling Range National Park

This park has stunning mountain scenery. From a distance the range changes colour, depending on the weather, season and time of day. The spectacular jagged peaks, including the great Bluff Knoll, are popular with walkers and climbers.

### Great Southern wineries

This region has over 30 wineries, most open for sales. The dozen that extend from the Frankland River east through Mount Barker to Porongurup are noted for aromatic rieslings grown on well-drained, gravelly-sandy soils. The region's unwooded chardonnay, shiraz and light reds are also popular.

### Albany Whaleworld

The bloody realities of whaling are displayed at the old Cheynes Beach Whaling Station on Frenchman Bay, 25 km south-east of Albany. Visitors can explore *Cheynes IV*, a restored whalechaser, and relive the sights and sounds of the hunt. Recorded songs of whales at sea provide background music.

# ESPERANCE & NULLARBOR

This is a coastline of rare and remote beauty. The beaches of Esperance are among the most spectacular in Australia, famed for their white sand, brilliant turquoise waters, and views across a network of offshore islands. To the north-east, beyond the desert beaches, underwater caves, sheer fossil-encrusted cliffs and drifting dunes lies the vast Nullarbor Plain. While Esperance is a large and well-serviced holiday centre, the Nullarbor is remote touring country. Advance bookings should be made for the limited accommodation en route, and travellers should observe basic outback travel precautions such as ensuring adequate fuel and water supplies.

## TOP EVENTS

| | |
|---|---|
| Jan. | Summer Festival (Hopetoun) |
| Feb. | Offshore Angling Classic (Esperance) |
| May | Golf Classic (Eucla) |
| Sept. | Wildflower Show (Ravensthorpe) |
| Sept. | Wildflower Show (Esperance) |
| Oct. | Agricultural Show (Esperance) |
| Oct.–Nov. | Festival of the Wind (Esperance, even-numbered years) |
| Nov. | Border Dash (Border Village to Eucla) |

## EXPERIENCE IT!

❶ **Visit** the Esperance Municipal Museum to see debris from NASA's spaceship Skylab

❷ **See** the many species of orchids in spring in remote Cape Arid National Park

❸ **Ride** a camel and eat bush tucker at Eremia Camel Farm near Ravensthorpe

### CLIMATE ESPERANCE

| | J | F | M | A | M | J | J | A | S | O | N | D |
|---|---|---|---|---|---|---|---|---|---|---|---|---|
| Max. °C | 26 | 26 | 25 | 23 | 20 | 18 | 17 | 18 | 19 | 21 | 23 | 25 |
| Min. °C | 16 | 16 | 15 | 13 | 11 | 9 | 8 | 9 | 10 | 11 | 13 | 14 |
| Rain mm | 22 | 27 | 31 | 43 | 76 | 82 | 98 | 84 | 58 | 50 | 36 | 17 |
| Raindays | 6 | 6 | 8 | 11 | 14 | 16 | 17 | 17 | 14 | 12 | 10 | 7 |

## VISITOR INFORMATION

Esperance: (08) 9071 2330; 1300 664 455

Eucla: (08) 9039 3468

## FOCUS ON

### The Nullarbor

The Nullarbor is one of the country's premier touring experiences. It is a 250 000-sq-km, treeless limestone slab. Initially part of the seabed, it has been partly formed by deposits of marine fossils. The terrain is riddled with sinkholes, caverns and caves, the largest of which is the 6-km-long Cocklebiddy Cave (just north-west of the town of Cocklebiddy), one of the longest underwater caves in the world. Although it can seem featureless, the country is far from monotonous, particularly where the highway veers to the coast for a view of dramatic cliffs and the wild Southern Ocean, and perhaps a lucky sighting of migrating southern right whales.

### Great Ocean Drive

A 39-km circuit drive explores the coast west of Esperance. Attractions include Australia's first wind farm; sheltered swimming at Twilight Cove; and Pink Lake, rendered lipstick-coloured by algae. There are coastal lookouts and sightings of southern right whales from June to November.

### Cape Le Grand National Park

Swimming beaches, sheltered coves, heathlands, sandplains and the Whistling Rock are all features of this park, 56 km east of Esperance. There are easy walking trails and two camping areas. Good scenic spots include Lucky Bay (where you can launch a boat), Thistle Cove and Hellfire Bay.

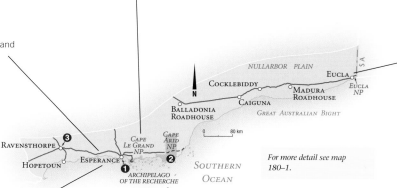

### Eucla

This isolated outpost was established in 1877 as a telegraph station. Coastal dunes partially obscure the ruins (pictured), 4 km from town. On the beach, a lonely jetty stretches out into startlingly blue waters. In Eucla National Park, under mallee scrub and heathland, lies the 45-m-high chamber of Koonalda Cave.

For more detail see map 180–1.

### Coastal delights

Esperance is a water-sports paradise. Wave-sail at Observatory and Fourth beaches; windsurf on the harbour; dive or snorkel around the islands. Fishing charters tour the islands for sampson fish, queen snapper and red snapper, while land-based anglers can cast a line from Tanker Jetty.

### Archipelago of the Recherche

This offshore nature reserve of 105 granite islands and 1500 islets runs 250 km along the Esperance coast. Boat tours, available from Esperance, may include sightings of fur seals, sea lions, dolphins and, in season, southern right whales. Visitors can stay overnight in safari huts or camp on Woody Island.

# THE GOLDFIELDS

**W**estern Australia's historic Goldfields region occupies a landscape of alluvial flats and saltplains broken by rocky outcrops and a surprising diversity of native vegetation – around 100 species of eucalypt as well as brilliant displays of wildflowers in spring. Gold continues to be mined here, while sheep stations the size of small nations produce fine wool. The area's main attractions are its fascinating heritage and the opportunity to tour Western Australia's vast outback, where April to October is the best time to visit. Those planning to explore beyond the main centres should observe basic outback safety precautions.

## TOP EVENTS

**Apr.** *Nullarbor Muster (Rawlinna, via Kalgoorlie)*

**Aug.** *Gwalia Market Day (Gwalia, near Leonora)*

**Sept.** *Kalgoorlie Cup (Kalgoorlie)*

**Sept.** *Spring Festival (Kalgoorlie)*

**Sept.** *Balzano Barrow Race (Kalgoorlie)*

**Sept.** *Fishing in the Desert (Kambalda)*

**Sept.** *Coolgardie Day (Coolgardie)*

**Sept.–** *Metal Detecting Championships and*
**Oct.** *Fun Day (Coolgardie)*

**Oct.** *Art Prize (Leonora)*

**Dec.** *St Barbara's Festival (Kalgoorlie)*

## EXPERIENCE IT!

❶ **Drive** *to Kambalda's Red Hill Lookout for the view of Lake Lefroy*

❷ **Experience** *the Ngaanyatjarraku people's art and culture at the Tjulyuru Cultural and Civic Centre, Warburton*

❸ **Board** *the Loopline Tourist Railway, Kalgoorlie, for a circuit of the Golden Mile*

## VISITOR INFORMATION

Kalgoorlie–Boulder: (08) 9021 1966
Norseman: (08) 9039 1071
www.kalgoorlieandwagoldfields.com.au

## FOCUS ON

### Goldfields history

The discovery of gold in the region in 1892 secured the economic success of Western Australia. Since then, goldmines from Norseman to Laverton have yielded well over 1000 tonnes. A railway from Perth in 1896 and a water pipeline in 1903 helped Kalgoorlie and Boulder to sustain a population of 30 000, the liquor requirements of which were met by 93 hotels. By 1900 surface gold was exhausted and big companies went underground. Exhausted mines have left a belt of ghost towns north of Kalgoorlie, while nickel mining since the 1960s has allowed towns such as Kambalda and Leonora to survive.

### North of Kalgoorlie

Menzies has 230 people and several intact old buildings; Kookynie has retained its spacious 1894 Grand Hotel. Gwalia, almost a ghost town, has a museum, a restored State Hotel and tin houses preserved in their lived-in state (pictured). Laverton, 100 km east, has historic buildings saved by the nickel industry.

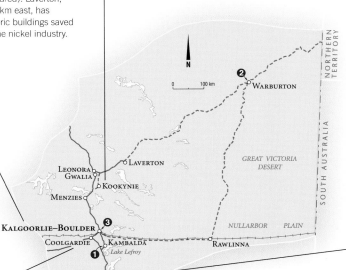

### CLIMATE KALGOORLIE–BOULDER

|          | J  | F  | M  | A  | M  | J  | J  | A  | S  | O  | N  | D  |
|----------|----|----|----|----|----|----|----|----|----|----|----|----|
| Max. °C  | 34 | 32 | 30 | 25 | 20 | 18 | 17 | 18 | 22 | 26 | 29 | 32 |
| Min. °C  | 18 | 18 | 16 | 12 | 8  | 6  | 5  | 5  | 8  | 11 | 14 | 17 |
| Rain mm  | 22 | 28 | 19 | 19 | 28 | 31 | 26 | 20 | 15 | 16 | 18 | 15 |
| Raindays | 3  | 4  | 4  | 5  | 7  | 8  | 9  | 7  | 5  | 4  | 4  | 3  |

*For more detail see maps 180–1 & 183.*

### Kalgoorlie–Boulder

Kalgoorlie–Boulder produces half Australia's gold; the adjacent Golden Mile is the world's richest square mile of gold-bearing ore. Visitors to Hannans North Historic Mining Reserve can sample the rigours of mining in the 1800s. Don't miss the gold vault at the Museum of the Goldfields.

### Norseman, gateway to the West

The Eyre Highway across the Nullarbor ends at Norseman, once the centre of the second richest goldfield in Western Australia; some mines still operate here. The Historical Collection has displays of memorabilia and geological specimens. Beacon Hill Lookout offers views of the town and surrounding salt lakes.

### Coolgardie

Historical street markers are a good introduction to this first town in the eastern goldfields, with its splendid, historic public buildings. Examples include The Marble Bar Hotel now the RSL (pictured), and the 1898 Warden's Court. The latter, an architectural treasure, houses the comprehensive Goldfields Exhibition museum and the Tourist Bureau.

### Peak Charles National Park

South-west of Norseman, granite mountains rise in wave-cut platforms to a height of 651 m. A track, suitable only for experienced walkers and climbers in favourable weather, leads from the carpark up to the south ridge for views across saltpans, sand plains and dry woodlands to Peak Eleanora.

# THE HEARTLANDS

Western Australia's wheat belt dominates in this region: a vast golden landscape of historic towns, windmills and broad-verandahed homesteads. A string of surf beaches extends north from Perth. Major lobster ports are also attractive holiday centres, and a number of national parks protect spectacular landscapes, including one of the State's must-see features – The Pinnacles. Inland lie pockets of forested country with something English about them, while Spanish Colonial is the main style of one of Australia's most unusual towns. Each spring, from the coast to the wheat fields, wildflowers provide a common theme for this otherwise diverse region.

## TOP EVENTS

| | |
|---|---|
| *Jan.* | *State Gliding Championships (Narrogin)* |
| *Mar.* | *Autumn Alternative Agricultural Show (Pingelly)* |
| *Aug.* | *Daffodil Festival (York)* |
| *Aug.* | *Avon River Festival (Northam)* |
| *Sept.* | *Jazz Weekend (York)* |
| *Oct.* | *Bush Races Weekend (at Jilakin Rock, near Kulin)* |
| *Oct.* | *Spring Festival (Narrogin)* |
| *Oct.* | *Multicultural Festival (Northam)* |
| *Nov.* | *Marine Expo and Blessing of the Fleet (Jurien Bay)* |

## EXPERIENCE IT!

❶ *Go rowing on Loch McNess at the heart of Yanchep National Park*

❷ *Drive through pretty Chittering Valley, near Gingin, to see wildflowers and visit the wineries*

❸ *Observe rare wildlife in natural surroundings at Dryandra Woodland, north-west of Narrogin*

## VISITOR INFORMATION

Northam: (08) 9622 2100
York: (08) 9641 1301
www.heartlands.com.au

## FOCUS ON

### Wildflowers

There are over 9000 named species and 2000 unnamed species of wildflowers in Western Australia, giving the State one of the richest floras in the world. Most wildflowers occur in the south-west of the State and about 75 per cent of the species are unique to this region. Flowering begins in August and continues through spring and early summer. The Heartlands is one of the best and most accessible places to see wildflower displays. Top spots include: Lesueur and Badgingarra national parks near Jurien Bay, the Chittering Valley near Gingin, and the sand plains around Southern Cross.

### CLIMATE NORTHAM

| | J | F | M | A | M | J | J | A | S | O | N | D |
|---|---|---|---|---|---|---|---|---|---|---|---|---|
| Max. °C | 34 | 34 | 31 | 26 | 21 | 18 | 17 | 18 | 20 | 24 | 28 | 32 |
| Min. °C | 17 | 17 | 15 | 12 | 9 | 7 | 5 | 6 | 7 | 9 | 12 | 15 |
| Rain mm | 10 | 13 | 19 | 23 | 57 | 83 | 84 | 62 | 37 | 25 | 12 | 9 |
| Raindays | 2 | 2 | 3 | 6 | 11 | 15 | 16 | 14 | 11 | 7 | 4 | 2 |

### New Norcia

This town, Spanish Colonial in style, was built in 1846 by Benedictine monks who aimed to establish a mission for the local indigenous population. It remains Australia's only monastic town. Visitors can tour the buildings (pictured) and visit the fascinating Museum and Art Gallery.

### The Pinnacles Desert

Thousands of limestone pillars, the eroded remnants of what was once a thick bed of limestone, create this weirdly beautiful landscape in what is now Nambung National Park. Other park attractions include a beautiful coastline with superb beaches where visitors can fish, swim, snorkel, walk or picnic.

### Central wheat belt

This is an area of endless horizon, dusty golden paddocks and brilliant wildflower clusters in spring. Attractions include Kellerberrin Hill, the third-largest monolith in Australia, and Meckering where a 1968 earthquake has left an impressive fault line.

*For more detail see maps 178 & 180.*

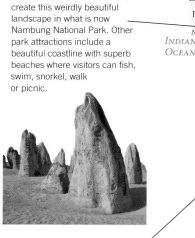

### Avon Valley

In the 1860s bushranger Moondyne Joe hid in the forests, caves and wildflower fields of this lush valley. Now Avon Valley National Park preserves much of the landscape. In the valley's heart, and marking the start of the wheat belt, are the historic towns of Northam and York.

### Wave Rock and Mulka's Cave

Wave Rock, east of Hyden, is a 2.7 billion-year-old piece of granite, 15 m high and 100 m long. It looks like a giant wave frozen at the moment of breaking and has vertical bands of colour caused by algal growth. To the north is Mulka's Cave, featuring Aboriginal rock art.

# OUTBACK COAST & MID-WEST

The ancient landforms of Western Australia's interior meet the startlingly blue waters of the Indian Ocean in this vast area known for the richness and rarity of its natural features. Reefs, eroded cliffs and gorges, ancient rocks, life forms billions of years old, sea mammals, diverse flora, and stretches of red outback are all to be found. A series of towns (mostly coastal) offer good holiday facilities as well as glimpses of Western Australia's pioneer and maritime history. Much of this country is remote; for those planning to explore beyond the main tourist routes, safety precautions for outback travelling are essential.

## TOP EVENTS

| | |
|---|---|
| Mar. | Sport Fishing Classic (Kalbarri) |
| Mar. | Sea Jazz Spectacular (Geraldton) |
| June | Batavia Celebrations (Geraldton) |
| Aug. | Wildflower Show (Mullewa) |
| Aug. | Festival (Carnarvon) |
| Oct. | Airing of the Quilts (Northampton) |
| Oct. | Octoberfest (Exmouth) |
| Oct. | Sunshine Festival (Geraldton) |
| Nov. | Blessing of the Fleet (Kalbarri) |

## EXPERIENCE IT!

❶ **Visit** Peron Homestead in Francois Peron National Park, once part of a sheep station

❷ **Dive** around the Houtman Abrolhos Islands, a group of more than 100 coral islands

❸ **Stay** at Wooleen Station, near Murchison, in the shearers' quarters or the National Trust-listed homestead

## VISITOR INFORMATION

Carnarvon: (08) 9941 1146
Geraldton: (08) 9921 3999
www.outbackcoast.com

## FOCUS ON

### Shark Bay

World Heritage-listed Shark Bay is a sunny paradise of shallow azure waters, bays and inlets, blessed with a great complement of unusual and interesting natural features. It supports the world's most diverse and abundant examples of stromatolites – sedimentary rocks made up of layers of 3.5 billion-year-old fossilised blue-green algae. It has 12 species of seagrass, the world's greatest collection. It also boasts an extraordinary marine population: 10 000 or so dugongs (ten per cent of the world's population); humpback whales resting on their long migrations; green and loggerhead turtles; and, most famously, a large pod of dolphins.

### CLIMATE CARNARVON

| | J | F | M | A | M | J | J | A | S | O | N | D |
|---|---|---|---|---|---|---|---|---|---|---|---|---|
| Max. °C | 31 | 33 | 31 | 29 | 26 | 23 | 22 | 23 | 24 | 26 | 27 | 29 |
| Min. °C | 22 | 23 | 22 | 19 | 15 | 12 | 11 | 12 | 14 | 16 | 19 | 21 |
| Rain mm | 12 | 21 | 16 | 14 | 38 | 48 | 47 | 19 | 6 | 6 | 4 | 2 |
| Raindays | 2 | 3 | 2 | 3 | 5 | 7 | 7 | 5 | 3 | 2 | 1 | 1 |

### Reef to range

Ningaloo Marine Park protects Western Australia's largest reef. Along the coast is Cape Range National Park, where beach campsites are ideal for visitors wanting to explore the corals and fish of the stunning underwater landscape, as well as the gorges and rivers of the landscape beyond the coast.

### Kalbarri National Park

Kalbarri is best known for its 80 km of gorges, carved out by the Murchison River. Water sports are popular on the river's lower reaches. The park is also one of the world's richest wildflower areas. Dolphins, whale sharks and whales frequent the coastal waters and fishing is excellent.

### Mount Augustus National Park

Mount Augustus, or Burringurrah as it is known by the Watjarri people, rests on an ancient piece of granite twice the size of Uluru. The park also features Aboriginal art sites and walking trails. Camping is available nearby. Travellers in 2WD vehicles should check road conditions before departure.

### Geraldton

This large town is a suitable base for exploring the Batavia Coast's swimming and surfing beaches. In town, Mahomets Beach is one of Australia's top windsurfing destinations. The town has a good regional gallery, and a number of impressive buildings including a Byzantine-style cathedral (pictured) built in the early 1900s.

*For more detail see maps 179 & 180.*

### Monkey Mia

About 400 bottlenose dolphins live around Monkey Mia in the Shark Bay World Heritage Area. Each morning, several dolphins drift into the shallows to be hand-fed with fish, which they occasionally offer back. The world's largest population of dugongs lives here. Take a dugong-watching cruise to see them.

# THE KIMBERLEY

The Kimberley, bigger than Germany, has a population of just 25 000 people. It is one of Australia's true frontiers, with an ancient, reddened landscape of rivers and gorges, a wild inhabited coastline, and the signature beehive shapes of the Bungle Bungles. At the time of white colonisation there were around two dozen Aboriginal language groups. Early white explorers were enchanted by the romantic grandeur of The Kimberley and appalled by the distances, hardships and dangers. Visitors today will find the grandeur largely untouched and travelling conditions highly variable. While the coastal town of Broome is becoming increasingly well known as a resort destination, there are large tracts of this region that are completely inaccessible by road – or accessible by 4WD only – and offering only the most basic of facilities. Travellers should familiarise themselves with prevailing conditions and carry adequate supplies.

**CLIMATE HALLS CREEK**

|  | J | F | M | A | M | J | J | A | S | O | N | D |
|---|---|---|---|---|---|---|---|---|---|---|---|---|
| Max. °C | 37 | 36 | 36 | 34 | 30 | 27 | 27 | 30 | 34 | 37 | 38 | 38 |
| Min. °C | 24 | 24 | 23 | 20 | 17 | 14 | 13 | 15 | 19 | 23 | 25 | 25 |
| Rain mm | 153 | 137 | 74 | 22 | 13 | 5 | 6 | 2 | 4 | 17 | 37 | 77 |
| Raindays | 13 | 13 | 8 | 3 | 2 | 1 | 1 | 1 | 1 | 3 | 6 | 11 |

## FOCUS ON

### Aboriginal art

The Kimberley is one of Australia's most important regions for Aboriginal rock art and is renowned for two styles – the Bradshaw and the Wandjina. The Bradshaw 'figures' as they are known, are painted in red ochre. According to one Aboriginal legend, birds drew the figures using their beaks. One rock-face frieze shows figures dancing and swaying; another depicts figures elaborately decorated with headdresses, tassels, skirts and epaulets. Significant Bradshaw sites have been found on the Drysdale River. The more recent Wandjina figures, named for ancestor spirits from the sky and sea who brought rain and fertility, are in solid red or black, outlined in red ochre, and sometimes on a white background. Wandjina figures are typically human-like, with pallid faces and wide, staring eyes and, for reasons of religious belief, no mouth. Good examples of Wandjina art have been found near Kalumburu on the King Edward River and at the burial site known as Panda-Goornnya on the Drysdale River.

## TOP EVENTS

**Easter** *Dragon Boat Regatta (Broome)*

**May** *Ord Valley Muster (Kununurra)*

**May** *King Tide Day (festival celebrating highest tide in Australia, Derby)*

**June** *Dam to Dam Dinghy Race (Kununurra)*

**June** *Moonrise Rock Festival (Derby)*

**June** *Mowanjum Festival (indigenous art and culture, Derby)*

**June–July** *Race Round (horseracing week, Broome)*

**Aug.** *Rodeo (Kununurra)*

**Aug.** *Opera Under the Stars (Broome)*

**Aug.–Sept.** *Shinju Matsuri (Festival of the Pearl, Broome)*

**Sept.** *Munumburra Music Festival (Wyndham)*

**Sept.** *Night Rodeo (Kununurra)*

**Nov.** *Mango Festival (Broome)*

## EXPERIENCE IT!

❶ *Take a scenic flight from Derby over the Buccaneer Archipelago, with a swim and refreshments at Cape Leveque*

❷ *Inspect 130-million-year-old dinosaur footprints at Gantheaume Point near Broome*

❸ *Stay at El Questro Station, Australia's most luxurious outback resort, and enjoy the hot springs*

❹ *Ride a camel along the magnificent Cable Beach in Broome*

❺ *Fly from Kununurra to a camp on the remote Mitchell Plateau and see rainforest, waterfalls, birdlife and Aboriginal art*

**VISITOR INFORMATION**
Broome: (08) 9192 2222
Kununurra: (08) 9168 1177

### Gibb River Road

This unsealed road, starting at Derby and running 649 km through The Kimberley, provides a true outback adventure. River crossings, passable only during the Dry, offer scenic campsites. Along the way are spectacular gorges, and swimming spots with waterlilies. Read the *Gibb River Road Guide* before commencing your journey.

### Dampier Peninsula

The 200-km unsealed Broome–Cape Leveque route traverses open eucalypt country and Aboriginal Reserve land. Within the reserve land are a church at Beagle Bay with an unusual mother-of-pearl altar (pictured) and a church at Lombadina–Djarindjin. See unique pindan vegetation in Point Coulomb Nature Reserve and perhaps humpback whales from Cape Leveque Lighthouse.

### Port of pearls

Broome has a balmy winter climate, the white, palm-fringed Cable Beach, and a multicultural heritage. In Chinatown there are Chinese merchants, pearl dealers, and restaurants serving a variety of cuisines. The history of pearling is told at the old customs house, the pearling luggers display, and the Japanese Cemetery (pictured).

**Cruising the
Wandjina Coast**
This coastline is a succession
of capes, gulfs, bays and
mangrove swamps, and rivers
emptying onto mudflats.
There are 3000 islands and
countless reefs. A good way to
see the 11-m tide running
over Montgomery Reef and
into the bays and estuaries is
on a cruise from Broome.

**Lake Argyle and Kununurra**
Lake Argyle was formed in the
1960s as part of the Ord River
Scheme, the success of which is
evident in the lush crops of the
area (pictured). The lake is so
large that it has developed its own
ecosystems. By taking a boat
cruise you can experience the
magnificent scenery and
abundant wildlife of the area.
Start from Kununurra, which has
excellent tourist facilities.

*For more detail see map
184–5.*

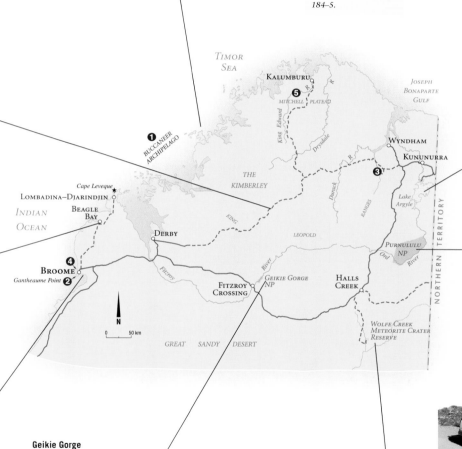

**Purnululu National Park**
A rough 50-km track off the
Great Northern Highway leads
to the spectacular Bungle
Bungle Range in Purnululu
National Park on the Ord River.
A fantastic landscape of huge
black-and-orange sandstone
domes is intersected by
narrow, palm-lined gorges
where pools reflect sunlight off
sheer walls.

**Geikie Gorge**
North-east of Fitzroy Crossing
the Fitzroy River cuts through
the Geikie Range to create a
7-km gorge with sheer walls
bleached by annual flooding.
The riverbanks are inhabited
by freshwater crocodiles, fruit
bats and many bird species.
The only way to see the gorge
is by boat – during the Dry.

**Wolfe Creek Meteorite Crater**
Two hours by unsealed road south of
Halls Creek, and across some inhospitable
country, is the world's second largest
meteorite crater. It is 850 m across and was
probably formed by a meteorite, weighing at
least several thousand tons, crashing to
earth a million years ago.

# THE PILBARA

This region's centrepiece is the vivid, ochre-hued Hamersley Range, which stretches 300 km through this mineral-rich area. In the 1860s pastoralists settled in the western Pilbara and established Roebourne and Cossack. Iron-ore discovery in the 1960s saw the establishment of modern towns such as Tom Price and Newman, which today provide comfortable bases for touring the area's magnificent landscapes, including the gorges and waterfalls of Karijini National Park. The Pilbara coast from Exmouth Gulf to Eighty Mile Beach is a place of vast tidal flats broken by mangroves. Coral reefs and offshore islands offer swimming, boating and beachcombing.

## TOP EVENTS

**June** *Pilbara Pursuit Jetboat Classic (Karratha)*

**June** *Black Rock Stakes (wheelbarrow race, Port Hedland)*

**Aug.** *FeNaCLNG Festival (Annual Show, Karratha)*

**Aug.** *Game-fishing Classic (Dampier, near Karratha)*

**Aug.** *Campdraft and Rodeo (Newman)*

**Aug.** *Spinifex Spree (Port Hedland)*

**Aug.** *Royal Show (Roebourne)*

**Aug.** *Roebourne Cup and Ball (Roebourne)*

**Aug.** *Nameless Festival (Tom Price)*

## EXPERIENCE IT!

**❶** *Swim in the Chinderwarriner Pool in Millstream–Chichester National Park, 150 km south of Roebourne*

**❷** *Take Karratha's 3-hour Jaburara Heritage Trail to Aboriginal rock carvings and artifact scatters*

**❸** *Follow the 52-km Emma Withnell Heritage Trail around Roebourne, Cossack and Point Samson's historic sites*

## VISITOR INFORMATION

Karratha: (08) 9144 4600
Tom Price: (08) 9188 1112
www.pilbara.com

## FOCUS ON

### Hamersley Range resources

One of the world's richest deposits of iron ore was discovered in 1962 in the Hamersley, spearheading the Hamersley Iron Project. Towns with swimming pools, gardens and golf courses sprang up in this landscape of mulga scrub, spinifex and red mountains. Visitors can inspect open-cut mines at Tom Price. At Dampier and Port Hedland there are iron-ore shipping ports; the latter boasts the largest iron-ore export tonnage in Australia. Offshore from Karratha is the massive North West Shelf Gas Project; a visitors' centre on Burrup Peninsula explains the project.

### CLIMATE ROEBOURNE

|  | J | F | M | A | M | J | J | A | S | O | N | D |
|---|---|---|---|---|---|---|---|---|---|---|---|---|
| Max. °C | 39 | 38 | 38 | 35 | 30 | 27 | 27 | 29 | 32 | 35 | 38 | 39 |
| Min. °C | 26 | 26 | 25 | 22 | 18 | 15 | 14 | 15 | 17 | 20 | 23 | 25 |
| Rain mm | 59 | 67 | 63 | 30 | 29 | 30 | 14 | 5 | 1 | 1 | 1 | 10 |
| Raindays | 3 | 5 | 3 | 1 | 3 | 3 | 2 | 1 | 0 | 0 | 0 | 1 |

### Pilbara islands

Dampier Archipelago's nearest islands are 20 minutes by boat from Dampier. The islands' cliffs and sand plains are the focus for bushwalkers and birdwatchers, while pristine beaches offer swimming and fishing. Turtles and seabirds nest on the islands, and dolphins and humpbacked whales can be seen offshore.

### Cossack

This first port in the north-west was built between 1870 and 1898 and is now a ghost town. Many buildings have been restored including Galbraiths Store (pictured). The old post office houses a gallery and the courthouse a museum, while police barracks offer budget accommodation.

*For more detail see maps 179, 182–3 & 184.*

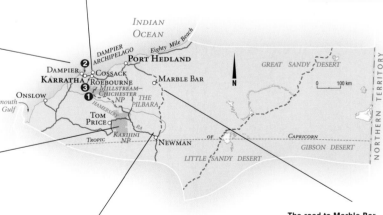

### Karijini National Park

Karijini is the name given to this area by the original inhabitants, the Banjima. It is renowned for extraordinary gorges, multicoloured walls and hidden pools and waterfalls. Brilliant wildflowers carpet the rust-red hills in spring. Camping is available inside the park.

### The Newman waterholes

Kalgans Pool, Eagle Rock Falls, Punda Pool and Weeli Wolli Spring are waterhole areas north-west of Newman. Some have spectacular gorges, others feature waterfalls and river-gum scenery. Wanna Munna is an interesting rock-art site. All these areas can be reached from Newman within 90 minutes, but most are accessible by 4WD only.

### The road to Marble Bar

Australia's hottest town was named for a unique bar of red jasper. Marble Bar is a mining and pastoral centre in the eastern Pilbara, and popular with tourists. The 184-km route from Port Hedland, sealed for about two thirds of the journey, crosses a landscape of gorges, spinifex and red and purple rocks.

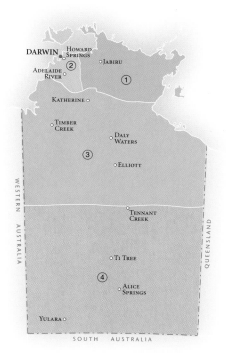

# NORTHERN TERRITORY

The Northern Territory lies midway across the continent. Its Top End includes the steamy tropics to the far north and its southern extremity reaches into Australia's desert heart. It is a frontier of sometimes extraordinary remoteness where vast tracks of land are unsettled and where some of the country's most remarkable natural landscapes are to be found.

## Floodplains to desert plains

The Timor Sea, the Arafura Sea and the Gulf of Carpentaria, scattered with islands, front the Northern Territory's tropical coastline. Flood plains, mudflats and mangroves dominate the coast, and some of Australia's most significant wetland areas are found just east of Darwin. Rivers near the coast, ranging from tidal waterways in the west to small crystal flows in the east, support big populations of barramundi and other freshwater species.

The western border of the Territory abuts Western Australia's Kimberley region and shares much of its ancient, rugged character. South from the coast the land rises gently to the low, sandstone Barkly Tableland, where millions of hectares of tussock grassland are watered for cattle pasture by artesian bores in the dry season. Much of the interior tableland is desert or semi-arid. Viewed from above, it is a landscape wrinkled with the shapes of ancient landforms such as the MacDonnell Ranges.

## Lands and landscapes

Some 50 per cent of the Territory's area is Aboriginal land or land under claim. This includes most of the offshore islands, the north-east corner of Arnhem Land, part of the west coast and a piece of the eastern half stretching from Timber Creek to the South Australian border.

The Territory's most distinctive landscapes are protected by national parks, some in remote regions. Two of the parks are World Heritage areas. The first, Kakadu in the tropical north, is a wonderland of diversity and contains one of the world's oldest and largest Aboriginal rock-art galleries. The second, Uluṟu–Kata Tjuṯa, which lies in The Red Centre, is home to Uluṟu, the monolith that has become Australia's most recognised natural symbol.

## First peoples

Archaeological evidence points to a human presence in Australia that goes back at least 50 000 and possibly 80 000 years. At the time of white settlement there was an estimated population in the Territory of 35 000 Aboriginal people living in 126 tribal groups, broken down into family groups of about twenty. As in other parts of Australia, the Aboriginal people made good use of the available resources and were able to cope with the climatic extremes.

Aboriginal rock art, Northern Territory

## A faltering foothold

A Dutch ship, the *Arnhem*, sighted the Territory coast in 1623. The British, concerned about Dutch interest in northern Australia, established three settlements on the coast between 1824 and 1849. All three struggled against environment and remoteness, and failed.

In 1863 the Northern Territory became part of South Australia. Palmerston, renamed Darwin in 1911, became the main town in 1869. A telegraph line linking Adelaide to Palmerston and the overseas cable was completed in 1872. A gold rush at Pine Creek in 1874 attracted prospectors and in the 1880s pastoralists settled on the Barkly Tableland to raise cattle for live export to Asia.

The Territory's post-colonial history has been one of the most turbulent in Australia. Apart from the struggle to maintain settlement in a forbidding landscape, the Territory was bombed extensively by the Japanese in the 1940s and has faced three major cyclones. Cyclone Tracy effectively destroyed the capital Darwin in 1974.

## Governing the Never Never

In 1911 South Australia surrendered the Northern Territory to the Commonwealth. An administrator then ran the Territory until a partly elected Legislative Council was established in 1947. From 1922, voters elected a member of the House of Representatives in Canberra but that member could vote only on matters relating to the Territory. Aboriginal adults were given the vote in 1962. The Territory was granted full self-government in 1978, but a referendum in October 1998 voted against its becoming a State.

## Territorians

The Territory has a population of 192 000, the lowest of any State or Territory. Darwin has around 90 000 people and Alice Springs 26 000. Around 20 per cent of the population claim an overseas birthplace, mainly the United Kingdom and New Zealand but increasingly the Philippines, East Timor and Indonesia.

Nearly a quarter of all Territorians, around 47 000 people, identify as Aboriginal people. Historically, the remoteness of Arnhem Land and the deserts kept Europeans at bay, although missionaries did penetrate some remote regions. The Territory's indigenous communities retain their language and culture to a far greater degree than elsewhere in Australia.

## Visitors by the million

The Territory's main industries are mining, beef cattle, pearl farming, fishing, crocodile farming and tourism. One and a quarter million visitors, nearly half from overseas, arrive each year to experience the Territory's unique natural and cultural features. Activities tend to be based around the two main centres 1500 kilometres apart: Darwin in the tropical north and Alice Springs in the desert centre. The peak time to visit is May to October, during the Top End's dry season and the Centre's pleasantly warm winter.

For more information on the Northern Territory, see Tourist Bureaus, opposite page 236.

# DARWIN

Darwin is about the size of a large provincial town, with all the facilities you would expect of a capital city. Its climate changes from hot and dry to hot and humid later in the year. Twice rebuilt, Darwin has a spacious, ordered feel thanks to the wide streets, low buildings and expansive manicured lawns. But it is also a city with a magnificent tropical chaos as streets give way to mangrove estuaries, brightly coloured foliage and huge ocean tides.

## CITY CENTRE

See map on page 213.

**Aquascene** 213 B7
Handfeed Darwin's many fish species at high tide.

**Australian Pearling Exhibition** 213 I11
Exhibits on the history and science of this important industry.

**Bicentennial Park** 213 D9
Take a stroll on the Esplanade at sunset; extensive trails, memorial sites and brilliant views.

**Christ Church Cathedral** 213 G10
Built in 1902, hit by Japanese gunfire in 1942 and destroyed by Cyclone Tracy in 1974; the new building incorporates the original porch and an incredible altar that was hewn from a jarrah log over 400 years old.

**Darwin Botanic Gardens** 213 D1
Lush gardens that date back to a vegetable patch established in the 1870s; impressive tropical, orchid and palm collections, and a self-guided Aboriginal plant-use trail.

**Deckchair Cinema** 213 I9
Dry-season screenings of alternative films under the stars (May to October).

**Lyons Cottage** 213 E10
Built in 1925 to house British and Australian Telegraph Company staff; now a museum on the history of the city.

**Mindil Beach Sunset Market** 213 B1
Live entertainment, exotic foods, art and craft, a tropical sunset and beach fireworks; Thursday nights, May to October, and Sunday nights, June to September.

**Overland Telegraph Memorial** 213 G11
Marks the centenary of significant Darwin events, including the completion of the Overland Telegraph line between Adelaide and Darwin, and the laying of the overseas cable to Java.

**Parliament House** 213 F10
Darwin's most imposing modern building; free guided tours on Saturdays at 10 a.m. and 12 noon.

**VISITOR INFORMATION**
**Tourism Top End**
Cnr Mitchell and
Knuckey sts, Darwin
(08) 8936 2499
www.nttc.com.au

**TOP EVENTS**
**Touring Car Championships** (May)
V8 supercars in a 3-day contest

**Royal Darwin Show** (July)
Darwin's premier event

**Darwin Rodeo and Country Music Concert** (July or Aug.)
Three days of 'yee-ha', Top End style

**Darwin Cup Carnival** (Aug.)
The city's premier horse race

**Festival of Darwin** (Sept.)
A feast of visual and performing arts

**Stokes Hill Wharf** 213 H12
Once the main port of the city, now a popular leisure area with food outlets, a pearl store and a bar.

**World War II Oil Storage Tunnels** 213 G11
Network of five concrete tunnels built to store oil for the navy; one tunnel is open to the public and features photographs and stories of the war years.

## SUBURBS AND SURROUNDS

See map on page 99.

**Australian Aviation Heritage Centre** 99 D4
Impressive list of exhibits including a massive B52 bomber and the wreckage of a Zero fighter shot down over Darwin in 1942.

**Casuarina Coastal Reserve** 99 C2
Long, white sandy beach, dunes, and mangrove and monsoon vine thickets; walking and cycling track to Nightcliff; includes Aboriginal sacred site, Old Man Rock.

**Crocodylus Park** 99 E3
For a safe encounter with these prehistoric monster reptiles, among other wildlife; also a research centre and museum.

**Cullen Bay Marina** 99 B5
Wonderful views, waterfront dining, shops and boardwalk; departure point for sunset cruises.

**Darwin Crocodile Farm** 99 I10
Houses 7000 estuarine and freshwater crocodiles combined; tours and feeding displays.

**Darwin Harbour Cruises** 99 B5
Explore the beautiful Darwin coastline.

**East Point Military Museum** 99 A3
Artillery, war planes, archival footage of Japanese bombings and an impressive photographic collection.

**Fannie Bay Gaol Museum** 99 B4
Darwin's prison from 1883 to 1979; displays on the region's history, and remnants of prison history such as old cells and gallows.

**Howard Springs** 99 H5
Nature reserve with a spring-fed, crocodile-free pool for swimming.

**Museum and Art Gallery of the Northern Territory** 99 B4
Features one of the most significant Aboriginal collections in the world, and the Cyclone Tracy gallery.

### GETTING AROUND

Darwin is very easy to negotiate either by car or on foot. The streets are well signed and traffic is light even at peak times. The Tour Tub is a service that provides a bus tour of the city's top sights. It departs daily from the north end of Smith Street Mall. The Darwin Bus Service provides a link between the city centre and outlying suburbs; the main terminal is on Harry Chan Avenue. A tour of the harbour is a must. Cullen Bay Marina is the departure point for cruises around Fannie Bay, Stokes Hill Wharf and Frances Bay, and for ferry trips to Mandorah on the Cox Peninsula.

**Airport shuttle bus**
Darwin Airport Shuttle (08) 8981 5066

**Motoring organisation**
AANT (08) 8981 3837

**Public transport**
Darwin Bus Service (08) 8924 7666

**Bus tours**
Tour Tub (08) 8981 5233

**Boat cruises**
City of Darwin Cruises 0417 855 829, Darwin Pearl Lugger Cruises (08) 8942 3131, Spirit of Darwin (08) 8981 3711

**Taxis**
Darwin Radio Taxis 13 10 08

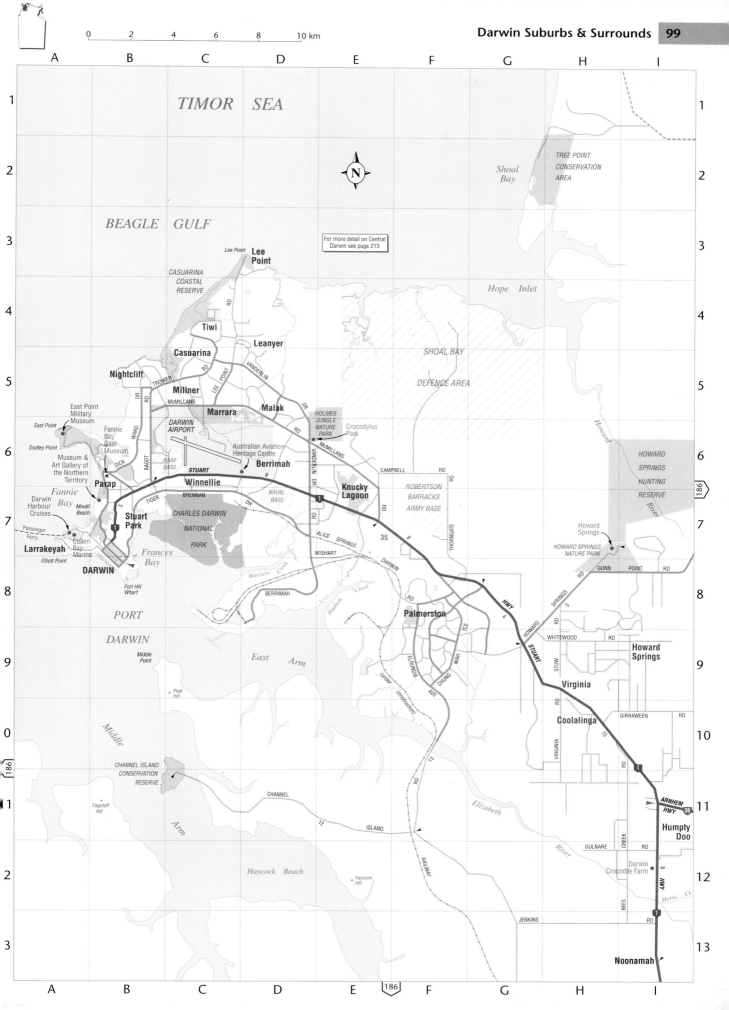

TIMOR SEA

BEAGLE GULF

Shoal Bay

TREE POINT CONSERVATION AREA

Hope Inlet

SHOAL BAY DEFENCE AREA

For more detail on Central Darwin see page 213

Lee Point

Lee Point

CASUARINA COASTAL RESERVE

Tiwi

Leanyer

Casuarina

Nightcliff

Millner

Marrara

Malak

McMILLANS

East Point Military Museum

East Point

Dudley Point

Fannie Bay Gaol Museum

DARWIN AIRPORT

Australian Aviation Heritage Centre

HOLMES JUNGLE NATURE PARK

Crocodylus Park

Howard

HOWARD SPRINGS HUNTING RESERVE

Museum & Art Gallery of the Northern Territory

RAAF BASE

STUART

Berrimah

Winnellie

CAMPBELL

RD

Howard Springs

Fannie Bay

Darwin Harbour Cruises

Mindil Beach

Parap

BRENNAN

NAVAL BASE

Knucky Lagoon

ROBERTSON BARRACKS ARMY BASE

HOWARD SPRINGS NATURE PARK

Cullen Bay Marina

Stuart Park

CHARLES DARWIN NATIONAL PARK

TIGER

ALICE SPRINGS

35

8

THORNGATE

GUNN POINT RD

Passenger Ferry

Larrakeyah

Elliott Point

DARWIN

Frances Bay

WISHART

DARWIN

SPRINGS

WHITEWOOD

RD

Howard Springs

Fort Hill Wharf

BERRIMAH

Hudson Creek

RD

HWY

STOW

Virginia

PORT

DARWIN

Middle Point

East Arm

Bleesers Creek

Palmerston

HOWARD

STUART

Coolalinga

Peak Hill

ELRUNDIE

CHUNG

WAH

TCE

AVE

GIRRAWEEN RD

RD

VIRGINIA

Middle

CHANNEL ISLAND CONSERVATION RESERVE

13

RD

10

RD

Flagstaff Hill

Arm

CHANNEL

Elizabeth

ARNHEM HWY

Humpty Doo

12

ISLAND

RAILWAY

River

GULNARE RD

CREEK

BEES

Darwin Crocodile Farm

Haycock Reach

Haycock Hill

Horns Ck

HWY

JENKINS

RD

Noonamah

# KAKADU & ARNHEM LAND

The ancient Arnhem Land escarpment meanders 500 km north to south, separating Kakadu National Park in the west from Arnhem Land in the east. World Heritage-listed Kakadu is of enormous cultural and environmental significance. The main access is via the sealed Arnhem Highway from Darwin. Some park areas are 4WD only. Facilities are excellent and park accommodation ranges from resort-style to camping. To the east is Aboriginal-owned Arnhem Land, traditional home to a number of language groups: this is one of Australia's most remote and least traversed regions. Within Arnhem Land Aboriginal Land, general access is limited to Cobourg Peninsula in the north-west and, on Gove Peninsula in the east, Nhulunbuy Town Lease and Buku-Larrnggay Mulka (the Aboriginal art museum at Yirrkala). Visitors can go to other areas on tours with Aboriginal guides, however. Permits are needed for the approaches by road to both peninsulas. During the Wet (November to April) some areas of the region may be inaccessible by road.

## FOCUS ON

### Natural and cultural Kakadu
Kakadu is one of only a few World Heritage sites worldwide that are listed for both their natural value and their cultural value. A place of enormous natural beauty and grand landscapes, it contains most habitats of northern Australia, including monsoonal rainforest, tidal estuary and floodplain, and riverine floodplain and woodland. It is one of the most biologically diverse areas of the country, home to 50 or more mammal species, 280 bird species, 123 reptile species, 52 freshwater fish species and 1600 plant species. Culturally, Kakadu's credentials are just as impressive. Because of its rich resources, Kakadu was one of the continent's most intensely populated areas before European settlement. With an estimated 5000 rock-art sites, it has the world's oldest and largest rock-art collection. As well as being aesthetically invaluable, some of the work records important events over the millennia, such as the presence and extinction of the thylacine and the contact between Aboriginal people and Macassan traders.

## TOP EVENTS

*July*    *National Aboriginal and Islander Day of Celebration (Nhulunbuy)*

*Aug.*    *Wind Festival (Jabiru)*

## EXPERIENCE IT!

**❶** *Walk* to Sunset Lookout at Ubirr for spectacular escarpment views at sunset

**❷** *Fish* for barramundi in one of the many beautiful billabongs

**❸** *Go* by boat to Cobourg Peninsula's Victoria Settlement, the ruins of a British garrison set up in 1838 to defend the north

**❹** *Take* an Aboriginal-guided cultural tour of the East Alligator River, via Border Store

**❺** *Enjoy* a vast and beautiful landscape on a scenic flight from Jabiru

### VISITOR INFORMATION
Tourism Top End
Darwin: (08) 8936 2499
www.ntholidays.com
Bowali Visitor Centre
Kakadu: (08) 8938 1121

CLIMATE **JABIRU**

| | J | F | M | A | M | J | J | A | S | O | N | D |
|---|---|---|---|---|---|---|---|---|---|---|---|---|
| Max. °C | 34 | 33 | 33 | 34 | 33 | 31 | 32 | 34 | 36 | 37 | 36 | 35 |
| Min. °C | 25 | 24 | 24 | 24 | 22 | 19 | 18 | 19 | 21 | 24 | 25 | 25 |
| Rain mm | 347 | 332 | 318 | 66 | 11 | 1 | 3 | 4 | 9 | 27 | 158 | 211 |
| Raindays | 22 | 21 | 20 | 7 | 2 | 0 | 0 | 0 | 1 | 3 | 12 | 16 |

**Walks at South Alligator River**
Towards the end of the Dry, thousands of waterbirds, including jabirus (pictured), congregate to feed in the Mamukala Wetlands. A short nature trail through the wetlands starts just east of the Arnhem Highway crossing of South Alligator River. In contrast, the Gungarre Monsoon Rainforest Walk (west of the river) passes through a closed forest environment.

**Bowali Visitor Centre**
Dynamic displays in Kakadu National Park's main visitor centre tell the story of Kakadu from indigenous and non-indigenous perspectives. An excellent first stop on any tour of the area, Bowali has a theatrette that shows audio-visuals of the park's highlights. Park headquarters is on the same site.

**Yellow Water**
Yellow Water (Ngurrungurrudjba) is a spectacular wetlands area with prolific birdlife, particularly in the dry season. Boat tours give visitors a close-up view of the birdlife and the Territory's crocodiles; the sunrise and sunset tours are particularly rewarding. Tours depart from Gagudju Lodge, Cooinda.

**Cobourg Peninsula**
Custodianship of this peninsula, protected by Gurig National Park, is shared by four Iwaidja clan groups. Visitors can fish, and explore the remote and beautiful landscape. Access is by 4WD through Arnhem Land, or by charter flight. Contact the Territory's Parks and Wildlife Commission for permits and campsite bookings.

**Ubirr**
Ubirr, on the Arnhem Land escarpment, houses one major rock-art gallery and some 36 smaller sites nearby. The paintings are predominantly in the X-ray style, although there are also Mimi paintings (depictions of delicate spirit figures), believed to be older. A circuit walk takes in the main sites.

**Gove Peninsula**
The Gove Peninsula is the traditional home of the Yolngu people, who have freehold title of the area. This remote paradise with its islands and cays, reefs and beaches is a frontier for anglers. Access is via charter flight, or by 4WD through Arnhem Land. Contact the Northern Land Council for permits.

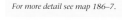

*For more detail see map 186–7.*

**Ranger Uranium Mine**
Uranium was discovered in the region in 1953. The Ranger mine opened in 1981 and the nearby township of Jabiru was established to accommodate mine workers. Tours of the mine are run in the Dry (May to October).

**Jim Jim and Twin Falls**
Jim Jim Falls (Barrkmalam) and Twin Falls (Gungkurdul) are reached via a 4WD track, 60 and 70 km respectively off the Kakadu Hwy. Both falls are best seen early in the Dry. Jim Jim, a 215-m drop, has a sand-fringed pool for year-round swimming. Twin Falls (pictured) has grand rock formations.

**Nourlangie Rock**
Nourlangie on the Arnhem Land escarpment is one of Kakadu's main Aboriginal rock-art areas. On the Nourlangie Art Site Walk visitors see a variety of styles, including prime examples of Kakadu X-ray art, which shows the anatomy of humans and animals in rich detail. Enjoy splendid views as you walk.

# AROUND DARWIN

The attractions within easy reach of Darwin provide an introduction to the natural wealth of the Territory and offer a glimpse of the local culture as well. Litchfield National Park showcases some extraordinary geological features, the wetlands of the Adelaide and Mary rivers teem with birdlife, and the Territory Wildlife Park offers up-close encounters with the creatures of northern Australia. During the Wet (November to April) some areas of the region may be inaccessible by road.

## TOP EVENTS

| | |
|---|---|
| *May* | *Gold Rush Festival (Pine Creek)* |
| *May* | *Races (horseracing, Pine Creek)* |
| *June* | *Bush Race Meeting (horseracing, Adelaide River)* |
| *June* | *Show (rodeo, country music, crafts, Adelaide River)* |
| *June* | *Rodeo (Pine Creek)* |
| *June/ July* | *International Skydiving and Parachuting Championships (Batchelor)* |

## EXPERIENCE IT!

❶ **Swim** in the crocodile-free, spring-fed natural pool at Howard Springs Nature Park.

❷ **Take** a 4WD tour to The Lost City, a landscape of sandstone block formations in Litchfield National Park.

❸ **Visit** Fogg Dam at sunrise or sunset to see the Top End's prolific wildlife in natural surroundings

## VISITOR INFORMATION

Tourism Top End
Darwin: (08) 8936 2499
www.ntholidays.com

## FOCUS ON

### Crocodiles

Crocodiles are both compelling and deadly creatures. Of the two types in northern Australia the most dangerous is the estuarine crocodile ('saltie'). This well-camouflaged reptile is found out at sea, along the coastline, in tidal rivers and creeks, and in rivers up to 100 km from the coast. Never go swimming where 'salties' have been seen. The freshwater crocodile ('freshie') inhabits rivers and lagoons; it is smaller, but can still inflict a serious wound. Both types nest and sun themselves near the water's edge. Always seek local advice before swimming, camping or boating. View these reptiles safely at Darwin Crocodile Farm, 40 km south of the city and Crocodylus Park, an education and research centre in Darwin's north-eastern suburbs.

### CLIMATE ADELAIDE RIVER

| | J | F | M | A | M | J | J | A | S | O | N | D |
|---|---|---|---|---|---|---|---|---|---|---|---|---|
| Max. °C | 32 | 31 | 32 | 33 | 32 | 31 | 30 | 31 | 33 | 33 | 33 | 33 |
| Min. °C | 25 | 25 | 25 | 24 | 22 | 20 | 19 | 21 | 23 | 25 | 25 | 25 |
| Rain mm | 429 | 353 | 322 | 103 | 21 | 1 | 1 | 6 | 16 | 73 | 141 | 250 |
| Raindays | 21 | 20 | 19 | 9 | 2 | 1 | 1 | 1 | 2 | 7 | 12 | 16 |

### Territory Wildlife Park

This award-winning park shows Northern Australia's native fauna and flora. Features include aviaries, raptor displays (pictured), an aquarium tunnel and a large nocturnal house. Nearby, Berry Springs Nature Park features a spring-fed pool – safe for swimming – in natural bushland.

### Tiwi Islands

Bathurst and Melville islands form the Tiwi Islands, 80 km offshore from Darwin. They belong to the Tiwi people, whose unique culture results from their historic isolation. The spectacular landscape offers escarpments, lakes, waterfalls, pristine beaches and forests. One- and two-day Tiwi-led tours are run during the Dry.

### Adelaide River wetlands

Central to this wetland area is Window on the Wetlands Visitor Centre, which provides an overview of the ecology of wetlands as well as stunning views across floodplains. For waterlilies in bloom, visit mid-year.

TIMOR SEA

TIWI ISLANDS

Bathurst Island

Melville Island

VAN DIEMEN GULF

BEAGLE GULF

DARWIN

❶ HOWARD SPRINGS

❸

NOONAMAH

MARY RIVER NP

BATCHELOR

MARY RIVER CROSSING

MARY RIVER NP

❷

ADELAIDE RIVER

LITCHFIELD NATIONAL PARK

N

0    30 km

PINE CREEK

*For more detail see map 186.*

### Litchfield National Park

Litchfield, 2 hours from Darwin, has waterfalls, gorges, pockets of rainforest, giant termite mounds, walks and campsites. Enjoy the scenic pools at the bottom of the park's waterfalls; most offer crocodile-free swimming, but read the signs before you take the plunge.

### Mary River wetlands

Monsoon and paperbark forests fringe the billabongs and riverbanks of this magnificent wetland. Visitors in 2WD vehicles can picnic and fish at Mary River Crossing on Arnhem Highway. Those with 4WDs can head further north to the famed fishing spots of Corroboree Billabong, North Rockhole and Shady Camp.

# GULF TO GULF

Lying between the major tourist areas of the Red Centre and Top End are places where visitors can experience the natural riches of the Territory away from crowds. Some of these places are well known, particularly the world-famous gorges of Nitmiluk National Park. Other attractions are scarcely on the map: the rugged national parks of the far west; the string of remote barramundi fishing destinations along the east and west coasts; and a number of 4WD destinations. Long distances separate towns in these areas; travellers should familiarise themselves with prevailing conditions and carry adequate supplies.

## TOP EVENTS

**Easter** *Fishing Classic (Borroloola)*

**Apr.– May** *Fishing competitions (Timber Creek)*

**May** *Back to the Never Never Festival (Mataranka)*

**May** *Art Show (Mataranka)*

**June** *Burunga Sport and Cultural Festival (Katherine)*

**June** *Katherine Cup (horseracing, Katherine)*

**June** *Canoe Marathon (Katherine)*

**Aug.– Sept.** *Flying Fox Festival (Katherine)*

**Sept.** *Races (horseracing, Timber Creek)*

## EXPERIENCE IT!

❶ *Explore* Cutta Cutta Caves, a 2-km-long underground limestone formation, south-east of Katherine

❷ *Fly,* via Cape Crawford, to Lost City, an eerie landscape of pillars rising out of the plain

❸ *Try* bush tucker and learn traditional crafts at Manyallaluk Aboriginal community

## VISITOR INFORMATION

Katherine: (08) 8972 2650

Tourism Top End
Darwin: (08) 8936 2499
www.ntholidays.com

## FOCUS ON

### Barramundi fishing

Barrumundi, Australia's premier native sports fish, is nowhere as prolific or accessible to anglers as it is in the Northern Territory. There is good barra fishing along both east and west coasts. The rugged west features tropical wetlands and a network of waterways. Popular spots include Daly River (known for the size of its barramundi and its fishing lodges), Nitmiluk (Katherine Gorge), and Victoria River via Timber Creek. The numerous eastern rivers are smaller, with minimal tides but very clear water. Top spots here are Borroloola on McArthur River and Roper Bar on Roper River.

### Nitmiluk National Park

The traditional home of the Jawoyn people, this park is world-renowned for its 13 stunning gorges, carved from red sandstone over 20 million years. Visitors can navigate the gorges in canoes, take a boat tour with a Jawoyn guide, swim in the pools or explore the 100-km network of walking tracks.

### Keep River National Park

This remote park includes the traditional land of the Miriwoong and Kadjerong peoples and contains many important art sites, including the accessible Nganalam site. A major attraction is the park's rugged sandstone formations, similar to those of Purnululu National Park's Bungle Bungles. There are designated camping areas and good walks.

### Gregory National Park

Forming a transitional zone between the tropics and the Central Australian desert, Gregory's two sectors offer a rugged, remote landscape of sandstone escarpments, limestone gorges, billabongs and woodlands. There are 4WD scenic routes, walking tracks and interesting Aboriginal and European heritage sites.

| CLIMATE KATHERINE | | | | | | | | | | | | |
|---|---|---|---|---|---|---|---|---|---|---|---|---|
| | J | F | M | A | M | J | J | A | S | O | N | D |
| Max. °C | 35 | 34 | 35 | 34 | 32 | 30 | 30 | 33 | 35 | 38 | 38 | 37 |
| Min. °C | 24 | 24 | 23 | 20 | 17 | 14 | 13 | 16 | 20 | 24 | 25 | 24 |
| Rain mm | 235 | 213 | 161 | 33 | 6 | 2 | 1 | 1 | 6 | 29 | 87 | 197 |
| Raindays | 15 | 13 | 10 | 2 | 1 | 0 | 0 | 0 | 1 | 3 | 7 | 12 |

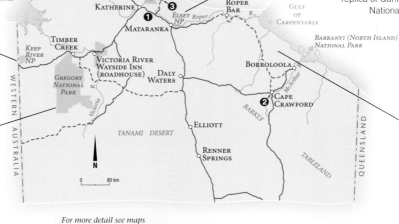

### Never Never country

Jeannie Gunn wrote *We of the Never Never* (1908) after living at Elsey Station. Now you can visit Mataranka Homestead, a faithful replica of Gunn's home. Nearby in Elsey National Park visitors can enjoy the Mataranka thermal pool (pictured), which pumps out 20 million litres of water daily.

### Eastern frontiers

The area adjoining the Gulf of Carpentaria is popular with 4WD travellers seeking new frontiers. The main settlement, Borroloola, is central for barramundi anglers and offers access to the waters around Barranyi (North Island) National Park.

*For more detail see maps 186–7 & 188–9.*

0    80 km

N

# THE RED CENTRE

This is Australia's geographical, scenic and mythic heart. With its spectacular landforms, deserts, blue skies and monumental sense of scale, it has become a powerful symbol of the ancient grandeur of the Australian continent. For many thousands of years the region has been home to Aboriginal people from numerous groups – including the Arrernte and the Anangu – who named, mapped and inscribed with spiritual meaning almost every one of the landforms, from the massive Uluru to ancient riverbeds and obelisks. The Europeans colonised the area in the 1870s with the building of the Overland Telegraph Line. Tourism began in the 1940s and has flourished since the 1970s; facilities range from excellent at Alice Springs and Yulara to non-existent at some of the far-flung attractions. The best time to visit is during the winter months; the summer is very hot. Visitors intending to explore beyond the beaten track need to be fully self-sufficient.

## TOP EVENTS

**Jan.** Lasseter's Indoor Challenge (Alice Springs)

**Apr.** Country Music Festival (Alice Springs)

**Apr.– May** Racing Carnival (horseracing, Alice Springs)

**May** Bangtail Muster (Alice Springs)

**May** Cup Day (horseracing, Tennant Creek)

**May** Go-Kart Grand Prix (Tennant Creek)

**June** Finke Desert Race (vehicle-racing, Alice Springs)

**July** Camel Cup (Alice Springs)

**July** Show (Alice Springs)

**July** Show (Tennant Creek)

**Aug.** Rodeo (Alice Springs)

**Aug.** Henley-on-Todd Regatta (Alice Springs)

**Sept.** Desert Harmony Festival (Tennant Creek)

**Oct.** Masters Games (mature-age athletics, Alice Springs, even-numbered years)

**Nov.** Corkwood Festival (Alice Springs)

## VISITOR INFORMATION

Central Australian Tourism Industry Association
Alice Springs: (08) 8952 5800
www.centralaustraliantourism.com

### CLIMATE ALICE SPRINGS

|          | J  | F  | M  | A  | M  | J  | J  | A  | S  | O  | N  | D  |
|----------|----|----|----|----|----|----|----|----|----|----|----|----|
| Max. °C  | 36 | 35 | 32 | 28 | 23 | 20 | 19 | 22 | 27 | 31 | 33 | 35 |
| Min. °C  | 21 | 21 | 17 | 13 | 8  | 5  | 4  | 6  | 10 | 15 | 18 | 20 |
| Rain mm  | 36 | 42 | 37 | 14 | 17 | 15 | 16 | 12 | 9  | 21 | 26 | 37 |
| Raindays | 5  | 5  | 3  | 2  | 3  | 3  | 3  | 2  | 2  | 5  | 6  | 5  |

**Kings Canyon**
Spectacular Kings Canyon features sandstone walls rising to 100 m. A 6-km-return trail scales the side of the canyon and leads past beehive formations to the Garden of Eden. The surrounding Watarrka National Park, traditional land of the Luritja people, includes lush relic vegetation and classic red sand dunes.

**Kata Tjuta**
Uluru's sister rock formation Kata Tjuta, meaning 'many heads' comprises 36 magnificently rounded and coloured dome-like shapes covering about 35 sq km. The 3-hour Valley of the Winds walk winds through the crevices and gorges of the rock system.

## FOCUS ON

### The story of Uluru

Uluru lies in the territory of the Anangu people. European explorer William Gosse named it Ayers Rock in 1873. Along with The Olgas (now Kata Tjuta) and surrounding land it became a national park in 1958. In 1985 it was returned to its traditional owners and was gazetted as Uluru. The rock is Australia's most identifiable natural icon. It is a massive, red, rounded monolith rising 348 m above the plain and 863 m above sea level, and reaching 6 km below the earth's surface. Uluru's circumference measures 9.4 km. It has no joints so, despite its valleys, fissures and caves it is a true monolith. Uluru attracts tourists because of its size and singularity. For the Anangu, however, the rock is not a single spiritual object but a thing of many parts: along with Kata Tjuta, it is the physical evidence of the deeds, actions, journeys and artifacts of the Tjukurpa, the ancestral beings of creation times.

### Exploring Uluru

The Anangu prefer tourists not to climb Uluru. There are four guided walks: a 9.4-km walk around the base; the Mala walk to art sites; the Liru walk explaining the use of bush materials; and the Kuniya walk, during which creation stories are told. Pictured here are quandong fruit.

### West MacDonnell Ranges
The traditional home of the Arrernte people, these ranges offer extraordinarily diverse flora (about 600 species, 75 of them rare) and some of Australia's best gorge scenery. Sites to visit include Simpsons Gap, Ellery Creek Big Hole, Serpentine Gorge and Ormiston Gorge. All are accessible in a 2WD vehicle. For walkers, there is the Larapinta Trail.

### Devils Marbles
This collection of huge, precarious-looking spherical boulders lies in clusters in a shallow valley. The area is protected as an Aboriginal site. According to legend, the Marbles are the Rainbow Serpent's eggs.

### EXPERIENCE IT!

❶ *Taste* the wines at Chateau Hornsby, Northern Territory's only winery

❷ *Inspect* the ruins at Arltunga Historical Reserve, site of Central Australia's first gold rush in 1887

❸ *Discover* the cultural and environmental history of Uluṟu–Kata Tjuṯa National Park at its award-winning Cultural Centre

❹ *Swim* in the refreshingly cold waters of Trephina Gorge

❺ *Take* a 4WD trip to Tnorala (Gosse Bluff), a massive crater formed when a comet crashed to earth over 130 million years ago

For more detail see maps 188–9 & 190–1.

### Ruby Gap Nature Park
This far-flung park in the East MacDonnell Ranges is well worth the 4WD trip. Its 850 million-year-old landscape includes the garnet-strewn gorge at Glen Annie and, on the Hale River, another that is often considered to be Australia's most beautiful gorge. There are no facilities, although bush camping is permitted.

### Alice Springs
Australia's best-known country town was originally a waterhole, named for a telegraph official's wife. Alice Springs today is a lively, well-serviced centre with around 400 000 visitors each year. Attractions include the Museum of Central Australia, Araluen Galleries (pictured) and the Telegraph Station Historical Reserve.

### Finke Gorge National Park
This park is 4WD access only. Its unique feature is Palm Valley, a 10 000-year-old oasis where 3000 red fan palms cluster in a valley. The Finke River, which has carved out Finke Gorge, has maintained its course for over 100 million years and is possibly the world's oldest river.

### Simpson Desert and Chambers Pillar
The world's largest sand-dune desert was formed around 18 000 years ago after the continent's central lakes had dried up. Much of the desert is impossibly remote; however, this northern section is accessible by 4WD. The main attraction is Chambers Pillar, a sandstone obelisk towering 50 m above the plain.

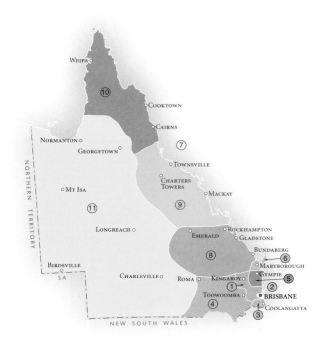

# QUEENSLAND

Queensland is Australia's second-largest State, covering 1 727 200 square kilometres in the continent's north-east corner. Of its 3 500 000 residents, 54 per cent live outside the capital Brisbane, making Queensland Australia's most decentralised State. World-famous natural features have earned Queensland a reputation as a premier holiday destination with both interstate and international tourists.

## Natural wonders

Queensland's east coast is a narrow strip of beaches, headlands, lagoons, estuaries and mangrove swamps between the Pacific Ocean and the Great Dividing Range. Offshore, the islands and coral reefs of the Great Barrier Reef form one of the great wonders of the natural world. Ancient rainforests cover the Great Dividing Range and west of the range, tableland country supports some of Australia's most productive agricultural regions. Inland lie the vast plains of the Gulf and Channel country. Meandering rivers, dry for much of the year, empty into the mangrove swamps and tidal flats of the Gulf and wind towards Australia's interior in a maze of channels. Run-off from tropical rains on the western slopes of the Great Dividing Range over millions of years has seeped under the plains to create the Great Artesian Basin.

Two-thirds of Queensland is in the tropics. The north-east coast is subject to monsoon conditions during the Wet, which runs from November to April. The subtropical south-east coast has warm, humid summers tempered by sea breezes, while summers on the plains are hot and dry. Queensland – from the outback to the tropics – is best visited from May to October, when the climate is pleasantly mild and dry.

## Early Days

The first inhabitants of what is now Queensland were the Aboriginal people, spread across six geographical and cultural regions each containing several different language groups. About 5000 Torres Strait Islander people inhabited some of the many islands between Cape York and Papua New Guinea.

Willem Jansz was the first known European to sight Australia when he sailed down the west coast of Cape York Peninsula in March 1606. The British established a penal settlement at Moreton Bay in 1824. The district opened to 'free settlers' in 1842 who quickly occupied the Brisbane River valley, the Darling Downs, and the Burnett country to the north. These areas became the colony of Queensland in 1859 and Queensland achieved statehood as part of the Commonwealth of Australia in 1901.

## Troubled times

White settlement was not to the benefit of the indigenous population. Conflict between the Aboriginal people and settlers was brutal in central and northern Queensland. Massacres at Hornet Bank in 1857 and near Emerald in 1861 resulted in indiscriminate reprisals led by the Native Police. Legislation in 1897 confined Queensland's Aboriginal people to mission stations and government reserves. Government protectors could remove Aboriginal children from their families without right of appeal.

## Sunshine democracy

On the colony's separation in 1859, Queensland's constitution was similar to that of New South Wales: an elected Legislative Assembly and an appointed Legislative Council. The world's first Labor government held office in Queensland for seven days in December 1899. Labor governed Queensland from 1915 to 1957, except for the period from 1929 to 1932. Labor abolished the Legislative Council in 1922, the only Australian State to do so. The Country–Liberal coalition, first elected 1957, was voted out in 1989 following corruption allegations and inquiries. A minority Labor government was elected in November 1999; Labor recorded a landslide victory in February 2001.

## Capital and cultural wealth

Queensland occupies one of Australia's richest pockets of land in terms of resources. Sheep, cattle and sugar farming were established in the first half of the 19th century and have remained strong industries. The rich volcanic soils of the Darling Downs tableland have provided huge crops of wheat, oil, fruit, tobacco, cotton and most recently wine. Tropical fruit orchards are found along the coast. The discovery of gold and copper in 1867 set off the first Queensland mining boom. Production of coal, gold, copper, silver, lead, zinc, bauxite, mineral sands and natural gas currently contributes over six billion dollars to the State's income.

Recently, Queensland's indigenous people began voicing their rights to their traditional lands. Much of Cape York Peninsula has been subject to native title claims in the last decade and thousands of square kilometres along the west coast were returned to traditional owners. Australia's two most significant land rights claims, Mabo (1992) and Wik (1996), were Queensland claims.

## Welcoming the world

Tourism now accounts for about 10 per cent of Queensland's gross product. About 30 per cent of all overseas visitors to Australia specify Queensland as their main destination. The often unique natural scenery, an ancient culture's artifacts, an easy pace and affordable facilities are attracting increasing numbers of visitors from around the world. Eco-tourists, backpackers, jetsetters and old-fashioned sun-and-surf-lovers are just some of the types of people drawn to the self proclaimed sunshine state.

Imperial Hotel in the old goldmining town of Ravenswood

For more information on Queensland, see Tourist Bureaus, opposite page 236.

# BRISBANE

The city of Brisbane straddles the lazy curves of the Brisbane River, which winds its way through the suburbs to Moreton Bay. The long fingers of Moreton and Stradbroke islands create a barrier to the Pacific Ocean, providing the city with a vast body of calm water at its foreshore. Inland, a hilly, subtropical terrain provides breathing space and a beautiful backdrop for a city with a population of more than 1.6 million.

## VISITOR INFORMATION

**Brisbane Visitor Information Centre**
Queen Street Mall (07) 3006 6290
www.brisbanetourism.com.au

**South Bank Parklands Visitor Centre**
Allgas building, Stanley Street Plaza
(07) 3867 2051

**Redlands Tourism Centre**
1 Passage St, Cleveland
(07) 3821 0057

**Bayside Information Centre**
66 Bay Tce, Wynnum
(07) 3893 0589

**Redcliffe Tourist Information Centre**
Pelican Park, Hornibrook Esplanade
(07) 3284 3500

## TOP EVENTS

**Queensland Winter Racing Carnival**
(May–June)
Two months of excitement on and off the racecourse

**Brisbane International Film Festival** (Aug.)
A showcase of Australian and international cinema

**'The Ekka' – Royal Brisbane Show** (Aug.)
An ideal event for families

**Brisbane River Festival** (Sept.)
Regattas, aquatic feats and Dragon Boats

**Spring Hill Fair** (Sept.)
Two days of markets, performers and cuisine

## CITY CENTRE

See map on page 214.

**Brisbane City Hall** 214 D6
Architectural landmark of the city centre; also houses the contemporary work of the Brisbane City Gallery.

**Brisbane Cricket Ground ('The Gabba')** 214 I13
Home to the Brisbane Lions; hosts international and State cricket games.

**Brunswick Street Mall** 214 H2
Part of a lively inner-city neighbourhood with reasonably priced cuisine from all corners of the world; fascinating markets on Sundays.

**City Botanic Gardens** 214 F9
Ornamental plantings, glittering ponds, a mangrove boardwalk and broad sweeps of lawn on the banks of the Brisbane River.

**Commissariat Stores** 214 E8
Early colonial building, today housing a small museum run by the Royal Historical Society of Queensland.

**Customs House** 214 G5
Gallery and restaurant in historic riverside setting.

**Eagle Street Pier** 214 G6
Popular gathering spot with restaurants, bars and cafes; on Sundays, setting for Brisbane's largest open-air market.

**Old Windmill** 214 D5
Brisbane's oldest structure; built by
convicts in 1828 to grind wheat
and maize.

**Parliament House** 214 E9
A grand old French Renaissance-style
building; tours through here offer a
glimpse into the world of
Queensland politics.

**Queensland Art Gallery** 214 C8
Renowned artists represented from
Australia and abroad; features a
meditative Water Mall.

**Queensland Maritime
Museum** 214 E11
Seafaring relics charting
Queensland's maritime history from
the Dutch landing at Cape York in
1606; includes dry dock with World
War II frigate.

**Queensland Museum** 214 B8
Extensive natural history collection
with endangered species display and
a virtual 'trip' back 220 million years.

**Roma Street Parklands** 214 C4
Recent development on the former
rail yards with shops, restaurants, a
lake and tropical rainforest.

**St John's Cathedral** 214 F4
Gothic-style building with the only
stone-vaulted ceiling in a cathedral in
the Southern Hemisphere.

**Sciencentre** 214 E8
Interactive science displays for all the
family.

**South Bank Beach** 214 D10
A palm-fringed, sandy beach,
practically in the middle of the city.
Lifeguards are an added bonus for
families.

**South Bank Parklands** 214 D9
Beach, rainforest and butterfly house
in the city; on Friday evenings, a
magical setting for Lantern Village
Market; Craft Village on Saturdays
and Sundays.

**Story Bridge** 214 H4
The city's best-known landmark and
largest steel cantilever bridge in
Australia.

## SUBURBS AND SURROUNDS

See map on page 111.

**Alma Park Zoo** 111 C5
Exotic animals in subtropical
surrounds; Australian native animals
in hands-on enclosures.

**Bribie Island** 111 D1
Excellent for bushwalking, crabbing,
fishing and boating; access from
Caboolture–Bribie Island Road (via
bridge).

**Brisbane Powerhouse** 111 C8
An exciting centre for live arts; the
site of a popular Farmers' Market on
the second Saturday of each month.

**Fortitude Valley** 111 C8
An inner-city suburb with a rich
history. Today 'the valley' is one of
Brisbane's best night and shopping
spots.

**Lone Pine Koala Sanctuary** 111 C9
Visit the world's largest koala
sanctuary.

**Manly** 111 E8
Good swimming and fishing beaches,
and fine places to enjoy a picnic;
historical sites nearby to explore on
foot.

**Miegunyah** 111 C8
Historic house with displays
commemorating Queensland's
pioneering women.

**Mount Coot-tha Forest Park** 111 B8
Take in the sensational views from
the summit; wander through Mount
Coot-tha Botanic Gardens and visit
the Tropical Dome, Japanese Garden
(pictured below) and Australian Plant
Community area.

**Mount Glorious** 111 A6
Dense forests and spectacular views;
visit Walk-about Creek Wildlife
Centre en route.

**New Farm Park** 111 C8
Nestled on the river bend at the end
of Brunswick Street; garden oasis of
tropical and ornamental species;
restaurant in attractive garden
setting.

**Newstead House** 111 C8
A classic Australian homestead on the
banks of the river at Breakfast Creek.

**North Stradbroke Island** 111 H8
Popular destination for fishing,
surfing, swimming, horseriding and
canoeing; includes national park;
access by ferry from Cleveland.

**Ormiston House** 111 F8
Former home of the founder of
Queensland's big sugar industry
(open Sundays, March to November).

**Redcliffe Peninsula** 111 D5
Juts out into Moreton Bay, providing
beautiful sandy beaches; swimming is
generally safe and fishing is excellent.

**Redland Bay** 111 F10
A peaceful outer suburb of Brisbane,
renowned for its markets, gardens
and the strawberry festival in
September.

**St Helena Island** 111 E7
Former penal settlement, now a
national park; cruises to the island
depart from the Manly Boat Harbour.

**GETTING AROUND**

Brisbane has well-signed roads and little
traffic congestion, yet it is not an easy
city for the first-time visitor to negotiate.
There is a criss-crossing network of
major motorways and a number of one-
way streets. An up-to-date road map and
some careful planning are necessary.
Brisbane's best through-routes are all
multi-lane motorways with staffed
tollgates. The Gateway Motorway also
provides excellent access to Brisbane
Airport. The transport system (bus, rail
and ferry) is efficient, with a couple of
excellent bus routes specifically for
tourists. A boat trip on the Brisbane
River is a must, and there is a very good
commuter ferry service that stops at key
destinations around the city.

**Airport shuttle bus**
Coachtrans Skytrans Airport Service
(07) 3860 6999

**Motoring organisation**
RACQ 13 19 05

**Public transport**
TransInfo (bus, ferry, rail) 13 12 30

**Bus tours**
City Sights and City Lights tourist trips
aboard open-air tram replicas around
the city and suburban sights 13 12 30

**Brisbane River trips**
Kookaburra River Queens
(07) 3221 1300,
Mirimar Cruises (07) 3221 0300

**Taxis**
Black & White Cabs 13 10 08,
Yellow Cabs 13 19 24

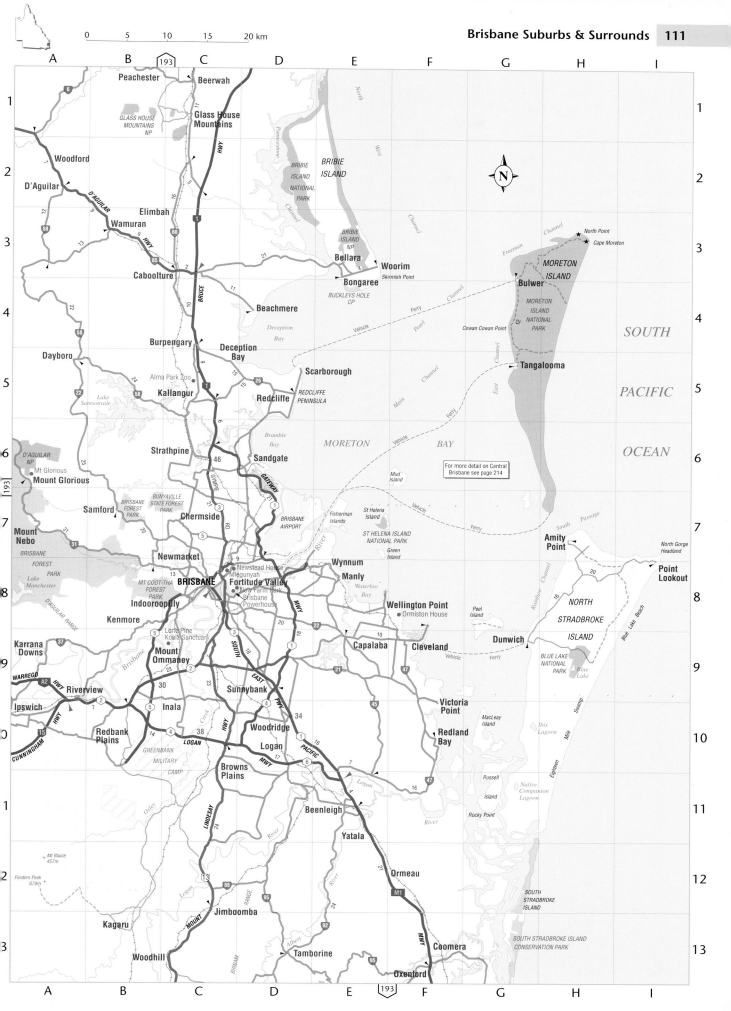

0   5   10   15   20 km

**A    B    C    D    E    F    G    H    I**

Peachester    Beerwah

Glass House
Mountains
GLASS HOUSE
MOUNTAINS
NP

BRIBIE
ISLAND

BRIBIE
ISLAND

Woodford

D'Aguilar

Elimbah

Wamuran

BRIBIE
ISLAND
NATIONAL
PARK

North

West

Dayboro

Caboolture

Bellara

BRIBIE
ISLAND
NP

Woorim

Bongaree

Skirmish Point

MORETON
ISLAND

North Point
Cape Moreton

Beachmere

BUCKLEYS HOLE
CP

Channel

Freeman

Bulwer

Burpengary

Deception
Bay

Deception
Bay

Scarborough

Vehicle

Ferry

Pearl

MORETON
ISLAND
NATIONAL
PARK

Cowan Cowan Point

Kallangur

Alma Park Zoo

Lake
Samsonvale

Redcliffe

REDCLIFFE
PENINSULA

Channel

Tangalooma

SOUTH

Strathpine

Bramble
Bay

MORETON    BAY

Main

Vehicle

Ferry

East Channel

PACIFIC

Mount Glorious

D'AGUILAR
NP

Mt Glorious

Sandgate

Mud
Island

Channel

OCEAN

Samford

BRISBANE
FOREST
PARK

BUNYAVILLE
STATE FOREST
PARK

Chermside

St Helena
Island

Vehicle

For more detail on Central
Brisbane see page 214

Mount
Nebo

BRISBANE
FOREST
PARK

Lake
Manchester

Newmarket

Newstead House
Miegunyah

Fisherman
Islands

St Helena Island

ST HELENA ISLAND
NATIONAL PARK

Green Island

Ferry

Amity
Point

North Gorge
Headland

BRISBANE

Fortitude Valley

New Farm Park
Brisbane
Powerhouse

Wynnum

Manly

Point
Lookout

Indooroopilly

MT COOT-THA
FOREST
PARK

Waterloo
Bay

Wellington Point

Ormiston House

Peel
Island

Dunwich

NORTH
STRADBROKE
ISLAND

Blue Lake Beach

Kenmore

Lone Pine
Koala Sanctuary

Capalaba

Cleveland

Vehicle

Ferry

BLUE LAKE
NATIONAL
PARK

Blue
Lake

Karrana
Downs

Mount
Ommaney

Sunnybank

Victoria
Point

MacLeay
Island

Ibis
Lagoon

Riverview

Ipswich

Inala

Woodridge

Redland
Bay

Russell
Island

Native
Companion
Lagoon

Redbank
Plains

GREENBANK
MILITARY
CAMP

Logan

Rocky Point

River

SOUTH
STRADBROKE
ISLAND

Browns
Plains

Beenleigh

Yatala

Mt Blaine
457m

Flinders Peak
679m

Ormeau

Kagaru

Jimboomba

Tamborine

Coomera

SOUTH STRADBROKE ISLAND
CONSERVATION PARK

Woodhill

Oxenford

# BRISBANE HINTERLAND

This region offers a number of easily reached attractions. The heavily forested hills of the D'Aguilar Ranges create a subtropical haven just 20 minutes west of the city; the main access point is the hamlet of Mount Glorious, in Brisbane Forest Park. Also to the west is the heritage city of Ipswich. Further north-west, the diverse crops and heritage villages in the area known as South Burnett offer pleasant rural touring while the native landscape, including stands of rare pine rainforest, is preserved in Bunya Mountains National Park. Scattered throughout the region are attractions that include animals – perfect for families.

## TOP EVENTS

**Mar.** Peanut and Harvest Festival (Kingaroy, odd-numbered years)

**Mar.** Pine Rivers Heritage Festival (Strathpine)

**Apr.** Food and Wine Fest (Kingaroy)

**Apr.** Great Horse Ride (Kilkivan, near Murgon)

**May** Pumpkin Festival (Goomeri, near Murgon)

**Aug.** Camp Oven Bush Poets Festival (Strathpine)

**Oct.** Potato Carnival (Gatton)

**Oct.** Bjelke-Petersen Dam Fishing Competition (Murgon)

**Oct.** Pioneer Festival (Nanango)

## EXPERIENCE IT!

**❶ Tour** the rail workshops in Ipswich, where Queensland's first train line was launched in 1864

**❷ Take** a balloon flight from Laidley, over orchards and market gardens

**❸ Drive** the Mount Glorious–Samford Road, one of the State's most scenic routes

**Booubyjan Homestead**

Two Irish brothers, the Clements, took up this run near Goomeri in 1847, replacing sheep with cattle in the 1880s. The property is still owned by the family. The homestead, open daily, provides a glimpse of pioneering life and the changes wrought by five generations of continuous occupation.

## VISITOR INFORMATION

Brisbane Tourism
Brisbane: (07) 3006 6290
www.brisbanetourism.com.au

South Burnett Visitor Information Centre
Kingaroy: (07) 4162 3199
www.southburnett.com.au

## FOCUS ON

### Animal antics

The Walk-about Creek Wildlife Centre, in Brisbane Forest Park, features a freshwater creek environment populated with water dragons, frogs, platypuses, pythons and fish. The Australian Woolshed, just past Samford, re-creates life on a sheep station. Shearing demonstrations, ram shows and cattle-dog demonstrations are staged daily, while native animals roam freely. Daisy Hill State Forest is a pocket of eucalypt forest and acacia scrub 25 km south of Brisbane, where visitors can scan the canopy for koalas from a treetop tower. The Daisy Hill Koala Centre in the central picnic area has information about koalas and their habitats.

### CLIMATE MOUNT GLORIOUS

| | J | F | M | A | M | J | J | A | S | O | N | D |
|---|---|---|---|---|---|---|---|---|---|---|---|---|
| **Max.°C** | 25 | 24 | 24 | 21 | 18 | 16 | 15 | 17 | 20 | 22 | 24 | 25 |
| **Min. °C** | 18 | 17 | 17 | 15 | 12 | 10 | 9 | 9 | 11 | 14 | 15 | 17 |
| **Rain mm** | 238 | 252 | 222 | 129 | 126 | 84 | 86 | 56 | 57 | 114 | 123 | 167 |
| **Raindays** | 15 | 16 | 16 | 12 | 11 | 8 | 8 | 7 | 7 | 10 | 11 | 13 |

**South Burnett**

This comfortable slice of rural Queensland invites you to the historic timber towns of Blackbutt and Yarraman or to wineries along the scenic Barambah Wine Trail. Go to the Nanango or Kilkivan areas to fossick for gold, or to Kingaroy, a prosperous agricultural centre. Accommodation includes B&Bs and farmstays.

**Bunya Mountains**

This isolated spur of the Great Dividing Range is a cool, moist region of waterfalls, green and scarlet king parrots and the remaining stands of bunya pine (pictured), a species much depleted by early timber-getters. Walk the easy 4-km Scenic Circuit from the Dandabah camping area, through rainforest to Pine Gorge Lookout.

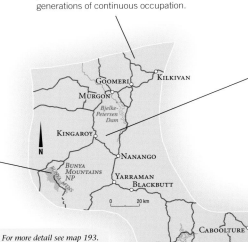

*For more detail see map 193.*

**Ipswich**

Ipswich, Queensland's oldest provincial city, was established in 1827 as a convict outstation, but soon thrived as a river port. Its early wealth and confidence is reflected in its 19th-century buildings, which include grand public edifices, several of the State's oldest churches and some impressive mansions. A self-guide walk is available.

**Brisbane Forest Park**

Few cities have on their doorstep the diverse, pristine rainforest, towering trees, cascading waterfalls, deep pools, mountain streams and incredible wildlife (pictured) offered by the Brisbane Forest Park. The small settlement of Mount Glorious is a base for forest walking tracks. Wivenhoe Lookout, 10 km further on, has superb views west to Lake Wivenhoe.

# BRISBANE ISLANDS

The calm blue waters of Moreton Bay encircle the mouth of the Brisbane River and extend along the Brisbane coastline and beyond. There are over 350 islands in this touring region, including the sizeable islands of Moreton, North Stradbroke, St Helena and Bribie. Despite some development, these islands have managed to retain an aura of wilderness, with endless white beaches, creeks, lakes, pockets of eucalpyt forest, wildflowers and wildlife. All, with the exception of St Helena, are major holiday destinations with a range of accommodation and facilities. They offer surfing, snorkelling, diving, fishing, bushwalking and scenic touring.

## TOP EVENTS

**Aug.** Fishing Classic (North Stradbroke Island, biggest fishing competition in Australia)

**Sept.** River Festival (celebrates Brisbane River and Bay area)

**Sept.** Festival in Ruins (celebrates history and ecology of St Helena Island)

**Sept.–** Festival (including mullet throwing
**Oct.** competition, Bribie Island)

## EXPERIENCE IT!

**❶ Swim** in the beautiful freshwater Blue Lake on North Stradbroke Island

**❷ Walk** to Queensland's oldest operating lighthouse (1857) at the tip of Cape Moreton

**❸ Go** crabbing in Pumicestone Channel off Bribie Island

### Bribie Island
Bribie is connected to the mainland at Caboolture by bridge. Magnificent birdlife and wildflowers are the main attractions, while fishing, boating and crabbing are popular activities. Woorim, in the south-east, is an old-fashioned resort with great surfing beaches. Nearby, Buckleys Hole Conservation Park is a good picnic spot for daytrippers, and has walking tracks to the beach and through various vegetation types.

## VISITOR INFORMATION
Brisbane Tourism
Brisbane: (07) 3006 6290
www.brisbanetourism.com.au

## FOCUS ON

### Marine life
Moreton Bay supports a marine population that includes dolphins, whales, dugongs and turtles. Visitors to Moreton Island can see dolphins at the Tangalooma Wild Dolphin Resort, where a care program has been developed, or at several spots along the western shore. Migrating humpback whales can be seen between June and November from Cape Moreton and from North Gorge Headland on North Stradbroke Island. Pumicestone Channel, between Bribie and the mainland, is a haven for turtles, dolphins and dugongs. Diving and snorkelling are available on all three islands, allowing visitors to explore the crystal waters and rich underwater life of this magnificent bay.

### CLIMATE MORETON ISLAND

|  | J | F | M | A | M | J | J | A | S | O | N | D |
|---|---|---|---|---|---|---|---|---|---|---|---|---|
| Max.°C | 33 | 32 | 32 | 32 | 31 | 30 | 30 | 31 | 32 | 34 | 35 | 34 |
| Min. °C | 23 | 23 | 23 | 21 | 19 | 18 | 17 | 16 | 18 | 20 | 21 | 23 |
| Rain mm | 326 | 331 | 287 | 115 | 22 | 10 | 8 | 4 | 5 | 17 | 65 | 198 |
| Raindays | 20 | 20 | 19 | 11 | 6 | 4 | 4 | 2 | 2 | 2 | 5 | 12 |

### Moreton Island
Almost all this large sand island is national park. Its 280-m Mt Tempest is probably the world's highest stable sandhill; on the east coast is an unbroken 36-km surf beach, with calmer beaches on the west coast (pictured). Get to the island by passenger or vehicular ferry from Scarborough or the Brisbane River. A 4WD and a permit are required for self-drive touring; or you can take a guided tour.

*For more detail see map 193.*

CABOOLTURE
BRIBIE ISLAND
❸
WOORIM
BUCKLEYS HOLE CP
Ferry
★ Cape Moreton
MORETON ISLAND
❷
SCARBOROUGH
MORETON BAY
Mt Tempest 280m
TANGALOOMA
Ferry
MORETON ISLAND NP
N
Ferry
St Helena Is
Ferry
BRISBANE
Brisbane River
MANLY
DUNWICH
North Gorge
CLEVELAND
Ferry
BLUE LAKE NP
❶ Blue Lake
NORTH STRADBROKE ISLAND

0    10 km

### St Helena Island
This low sandy island, 8 km from the mouth of the Brisbane River, was used as a prison from 1867 to 1932, during which time it was dubbed 'the hell-hole of the South Pacific'. Historic ruins remain and are protected in the island's national park. Tours of the island depart from the Brisbane suburbs of Manly and Breakfast Creek.

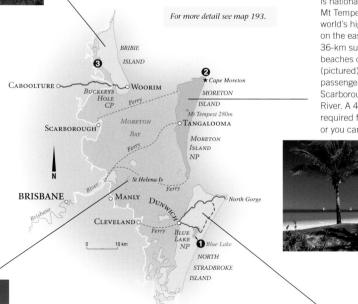

### North Stradbroke Island
'Straddie' is a coastal and bushland paradise, with contained pockets of development. Blue Lake National Park is an ecologically significant wetland; access is by 4WD or a 45-minute walk. Other island walking trails include the popular North Gorge Headland Walk. Travel to North Stradbroke by vehicular ferry from Cleveland to Dunwich, the site of a 19th-century quarantine and penal centre.

# GOLD COAST & HINTERLAND

Some 4 million visitors arrive each year to holiday along the Gold Coast's 70 km of coastline, which includes no less than 35 famously beautiful beaches stretching from South Stradbroke Island to the New South Wales border. Shopping, restaurants, nightlife, family entertainment, high-rise hotels, golf, fishing, sailing, surfing and unbelievably good weather – around 300 days of sunshine per year – are the trademark features of what has become Australia's biggest and busiest holiday destination. To the west lies the Gold Coast hinterland, another kind of world altogether. Here a superb natural landscape of tropical rainforests, unusual rock formations and cascading waterfalls – much of it protected by national park – offers visitors opportunities for such nature-based activities as bushwalking, camping, and wildlife-watching.

## CLIMATE COOLANGATTA

|         | J   | F   | M   | A   | M   | J   | J   | A   | S   | O   | N   | D   |
|---------|-----|-----|-----|-----|-----|-----|-----|-----|-----|-----|-----|-----|
| Max.°C  | 28  | 28  | 27  | 25  | 23  | 21  | 20  | 21  | 22  | 24  | 26  | 26  |
| Min. °C | 20  | 20  | 19  | 17  | 13  | 11  | 9   | 10  | 12  | 15  | 17  | 19  |
| Rain mm | 184 | 181 | 213 | 114 | 124 | 122 | 96  | 103 | 49  | 108 | 137 | 166 |
| Raindays| 14  | 15  | 16  | 14  | 10  | 9   | 7   | 9   | 9   | 11  | 11  | 13  |

## TOP EVENTS

| | |
|---|---|
| **Jan.** | New Age of Aquarius Expo (Southport) |
| **Jan.** | Australian Open Beach Volleyball (Surfers Paradise) |
| **Mar.** | Somerset Celebration of Literature (Mudgeeraba) |
| **Apr.** | Rathdowney Heritage Festival (Beaudesert) |
| **May– June** | Gold Coast Cup Outrigger Canoe Ultra Marathon (Coolangatta) |
| **June** | Wintersun Festival (Coolangatta) |
| **June** | Philippine Festival (Bundall, near Surfers Paradise) |
| **June** | Gold Coast City Marathon (Runaway Bay, near Main Beach) |
| **June** | Country and Horse Festival (Beaudesert) |
| **Aug.** | Australian Arena Polo Championships (Nerang) |
| **Aug.– Sept.** | Gold Coast Show (Southport) |
| **Sept.** | Springfest (Palm Beach) |
| **Oct.** | Gold Coast Tropicarnival (Surfers Paradise) |
| **Oct.** | Honda Indy 300 (Surfers Paradise) |
| **Nov.** | Australian Music Week (Surfers Paradise) |

## EXPERIENCE IT!

❶ **Try** your luck at the popular Conrad Jupiters Casino at Broadbeach

❷ **Learn** to water-ski at Cable Ski World, Runaway Bay

❸ **Stroll** across the treetops on the rainforest canopy walk at Green Mountains in Lamington National Park

❹ **Board** a charter to fish for mackerel, tuna, bonito and snapper, just offshore at Surfers Paradise

❺ **Take** a scenic flight from Broadbeach, aboard a Tiger Moth plane

## VISITOR INFORMATION

Gold Coast Tourism Bureau
Coolangatta: (07) 5536 7765
Surfers Paradise: (07) 5538 4419
www.goldcoasttourism.com.au

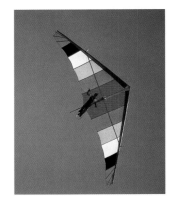

**Tamborine Mountain**
This 552-m plateau lies on the Darlington Range, a spur of the McPherson Range. It is a picturesque and popular spot for hang-gliders (pictured). Tamborine National Park comprises seventeen small areas including Witches Falls, the first national park area in the State. Visitors will also find villages full of galleries, cafes, antique stores and craft shops, and a couple of splendid gardens.

## FOCUS ON

### Theme parks and family attractions

The Gold Coast theme parks have become, since the 1980s, one of the region's most popular attractions. Warner Bros Movie World, south of Oxenford, is based on the legendary Hollywood movie set. It is a fully operational film set as well as a theme park. Nearby is Wet 'n' Wild Water World, Australia's largest aquatic park. At Coomera to the north is Dreamworld, which includes Tiger Island, the Tower of Terror and the Giant Drop. Sea World, north of Main Beach, is the region's oldest 'world', having begun in the 1950s as a water show on the Nerang River. Today it is the largest marine park in the Southern Hemisphere, offering performances by dolphins, seals, sea-lions and penguins, among others. At Surfers Paradise, Ripleys Believe it or Not Museum exhibits oddities that stretch credibility. Other attractions in the region include the David Fleay Wildlife Park at West Burleigh, Currumbin Wildlife Sanctuary and, further south, Tropical Fruit World (in NSW).

**Lamington National Park**
Part of a World Heritage area, this popular park preserves a wonderland of rainforest and volcanic ridges, criss-crossed by 160 km of walking tracks. Visitors will experience rich plant and animal life. The main picnic, camping and walking areas are at Binna Burra and Green Mountains, sites of the award-winning Binna Burra Lodge and O'Reilly's Rainforest Guest House.

**Warner Bros Movie World**
This popular theme park, south of Oxenford, offers visitors the chance to 'meet' their favourite Hollywood characters and see the business of movie-making up close. Studio tours, stunt shows and Looney Tune characters are a few of the many features. Rides include the Batman, Lethal Weapon, Wild West Adventure and the Road Runner Rollercoaster (for the toddlers).

**Golf at Sanctuary Cove**
With 40 courses, the Gold Coast is one of the Southern Hemisphere's great golfing destinations. Sanctuary Cove boasts two championship courses: the exclusive Pines, one of the toughest; and the immaculate Palms, designed around groves of cabbage palms. Pick up a golfing guide from the Gold Coast Tourism Bureau.

**South Stradbroke Island**
South Stradbroke, separated from North Stradbroke by the popular fishing channel Jumpinpin, is a peaceful alternative to the Gold Coast. Access is by launch from Runaway Bay. Cars are not permitted; visitors walk or cycle. There are two resorts, a camping ground, a range of leisure activities, and beautiful beaches.

**The Broadwater**
This calm expanse, fringed by waterfront houses and protected by the long finger of South Stradbroke Island, is popular for boating and fishing. Land-based anglers can try the breakwalls inside the Broadwater entrance. Here visitors can hire boats to explore this waterway, as well as its tributaries and the Nerang River.

*For more detail see map 193.*

**Surfers Paradise**
Surfers Paradise is the Gold Coast's signature settlement. The first big hotel was built here in the 1930s among a clutch of shacks along one of the State's most beautiful beaches. Since then the area has become an international holiday metropolis attracting every kind of visitor, from backpacker to jetsetter.

**Springbrook National Park**
Volcanic gorges and forests of 4000-year-old beech trees are among the attractions of this magnificent park on the State border. Other highlights include the spectacular Purlingbrook Falls (pictured), and Natural Bridge (in the park's remote western section), an unusual-looking rock arch spanning a mountain creek.

**Standout beaches**
The Gold Coast is a surfers' mecca. The southern beaches are the best, including Currumbin (pictured), and Kirra Point (in Coolangatta) said to have one of the 10 best breaks in the world. Greenmount Beach (also in Coolangatta) is great for families, as is Tallebudgera (north of Palm Beach), offering both estuary and ocean swimming.

# DARLING DOWNS

The Darling Downs, beginning 100 km west of Brisbane, is a huge agricultural district spread across 72 000 sq km of undulating plains, 900 m above sea level. The region's rich black volcanic soil yields grapes, oil seeds and wheat, as well as some of the country's most magnificent gardens, particularly around the large city of Toowoomba. Throughout the countryside, English-style plantings of elms, plane trees and poplars, along with lush tropical growth, fringe green pastures, neat grainfields and historic towns. National parks preserve a native landscape of eucalypt forests and granite outcrops, and provide opportunities for camping and walking.

### TOP EVENTS

**Feb.** Melon Festival (Chinchilla, odd-numbered years)

**Mar.** Cotton Week (Dalby)

**Easter** Easter in the Country (Roma)

**Apr.** National Rock Swap Festival (Warwick)

**June–Aug.** Brass Monkey Season (winter festival, Stanthorpe and Warwick)

**Sept.** Carnival of Flowers (Toowoomba)

**Oct.** Festival of the Horse (Toowoomba)

**Oct.** Granite Belt Spring Wine Festival (Stanthorpe)

**Oct.** Australia's Famous Rose and Rodeo Festival (Warwick)

### EXPERIENCE IT!

❶ **Enjoy** magnificent views of the Lockyer Valley from Toowoomba's Picnic Point

❷ **Visit** Queen Mary Falls in the southern part of Main Range National Park

❸ **Take** the Warwick City Walk Tour to see the town's historic architecture

### CLIMATE TOOWOOMBA

|          | J   | F   | M   | A  | M  | J  | J  | A  | S  | O  | N  | D   |
|----------|-----|-----|-----|----|----|----|----|----|----|----|----|-----|
| Max.°C   | 28  | 27  | 26  | 23 | 20 | 17 | 16 | 18 | 21 | 24 | 26 | 28  |
| Min. °C  | 17  | 17  | 15  | 12 | 9  | 6  | 5  | 6  | 9  | 12 | 14 | 16  |
| Rain mm  | 135 | 122 | 95  | 63 | 60 | 58 | 54 | 40 | 48 | 73 | 89 | 120 |
| Raindays | 12  | 11  | 11  | 8  | 8  | 8  | 7  | 6  | 7  | 8  | 10 | 11  |

*For more detail see map 192–3.*

### FOCUS ON

**Gardens of the Downs**
The climate and soils of the Darling Downs have created one of Australia's great gardening districts. Toowoomba has 150 public parks and gardens, including the Japanese Garden, the Wetlands of the World Park, the Scented Garden – for visually impaired people – and the 6-ha mountainside Boyce Gardens (Monday to Friday), with 700 species of trees, shrubs and perennials. Warwick is known for its roses, particularly the red 'City of Warwick', best seen in Leslie Park. There are superb private gardens throughout the region. Some open daily, some seasonally and some as part of the Open Garden Scheme; check with the information centre for details.

### Jondaryan Woolshed

This 1859 woolshed on historic Jondaryan Station, 45 km north-west of Toowoomba, is the centrepiece of a complex of old farm buildings. Blacksmithing and shearing demonstrations are held daily. The shearers' quarters is now a youth hostel, featuring iron beds and a cooking and dining area with a sawdust-covered floor.

**The Toowoomba Japanese garden**
A thousand visitors a week stroll the 3 km of paths at Ju Raku En, a Japanese garden at the University of Southern Queensland. Opened in 1989, it showcases the harmony and beauty of ancient Japanese garden design with its lake, willowy beeches, islands, bridges, stream and pavilion.

### Granite Belt wineries

Queensland's only significant wine region is on an 800-m plateau in the Great Dividing Range around Ballandean and Stanthorpe. About 28 boutique wineries, most with tastings and sales, grow major grape varieties on the well-drained granite soils, favouring soft, low-tannin reds made from shiraz and merlot grapes.

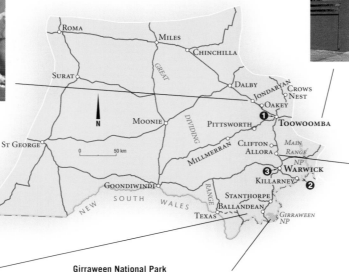

### Allora

This evocative town lies just off the highway between Toowoomba and Warwick. Victorian verandahed shopfronts and three old timber hotels line the main street. St David's Anglican Church (1888), is one of Queensland's finest timber churches. Glengallan Homestead, north of town, was built in 1867, during pastoralism's golden age.

### Girraween National Park

This 11 700-ha national park is on the edge of the New England Tableland. Granite outcrops and strangely balanced boulders sit among eucalypt forest and heath that comes alive with colour in spring. There are walking tracks, and camping and picnic facilities at Bald Rock Creek and Castle Rock.

# SUNSHINE COAST

Beautiful beaches, bathed by the blue South Pacific and fringed by native bush, stretch from Rainbow Beach southward to the tip of Bribie Island to form the Sunshine Coast. The weather is near perfect, with winter temperatures around 25°C. Well-serviced holiday towns cater to all interests from golf and fishing to fine dining and cafe-squatting. Inland lie the forested folds and ridges of the hinterland, where visitors can enjoy hillside villages, waterfalls, walks, scenic drives, superb views and a couple of trademark Queensland holiday attractions. In the south of this area, the Glass House Mountains loom above the surrounding plains.

## TOP EVENTS

**Jan.**   Ginger Flower Festival (Yandina)

**Easter**   Easter Festival (Tin Can Bay)

**Apr.**   Sunshine Coast Festival of the Sea

**June**   William Landsborough Day (Landsborough)

**Aug.**   National Country Music Muster (Gympie)

**Sept.–**   Jazz Festival
**Oct.**   (Noosa Heads)

**Oct.**   Gold Rush Festival (Gympie)

**Oct.**   Nambour Yarn Festival (Mapleton, near Nambour)

**Oct.–**   Triathlon Multi Sport Festival
**Nov.**   (Noosa Heads)

## EXPERIENCE IT!

**❶ Glide** along Noosa River in a gondola at sunset, with champagne and music

**❷ Experience** the transparent tunnel at the UnderWater World complex at Mooloolaba

**❸ Fish** for bream, flathead, whiting and dart in the surf along Rainbow Beach

### CLIMATE NAMBOUR

|  | J | F | M | A | M | J | J | A | S | O | N | D |
|---|---|---|---|---|---|---|---|---|---|---|---|---|
| **Max.°C** | 30 | 29 | 28 | 26 | 24 | 22 | 21 | 22 | 25 | 27 | 28 | 29 |
| **Min. °C** | 19 | 20 | 18 | 15 | 12 | 9 | 8 | 8 | 10 | 14 | 16 | 18 |
| **Rain mm** | 242 | 262 | 236 | 149 | 143 | 91 | 92 | 53 | 48 | 105 | 141 | 176 |
| **Raindays** | 16 | 18 | 18 | 13 | 13 | 9 | 9 | 8 | 9 | 12 | 12 | 13 |

## VISITOR INFORMATION

Caloundra: (07) 5491 0202;
1800 644 969

Cooloola area: (07) 5483 5554

Maroochydore: (07) 5479 1566;
1800 882 032

Noosa Heads: (07) 5447 4988;
1800 448 833

www.sunshinecoast.org

## FOCUS ON

### Tropical produce

The Sunshine Coast hinterland, with its subtropical climate and volcanic soils, is renowned for its produce. Nambour's Big Pineapple symbolises the importance of food as a tourist attraction in the region. Visitors can take a train, trolley and boat through a plantation growing pineapples and other fruit, macadamia nuts, spices and flowers. Yandina's Ginger Factory, the world's largest, sells ginger products including ginger ice-cream. For freshly picked local fruit and vegetables, visit the Saturday morning markets at Eumundi, north of Yandina. The Superbee Honey Factory, south of Buderim, has beekeeping demonstrations and 28 varieties of honey for tasting.

### The coloured sands of Teewah

Located in the Cooloola section of Great Sandy National Park, the coloured sands rise in 40 000-year-old, 200-m-high multicoloured cliffs. It is thought that oxidisation or the dye of vegetation decay has caused the colouring; Aboriginal legend attributes it to the slaying of a rainbow serpent.

### Mountain villages

The 70-km scenic drive here is one of Queensland's best. Starting on the Bruce Highway near Landsborough, it passes the antiques shops, B&Bs, galleries and cafes of the pretty mountain villages of Maleny, Montville, Flaxton and Mapleton, offering beautiful coastal and mountain views as well. The drive ends near the town of Nambour.

### Noosa Heads

Noosa Heads offers luxury hotels, top restaurants, hip bars and stylish boutiques. The town is flanked by ocean on one side and an estuary on the other, and is overlooked by the headland of Noosa National Park with its pandanus-fringed beaches.

*For more detail see map 193.*

### Southern coastal

The towns of Caloundra, Mooloolaba and Maroochydore make a pleasant daytrip from Brisbane, as well as being good spots for a family holiday. The area offers patrolled surfing beaches, protected lakes and rivers for boating and fishing, holiday flats and caravan parks, boat hire, and a range of child-friendly attractions.

### Glass House Mountains

These 20-million-year-old crags, the giant cores of extinct volcanoes, mark the southern entrance to the Sunshine Coast. Glasshouse Mountains Road leads to sealed and unsealed drives through the mountains, with some spectacular lookouts along the way. There are walking trails, picnic grounds and challenges aplenty for rock-climbers.

# FRASER ISLAND & COAST

This region has two of Queenland's signature attractions: Hervey Bay, a large resort town with the best whale-watching in Australia, and offshore, the nature-based holiday destination of Fraser Island. Offering spectacular white beaches and coloured sand cliffs, and dunes, creeks, lakes, wildflower heathland and rainforest, Fraser is reached by vehicular barge from Hervey Bay or Rainbow Beach further south; a 4WD is essential. Hervey Bay offers a range of accommodation and other facilities, Fraser a narrower choice. The heritage town of Maryborough and the calm waters of Great Sandy Strait are among the region's other attractions.

## TOP EVENTS

**Feb.**   Yagubi Festival (multicultural festival, Hervey Bay)

**Easter** Amateur Fishing Classic (Burrum Heads)

**Apr.**   Gladstone–Hervey Bay Blue Water Classic (Hervey Bay)

**May**    Best of Brass (Maryborough)

**Aug.**   Whale Festival (Hervey Bay)

**Sept.**  Heritage City Festival (Maryborough)

**Oct.**   Masters Games (Maryborough)

**Oct.**   Seafood Festival (Hervey Bay)

## EXPERIENCE IT!

**❶ Visit** the Thursday heritage market in Maryborough

**❷ Catch** the July–October run of tailor on the northern half of Fraser Island's Seventy Five Mile Beach

**❸ Swim** in the dazzling sand-bottomed Lake McKenzie on Fraser Island

### CLIMATE MARYBOROUGH

|          | J   | F   | M   | A  | M  | J  | J  | A  | S  | O  | N  | D   |
|----------|-----|-----|-----|----|----|----|----|----|----|----|----|-----|
| Max.°C   | 31  | 30  | 29  | 27 | 25 | 22 | 22 | 23 | 26 | 28 | 29 | 31  |
| Min. °C  | 21  | 21  | 19  | 17 | 13 | 10 | 9  | 9  | 12 | 15 | 18 | 20  |
| Rain mm  | 166 | 173 | 159 | 90 | 80 | 67 | 54 | 40 | 43 | 75 | 85 | 128 |
| Raindays | 13  | 14  | 14  | 12 | 11 | 8  | 7  | 6  | 6  | 8  | 9  | 11  |

## VISITOR INFORMATION

Hervey Bay: (07) 4124 4050; 1800 811 728

Maryborough: (07) 4121 4111

www.frasercoast.org

## FOCUS ON

### Fraser Island

World Heritage-listed in 1992, this is the world's largest sand island, covering 184 000 ha. It has dunes that reach 240 m in height, and about 40 dune lakes, approximately half the number in the world. Fraser supports an extraordinary diversity in rainforest, wildflower heath, mangroves, 350 bird species and a large population of dingoes, said to be the purest strain in Australia. The island was home to the Badtjala Aboriginal people for some 5000 years, during which time it was known as K'gari. The *Stirling Castle* was wrecked here 1836, and Europeans named the island after Eliza Fraser, the captain's wife.

### Hervey Bay

This once sleepy settlement is now a booming resort town of over 43 000 people. The bay itself is a large, calm body of water warmed by tropical currents. The area's protected beaches are perfect for family swimming. Other popular activities include sailing, diving, windsurfing, fishing, kayaking and skydiving.

### Whale-watching

Each year around 2000 humpback whales migrate from the Antarctic to Australia's eastern subtropical coast. On their return, between August and October, up to 400 rest and regroup in Hervey Bay. For an up-close view, visitors can take a whale tour from Urangan Boat Harbour.

### Great Sandy Strait

This narrow strait between the mainland and Fraser Island makes for good boating; houseboats and other vessels are for hire. Drop into the Kingfisher Bay Resort and Village on Fraser Island. Look out for dugongs, the world's only plant-eating marine mammals, and fish in the estuary of Mary River, around River Heads.

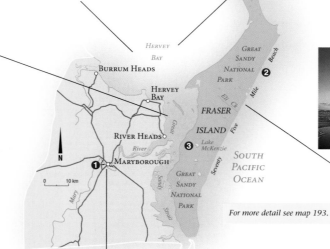

For more detail see map 193.

### Fraser Island's east coast

Fraser Island's surf coast takes in the beautiful Seventy Five Mile Beach; The Cathedrals, 15-m sheer cliffs composed of different coloured sands; the wreck of the *Maheno* (pictured), a trans-Tasman luxury liner; and Eli Creek, a freshwater creek filtered through the dunes, where visitors can float beneath the pandanus trees.

### Maryborough Heritage Walk and Drive

A European settlement since 1847, Maryborough is one of Queensland's oldest and best-preserved provincial cities. A self-guide brochure leads visitors through tree-lined streets past heritage sites and well-restored Queenslander-style houses, and along the historic streetscape of Wharf Street (pictured).

# GREAT BARRIER REEF

The reef is Australia's most prized and visited natural destination. Extending over 2000 km along the coast of Queensland, this breathtakingly beautiful marine environment features tropical islands, aquamarine waters, rare and brilliantly coloured corals, sea grass beds, fish, sea-going mammals and birds. It is considered to be one of the world's great destinations for diving, sailing and a large number of other activities including fishing, swimming, walking, windsurfing, kayaking and even horseriding. Only 22 of the reef's 900 islands cater for tourists. Some islands support large resorts with every level of accommodation, whilst others are completely protected by national park and offer camping only. Day trips from the mainland are a popular way of seeing the reef for those with limited time.

## VISITOR INFORMATION

Great Barrier Reef Central
Reservations Office
Milton: (07) 3876 4644
www.great-barrier-reef.com

**Southern Reef Islands**
Bundaberg: (07) 4152 9289
www.bdtdb.com.au

Gladstone: (07) 4972 4000
www.gladstoneregion.org.au

Rockhampton: (07) 4922 5339

**Whitsunday Islands**
Proserpine: (07) 4946 6673;
1800 801 252
www.whitsundayinformation.com.au

**Tropical North Islands**
Cairns: (07) 4051 3588
www.tnq.org.au

**Queensland National Parks and
Wildlife Service offices**
Airlie Beach: (07) 4946 7022
Cairns: (07) 4053 4533
Gladstone: (07) 4971 6500
Ingham: (07) 4077 2822
www.env.qld.gov.au

## ISLAND ACCESS

### TROPICAL NORTH ISLANDS

**MAGNETIC ISLAND**  *8 km NE of Townsville*
From Townsville, by vehicular ferry, catamaran or water taxi.

**ORPHEUS ISLAND**  *80 km N of Townsville*
From Townsville or Cairns, by sea plane.

**HINCHINBROOK ISLAND**  *5 km E of Cardwell*
From Cardwell, by launch.

**BEDARRA ISLAND**  *35 km NE of Cardwell*
From Dunk Island, by launch.

**DUNK ISLAND**  *5 km SE of Mission Beach*
From Cairns, by plane. From Clump Point near Mission Beach, by launch. From Wongaling Beach and South Mission Beach, by water taxi.

**FITZROY ISLAND**  *30 km SE of Cairns*
From Cairns, by catamaran.

**GREEN ISLAND**  *27 km NE of Cairns*
From Cairns, by catamaran, sea plane or helicopter.

**LIZARD ISLAND**  *93 km NE of Cooktown*
From Cairns or Cooktown, by plane or sea plane.

### WHITSUNDAY ISLANDS

**BRAMPTON ISLAND**  *32 km NE of Mackay*
From Mackay, by light plane or launch, or from Hamilton Island by plane.

**LINDEMAN ISLAND**  *67 km N of Mackay*
From Airlie Beach or Shute Harbour, by light plane or boat. From Mackay by plane, or Hamilton Island by boat or plane.

**HAMILTON ISLAND**  *16 km SE of Shute Harbour*
Direct flight from Sydney, Brisbane and Melbourne; connections to all major cities. From Shute Harbour, Whitsunday Coast, by launch.

**LONG ISLAND**  *9 km from Shute Harbour*
From Shute Harbour or Hamilton Island, by launch or helicopter. From Whitsunday Airport by sea plane.

**SOUTH MOLLE ISLAND**  *8 km from Shute Harbour*
From Shute Harbour, Whitsunday coast or Hamilton Island, by launch.

**DAYDREAM ISLAND**  *5 km from Shute Harbour*
From Shute Harbour or Hamilton Island, by launch or helicopter.

**WHITSUNDAY ISLAND**  *25 km E of Shute Harbour*
From Shute Harbour or Able Point Marina, Airlie Beach, by boat.

**HOOK ISLAND**  *20 km NE of Shute Harbour*
From Shute Harbour or Able Point Marina, Airlie Beach, by launch.

**HAYMAN ISLAND**  *25 km NE of Shute Harbour*
Direct flight to Hamilton Island from Sydney and Brisbane (connections to all major cities), then by launch to Hayman Island. From Airlie Beach, by water taxi.

### SOUTHERN REEF ISLANDS

**LADY ELLIOT ISLAND**  *80 km NE of Bundaberg*
From Bundaberg or Hervey Bay, by plane.

**LADY MUSGRAVE ISLAND**  *105 km N of Bundaberg*
From Bundaberg, by sea plane, catamaran or trimaran. From Seventeen Seventy, by catamaran.

**HERON ISLAND**  *72 km NE of Gladstone*
From Gladstone, by catamaran or charter helicopter.

**NORTH WEST ISLAND**  *75 km NE of Gladstone*
From Gladstone, by charter boat.

**GREAT KEPPEL ISLAND**  *48 km NE of Rockhampton*
From Rockhampton, by light plane. From Yeppoon by launch.

*For more detail see maps 193, 195 & 197.*

COOKTOWN

TROPICAL NORTH ISLANDS

CAIRNS

TOWNSVILLE
SHUTE HARBOUR          WHITSUNDAY ISLANDS

MACKAY

SOUTHERN REEF ISLANDS

ROCKHAMPTON
GLADSTONE
BUNDABERG

# TROPICAL NORTH ISLANDS

**CLIMATE FITZROY ISLAND**

|          | J  | F  | M  | A  | M  | J   | J   | A   | S   | O  | N  | D  |
|----------|----|----|----|----|----|-----|-----|-----|-----|----|----|----|
| Max. °C  | 31 | 30 | 29 | 28 | 26 | 24  | 24  | 25  | 27  | 29 | 30 | 31 |
| Min. °C  | 12 | 12 | 10 | 8  | 7  | 5   | 4   | 5   | 6   | 7  | 9  | 10 |
| Rain (mm)| 27 | 25 | 31 | 60 | 89 | 100 | 106 | 103 | 86  | 68 | 40 | 35 |
| Raindays | 6  | 5  | 7  | 11 | 15 | 18  | 17  | 18  | 15  | 13 | 9  | 7  |

## Lizard Island
Game-fishing, excellent reef surrounds, snorkelling and diving, and national park walks. Small, luxurious resort with bungalow-style lodgings (max. 80 people) or camping (max. 20 people); camping permits from Cairns parks office.

## Fitzroy Island
Low-key destination with national park, white coral beaches and magnificent flora and fauna. Bushwalking, diving and snorkelling. Hostel-style and cabin accommodation (max. 160 people) and camping (max. 60 people).

## Green Island
True coral cay covered with thick tropical vegetation. Glass-bottomed boats for reef viewing and underwater observatory. Popular day-trip destination with small resort (max. 90 people).

## Bedarra Island
Island of untouched tropical beauty, off-limits to day visitors and children under 15. Bushwalking, snorkelling, fishing, swimming, windsurfing, sailing and tennis. Exclusive resort (max. 30 people).

## Dunk Island
National park with walking tracks through rainforest and prolific birdlife, butterflies and wild orchids. Parasailing, water-skiing, sailing, clay target shooting and horseriding. Resort accommodation (max. 360 people) and camping (max. 30 people).

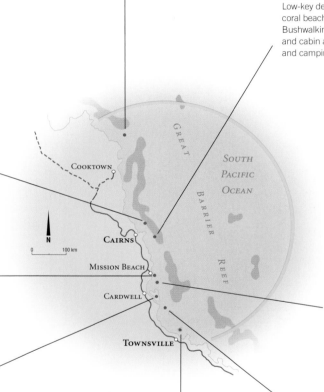

## Hinchinbrook Island
National park with wonderland of mountains, tropical vegetation, waterfalls and sandy beaches. Snorkelling, swimming, fishing and bushwalking. Small, low-key resort (max. 45 people).

## Orpheus Island
Small island surrounded by coral reefs and protected by national park. Birdwatching, water sports, glass-bottomed boats, island walks and fishing. 5-star resort (max. 74 people) or bush camping (max. 54 people); camping permits from Ingham parks office.

## Magnetic Island
National park and beautiful beaches. Horseriding, bushwalking, snorkelling, parasailing, swimming, fishing, sea kayaking and reef excursions. Permanent population and range of accommodation from budget to deluxe.

# WHITSUNDAY ISLANDS

**CLIMATE HAMILTON ISLAND**

| | J | F | M | A | M | J | J | A | S | O | N | D |
|---|---|---|---|---|---|---|---|---|---|---|---|---|
| Max. °C | 30 | 30 | 29 | 27 | 25 | 23 | 22 | 23 | 25 | 28 | 29 | 30 |
| Min. °C | 25 | 25 | 24 | 23 | 21 | 19 | 18 | 18 | 20 | 22 | 23 | 24 |
| Rain (mm) | 13 | 322 | 262 | 242 | 159 | 100 | 80 | 59 | 23 | 52 | 89 | 215 |
| Raindays | 15 | 18 | 19 | 19 | 18 | 12 | 10 | 11 | 7 | 8 | 8 | 13 |

**Daydream Island**
Small island of volcanic rock, coral and dense tropical foliage. 'Kids Club', tennis, outdoor cinema, water sports centre, snorkelling, diving and reef and island trips. Luxurious resort (max. 900 people).

**Long Island**
Part of Conway National Park. Walking tracks leading to scenic lookouts. Water sports, fishing and resort activities. Three resorts: Club Crocodile (max. 400 people), Palm Bay (max. 60 people) and Whitsunday Wilderness Lodge (max. 16 people).

**Brampton Island**
National park, wildlife sanctuary and fine golden beaches. Snorkelling trail, bushwalking, sea-plane trips and water-sports. Resort-style accommodation (max. 280 people).

**Hayman Island**
Close to the outer reef. Fishing, sightseeing trips, scenic flights, diving, water sports, 'Kids Club' and whale-watching excursions. Luxury resort (max. 450 people).

**Hook Island**
Small low-key wilderness resort with cabins and campsites (max. 140 people). Snorkelling, scuba diving, fishing, reef trips, coral submarine trips and fish-feeding.

**South Molle Island**
Small, lightly timbered island. Numerous inlets and splendid views of Whitsunday Passage. Golf, bushwalking, snorkelling, scuba diving, windsurfing and sailing. Medium-size resort (max. 520 people).

**Whitsunday Island**
Entire island is uninhabited national park. Beautiful 7-km white silica beach and complex mangrove system. Camping only (max. 40 people); details from Airlie Beach parks office.

**Hamilton Island**
Large island with wide range of facilities and activities. Shops, marina and fauna park. Windsurfing, sailing, fishing, scuba diving, parasailing, helicopter rides, tennis, squash, and reef and inter-island trips. Resort (max. 1500 people).

**Lindeman Island**
Secluded beaches, national park, and prolific birds and butterflies. Golf course, full range of water sports and other island activities. Club Med resort (max. 460 people).

SHUTE HARBOUR
AIRLIE BEACH

MACKAY

N

0   100 km

# SOUTHERN REEF ISLANDS

**CLIMATE LADY ELLIOT ISLAND**

| | J | F | M | A | M | J | J | A | S | O | N | D |
|---|---|---|---|---|---|---|---|---|---|---|---|---|
| Max. °C | 29 | 29 | 28 | 27 | 24 | 22 | 21 | 22 | 24 | 25 | 27 | 28 |
| Min. °C | 24 | 24 | 23 | 22 | 20 | 18 | 17 | 17 | 19 | 20 | 22 | 23 |
| Rain (mm) | 27 | 174 | 133 | 106 | 120 | 93 | 99 | 58 | 38 | 59 | 71 | 86 |
| Raindays | 13 | 15 | 15 | 15 | 15 | 12 | 10 | 9 | 8 | 9 | 8 | 10 |

**North West Island**
Second largest coral cay on reef. Superb bird- and turtle-watching opportunities. Camping only (max. 150 people); permit details from Gladstone parks office.

**Heron Island**
Small coral cay, entirely national park. Turtle-nesting site, birdwatching and prolific flora. Diving, snorkelling, reef and ecology walks. Resort-style accommodation (max. 250 people).

**Great Keppel Island**
White, sandy beaches and unspoiled tropical island scenery. Tennis, water-skiing, diving, snorkelling, fishing, sea kayaking, golf, parasailing, coral viewing and island cruises. 'Kids Club' during holidays. Camping, cabins and lodge-style accommodation (max. 650 people).

**Lady Musgrave Island**
Coral cay with navigable lagoon. Glass-bottomed boats, floating pontoon, semi-submersible submarine, prolific birdlife and turtle-nesting site. Camping only (max. 50 people); permit details from Gladstone parks office.

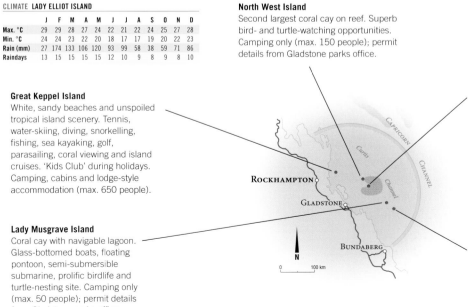

ROCKHAMPTON

GLADSTONE

CAPRICORN CHANNEL

Curtis Channel

CHANNEL

BUNDABERG

N

0   100 km

**Lady Elliot Island**
Small coral cay with 19 major dive areas. Bird rookeries, turtle-nesting site and whale-watching opportunities. Low-key resort (max. 140 people), ranging from budget to island suites.

# CAPRICORN

Spanning the Tropic of Capricorn, this highly productive region combines mining, industry, agriculture and cattle-raising with tourism. Offshore lie the southernmost islands of the Great Barrier Reef. The coastline is relatively untouched by commercial development. Remote beaches and river estuaries with unspoilt coastal bushland are found in the national parks of the Discovery Coast south of Gladstone. Inland, the eroded sandstone plateaus of the Great Dividing Range rise abruptly from the plains, most notably in the Carnarvon and Blackdown Tableland national parks. Most of Queensland's coal exports come from open-cut mines around Blackwater. Mining also occurs in gemfields west of Emerald. The area has three big towns: Bundaberg is a centre for sugarcane, subtropical fruits and vegetables; Gladstone is a major port and industrial centre; and Rockhampton is a cattle town, servicing properties in the Fitzroy River valley and to the west.

## EXPERIENCE IT!

❶ *Visit* the Aboriginal Dreamtime Cultural Centre, north of Rockhampton, and learn about the Darumbal people, the original inhabitants of the Fitzroy River area

❷ *Savour* a mud crab sandwich at Miriam Vale's Shell Roadhouse

❸ *Watch* crocodiles feeding and baby crocs hatching at the Koorana Crocodile Farm, Keppel Sands

❹ *Canoe*, fish, ski, sail or swim in the vast, calm Lake Awoonga

❺ *See* the 25-million-year-old Mystery Craters, north-east of Gin Gin

## VISITOR INFORMATION

Bundaberg: (07) 4152 9289;
1800 060 499
www.bdtdb.com.au

Gladstone: (07) 4972 4000
www.gladstoneregion.org.au

Rockhampton: (07) 4922 5339
www.rockhampton-qld.gov.au

### The gemfields

Some of the world's richest sapphire fields are found around the tiny, ramshackle settlements of Anakie, Sapphire, Rubyvale and Willows Gemfields, some 50 km west of Emerald. The same area yields zircons, amethysts, rubies and topaz. Fossicking licences can be bought on the gemfields for a small fee. If you don't find what you're after, the area also has plenty of gemstone outlets.

### Blackdown Tableland National Park

This undulating 800-m high sandstone plateau of open forest, heath, waterfalls and gorges lies 50 km south-east of Blackwater. There is a camping ground at Mimosa Creek, a gorge with swimming holes at Rainbow Falls, and a number of scenic trails. Visit Sunset Lookout for superb sunrise and sunset views.

## CLIMATE ROCKHAMPTON

| | J | F | M | A | M | J | J | A | S | O | N | D |
|---|---|---|---|---|---|---|---|---|---|---|---|---|
| Max.°C | 32 | 31 | 30 | 29 | 26 | 23 | 23 | 25 | 27 | 30 | 31 | 32 |
| Min. °C | 22 | 22 | 21 | 18 | 14 | 11 | 9 | 11 | 14 | 17 | 19 | 21 |
| Rain mm | 136 | 141 | 103 | 47 | 52 | 35 | 31 | 29 | 24 | 48 | 68 | 105 |
| Raindays | 11 | 12 | 10 | 7 | 7 | 5 | 5 | 4 | 4 | 7 | 8 | 10 |

## FOCUS ON

### Discovery Coast

Seventeen Seventy, a small town on a narrow, hilly peninsula above an estuary, was named to mark Captain Cook's landing at Bustard Bay on 24 May 1770. The main access is from Miriam Vale on the Bruce Highway (about 60 km on a partly sealed road). Today's visitors come for the views from the headland north across the bay, and for fishing, mud crabbing and boating. Agnes Water, a few kilometres south, has Queensland's northernmost surfing beach; rolling surf and a balmy climate attract visitors all year round. Eurimbula National Park, just across Round Hill Inlet from Seventeen Seventy, has dunes, mangroves, salt marshes and eucalypt forests. From Agnes Water an 8-km track south to Deepwater National Park is suitable for 4WD vehicles only. The long beaches of this park, broken by the estuaries of freshwater creeks, form a breeding ground for loggerhead turtles.

### Carnarvon National Park

The towering sandstone cliffs rise abruptly from the plain in Carnarvon National Park, 250 km south of Emerald. The Art Gallery and Cathedral Cave, major Aboriginal art sites, contain countless stencils and engravings. The signature attraction is Carnarvon Gorge, a twisting sandstone chasm with lush eucalypt forest. Camping (pre-book with the ranger), cabins and tours are all available.

### Mount Morgan

This goldmining town south of Rockhampton has hardly changed in a century. Take the town heritage tour, or visit the goldmines and the caves excavated for brick clay. The cemetery, containing graves of Chinese workers and other nationals, tells the town's history, as do the Railway Station and the Historical Museum.

## Australia's beef capital

Over two million cattle graze in the Fitzroy River valley and the lovely country west of Rockhampton (pictured). The town has many heritage buildings, a good regional art gallery and historic botanic gardens. Large numbers of barramundi are found in the Fitzroy River, often in the section close to town.

## Capricorn Coast

Thirteen beaches stretch out along Keppel Bay, taking in Yeppoon (pictured), Emu Park and Keppel Sands. Picturesque bays are framed by rocky headlands, pockets of rainforest, peaceful estuarine waters and wetlands – some of the natural features that have helped make sunny Capricorn Coast a popular resort area.

## TOP EVENTS

| | |
|---|---|
| **Easter** | Harbour Festival (Gladstone, includes finish of Brisbane–Gladstone Yacht Race) |
| **May** | Seventeen Seventy Commemorative Festival (Gladstone) |
| **June** | Country and Western Muster (Biloela) |
| **June** | Orange Festival (Gayndah, odd-numbered years) |
| **June** | Rocky Rush Rodeo (Rockhampton) |
| **July** | Multicultural Food and Wine Festival (Childers) |
| **Aug.** | Gemfest (Emerald) |
| **Sept.** | Music Spectacular (Emerald) |
| **Sept.** | Pineapple Festival (Yeppoon) |
| **Sept.** | Bundy in Bloom Festival (Bundaberg) |
| **Oct.** | Octoberfest (Yeppoon) |
| **Oct.** | Seafood Festival (Gladstone) |
| **Oct.** | Barra Bounty (Rockhampton) |
| **Dec.** | Summer Solstice Light Spectacular (Rockhampton) |
| **Dec.– Jan.** | Bent Wing Bat Flight Emergence (Rockhampton) |

## Industrial powerhouse

Gladstone has Queensland's biggest power station, the world's largest alumina plant (pictured) and aluminium refinery, Australia's biggest cement plant and Queensland's largest multi-cargo port. Tours of the major industries are available. The town is built around a magnificent deep-water harbour, which, despite the industry, retains much of its natural beauty.

*For more detail see maps 192–3 & 194–5.*

RUBYVALE
SAPPHIRE    EMERALD
WILLOWS    ANAKIE    BLACKWATER
GEMFIELDS
ROCKHAMPTON
TROPIC    OF
YEPPOON
Gt Keppel Is
EMU PARK
KEPPEL SANDS
CAPRICORN
GREAT BARRIER REEF
Fitzroy R.
BLACKDOWN
TABLELAND
NP
Dawson
MOUNT
MORGAN
GLADSTONE
GREAT
CARNARVON
NATIONAL
PARK
BILOELA
Lake Awoonga
EURIMBULA NP
Bustard Bay
SEVENTEEN SEVENTY
AGNES WATER
DEEPWATER NP
MIRIAM
VALE
THEODORE
EXPEDITION
NATIONAL
PARK
MONTO
GIN GIN
MON REPOS CP
BUNDABERG
CHILDERS
DIVIDING
TAROOM
Burnett River
MUNDUBBERA
GAYNDAH
BIGGENDEN
RANGE
0    50 km
N

## Mon Repos turtle rookery

Mon Repos Conservation Park, 15 km north-east of Bundaberg, is one of Australia's most important turtle rookeries. Sea turtles lay eggs in the sand from November to January and the young emerge and make for the sea from mid-January to March. In season there is an on-site interpretative centre and supervised viewing.

## Rum town

On the southern coast of the Capricorn region is Bundaberg, home of 'Bundy' rum. The rum distillery (pictured) runs daily tours. In the Botanical Gardens are the Hinkler House Memorial and Fairymead House Sugar museums, and steam train rides on Sundays. Around the town are sugar plantations, avocado orchards and market gardens.

# THE MID-TROPICS

Gold, cattle and sugar spearheaded the settlement of this area and established the towns of Mackay and Townsville in the 1860s. Today cattle and sugar remain key industries. Much of the coast – stretches of sandy shoreline, warm tropical waters, bush-covered headlands and large pockets of rainforest – remains intact despite development, and the district provides a great holiday alternative to some of Queensland's busier coastal areas. Accessible from several coastal points is the Great Barrier Reef and its islands. Inland, on the edge of the Outback, are a couple of the State's best-preserved historic towns.

## TOP EVENTS

| | |
|---|---|
| *Jan.* | Goldfield Ashes Cricket Carnival (Charters Towers) |
| *Mar.* | Greek Festival (Townsville) |
| *May* | Australian–Italian Festival (Ingham) |
| *May* | Country Music Festival (Charters Towers) |
| *July* | Australian Festival of Chamber Music (Townsville) |
| *July* | Troy Dunn International Bull Riding (Mackay) |
| *July* | Camp Draft (Nebo, near Mackay) |
| *Aug.* | Sarina Annual (Agricultural Show, Sarina) |
| *Aug.* | Gold Festival (Clermont) |

## EXPERIENCE IT!

❶ **Tour** the Fairleigh Sugar Mill near Mackay, July–October

❷ **Swim**, saunter and savour the atmosphere at The Strand waterfront development, Townsville

❸ **Dive** to the wreck of the SS *Yongala*, 16 km off Cape Bowling Green

### Marine attractions
At Reef HQ in Townsville, touch-tanks and underwater viewing-tunnels reveal some of the Great Barrier Reef's ecological mysteries. Next door, the Museum of Tropical Queensland features a full-scale reproduction of the bow of the HMS *Pandora* (pictured), a British vessel wrecked on the reef in 1791.

## VISITOR INFORMATION
Mackay: (07) 4952 2677
www.mackayregion.com
Townsville: (07) 4721 3660;
1800 801 902.
www.townsvilleonline.com.au

## FOCUS ON

### Heritage
This region preserves some interesting pockets of heritage. Ravenswood, east of Charters Towers, is now almost a ghost town. It flourished in the second half of the 19th century as a centre for the surrounding goldfields and many of its buildings from this period are in a near-original state. West of Mackay is Greenmount Historic Homestead – now a museum – built in 1915 on the Cook family's grazing property. Bowen, established in the 1860s, is North Queensland's oldest town. History here is recorded in 22 murals detailing the stories, personalities and events of the town.

### CLIMATE MACKAY

| | J | F | M | A | M | J | J | A | S | O | N | D |
|---|---|---|---|---|---|---|---|---|---|---|---|---|
| Max.°C | 30 | 29 | 28 | 27 | 24 | 22 | 21 | 22 | 25 | 27 | 29 | 30 |
| Min. °C | 23 | 23 | 22 | 20 | 17 | 14 | 13 | 14 | 16 | 20 | 22 | 23 |
| Rain mm | 293 | 311 | 303 | 134 | 104 | 59 | 47 | 30 | 15 | 38 | 87 | 175 |
| Raindays | 16 | 17 | 17 | 15 | 13 | 7 | 7 | 6 | 5 | 7 | 9 | 12 |

### Wallaman Falls
In Lumholz National Park, part of the Wet Tropics World Heritage area, Wallaman Falls has a 305-m sheer drop, the longest in Australia. Most of the park, named for a 19th-century Norwegian explorer, is trackless wilderness. The 1-hour drive from Ingham is mostly on unsealed road. Camp near the falls.

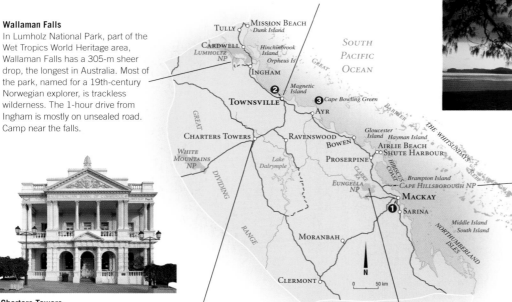

*For more detail see maps 194–5 & 197.*

### Cape Hillsborough and the Hibiscus Coast
Steep rainforest-clad hills plunge to rocky headlands linked by white sandy beaches in this lovely and surprisingly peaceful district north of Mackay. Wildlife, walking trails and camping are among the features of Cape Hillsborough National Park.

### Charters Towers
Charters Towers was Queensland's second largest city during the 1870s gold rush; then, it was known as 'The World' because of its size and cosmopolitan population. Today it is a showpiece of the original, with many beautifully preserved buildings including the Bank of Commerce (pictured), now restored as the New World Theatre Complex. The surrounding cattle country provides a scenic backdrop to this major settlement.

### Eungella National Park
This national park, spanning the Clarke Ranges, preserves 50 000 ha of rainforest, gorges, clear pools and tumbling falls. Much of the park remains wilderness, accessible only to experienced walkers. There are easier walking tracks around Broken River and Fern Flat in the south-west, and limited camping at Fern Flat.

# THE FAR NORTH

The Far North is a region of ancient rainforest, remote islands and a coastline that fronts the world's most spectacular reef. National parks, some of which are part of the World Heritage Wet Tropics, protect the superb beauty and natural value of the landscape and offer extensive opportunities for camping, fishing, walking and 4WD touring. Cape York is a vast undeveloped region with a population of just 10 000. On the west coast lie the frontier mining town of Weipa and several Aboriginal communities. At the northern tip, via often impassable roads, is the town of Bamaga, and beyond, the Torres Strait Islands. Some of the country's finest Aboriginal rock art is found near Laura, and the region generally is richly inscribed with the heritage of its original occupants. To the south, the coast between Innisfail and Mossman is the Riviera of tropical Australia. The 'capital' of the tropics, Cairns, is a major destination for tourists from around the world.

Daintree National Park

## TOP EVENTS

| | |
|---|---|
| *May* | *Village Carnivale (Port Douglas)* |
| *May* | *Races, Concert and Rodeo (Chillagoe)* |
| *May* | *Folk Festival (Kuranda)* |
| *June* | *Endeavour Festival (Cooktown)* |
| *June* | *Yuletide (Yungaburra)* |
| *July* | *Jazz Festival (Yungaburra)* |
| *July* | *Agricultural Show (Cairns)* |
| *July* | *Polocrosse Carnival (Cooktown)* |
| *July* | *Harvest Festival (Innisfail)* |
| *July* | *Laura–Cape York Aboriginal Dance Festival (Cooktown, odd-numbered years)* |
| *July* | *Rodeo (Mareeba)* |
| *Sept.* | *Air Show (Mareeba)* |
| *Oct.* | *Reef Festival and Hook, Wine and Sinker Festival (Cairns)* |
| *Oct.* | *Country Music Festival (Mareeba)* |
| *Oct.* | *Folk Festival (Yungaburra)* |

## VISITOR INFORMATION

Tourism Tropical North Queensland
Cairns: (07) 4051 3588
www.tnq.org.au

Cotton trees are found along this coast, and flower for most of the year

## FOCUS ON

### Tropical rainforests

The World Heritage Wet Tropics area covers 894 000 ha along the eastern escarpment of the Great Dividing Range between Townsville and Cooktown, and features rainforest, mountains, gorges, fast-flowing rivers and numerous waterfalls. The rainforest here is one of the most biologically diverse and ancient environments on Earth. It represents the major stages in Earth's evolutionary history and has the world's greatest concentration of primitive flowering plants or 'green dinosaurs', as they are known. Australia's largest area of rainforest wilderness is in the Daintree River valley just north of Mossman. At Cape Tribulation two World Heritage areas come together: rainforest and reef along the coast. Queensland's tropical rainforests can be seen on short walks, or on hikes lasting days; on sealed roads or 4WD treks along rutted tracks that cross creek fords; from scenic railways and cableways; and by boat or raft on forest rivers.

Whitewater rafting on the Tully River

## EXPERIENCE IT!

❶ *Ride* a raft on the white water of the Tully River (via Tully in The Mid-Tropics touring region), which descends from the Atherton Tableland through rainforest gorges

❷ *Marvel* at The Boulders (west of Babinda), rounded by fast-flowing river waters

❸ *Climb* Mount Bartle Frere, Queensland's highest mountain, on a 12-hour walk through Wooroonooran National Park

❹ *Enjoy* more than 200 species of palms at the Flecker Botanic Gardens in Cairns, established in 1886

❺ *Shop* for arts, crafts, fashions and food at the Kuranda country markets, the largest in the region

### CLIMATE CAIRNS

| | J | F | M | A | M | J | J | A | S | O | N | D |
|---|---|---|---|---|---|---|---|---|---|---|---|---|
| Max.°C | 31 | 31 | 30 | 29 | 28 | 26 | 26 | 27 | 28 | 29 | 31 | 31 |
| Min. °C | 24 | 24 | 23 | 22 | 20 | 18 | 17 | 18 | 19 | 21 | 22 | 23 |
| Rain mm | 413 | 435 | 442 | 191 | 94 | 49 | 28 | 27 | 36 | 38 | 90 | 175 |
| Raindays | 18 | 19 | 20 | 17 | 14 | 10 | 9 | 8 | 8 | 8 | 10 | 13 |

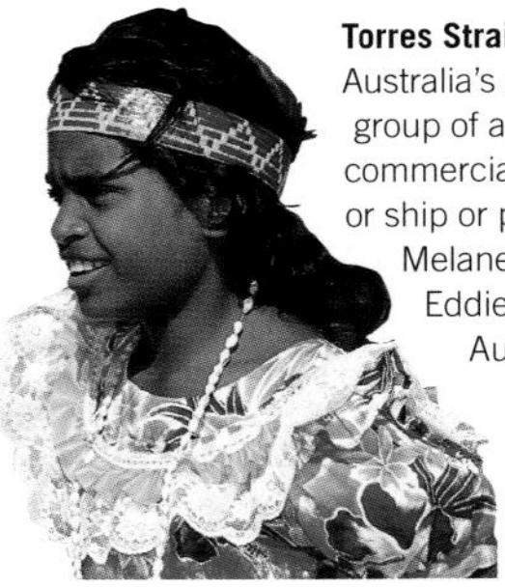

**Torres Strait Islands**
Australia's only non-Aboriginal indigenous people come from this group of around 100 islands off the northern tip of Cape York. The commercial centre is Thursday Island, reached by ferry from Seisia, or ship or plane from Cairns. The Torres Strait Islander people are of Melanesian descent and include among their number the late Eddie Mabo, famous for his successful 1992 land claim in Australia's High Court.

**Weipa**
The world's largest bauxite deposits are found around Weipa on the west coast of Cape York. In 1961 Comalco built a modern mining town with all facilities on the site of an Aboriginal mission station and reserve. The company offers tours of its mining operations. The fishing in the rivers and the waters of the Gulf is excellent.

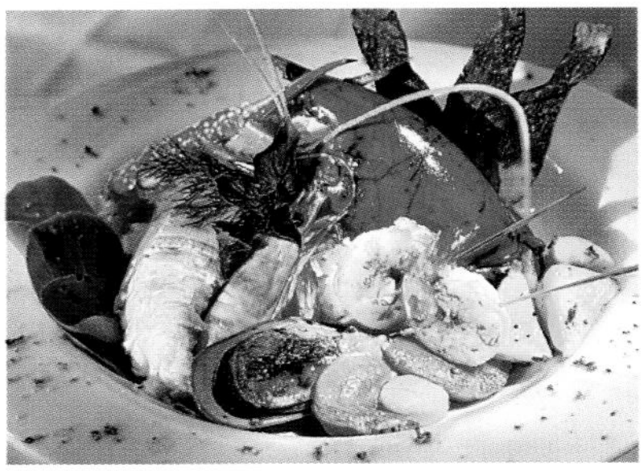

**Tropical cuisine**
A menu at a restaurant in the exclusive holiday town of Port Douglas might offer Gulf bug tempura skewered on lemongrass accompanied by a Tableland salad of greens, mango slices, coconut slivers and wasabi mayonnaise, and with a tropical-fruit ice-cream for dessert. Chefs trained in the culinary styles of the east and west are using the abundant local produce to create a true regional cuisine.

*For more detail see maps 196–7 & 198.*

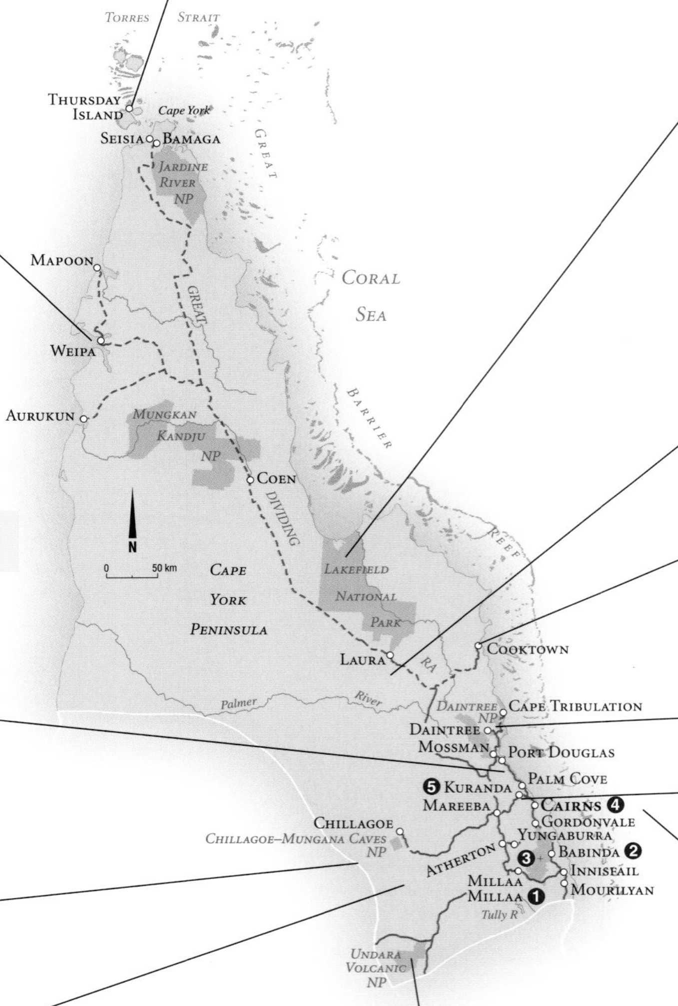
Torres Strait
Thursday Island
Cape York
Seisia
Bamaga
Jardine River NP
Great Barrier Reef
Coral Sea
Mapoon
Weipa
Great Dividing Range
Aurukun
Mungkan Kandju NP
Coen
N
0 50 km
Cape York Peninsula
Lakefield National Park
Laura
Cooktown
Palmer River
Daintree NP
Cape Tribulation
Daintree
Mossman
Port Douglas
Palm Cove
5 Kuranda
Mareeba
Cairns 4
Gordonvale
Yungaburra
Chillagoe
Chillagoe–Mungana Caves NP
Atherton
3
Babinda 2
Innisfail
Mourilyan
Millaa Millaa 1
Tully R
Undara Volcanic NP

**Chillagoe Caves**
This outstanding cave system is in a limestone belt extending north to the Palmer River. Vine thickets, towering above-ground structures, bat colonies and richly decorative stalactites and stalagmites create an unforgettable natural environment. There are regular tours of some caves, and visitors can wander through others without a guide.

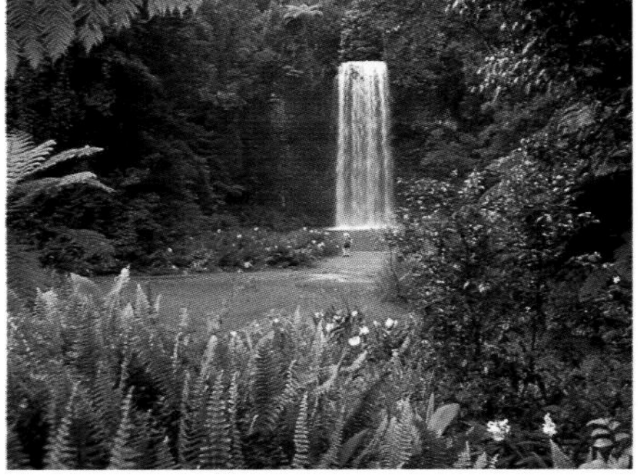

**Atherton Tableland**
This 900-m-high tableland south-west of Cairns is a productive farming district, thanks to its high rainfall and rich volcanic soil. The historic town of Yungaburra is listed with the National Trust. Nearby is the remarkable Curtain Fig Tree, a strangler fig that has subsumed its host, sending down a curtain of roots. Volcanic lakes and spectacular waterfalls, including Millaa Millaa Falls (pictured) and Zillie Falls, are among the other scenic attractions.

**Undara Lava Tubes**
These lava tubes are set in a beautiful national park expanse of savannah woodland and fringed with pockets of rainforest. Formed 190 000 years ago, Undara (an Aboriginal word for 'long') includes a 160-km lava tunnel, the longest on Earth. Accommodation, including camping, is available at Lava Lodge, also the starting point for tours of the area.

### Lakefield National Park

Lakefield is Queensland's second-largest national park. A near-wilderness of grassland, woodland, swamp and mangroves is cut by three major rivers and their tributaries. Access for conventional vehicles is via the township of Laura (during the Dry). Camping areas are at Hann and Kalpowar crossings. Visit the Old Laura Homestead, fish for barramundi and watch the wildlife.

### Aboriginal rock art

The Split Rock and Gu Gu Yalangi rock-art sites, south of Laura, are a sample of what the Laura and Cooktown region has to offer, namely one of the largest collections of prehistoric rock art in the world. The most distinctive works are the Quinkan figures, stick-like figures representing spirits that might emerge suddenly from rock crevices. Tours are available through the local Ang-Gnarra community.

### Cooktown

Captain Cook beached the *Endeavour* near the site of Cooktown in 1770. The town was built a century later when gold was discovered on the Palmer River to the south-west. Cooktown has botanic gardens dating from the 1880s, two museums, and a cemetery with hundreds of Chinese graves. Cruises along the river and out to the reef to experience the amazing marine life are available.

### Daintree National Park

The Mossman Gorge section of this World Heritage park takes visitors into the rainforest's green shady heart via an easy 2.7-km walk to the Mossman River. The Cape Tribulation section is a rich mix of coastal rainforest, mangroves, swamp and heath. There is camping at Noah Beach. From here, walking trails lead to spectacular reef and rainforest scenery.

### Scenic routes to Kuranda

Kuranda, an Aboriginal word for 'village in the rainforest', can be reached from Cairns via a couple of spectacularly scenic routes. A 19th-century steam-train carries visitors 34 km up steep slopes, through rainforest, along Barron Gorge and past Barron Falls. The Skyrail Rainforest Cableway (pictured) is a gondola cableway, passing through and above the rainforest canopy.

### Cairns

Cairns, located on the edge of two extraordinary natural environments, the reef and the rainforest, is an ideal base for activities ranging from big-game fishing to diving, walking and 4WD touring. A casino (pictured), five-star hotels, excellent restaurants and pulsating nightclubs cater for the most sophisticated travellers, while cafes, backpacker lodges and a lively atmosphere attract the backpacker crowd.

# OUTBACK & GULF COUNTRY

This is a remote, sparsely populated and – in parts – stunningly beautiful region extending west from the slopes of the Great Dividing Range. In the north, savannah grasslands give way to the lagoons and mangrove-lined estuaries of the Gulf of Carpentaria coastline. From the north to the centre, the low rise of fossil-strewn landforms punctuate the vastness of the surrounding plains. In the Channel Country of the south-west, dry waterholes and salt pans dominate the landscape, except when floodwaters from the north bring brilliant life to the country in the form of native flowers and grasses and flocks of birds. Many of the stories and legends of Australia's pioneering days were born here, and the themes of mateship, egalitarianism and a fair go are celebrated in the region's museums and monuments. Distances are vast and temperatures extreme: those intending to travel beyond sealed roads should plan their trips with care.

### CLIMATE NORMANTON

|         | J   | F   | M   | A  | M  | J  | J  | A  | S  | O  | N  | D   |
|---------|-----|-----|-----|----|----|----|----|----|----|----|----|-----|
| Max.°C  | 35  | 34  | 34  | 34 | 32 | 29 | 29 | 31 | 34 | 36 | 37 | 36  |
| Min. °C | 25  | 25  | 24  | 22 | 19 | 16 | 15 | 17 | 20 | 23 | 25 | 25  |
| Rain mm | 260 | 249 | 158 | 31 | 8  | 9  | 3  | 2  | 3  | 10 | 44 | 143 |
| Raindays| 14  | 14  | 9   | 2  | 1  | 1  | 1  | 0  | 0  | 1  | 4  | 9   |

## FOCUS ON

### Fishing the Gulf

The Gulf is one of Australia's true fishing frontiers. Anglers can fish the rivers – the Nicholson, Albert, Flinders, Norman and Gilbert – the coastal beaches, and the offshore waters and reefs of the Gulf via island resorts. Karumba, on the Norman River estuary, is a popular base for both river and offshore anglers. Sweers Island, in the Wellesley group, has a fishing resort offering access to thousands of hectares of reef where coral trout, parrotfish, sweetlip and sea perch (and in winter, pelagics such as mackerel and tuna) are plentiful. Mornington Island is home to the Birri Fishing Resort, offering crabbing, and sport and bottom fishing, all with professional masters. You can also stay at Escott Barramundi Lodge, on the Nicholson River, via Burketown. Fishing charters take you along the nearby lagoons and rivers, where you can catch barramundi, catfish and mangrove jack.

## EXPERIENCE IT!

**❶** *Drop* in on Minmi, Australia's best-preserved dinosaur, at Kronosaurus Korner Fossil Centre in Richmond

**❷** *Visit* the Burke and Wills Cairn, site of the explorers' most northerly camp, on the Normanton–Burketown Road

**❸** *Travel* from Boulia by 4WD to see billabongs, coolibahs and waterbirds in Diamantina National Park

**❹** *Experience* the Gulf country's birdlife, aboard a river cruise via Karumba

**❺** *Trace* the history of Australia's famous medical service at the Royal Flying Doctor Service Museum in Cloncurry

### Riversleigh fossil fields

The fossils in this World Heritage-listed part of Lawn Hill National Park record the evolution of mammals over 20 million years as the vegetation changed from rainforest to semi-arid grassland. Tours run from Mount Isa, where there is an interpretive centre featuring displays of local fossil discoveries (pictured), and Adels Grove near the park entrance.

## VISITOR INFORMATION

Gulf Savannah Tourist Organisation
Cairns: (07) 4031 1631
www.gulf-savannah.com.au

The Outback Queensland
Tourism Authority
Mount Isa: (07) 4743 7966
www.outbackholidays.tq.com.au

### Lawn Hill National Park

Lawn Hill Gorge, about 205 km from Burketown, is this remote park's main attraction. The gorge area protects an oasis of lush rainforest. Canoeing, swimming and walking are the main activities and there are two accessible Aboriginal art sites. Campsite bookings should be made 6 to 8 weeks ahead.

### Mount Isa

This is Queensland's largest inland town. The mine, dating from 1924 and with 4600 km of tunnels, produces lead, silver, copper and zinc. Take a 3-hour hard-hat mine tour (adults only), inspect the National Trust-owned early-settler tent house, or visit the Riversleigh Fossils Centre and Mount Isa Tourist Information.

### Channel Country

Monsoon rains in the tropical north flood the hundreds of inland river channels that meander through Queensland's south-west corner. Here cattle graze on huge semi-desert pastoral holdings. Spectacular red sandhills (pictured) are found in the area, particularly in Simpson Desert National Park in the far west beyond Birdsville, Queensland's most isolated settlement.

**Tourist train**
Every Wednesday the *Gulflander* leaves Normanton for the 153-km journey through the Gulf to the historic goldmining town of Croydon. With stops at points of interest along the line, the trip takes 4 hours. Travellers can explore Croydon with a local guide and return to Normanton on Thursday.

## TOP EVENTS

*May* Gregory River Canoe Races (Gregory, near Burketown)

*May* Dirt and Dust Triathlon (Julia Creek)

*May* Outback Muster and Drovers Reunion (Longreach)

*June* Waltzing Matilda Festival (Winton)

*July* Black Stump Camel Races (Blackall)

*July* Drovers Reunion Festival (Camooweal)

*July* Great Matilda Camel Races and Festival (Charleville)

*July* Desert Sands Camel Race and Festival (Boulia)

*Aug.* 'Surf' Carnival (inland Iron Man contest, Kynuna)

*Aug.* Isa Rodeo (Mount Isa)

*Aug.* World Lizard Races (Cunnamulla)

*Aug.* World Lizard Races (Eulo)

*Sept.* Outback Festival (Winton, odd-numbered years)

*Sept.* Birdsville Races (Birdsville)

*Oct.* Lake Moondarra Fishing Classic (Mount Isa)

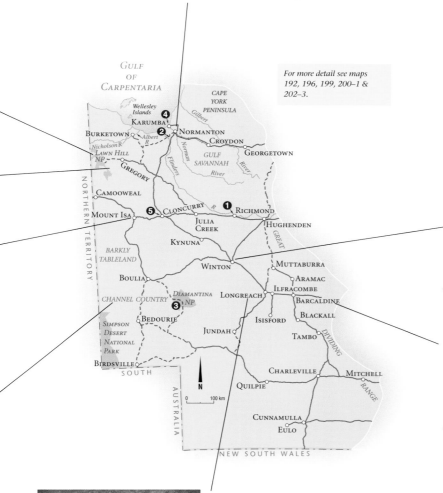

For more detail see maps 192, 196, 199, 200–1 & 202–3.

**Waltzing Matilda country**
Winton, the railhead town for sheep and cattle from the Channel Country, is the birthplace of 'Waltzing Matilda', Australia's favourite ballad. The song was penned at nearby Dagworth Station by bush poet Banjo Paterson and performed in the area in 1895. Winton's Waltzing Matilda Centre charts the song's history.

**Barcaldine**
The 'Garden City of the West' was the first Australian town to tap the waters of the Great Artesian Basin, an event commemorated by the town's giant windmill. The Australian Workers Heritage Centre recollects the 1891 shearers' strike and the Australian Workers Party, forerunner of the Australian Labor Party.

**Australian Stockman's Hall of Fame**
This impressive institution is just east of Longreach on the Matilda Highway. Imaginative displays show the development of white settlement in the Outback, including the contribution of women and Aboriginal people. Don't miss the nearby Qantas Founders Outback Museum, which tells the story of the English-speaking world's oldest airline.

# TASMANIA

Tasmania's beauty has won more hearts than it can claim square kilometres. The main island offers a multitude of attractions in an area that is a mere 296 kilometres north to south and 315 kilometres east to west. Hobart, Australia's second oldest and most southerly city, is situated on the broad estuary of the River Derwent under the spell of majestic Mount Wellington.

## Wild and rustic

In recent times, Tasmania has become known as one of the world's great wilderness destinations. The south-west and a section of the Central Plateau form one Tasmanian Wilderness World Heritage Area. This is landscape of dolomite mountains, glacial lakes, trackless rainforest and ancient Aboriginal art sites. The north-west, parts of the east coast, the Bass Strait islands, and areas around Hobart, including Bruny Island, are renowned for their wild coastal beauty.

Different, but equally attractive, is Tasmania's rural scenery. A decentralised population, good rainfall, short distances and a strong agricultural economy have translated into the establishment of numerous small rural settlements laid out in a pattern more European than Australian. Georgian and Victorian villages, freestone cottages, hedges, bridges, fields of hops and poppies and neatly tended orchards and vineyards dominate the Midlands south of Launceston, and the Derwent and Huon valleys north-west and south of Hobart respectively.

## The locals

Tasmania's population of 471 900 is the smallest of the Australian States. Overseas immigration to Tasmania has, for economic reasons, always been low, contributing only 0.05 per cent to its population increase in recent years. Tasmania has fewer residents born overseas than other States and so is less ethnically and culturally diverse.

Aboriginal people (Palawa) migrated to Tasmania about 35 000 years ago. There were up to 10 000 Aboriginal people on the island on the eve of white settlement. Divided into nine groups, they moved from place to place with the seasonal changes in the supply of shellfish, seals, birds, marsupials, and fruit and nuts.

The 1996 census counted 13 873 Aboriginal and Torres Strait Islander people in Tasmania. Many claim descent from the Palawa women who were kidnapped by sealers or who formed unions with settlers and convicts in remote districts. Tasmania's indigenous people are trying to strengthen their identity through language and cultural projects, and through land management assisted by the return of 12 significant sites under legislation passed in 1995.

## A dark past

Abel Tasman sighted and named Van Diemen's Land in 1642. French and British explorers followed from 1772. In 1803 the British, concerned at growing French interest in Van Diemen's Land, established a settlement on the River Derwent. The colony soon acquired a reputation for violence and lawlessness, plagued by escaped convicts. The reputation of the colony was particularly bad when it came to the treatment of the Palawa people.

White settlers drove the Palawa from their hunting grounds. Following the Black War of the 1820s, the government rounded up the few survivors and sent them to Flinders Island. After 13 years, only 47 of the original 133 sent there had survived, with most succumbing to disease and despair. The remaining few were later transfered to Oyster Bay near Hobart, where the last of the group, Truganini, died in 1876.

For fifty years Van Diemen's Land was a penal colony, and an infamously brutal one at that. Despite this, some semblance of normal society took root: houses were built, communities born, and whaling, sealing, shipbuilding and wool-growing industries established.

In 1825 Van Diemen's Land was separated from New South Wales and given its own nominated Legislative Council. A campaign by prominent residents resulted in no more convicts being sent to the colony after 1852. In 1856 the British government changed the colony's name to Tasmania and elections were held for a Legislative Assembly and Legislative Council. Unlike the other States, Tasmanian elections are now based on the Hare-Clark system. The present Labor government, elected in 1998, is the first in 16 years to command a Lower House majority.

## Niche markets

Two-thirds of Tasmania is too rugged and wet for farming or grazing; however, agriculture occupies 2 100 000 hectares of land in the north, Midlands and south-east. Unable to compete with the large-scale farming of the mainland, Tasmania has developed boutique agricultural and aqua-cultural industries producing high-quality gourmet fare. Cool-climate wines, lobster, abalone, oysters and Tasmanian salmon, apples, berries and other fruit, and quality dairy products are now being exported beyond Australia. Many visitors to Tasmania come to eat and drink their way around the island.

Tourism is Tasmania's fastest growing industry, with over half a million visitors now arriving each year. Tasmania is a niche rather than a mass tourist destination. It offers clean air and water, a choice of accessible or remote wilderness, beaches, historic sites and villages, quality food, distinctive cool-climate wines, and numerous fishing opportunities.

Tasmania's busy holiday period is December to March and bookings should be made well in advance. Travel options include a heavily subsided car ferry from Melbourne or the fly/drive packages, which are popular with travellers from further afield.

Early colonial building on Maria Island

For more information on Tasmania, see Tourist Bureaus, opposite page 236.

# HOBART

Hobart, Australia's second oldest and most southerly city, is situated on the broad estuary of the River Derwent under the spell of majestic Mount Wellington. A strong maritime flavour and sense of the past give Hobart an almost European air. This feeling is heightened in winter, when daytime temperatures drop to a crisp average 12 degrees Celsius. However, the city also has a strong Australian feel, surrounded as it is by bushland and boasting prime examples of distinctive colonial architecture.

**VISITOR INFORMATION**
**Tasmanian Travel and Information Centre**
Cnr Elizabeth and Davey sts, Hobart
(03) 6230 8233
www.discovertasmania.com.au

## CITY CENTRE

See map on page 215.

**Anglesea Barracks** 215 E9
The oldest military establishment in Australia, dating back to 1846, with beautiful Georgian buildings; guided tours on Tuesday mornings.

**Antarctic Adventure** 215 G9
Explore the world's most isolated continent; exhibits range from a blizzard simulator ride to evocative accounts of explorers and researchers.

**Battery Point** 215 G9
Former mariners' village; tearooms, restaurants and an antique shop around every corner.

**Constitution Dock** 215 G7
Historic hub of Hobart's busy waterfront; buy fresh seafood on the dock.

**Maritime Museum of Tasmania** 215 G7
Treasure chest of seafaring relics from when Hobart was a famous sea-port.

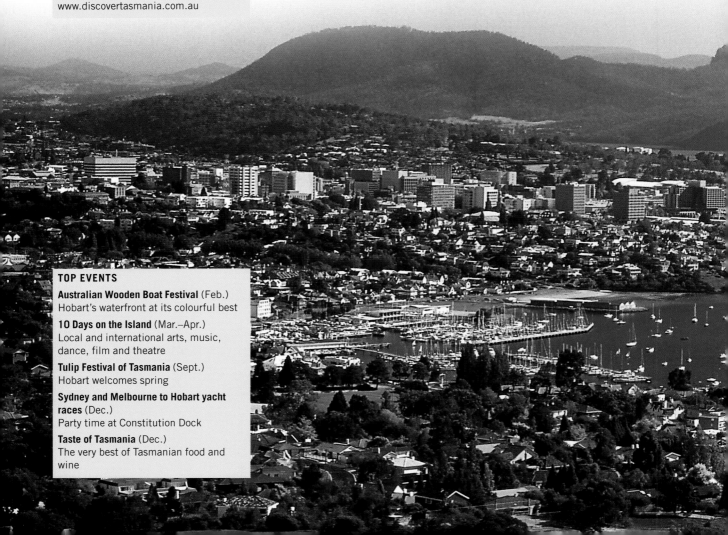

**TOP EVENTS**
**Australian Wooden Boat Festival** (Feb.)
Hobart's waterfront at its colourful best

**10 Days on the Island** (Mar.–Apr.)
Local and international arts, music, dance, film and theatre

**Tulip Festival of Tasmania** (Sept.)
Hobart welcomes spring

**Sydney and Melbourne to Hobart yacht races** (Dec.)
Party time at Constitution Dock

**Taste of Tasmania** (Dec.)
The very best of Tasmanian food and wine

**Parliament House** 215 F8
Originally a customs house designed by John Lee Archer and constructed by convicts in the late 1830s; visitors may inspect the restored Legislative Council Chamber.

**Penitentiary Chapel & Historic Site** 215 F6
View the tunnels, courtrooms and solitary confinement cells; ghost tours operate most evenings.

**Royal Tasmanian Botanical Gardens** 215 G2
The State's horticultural jewel, contained within convict-built walls; includes the Botanical Discovery Centre, which houses an Interpretation Gallery, a Plant House and a restaurant.

**St Davids Park** 215 F8
A good place to rest; Hobart's first colonial burial ground was here with gravestones dating back to 1804.

**Salamanca Place** 215 G8
Setting for the bustling Saturday market; historic 1830s warehouses now house quality arts and crafts, cafes and restaurants.

**Tasmanian Museum and Art Gallery** 215 G7
Notable for its magnificent colonial landscape paintings, Aboriginal history and the convict experience.

**Theatre Royal** 215 F6
Australia's oldest theatre still in operation.

**Van Diemen's Land Memorial Folk Museum (Narryna)** 215 F9
Colonial collection in historic townhouse.

## SUBURBS AND SURROUNDS

See map on page 134.

**Cadbury Schweppes Chocolate Factory** 134 F3
A chocolate-lover's dream come true; tours on weekdays and free samples.

**Cascade Brewery** 134 F5
Set in the foothills of Mount Wellington and over 150 years old; offers tours on weekdays.

**D'Entrecasteaux Channel** 134 D13
A leisurely drive from Hobart along the coastline of this stunning deep-blue channel takes you through tiny towns and boutique produce farms.

**Derwent Valley** 134 A2
Neat agricultural landscapes, rolling hills and historic buildings.

**Mount Wellington** 134 E5
Superb views of the D'Entrecasteaux Channel and the Derwent Valley, 1270 m above the city.

**Richmond** 134 H2
Probably Australia's best preserved Georgian Colonial village; boasts the country's oldest bridge, built by convicts in the 1820s; the local gaol pre-dates Port Arthur.

**Runnymede** 134 F4
National Trust Georgian-style house with lovely gardens.

**Tudor Court Model Village** 134 G6
Fascinating model of a Tudor Village: traditional thatched cottages, shingled shops, manor house, windmill and other period houses along with minute gardens and inhabitants dressed in historic costume.

**GETTING AROUND**
Traffic flows freely throughout Hobart; however, be warned that many of the streets are one way. Metered street parking is readily available and the Council operates several carparks at modest rates. Metro Tasmania operates a bus service that runs frequently during business hours, with a limited evening/weekend timetable. Walking is the best way to appreciate the rich history of the city centre, waterfront and Battery Point. Ferries and cruise boats leave regularly from Franklin Wharf and Brooke Street Pier at Sullivans Cove. During summer, sailing vessels run charter tours as far afield as Port Arthur and Bruny Island. There are also a number of coach tours, including a daily tour of the city and suburbs.

**Airport shuttle bus**
Tasmania's Own Redline Coach Services
1300 360 000

**Motoring organisation**
RACT 13 11 11

**Public transport**
Metro Tasmania 13 22 01

**Taxis**
City Cabs 13 10 08
Taxi Combined 13 22 27

**River Derwent cruises**
The Cruise Company (03) 6234 9294
Captain Fells Ferries (03) 6223 5893

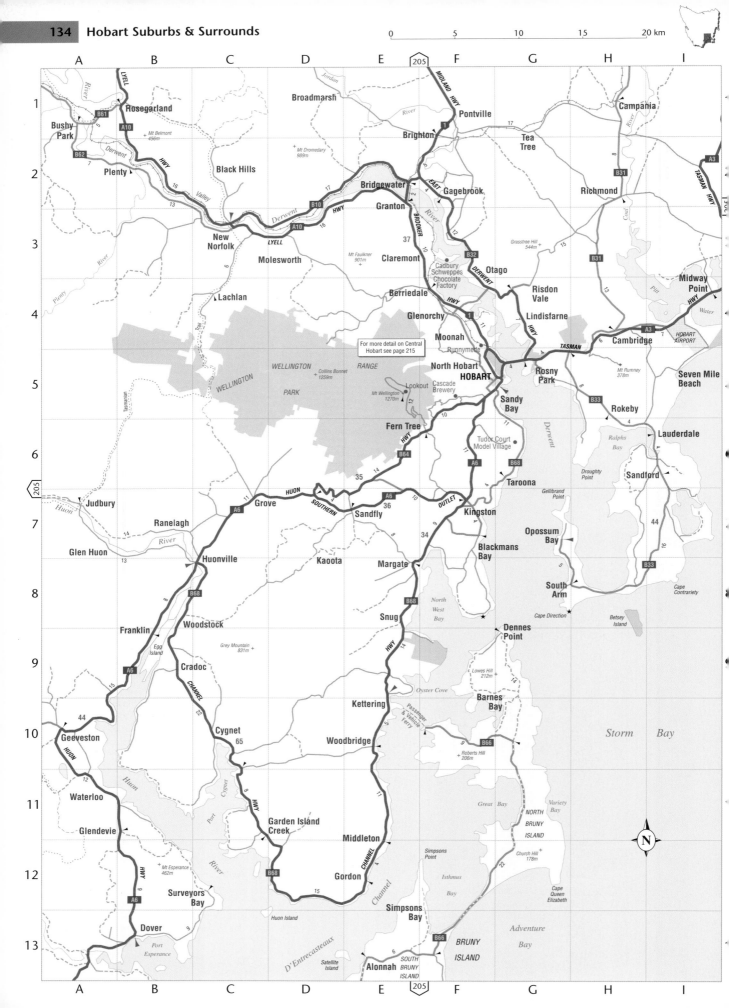

0    5    10    15    20 km

**A    B    C    D    E    F    G    H    I**

**1**

River

LYELL HWY

**B61**

Rosegarland

**A10**

Bushy Park

+ Mt Belmont 456m

Broadmarsh

River

Pontville

Campania

**205**

MIDLAND HWY

Tea Tree

**1**

Brighton

**B62**

Derwent

7

**2**

Plenty

HWY

16

Black Hills

+ Mt Dromedary 989m

Bridgewater

EAST

Gagebrook

Richmond

**B31**

**A3**

13

Valley

17

Granton

2

4

**B10**

HWY

BROOKER

12

TASMAN HWY

**3**

River

LYELL

16

New Norfolk

**A10**

Molesworth

37

Claremont

+ Mt Faulkner 901m

10

Cadbury Schweppes Chocolate Factory

**B32**

DERWENT

Otago

Grasstree Hill 544m +

15

**B31**

13

Midway Point

HWY

**4**

Plenty

Lachlan

Tall

Berriedale

HWY

Risdon Vale

Lindisfarne

6

Cambridge

**A3**

7

HOBART AIRPORT

Water

Glenorchy

**1**

11

TASMAN

Mt Rumney 378m +

**5**

WELLINGTON

Collins Bonnet 1259m +

RANGE

For more detail on Central Hobart see page 215

Moonah

Runnymede

North Hobart

**HOBART**

4

Rosny Park

Seven Mile Beach

WELLINGTON PARK

Mt Wellington 1270m +

Lookout

12

Cascade Brewery

10

Sandy Bay

**A6**

11

**B68**

Derwent

Ralphs Bay

Rokeby

**B33**

4

Lauderdale

**6**

**205**

Fern Tree

HWY

**B64**

14

35

Tudor Court Model Village

11

Droughty Point

Gellibrand Point

Sandford

**7**

Judbury

Huon

**A6**

11

Grove

HUON

SOUTHERN

4

36

**A6**

Sandfly

10

OUTLET

4

Taroona

**B68**

Kingston

Opossum Bay

44

**B33**

16

Ranelagh

River

14

Kaoota

34

Blackmans Bay

5

**7**

Glen Huon

13

Huonville

Margate

South Arm

**8**

**B68**

8

Woodstock

Grey Mountain 831m +

Egg Island

North West Bay

Snug

**B68**

Cape Direction

Dennes Point

Betsey Island

Cape Contrariety

Franklin

**9**

**A6**

15

Cradoc

CHANNEL

22

HWY

14

Oyster Cove

Passenger & Vehicle Ferry

Lowes Hill 212m +

Barnes Bay

14

**10**

Geeveston

44

HUON

Cygnet

65

CHANNEL

8

Woodbridge

Kettering

5

9

**B66**

Roberts Hill 206m +

Storm    Bay

Waterloo

12

**11**

Port

Cygnet

HWY

11

Garden Island Creek

Great Bay

NORTH BRUNY ISLAND

Variety Bay

Glendevie

Huon

River

Middleton

CHANNEL

Church Hill 178m +

22

**12**

HWY

9

**A6**

+ Mt Esperance 462m

**B68**

Gordon

15

4

Simpsons Point

Isthmus Bay

Cape Queen Elizabeth

Surveyors Bay

Dover

9

Huon Island

Simpsons Bay

**B66**

BRUNY ISLAND

Adventure Bay

**13**

Port Esperance

D'Entrecasteaux

Satellite Island

Alonnah

**205**

6

SOUTH BRUNY ISLAND

N

**A    B    C    D    E    F    G    H    I**

# SOUTH-WEST WILDERNESS

Tasmania's south-west is one of the planet's great wildernesses, an almost uninhabited landscape of fretted mountains, glacial lakes, majestic rivers, waterfalls, gorges, virgin temperate rainforest and 1000-year-old trees. In the valleys and along the coast are rock-art galleries and middens, representing some of Earth's best-preserved Ice Age sites. The region attracts nature lovers and adventurers from far afield. The Franklin River is one of the world's great whitewater destinations, and the network of wilderness tracks challenge the most experienced walkers. For the less adventurous there are shorter day walks, and guided extended walks on the coast.

## TOP EVENTS

**Jan.** Mount Lyell Picnic (Strahan)
**Mar.** Piners' Festival (Strahan)
**Oct.** Robert Sticht Festival (Queenstown)

## EXPERIENCE IT!

**❶ Go** fishing or horseriding along the 36-km Ocean Beach near Strahan, Tasmania's longest beach

**❷ Board** Queenstown's chairlift for views across the extraordinary surrounding landscape

**❸ Take** a self-guide tour of National Trust-classified Zeehan, once a large mining town

### CLIMATE STRATHGORDON

|  | J | F | M | A | M | J | J | A | S | O | N | D |
|---|---|---|---|---|---|---|---|---|---|---|---|---|
| Max. °C | 19 | 20 | 17 | 14 | 12 | 9 | 9 | 10 | 12 | 13 | 16 | 17 |
| Min. °C | 10 | 10 | 9 | 7 | 5 | 4 | 3 | 3 | 4 | 5 | 7 | 8 |
| Rain mm | 150 | 114 | 150 | 214 | 247 | 203 | 270 | 278 | 261 | 247 | 191 | 195 |
| Raindays | 17 | 14 | 18 | 21 | 22 | 21 | 25 | 25 | 24 | 23 | 20 | 20 |

### The Wilderness Railway
One of Tasmania's most recent tourist attractions is a restored 1896 rack-and-pinion railway, which travels a scenic 35 km across rivers and through forests. The journey begins at Queenstown, known for its landscape of bare multicoloured hills and gullies, and finishes at Strahan.

## VISITOR INFORMATION
Strahan: (03) 6471 7622
www.strahan.tco.asn.au

## FOCUS ON

### Preserving the wilderness
The 1972 flooding of Lake Pedder for the Gordon River hydro-electric scheme sparked a campaign to preserve the south-west wilderness from further inroads. Despite the region's 1982 World Heritage listing, the Tasmanian government pressed on. Conservationists blockaded a proposed dam site from December 1982 until the election of a new Federal Labor government in March 1983. Arrests and clashes with police made headlines and earned the movement support from mainstream Australia. Finally, Federal legislation to stop the project survived a High Court challenge. The historical and ecological significance of the south-west wilderness is imaginatively presented at Strahan Visitors Centre.

### Franklin–Gordon Wild Rivers National Park
One way to visit this grand wilderness is by boat from Strahan. Cruises run up the Gordon to Heritage Landing, where there is a short walk to a 2000-year-old Huon pine, a species unique to Tasmania. Guided rafting trips south along the Franklin River begin near Lyell Highway.

### Strathgordon and hydro-electricity
Strathgordon is the place to see Tasmania's massive hydro-electricity industry at work. Sights along Gordon River Road include the huge lakes Pedder and Gordon; Gordon Dam; and the underground Gordon Power Station, the biggest in Australia. Bushwalkers can enter Southwest National Park (pictured) via the Creepy Crawly Nature Trail.

### Macquarie Harbour and Strahan
Strahan (pictured) is a charming holiday town offering a huge range of outdoor activities. Originally a timber-milling town, today Strahan has a population of artists and craftspeople. Macquarie Harbour is best explored by boat; stop off at Sarah Island, which once housed the most intractable of the colony's convicts.

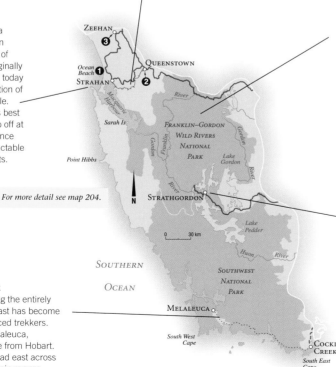

*For more detail see map 204.*

### The South Coast Track
This 10-day walk along the entirely uninhabited south coast has become a mecca for experienced trekkers. The walk starts at Melaleuca, reached by light plane from Hobart. From here walkers head east across a landscape of mountain ranges, rivers, swampy plains and wild beaches to reach Cockle Creek.

# THE NORTH-WEST

This region is a delight for bushwalkers as well as for more traditional holiday-makers. Along the north coast, a scenic road intersected by regional centres and holiday villages skirts the mountains that meet the waters of Bass Strait. The undulating country near the coast is a patchwork of farms producing vegetables, dairy products, honey and flowers. Further south are the dolomite peaks and still lakes of Cradle Mountain–Lake St Clair National Park, a World Heritage Area. On the west coast, the Arthur and Pieman rivers tumble through gorges and rainforest to a coastline of rolling breakers, dangerous headlands and rich Aboriginal sites.

## TOP EVENTS

| | |
|---|---|
| Feb. | Grande Fiesta Ng Filipino (Latrobe) |
| Feb. | Miners and Axemen Festival (Rosebery) |
| Feb. | Tasmazia Lavender Harvest Festival (near Sheffield) |
| Mar. | Taste the Harvest (Devonport) |
| Mar. | Splash of Colour Festival (Penguin) |
| Mar. | Ripcurl West Coast Classic (near Marrawah) |
| Mar. | Norwest Country Music Awards (Burnie) |
| July | North West Festival of Fire (Burnie) |
| Oct. | Taste of Ulverstone |

## EXPERIENCE IT!

**❶ See** rock engravings at Tiagarra Aboriginal Centre on Devonport's Mersey Bluff

**❷ Cruise** the Pieman River from Corinna

**❸ Taste** Mount Roland Cheese in Latrobe

## VISITOR INFORMATION

Burnie: (03) 6434 6111
Devonport: (03) 6424 4466
www.devonport.tco.asn.au/tourist.htm

## FOCUS ON

### Wilderness walks

An unforgettable way of seeing the lakes, tarns, buttongrass heaths, wildflowers, woodland and rainforest of Tasmanian alpine wilderness is by walking the 85-km Overland Track, one of Australia's most awe-inspiring treks. It runs the length of Cradle Mountain–Lake St Clair National Park and passes Mount Ossa, Tasmania's highest mountain. Each year about 5000 people attempt the 5 to 8-day walk. There are 12 unattended huts for overnight stays. These quickly fill up; be prepared to camp. In the park's northern half are shorter trail options, all of them through majestic landscapes. Summer is the best walking season in this area.

### CLIMATE WARATAH

| | J | F | M | A | M | J | J | A | S | O | N | D |
|---|---|---|---|---|---|---|---|---|---|---|---|---|
| Max. °C | 17 | 18 | 16 | 12 | 10 | 8 | 7 | 8 | 10 | 12 | 14 | 16 |
| Min. °C | 6 | 7 | 6 | 4 | 3 | 1 | 1 | 1 | 2 | 3 | 4 | 5 |
| Rain mm | 110 | 96 | 123 | 175 | 215 | 229 | 251 | 252 | 225 | 204 | 169 | 142 |
| Raindays | 16 | 14 | 18 | 21 | 23 | 23 | 25 | 25 | 24 | 23 | 20 | 18 |

### The Nut

Historic Stanley is dominated by the 152-m-high volcanic Circular Head (known as The Nut). A steep stairway and a chairlift go to the clifftop, where a 40-minute circuit walk offers views of coast and ocean.

### The fresh air of Woolnorth

The Van Diemen's Land Company, which was granted tracts of north-west Tasmania in the 1820s, still owns this sheep, cattle and plantation-timber property. Tours from Smithton include lunch and a visit to spectacular Cape Grim where the air is the world's cleanest.

### Bass Highway

The spectacular scenery on the Ulverstone to Stanley section of this highway recalls Victoria's Great Ocean Road. The route's highlights include: the little (fairy) penguins at the village of Penguin; the Lactos Cheese Tasting Centre in Burnie; and the colourful fields of Table Cape Tulip Farm near Wynyard.

*For more detail see map 206–7.*

### Arthur–Pieman Conservation Area

This reserve is reached via the scenic but controversial Western Explorer Road. This 3.5-hour route, steep sections of which are sealed, links Corinna and Arthur River. The conservation area was home to the Peerapper Aboriginal people, whose legacy is seen in middens and other archeological sites; access is limited.

### Cradle Mountain–Lake St Clair National Park

This glaciated landscape – rare in Australia – is part of the island's Wilderness World Heritage Area. Cradle Mountain (pictured) and Lake St Clair, in the north and south respectively, are both easily accessible.

# MIDLANDS & THE NORTH

The undulating Midland plains run south from Launceston, along the island's spine. This fertile region was developed in the 19th century by new arrivals who planted crops and grazed livestock. Colonial gentry built elegant mansions, such as Entally House, Woolmers, Brickendon and Clarendon, in an effort to re-create rural England. These days small-scale wine and gourmet food production captures something of the style of those early years, as do original buildings in towns like Westbury, Ross and Oatlands. Natural landscapes that have survived development are preserved in national parks and offer walking, skiing and, Tasmania's great recreation, trout fishing.

## TOP EVENTS

**Feb.** Launceston Cup (horseracing)

**Feb.** Festivale (food and wine, Launceston)

**Feb.** Village Fair and National Penny Farthing Championships (Evandale)

**Mar.** A Night in the Gorge (Launceston)

**Easter** Three Peaks Yacht Race (Beauty Point to Hobart)

**Apr.** Car Rally (Targa)

**May** Agfest (Carrick)

**Nov.** Craft Festival (Deloraine)

**Dec.** Gold Festival (Beaconsfield)

## EXPERIENCE IT!

❶ **Taste** leatherwood honey, unique to Tasmania, at Stephen's Honey Factory at Mole Creek

❷ **Take** a scenic cruise from Launceston along the Tamar River

❸ **Stroll** through lavender fields at Bridestowe Estate Lavender Farm near Nabowla (December–January)

**A stroll through Launceston**
Begin at Princes Square, a serene old park surrounded by Georgian churches. Walk north up John Street to one of Australia's oldest synagogues, and then to the Town Hall and some imposing Victorian bank buildings. Continue past a restored Georgian warehouse to the elegant Customs House facing the river.

## VISITOR INFORMATION
Gateway Tasmania Travel
Launceston: (03) 6336 3133;
1800 651 827
www.discovertasmania.com.au

## FOCUS ON

**Tasmanian Wine Route**
Northern Tasmania's 13 wineries are distributed between the west bank of the Tamar River, Pipers Brook and Lilydale. Pipers Brook Vineyard, started in 1974 and now a listed company, is the largest and best-known producer in the region. Cool-climate varieties ripen well in northern Tasmania and the local riesling, pinot noir and sparkling wines are gaining international recognition. Cabernet sauvignon, pinot gris, sauvignon blanc, chardonnay and gewurztraminer are also grown. The superb quality of the wine is due to the dry, warm autumn. Start by picking up a Tasmanian Wine Route brochure at a visitor information centre.

### CLIMATE LAUNCESTON

|  | J | F | M | A | M | J | J | A | S | O | N | D |
|---|---|---|---|---|---|---|---|---|---|---|---|---|
| Max. °C | 23 | 23 | 21 | 17 | 14 | 11 | 11 | 12 | 14 | 16 | 19 | 21 |
| Min. °C | 10 | 10 | 9 | 7 | 5 | 3 | 2 | 3 | 4 | 6 | 7 | 9 |
| Rain mm | 40 | 43 | 43 | 58 | 63 | 61 | 81 | 80 | 65 | 63 | 51 | 53 |
| Raindays | 8 | 7 | 9 | 11 | 13 | 13 | 16 | 16 | 13 | 13 | 11 | 10 |

## Woolmers Estate
Regarded as Australia's most significant colonial property, Woolmers (near Longford) has buildings, antique cars, photographs, art and furniture that reflect the life of six generations of one family, from 1817 to the present day.

*For more detail see maps 205 & 206–7.*

## Ben Lomond National Park
Tasmania's best snow skiing is to be found on Ben Lomond Range, a plateau rising to over 1575 m. The scenery is magnificent, especially the view from Legges Tor, Tasmania's second highest peak. The park offers easy bushwalking and is ablaze with wildflowers in spring and early summer.

## Trout fishing in the Central Highlands
Great Lake, Arthurs Lake, Lake Sorrell and Bronte Lagoon are renowned for their stocks of brown trout. January and February are the peak months for trout fishing.

## Ross
This tiny village (founded 1812) boasts the decoratively carved Ross Bridge (pictured), a fine example of convict building skill. The remains of Ross Female Factory, a prison for female convicts and their children, is nearby. Other points of interest include the barracks, the Uniting and Anglican churches and the Scotch Thistle Inn.

# THE SOUTH-EAST

Rivers, sea and mountains dominate the landscape of this extraordinarily rich and interesting region, one of Australia's most scenic touring destinations. The coastline fronting the Tasman Sea is a long, ragged and spectacularly beautiful strip of peninsulas, islands, inlets and channels. Imposing mountains shadow the coast in scenes more reminiscent of the seasides of Europe than those of Australia where the coastal plain is typically broad. Two major rivers, the Huon and Derwent, rise in the high country and meander through heavily pastured valleys. A leisurely pace of development over the last 200 years has kept much of the natural landscape intact. It has also ensured the preservation of many colonial sites, from the poignant sandstone ruins of Port Arthur to the elegant houses, public buildings, pubs and bridges of the small towns that dot the countryside.

## CLIMATE NEW NORFOLK

|  | J | F | M | A | M | J | J | A | S | O | N | D |
|---|---|---|---|---|---|---|---|---|---|---|---|---|
| Max. °C | 24 | 24 | 21 | 18 | 14 | 11 | 11 | 13 | 15 | 17 | 19 | 21 |
| Min. °C | 11 | 11 | 10 | 7 | 5 | 3 | 2 | 3 | 5 | 6 | 8 | 10 |
| Rain mm | 40 | 35 | 39 | 48 | 45 | 49 | 48 | 47 | 49 | 55 | 47 | 50 |
| Raindays | 8 | 7 | 9 | 10 | 11 | 12 | 13 | 14 | 13 | 14 | 12 | 11 |

## FOCUS ON

### The convict system

Reminders of Australia's convict years, long gone in other places, are a feature of Tasmania's south-east. The island was colonised in 1803 as a penal settlement and over the next 50 years 52 227 males and 12 595 females, 46 per cent of the entire Australian convict consignment, were transported to its remote shores. Many prisoners worked on public buildings and other infrastructure until the early 1820s, after which most were assigned to private settlers. Re-offending convicts from other prison colonies were sent to Port Arthur on the Tasman Peninsula from 1830 and, in the following years, a penal settlement for re-convicted criminals was built there. Transportation to Tasmania ended in 1852 after a bitter public campaign. Other convict sites on the Tasman Peninsula include the Coal Mines Historic Site (north of Port Arthur) and Eaglehawk Neck, while the fruits of convict labour can be seen in many early structures, such as those in the heritage town of Richmond.

## TOP EVENTS

| | |
|---|---|
| Jan. | Huon Valley Folk and Music Festival (Cygnet) |
| Feb. | Royal Hobart Regatta |
| Feb. | Country Music Festival (Richmond) |
| Mar. | Hop Harvest Festival (New Norfolk) |
| Mar. | International Highland Spin-In (wool-spinning competition, Bothwell) |
| Oct. | Village Fair (Richmond) |
| Oct. | Spring in the Valley (incl. open gardens, New Norfolk) |
| Oct. | Olie Bollen (Dutch community festival, Kingston) |
| Nov. | Agricultural Show (Brighton, near Pontville) |
| Nov. | Huon Agricultural Show (Huonville) |
| Dec. | Boxing Day Woodchop (Port Arthur) |

**VISITOR INFORMATION**
Tasmanian Travel and Information Centre
Hobart: (03) 6230 8233
www.discovertasmania.com.au

**Derwent Valley**
In the rolling country around New Norfolk rows of poplars mark the old hop fields. The Oast House at New Norfolk is a hop industry museum. Hops are still grown at Bushy Park, Glenora and Westerway, where shingled barns and waterwheels recall farming life over a century ago.

**Mount Field National Park**
Tasmania's oldest national park, 80 km north-west of Hobart, is a wilderness for beginners and daytrippers. The 40-m Russell Falls (pictured) is a wheelchair-friendly 15 minutes from the car park. Other trails wind through moorland, past lakes, and vistas of mountain and forest.

**D'Entrecasteaux Channel**
Between the Hartz Mountains and this deep-blue channel lies a world's-end coast of tiny towns in sheltered coves. The famous apple orchards are now complemented by boutique fruit and berry farms, salmon and wine. Woodbridge Hotel dining room, overlooking the channel, serves superb food based on local produce.

## Trout fishing

This region's lakes and rivers boast some of Australia's best freshwater fishing. A favourite among trout anglers is Ouse River, which joins the Derwent north of Hamilton. Other spots include Clyde, Jordan and Coal rivers east of the Derwent, and Tyenna, Styx and Plenty rivers west of the Derwent.

## Bothwell

In the 1820s Scottish immigrants settled the valley of the Clyde River, an area on the fringe of the central plateau that reminded them of their homeland. Bothwell has 53 National Trust-classified buildings, a hotel built in 1821, Australia's oldest golf course and good trout fishing.

## Richmond

This historic town 26 km from Hobart has 50 National Trust-classified 19th-century buildings. Some, like the courthouse and old post office, date from the 1820s. Convict-built Richmond Bridge (1823–25), is Australia's oldest bridge. Old Richmond Gaol (1825) retains its original cells and has displays on the convict system.

*For more detail see map 204–5.*

## EXPERIENCE IT!

❶ *Enjoy* the views in Hartz Mountains National Park, a window onto Tasmania's trackless wildernesses

❷ *Visit* Devils Kitchen, Tasman Blowhole and Tasmans Arch, dramatic rock formations on Tasman Peninsula

❸ *Swim* in the thermal pool and take an underground cave tour at Hastings Caves

❹ *Learn* about rainbow and mountain trout and Australian salmon at Salmon Ponds and Museum of Trout Fishing

❺ *Paddle* a sea-kayak in the D'Entrecasteaux Channel (from Kettering)

## Southern Tasmanian Wine Route

Tasmania's first vineyard was established at New Town in 1821. The modern industry began in 1958 when Claudio Alcorso set up the acclaimed Moorilla Estate on the Derwent. There are now about 18 boutique wineries fanning out from Hobart. Start with a map from information centres in the area.

## Tasmanian Devil Park

As well as other native creatures, at this park you can see the Tasmanian devil, a fierce-looking black furry creature the size of a small dog. The park also has interesting displays on the thylacine (Tasmanian tiger), a large marsupial regarded as extinct although unconfirmed sightings are still reported.

## Bruny Island

Bruny Island was home to the Nuenonne people, of whom Truganini, Tasmania's most famous Aboriginal, was one. Ferries run from Kettering. In the north are farms and holiday shacks; the south is part national park. Visitors can fish, swim, bushwalk and see penguins at The Neck Reserve (pictured) on the isthmus.

## Port Arthur Historic Site

Port Arthur is Tasmania's most popular tourist attraction and one of Australia's most significant historic sites. Imposing sandstone prison buildings are set in 40 ha of spectacular landscaping. There are ghost tours and summer boat trips to Isle of the Dead, final resting-place for convicts and prison personnel alike.

# THE EAST COAST

The East Coast is Tasmania's premier seaside destination for good reason. It boasts a mild sunny climate, some of Australia's most exquisite coastal scenery, historic sites, gourmet produce, and national park landscapes of peaks, gorges, waterfalls and forests. Many visitors come for a week or two, staying in one of a number of lovely low-key fishing and holiday villages; others choose to explore the coast in a leisurely manner, stopping off for a night here and there as the mood strikes them. There are many activities to enjoy, including diving and fishing in the rich marine environment directly offshore.

## TOP EVENTS

| | |
|---|---|
| **Mar.** | *Fingal Valley Festival (Fingal)* |
| **Mar.** | *Tasmanian Game-Fishing Classic (St Helens)* |
| **Easter** | *Jazz in the Vineyard (Freycinet Vineyard, near Bicheno)* |
| **June** | *Suncoast Jazz Festival (St Helens)* |
| **Nov.** | *Fun Fish (bream fishing competition, Swansea)* |
| **Dec.** | *Craft Fair (Cranbrook, near Swansea)* |

## EXPERIENCE IT!

**❶ Explore** the history of the East Coast in St Helens History Room

**❷ See** Aboriginal middens in the Bay of Fires Conservation Area

**❸ Meet** wombats, devils and birds at the East Coast Birdlife and Animal Park near Bicheno

### Mount William National Park

This fairly remote park, created in 1973, protects Tasmania's Forester kangaroo. Many bird species also enjoy a haven here. The view from Mount William takes in the sandy beaches and coastal heath of Tasmania's north-east corner and extends north to the Furneaux Group islands and south to St Marys.

### East Coast fishing

The fishing is excellent along this coast, and particularly around St Helens, which is the base for those planning to fish the East Australian Current for tuna, marlin and shark. For land-based and inshore anglers there is the long, narrow estuary of Georges Bay.

For more detail see maps 205 & 207.

### VISITOR INFORMATION

Gateway Tasmania Travel Centre
Launceston: (03) 6336 3133;
1800 651 827
www.discovertasmania.com.au

### FOCUS ON

**East Coast Gourmet Trail**
This region's indigenous Paredarerme people based their diet on shellfish. Fishing remains a vital industry. Visitors can taste and buy oysters at Freycinet Marine Farm near Coles Bay, or cray, oysters and scallops from Wardlaw's Cray Store at Chain of Lagoons, south of St Marys. The area is also known for its dairy produce – try the cheddar at Pyengana Dairy Company in the tiny river town of Pyengana. Kate's Berry Farm near Swansea is a gourmet institution, specialising in fresh berries and berry produce. At Swansea Wine and Wool Centre visitors can taste the pinots and chardonnays of the small local industry.

**CLIMATE BICHENO**

| | J | F | M | A | M | J | J | A | S | O | N | D |
|---|---|---|---|---|---|---|---|---|---|---|---|---|
| **Max. °C** | 21 | 21 | 20 | 19 | 16 | 14 | 14 | 14 | 16 | 17 | 18 | 20 |
| **Min. °C** | 13 | 13 | 12 | 10 | 8 | 7 | 6 | 6 | 7 | 8 | 10 | 11 |
| **Rain mm** | 55 | 59 | 56 | 61 | 58 | 61 | 55 | 49 | 45 | 55 | 58 | 73 |
| **Raindays** | 8 | 8 | 8 | 9 | 9 | 9 | 9 | 9 | 8 | 10 | 10 | 10 |

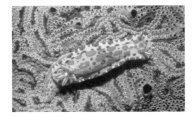

### Underwater wonders

The underwater landscape of the East Coast is an unsung wonder. Offshore from Bicheno is Governor Island Marine Reserve. Here, beneath clear waters, granite outcrops create underwater cliffs, caves and deep fissures, which provide a home for diverse marine communities. Glass-bottomed boat and diving tours are available.

### Maria Island

Maria Island, 20 km long and 13 km at its widest, combines history and natural beauty. A ferry from Louisville Point, 6 km north of Orford, goes thrice daily to Darlington, a restored penal settlement that operated 1825–51. The island, now national park, allows no private cars.

### Freycinet Peninsula

This long, narrow paradise features forests, cliffs, beaches and trails. The beautiful Peninsula Walking Track ends at Wineglass Bay (pictured), regarded by many as one of the world's best beaches. Coles Bay, which now has an upmarket resort, is a peaceful base from which to explore the area.

# BASS STRAIT ISLANDS

These islands, known for their produce, fauna and windswept beauty, are the remains of the land bridge between Tasmania and mainland Australia. They offer low-key holidays where the most energetic activity might be a coastal stroll, although more active experiences (game-fishing, diving and fossicking) are on offer. King and Flinders are the main islands. King, with 1700 residents, gets about 13 000 visitors a year, who mostly fly from Melbourne. Flinders (in the Furneaux Group of 53 islands) has 900 residents and welcomes 6000 or so visitors a year, most of whom fly in from Launceston or Melbourne.

### King Island produce

The Bass Strait islands have, in recent years, developed a strong reputation for quality food exports. The name King Island is synonymous with rich cheeses and creams made from unpasteurised milk. The matchless double brie and camembert can be sampled at the King Island Dairy, north of Currie.

### TOP EVENTS

| | |
|---|---|
| **Jan.** | King Island Racing Cup (Currie) |
| **Mar.** | Wybalenna Festival (Flinders Island) |
| **Mar.** | Agricultural Show (King Island) |
| **Mar.** | Imperial 20 (footrace, King Island) |
| **June** | Pheasant Season (King Island) |
| **Sept.** | Wind Festival (arts and crafts, Flinders Island) |
| **Oct.** | Agricultural Show (Flinders Island) |
| **Nov.** | Golf Open (King Island) |

### EXPERIENCE IT!

❶ **Fossick** for the elusive 'Killiecrankie diamond', a type of topaz, on Flinders Island

❷ **See** the Australian fur seals at Reid Rocks, a short boat ride from King Island

❸ **Enjoy** the view across to Victoria from Wickham Lighthouse (1861), tallest lighthouse in the Southern Hemisphere

### Furneaux Group boat tour

The Furneaux Group of islands, charted in 1798 by Matthew Flinders, became a base for sealers (called Straitsmen), many of whom were ex-convicts. Apart from Flinders, the only inhabited island is Cape Barren, where residents mostly fish and farm. Boat tours of the islands leave from Lady Barron on Flinders.

### VISITOR INFORMATION

Tasmanian Travel and Information Centre Hobart: (07) 6230 8233

Flinders Island Visitor Information Whitemark: (03) 6359 2380

www.focusonflinders.com.au
www.kingisland.net.au

### FOCUS ON

### Fishing

The Bass Strait islands offer superb coastal fishing. On Flinders Island, Australian salmon, flathead, gummy shark, silver trevally, pike and squid can be caught from rocks and beaches. From Lady Barron, Emita and Killiecrankie several charter boats take anglers offshore for catches of all the above as well as snapper, yellowtail kingfish, trumpeter and various kinds of tuna. On King Island there is excellent fishing for Australian salmon, flathead and whiting from the beaches along the east coast. South of Currie is British Admiral Reef, where boat anglers can try for morwong, warehou, yellowtail kingfish and squid.

### CLIMATE CURRIE

| | J | F | M | A | M | J | J | A | S | O | N | D |
|---|---|---|---|---|---|---|---|---|---|---|---|---|
| **Max. °C** | 20 | 21 | 20 | 17 | 15 | 14 | 13 | 13 | 14 | 16 | 17 | 19 |
| **Min. °C** | 13 | 13 | 13 | 11 | 10 | 9 | 8 | 8 | 8 | 9 | 10 | 11 |
| **Rain mm** | 36 | 39 | 48 | 68 | 99 | 102 | 124 | 115 | 84 | 75 | 60 | 52 |
| **Raindays** | 11 | 10 | 14 | 17 | 21 | 22 | 24 | 24 | 21 | 19 | 15 | 13 |

### Wybalenna Historic Site

Wybalenna ('black man's home'), was set up on Flinders Island in 1834 to house 133 Aboriginal people, survivors of Tasmania's pre-European population of over 4000. It is one of the most important historic sites in Tasmania. Nearby is a National Trust-restored church and cemetery (pictured).

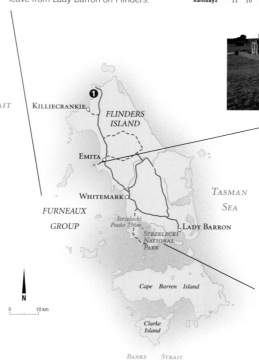

*For more detail see maps 204 (inset), 205 (inset) & 207.*

### Diving at wrecks

In the storm-lashed waters around King Island lie over 60 shipwrecks. The best known is the *Cataraqui* which sank in 1845 with the loss of 399 immigrants and crew, making it Australia's worst peacetime disaster. A number of wrecks around the island are accessible to scuba divers; diving tours are available.

### Strzelecki National Park

The granite Strzelecki Range occupies the south-west corner of Flinders Island. On a clear day, the highlight of this largely undeveloped park is a 5-hour-return walk to the summit of Strzelecki Peaks (pictured).

# Road Atlas of Australia

## Map Symbols

| | |
|---|---|
| Freeway; freeway under construction | |
| Highway, sealed | |
| Highway, unsealed | |
| Main road, sealed | |
| Main road, unsealed | |
| Secondary road, sealed, (suburbs maps only) | |
| Secondary road, unsealed, (suburbs maps only) | |
| Other road, sealed, with traffic direction arrow | |
| Other road, unsealed | |
| Mall | |
| Vehicle track | |
| National Highway Route Marker | M31  31 |
| National Route Marker | A1  1 |
| State Route Marker | C141  26 |
| Metroad Route Marker | 5 |
| Railway, with station | Paratoo |
| Total kilometres between two points | 114 |
| Intermediate kilometres | 45 |
| State border | |
| State capital city | ○ **SYDNEY** |
| Town, over 50 000 inhabitants | ○ **GEELONG** |
| Town, 10 000–50 000 inhabitants | ○ **Bundaberg** |
| Town, 5 000–10 000 inhabitants | ○ **Katherine** |
| Town, 1 000–5 000 inhabitants | ○ Narrogin |
| Town, 200–1 000 inhabitants | ○ Robe |
| Town, under 200 inhabitants | ○ Miena |
| Suburb, on state and region maps | ○ BELCONNEN |
| Suburb, on suburban maps | **Belconnen** |
| Locality (area name) | Williamsford |
| Pastoral station homestead | □ *Alroy Downs* |
| Major Aboriginal community | ○ Ngukurr |
| Aboriginal community | ○ Murgenella |
| Roadhouse | ▣ Fortesque Roadhouse |
| Commercial airport | ✈ |
| Place of interest | • |
| Landmark feature | ● |
| Adjoining map page number | 162 |
| National park | |
| Other reserve | |
| Aboriginal / Torres Strait Islander land | |
| Prohibited area | |

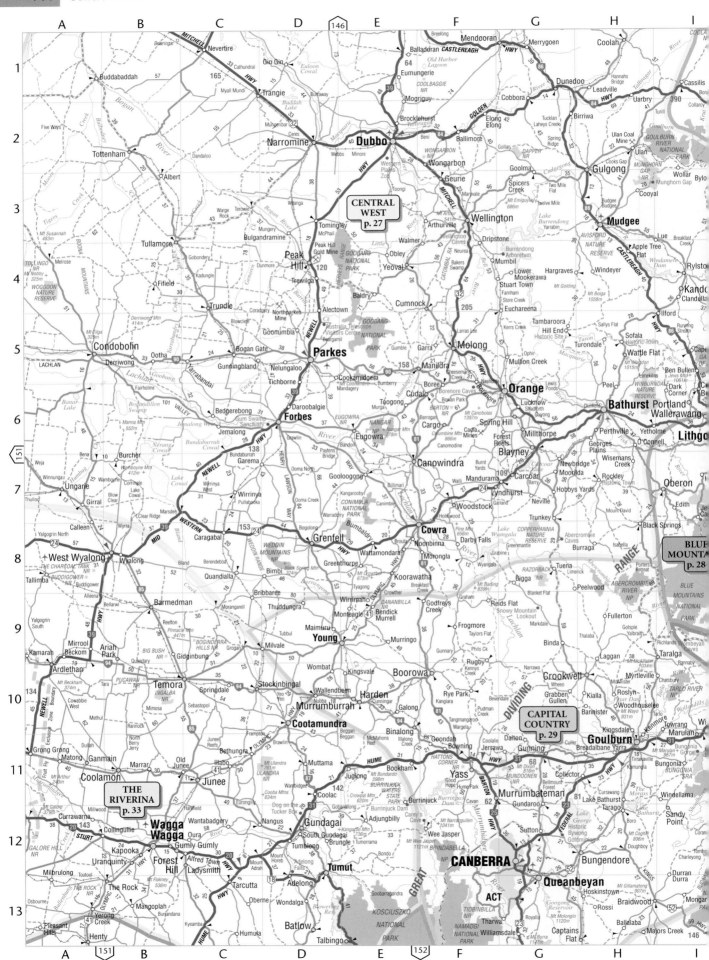

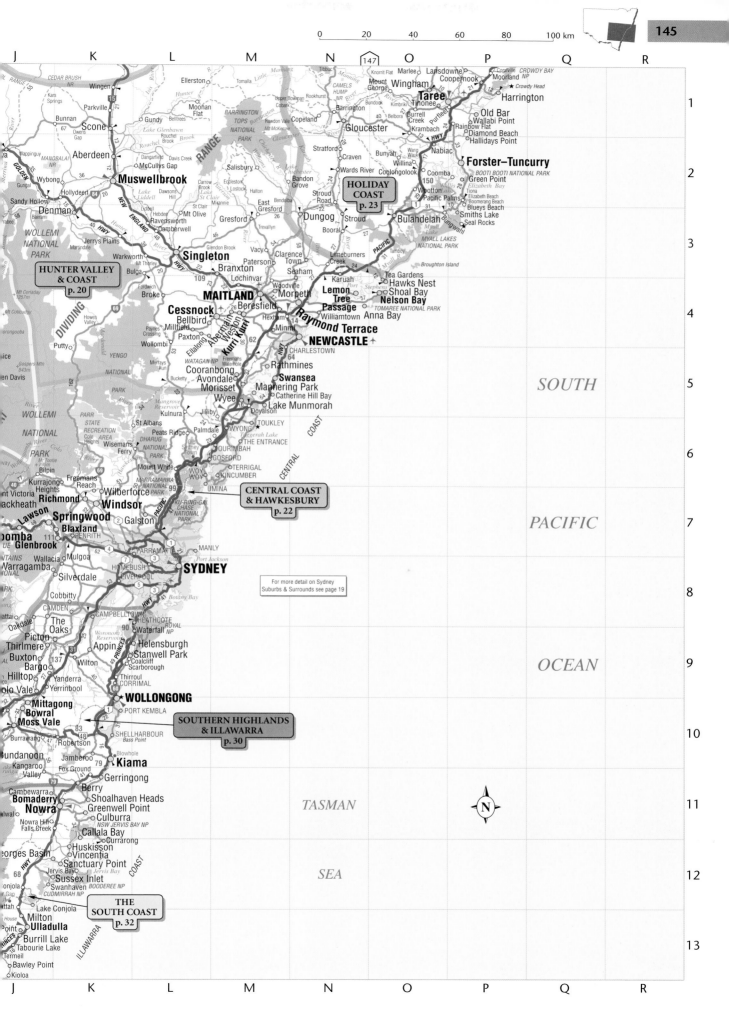

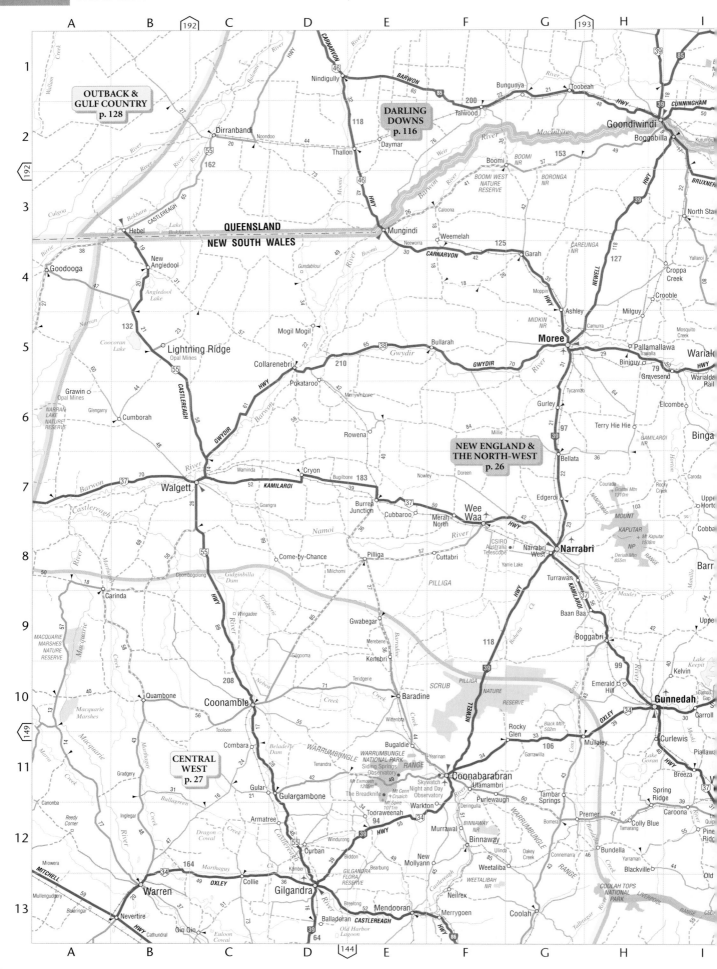

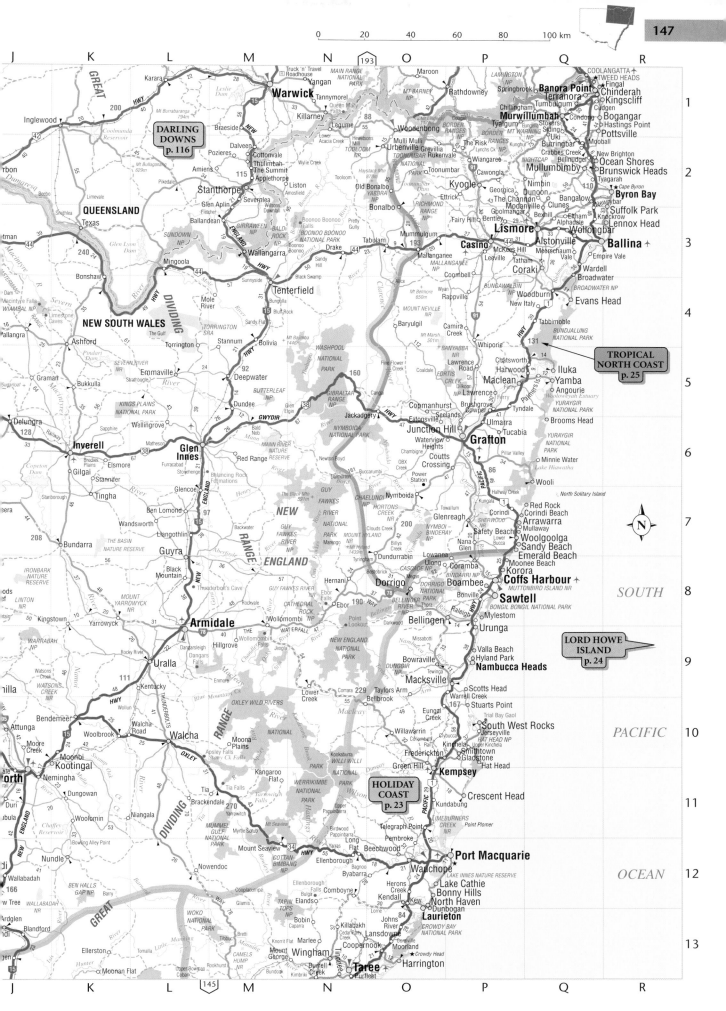

A 202 B C D E F 203 G H I

173

**OUTBACK & GULF COUNTRY p. 128**

QUEENSLAND
NEW SOUTH WALES

Lake Callamulcha

Moombidary

Corner Store
Cameron Corner
STURT

Binerah Downs
Warri Warri Gate
Dog Fence
Onepah
Adelaide Gate
Hamilton Gate
Waverley Gate

Berrawinnia Downs

Explorers Tree
NATIONAL
Fromes
PARK

Teurika

Ourimbah

Waka
133

Creek

Owen Downs

126

22

Pindera Downs

Barrajong

Tibooburra

53

Tilcha
GREY
Creek
Hewart Downs
Gun Vale
40
Clifton Downs
Colane
Koridina

Depot Glen Cairn
Poole's Cairn
Billabong
51
272
79
Wana

Yandama
Yandama
Poole's Grave
Milparinka
Whyjonta
Baronna Downs
102

Winnathee

Hawker Gate House
MT BROWN RIDGE
Yantara
Lake Altiboulka
Bundarra
NOCOLECHE

Mt Shannon 332m
72
Yantara Lake
Lake Ulenia
Petita
The Range

Smithville House
RANGE
Salt Lake
Turkey
Gumpopla
Nantilla

Lake Wallace
Pincally
Lake Bullea
Yancannia
138
Glendara
Tongo Lake
163

Big Salt Lake
Dalmuir
Cobham
Pulgamurtie
Allandy
Questa Park
Purnanga
McGurty Hill
Mullawoolka Basin

Starvation Lake
Turleys Gate
Pimpara Lake
HWY
47
Kooninberry Mtn
70
McCallum Park
Cawnalmurtee
254
Lake Yantabangee
Poloka Lake

Packsaddle
Pine Ridge
333
Pulchra
Caradec
Goodwood
Peery
Gilpoko Lake

Pine View
14
Packsaddle Roadhouse
65
Oak Vale
24
Peri Lake

Westwood Downs
16
Nundora
NOONTHORANGEE RANGE
17
Nuntherungie
19
44
White Cliffs Opal Mines
32
Mandalay

Boughams Gate
Teilta
CITY
The Selection
Koonawarra
Wertago
MUTAWINTJI NATURE RESERVE
Cootawundi
Tarella
Momba
THE OUTBACK p. 37

Floods Creek
46
73
MUTAWINTJI
Coona Coona
Nine Mile Lakes
Wild Duck

McDougalls Well
BENGORO RANGE
NATIONAL
BINGBANGO RANGE
PARK
Aboriginal Historic Site
Mt Daubeny
93
Lake Dick
Ulalie
Oulilla Lake

Morphetts
SILVER
45
Jones Lake
Coogee Lake
91
Mt Murchison 203m
Mena Murtee
Hamilton (ruin)
River
137

Wilangee
RANGE
73
61
Comarto
Wilcannia
Poopelloe Lake Gunyulka

MUNDI MUNDI PLAIN
Purnamoota
22
Glenora
HWY
119
Cawkers Well
19
BARRIER
32

Umberumberka Reservoir
Daydream Mine
Stephens Creek
31
Little Topar Roadhouse
Hazel Vale
196
32
Churinga
COBB
MACCULLOCHS

Silverton Historic Town
27
HWY
Stephens Creek Reservoir
77
BARRIER
Glen Lyon
SCOPES RANGE
Four Mile Lake
Talyawalka

49
32
Broken Hill
Fruit Fly Exclusion Zone Boundary
154
Malta Lake
Teraywynia
Cowary
186

Cockburn
79
Pine
Kinalung
Stephens
Horse Lake
Box Tank
Pamamaroo Lake
Annture Lake
Dry Lake
Nyngynderry
Glen Albyn
75
185

Mutooroo
Burta
Ascot Vale
SILVER
47
Quandong Roadhouse
60
Copi Hollow
Seven Mile
Dead Horse Lake
Wallace Lake
Albemarle
MANARA HILLS

Pine Point
CITY
HWY
Cawndilla Lake
Menindee Lake
KINCHEGA NATIONAL PARK
392
Amphitheatre Lake
Big Ampi
Victoria Lake
Glen Ora

SOUTH AUSTRALIA
NEW SOUTH WALES

A B C D 150 E F G H I

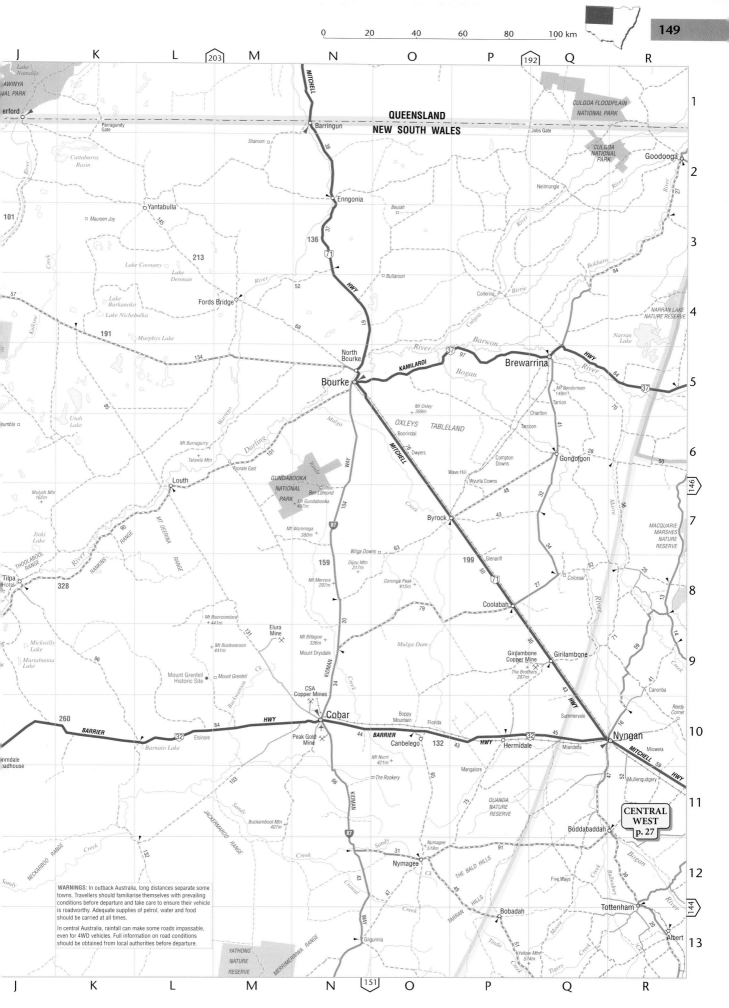

A B C D E F G H I

148

171

1

Pine Point
SILVER
Mutooroo
Burta
West
Fly
Fruit
Harry
Netley
Netley
Harry Creek
Coombah
Roadhouse
Menindee
KINCHEGA NATIONAL PARK
392
Cawndilla Lake
Stephens Ck
Amphitheatre Lake
Wallace Lake
Glen Ora
Teryawevnya Lake
Big Ampi
Albemarle
Victoria Lake
MANARA HILLS
71

2

Exclusion Zone Boundary
Olary Creek
Olary Ck
LANGWELL FLATS
75
CITY
Middle Camp
79
294
Tandou Lake
Redbank Lake
127
THE OUTBACK p. 37
Kaleentha Loop
Fruit Fly Exclusion Zone Boundary
Gum Lake
139
Savers Lake
Manara
Darnick
Beilpajah

3

SOUTH AUSTRALIA
NEW SOUTH WALES
Coombah Roadhouse
Coombah Lake
Woolcunda Lake
Popiltah Lake
Popio Ck
Popio Lake
Little Lake
Darling River
Lake Mindona
Yartla Lake
Great
Travellers Lake
Moornanyah Lake
Overnewton
Corinya
131

4

DANGGALI CONSERVATION PARK
BOOKMARK BIOSPHERE RESERVE
TARAWI NATURE RESERVE
74
HWY
Nialia Lake
Wyndham
Warrawenia Lake
Yelta Lake
NEARIE LAKE NATURE RESERVE
Lake Milkengay
Pooncarie
133
Garnpung Lake
Lake Leaghur
Malurulu Lake

5

CHOWILLA REGIONAL RESERVE
68
Darling
124
Lake Milkengay
Lake Arumpo
MUNGO NATIONAL PARK
Lake Mungo
The Walls of China
The Vale
Hatfield
Chibnalwood Lakes

6

169
Lake Litra
79
Lock 6
Chowilla
Lock 7
Rufus River
Lake Victoria
Lock 8
MURRAY RIVER NP
Wentworth
Coulnoa
Dareton
Burronga
Lake Gol Gol
Moonlight Lake
104

7

Paringa
Agricultural Check Point
Lindsay Point
Lock 9
Lake Wallawalla
STURT 144
A20
34
Meringur North
Meringur
Morkalla
Yarrara
Kulnine East
Merbein West
Birdwoodton
Merbein South
Cullulleraine
Lake Cullulleraine
HWY
24
21
Werrimull
Bambill
Karawinna
59
Koorlong
Cardross
Karweon
13
24
Merrinee
36
Merbein
Irymple
Mildura
Gol Gol
Nicholls Point
Billabong
Buronga
Coomealla
Sunny Cliffs
Red Cliffs
Karadoc
Yatpool
NEW SOUTH WALES
STURT
80
Pitarpunga Lake
Tin Tin Lake
Penarie
Redbank Weir
Ganawey Lake
Dundomallee Lake
Pringle Lakes
MALLEE CLIFFS NATIONAL PARK
Nicholls Point
Bunumburt Lake
69
Oxle

8

Yamba Roadhouse
Taldra
Noora
Nangari
Taplan
Tunart
Kumwall
SUNSET COUNTRY
MURRAY–SUNSET NATIONAL PARK
Rocket Lake
17
Carwarp
35
103
A79
HATTAH-KULKYNE NATIONAL PARK
Nangiloc
Colignan
KEMENDOK NR
MURRAY-KULKYNE PARK
Prill Lake
Lake Benanee
Euston
Robinvale
Bannerton
Weimby
Lake Caringay
Balranald
YANGA NATURE RESERVE
208
STURT
Loorica Lake
Lake Tala
76
HWY
20
28

9

VICTORIA
Meribah
Paruna
Peebinga
PEEBINGA CP
Pink Lakes
Mt Gnarr 980m
Fruit Fly Exclusion Zone Boundary
Hattah
112
Wemen
Kyndalyn
13
18
MURRAY
Kooloonong
Natya
Goodnight
Tooleybuc
94
B400
Kyalite
VALLEY
37
Yanga Lake
Impimi
Condoupie Lake
Condouple Lake
Lake Telbetts
Perekerten
Lake Lyle
Moolpa
62
Edward

10

29
31
Torrita
Walpeup
HWY
30
55
96
Ouyen
Kiamil
8
B12
Manangatang
Mittyack
Piangil North
Piangil
Wood Wood
24
Chinkapook
Nyah West
16
Natya
41
Woorinen
HWY
Nyah
42
Beverford
Cunninyeuk
70
Moulamein
Wako Irrigation Area
Nyah West
Vinifera
Pira

11

Pinnaroo
6
B12
24
MALLEE
Murrayville
Cowangie
Linga
140
20
Underbool
21
Boinka
B12
Mt Observatory
93m
Patchewollock
+Dunt Peak
Tempy
Speed
35
39
66
22
31
Turriff
Sea Lake
18
88
Liinduck 93m
40
Chillingollah
Waitchie
Ultima
43
Lake Boga
34
Swan Hill
Paddle-steamer
Tresco
Mystic Park
Murra
B400
Barb
Koondro

12

SCORPION SPRINGS CP
NGARKAT CP
BIG DESERT WILDERNESS PARK
BIG DESERT
WYPERFELD NATIONAL PARK
MALLEE COUNTRY p. 52
For more detailed coverage of localities in Victoria see pages 160-1
LAKE ALBACUTYA PARK
Lake Albacutya
Hopetoun
26
Lascelles
B220
Berriwillock
13
Culgoa
29
Lalbert
56
Nullawil
CALDER
16
Woomelang
Lake Charm
The Marsh
Lake Boga
Kerang
Kerang South
Quambatook
51

13

166
MOUNT SHAUGH CP
Mt Shaugh 184m
WIMMERA
Netherby
Yaapeet
45
Rainbow
17
Kenmare
26
Beulah
25
HWY
Curyo
40
Birchip
B220
Dumosa
31
Wycheproof
Glenloth
Nullawil
Lake Boort
Boort
Yando
B260
Durham
GOULBURN & MURRAY p. 53
158
159

N

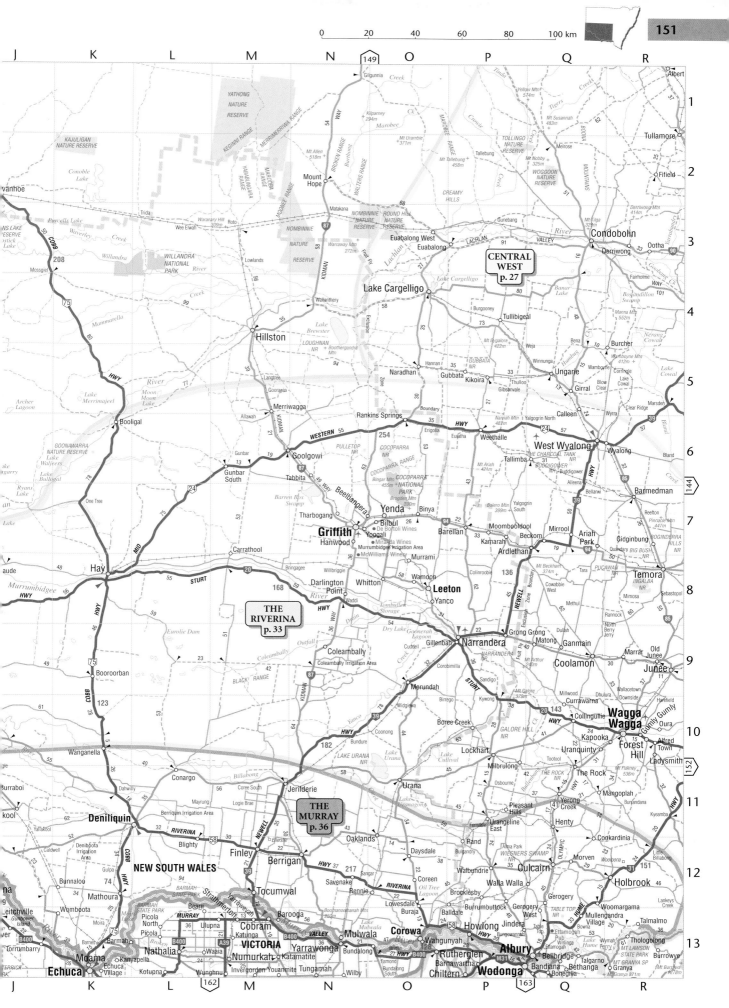

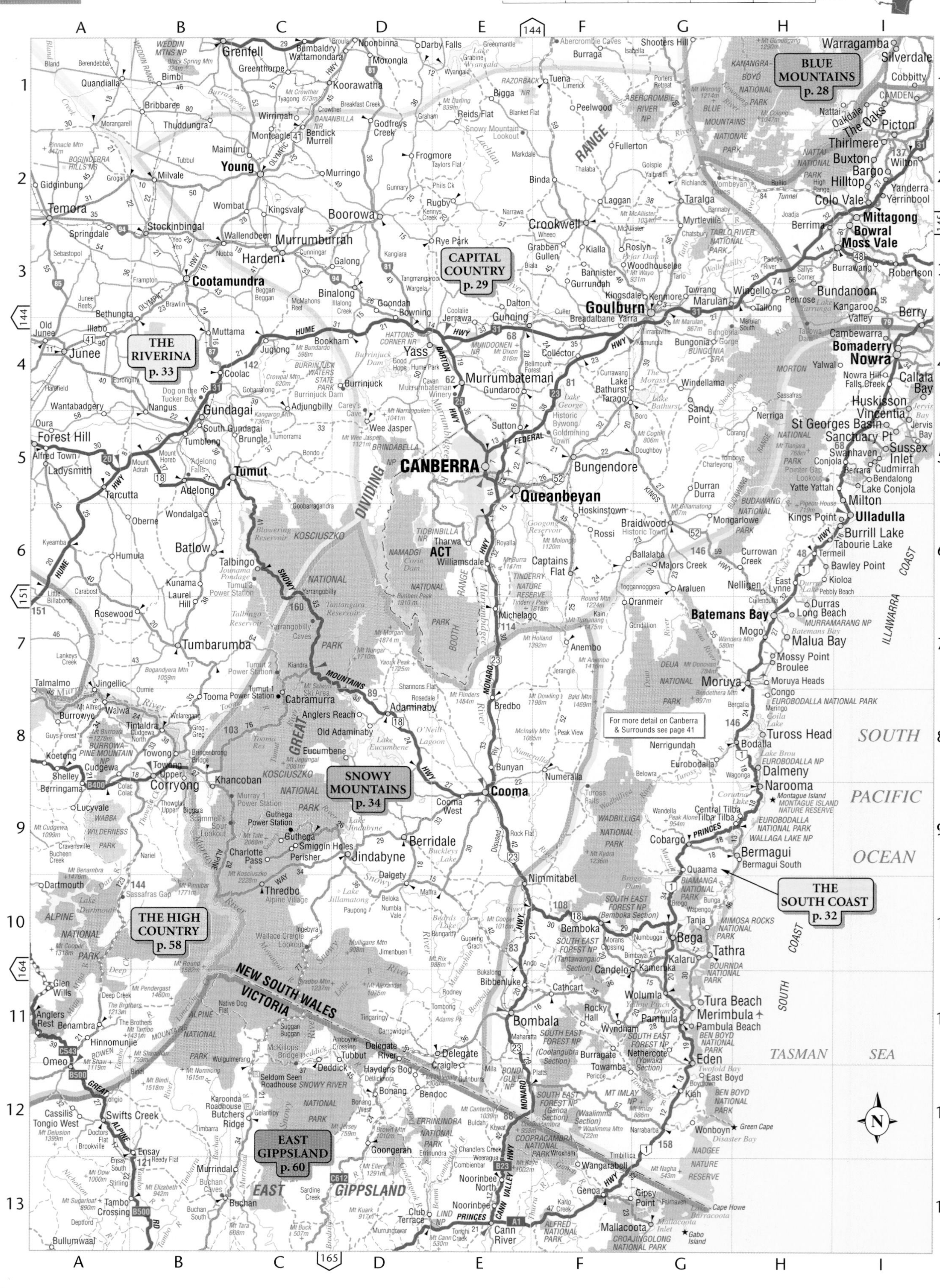

0 20 40 60 80 100 km

BLUE MOUNTAINS p. 28

CAPITAL COUNTRY p. 29

THE RIVERINA p. 33

SNOWY MOUNTAINS p. 34

THE HIGH COUNTRY p. 58

THE SOUTH COAST p. 32

EAST GIPPSLAND p. 60

SOUTH PACIFIC OCEAN

TASMAN SEA

NEW SOUTH WALES

VICTORIA

CANBERRA

Queanbeyan

Goulburn

Nowra

Batemans Bay

Cooma

Bega

Eden

N

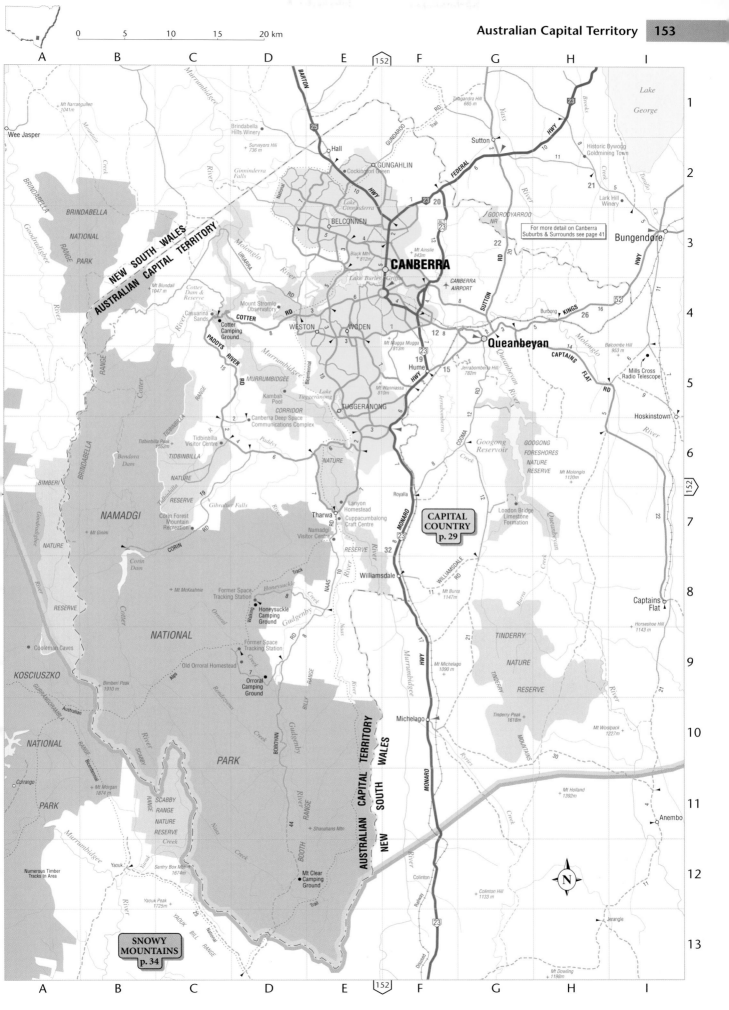

SPA & GARDEN COUNTRY p. 56

YARRA & DANDENONGS p. 57

WERRIBEE & BELLARINE PENINSULA p. 48

PHILLIP ISLAND & GIPPSLAND p. 62

MORNINGTON PENINSULA p. 61

For more detail on Melbourne Suburbs & Surrounds see page 47

MELBOURNE

GEELONG

PORT PHILLIP

BASS STRAIT

Tylden, Woodend, Newham, Hanging Rock, Romsey, Rochford, Darraweit Guim, Bylands, Wandong, Heathcote Junction, Flowerdale, Mt Caroline 515m, Break O'Day, Hazeldene, Murrindindi, Taggerty, Rubicon, Eildon, Lake Eildon NP, Mt Torbreck 1514m

Memorial Cross, Mount Macedon, Macedon, Monegeetta, Wallan, Upper Plenty, Mt Disappointment 793m, Kinglake West, Pheasant Creek, Kinglake, Glenburn, Mt Mitchell 957m, Mt Klondike 869m, Buxton, Mt Juliet 1105m, Mt Duffy 1028m

Bullengarook East, New Gisborne, Riddells Creek, Clarkefield, Kalkallo, Beveridge, Merriang, Glenvale, Kinglake National Park, Mt Robertson, State Forest, Marysville, Lake Mountain 1470m Ski Area

Macedon Regional Park, Macedon, Gisborne, Mickleham, Donnybrook, Woodstock, Whittlesea, St Andrews, Steels Creek, Dixons Creek, Narbethong, Granton, Black Spur

Toolern Vale, Sunbury, Yuroke, Yan Yean, Wollert, Mernda, Cottles Bridge, Smiths Gully, Panton Hill, Yarra Glen, Healesville, Mt Donna Buang 1250m

Bacchus Marsh, Diggers Rest, Melton, Bulla, Craigieburn, Hurstbridge, Sugarloaf Reservoir, Warrandyte, Coldstream, Woori Yallock, Millgrove, Warburton East, Warburton, McMahons Creek

Parwan, Rockbank, Exford, Keilor, Coburg, Thomastown, Lilydale, Seville, Launching Place, Yarra Junction, Gladysdale, Three Bridges, Powelltown, Great Dividing Range, Mt Little Joe 1134m

Rowsley, Balliang East, Tarneit, Footscray, Box Hill, Ringwood, Dandenong Ranges, Wandin North, Silvan, Olinda, Monbulk, Macclesfield, Avonsleigh, Hoddles Creek, Icy Creek, Noojee

Little River, Werribee, Werribee South, Altona, Point Cook, Brighton, Oakleigh, Belgrave, Emerald, Cockatoo, Gembrook, Upper Beaconsfield, Neerim, Neerim South, Crossover

Lara, Corio, Geelong, Clifton Springs, Portarlington, Bellarine, Indented Head, St Leonards, Drysdale, Frankston, Cranbourne, Dandenong, Lyndhurst, Berwick, Beaconsfield, Pakenham, Cranbourne South, Cardinia, Tooradin, Koo-wee-rup, Nar Nar Goon, Tynong, Bunyip, Longwarry, Drouin West, Brandy Creek, Buln Buln, Warragul, Nilma, Darnum, Yarragon, Trafalgar

Leopold, Ocean Grove, Barwon Heads, Breamlea, Point Lonsdale, Point Nepean, Portsea, Sorrento, Rosebud, Rye, Dromana, Safety Beach, Mount Martha, Mornington, Mount Martha, Baxter, Somerville, Tyabb, Hastings, Pearcedale, Warneet, Bittern, Crib Point, Stony Point, Tankerton, Grantville, The Gurdies, Nyora, Poowong, Loch, Bena, Korumburra, Jumbunna, Outtrim, Leongatha, Mirboo, Childers

Queenscliff, Sorrento, Rosebud, Balnarring, Somers, Shoreham, Flinders, Cape Schanck, Cowes, Ventnor, Rhyll, Newhaven, San Remo, Bass, Woolamai, Kongwak, Archies Creek, Kilcunda, Dalyston, Wonthaggi, Inverloch, Cape Paterson, Venus Bay, Tarwin Lower, Tarwin, Meeniyan

Corinella, Coronet Bay, Glen Forbes, Kernot, Modella, Ripplebrook, Athlone, Lang Lang, Heath Hill, Drouin South, Ellinbank, Yarragon South, Allambee, Seaview, Mt Worth State Park

PHILLIP ISLAND, Penguin Parade, The Nobbies, Churchill Island, Cape Woolamai, FRENCH ISLAND NATIONAL PARK, Western Port

Cape Paterson, Bunurong Marine and Coastal Park, Venus Bay, Tarwin Lower, Waratah North, Waratah Bay, Walkerville, Walkerville South, Cape Liptrap, Mt Liptrap 171m, Fish Creek, Buffalo, Stony Creek

BASS STRAIT, Spirit of Tasmania ferries, Station Pier to Devonport

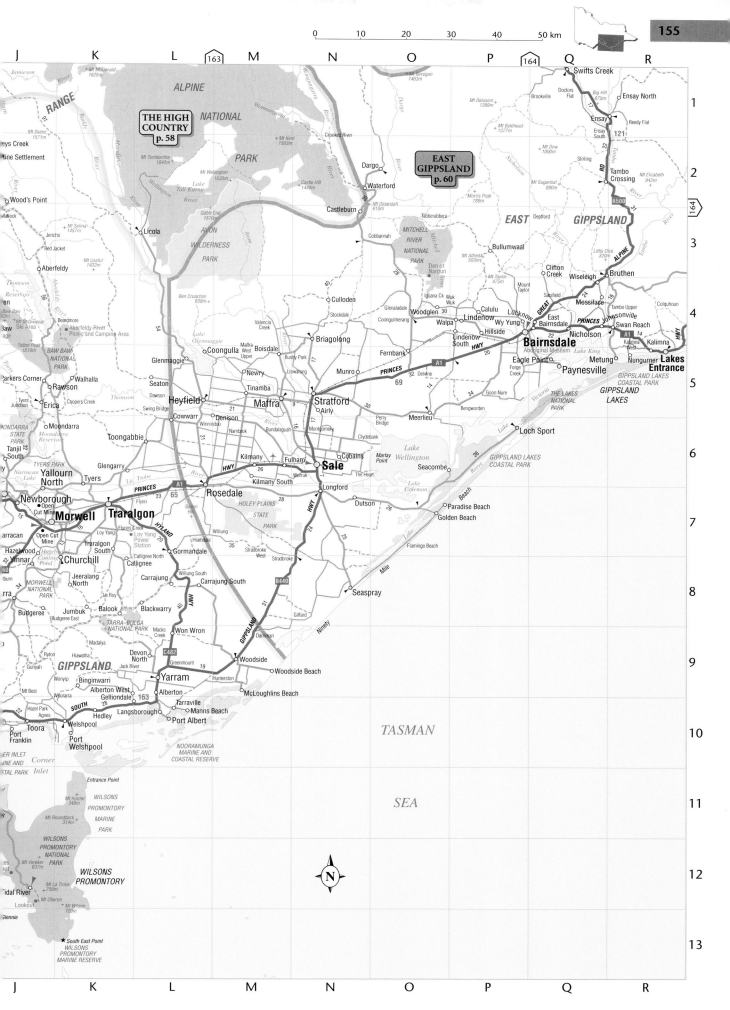

158

A B C D E F G H I

1 Joanna · Langkoop · Mackenzie Falls · Zumsteins · Halls Gap · Lake Wartook · Borokal Lookout
Wrattonbully · Kadnook · Powers Creek · Harrow · Reeds Lookout · BLACK RANGE STATE PARK · Mt Byron 549m · White Lake · River · GRAMPIANS · Brambuk Cultural C · Pomona · Mt Difficult / Mt Cassie 689m

2 Comaum · Poolaijelo · Connewirricoo · Moree · Culla · Pigeon Ponds · Englefield · Balmoral · Glendinning · Rocklands Reservoir · Woohlpooer · Billimina Shelter · Manja Shelter · Mt Thackeray 549m · VICTORIA RANGE · NATIONAL · Moora Moora Reservoir · THE · Mt Wa 1167
Coonawarra · DERGHOLM · STATE · Chetwynd · Tarrayoukyan · Coojar · Caddens Flat · Vasey · Gatum · Mooralla · A200 · Mt William

3 Penola · Dorodong · Dergholm · PARK · Roseneath · Warrock Homestead · Wando Bridge · Konong Wootong North · Brit Brit · Gringegalgona · Mt Dundas 466m · Mt Mackersey 552m · Glenisla · Victoria Point · Bryan Swamp · Karabeal · Mt Mundadjoog 828m · GRAMPIANS · Mirranatwa · SERRA
C198 · Lake Mundi · Dunrobin · Carapook · Wando Vale · Konong Wootong

4 Casterton · Heathfield · C198 · Sandford · Hilgay · Henty · 128 · Coleraine · Parkwood · Hensley Park · Moutajup · Warrayure · Dunkeld · Glenthompson 79
SOUTH AUSTRALIA · VICTORIA · GLENELG · B160 · Paschendale · Tahara Bridge · Wannon · HENTY · HWY · Kanawalla · Strathkellar · Bochara · Lake Linlithgow · Lake Repose
166 · Lindsay · Ardno · Strathdownie · Myaring · Merino · Digby · Tahara · DISTRICT · Grassdale · HWY · Hamilton · Tarrington · Yulecart · Yatchaw · Buckleys Swamp · Tabor · Croxton East · Penshurst · Mt Rouse 370m · B140

5 Mil Lel · WESTERN · Lake Kennedy · 88
Glenburnie · PRINCES · Puralka · Marp · Mt Napier STATE PARK · Byaduk North · Mt Napier 439m · Byaduk Caves · Warrabrook · Gazette · Caramut
Yahl · A1 · Caroline · Mumbannar · Dartmoor · Winnap · Hotspur · Branxholme · Wallacedale · Byaduk · Minhamite
Donovans Landing · C192 · Princess Margaret Rose Cave · Wanwin · Drik Drik · Greenwald · Lyons · Myamyn · Knebsworth · Macarthur · Hawkesdale

6 Nelson · LOWER GLENELG NATIONAL PARK · Milltown · MOUNT ECCLES NP · Broadwater · Dunmore · Willatook · Woolsthorpe
Oxbow Lake · DISCOVERY · Mt Van Dyke 183m · Drumborg · HENTY · Lake Condah · Eumeralla · Orford · Warrong · Winslow

7 Lake Bung Bung · Kentbruck · Homerton · Heywood · Bessiebelle · Codrington · St Helens · Kirkstall · Koroit · Southern Cross · Grassme
Mt Kincaid 197m · Mt Richmond 229m · Tyrendarra · Tyrendarra East · A1 · 97 · Yambuk · Toolong · Rosebrook · Woodford · Illowa · Bushfield · Dennington · Mailors Flat · Grassme Junctio

8 Discovery Bay · MT RICHMOND COASTAL NATIONAL PARK · Gorae West · Gorae · Narrawong · Tower Hill State Game Reserve · Killarney · Tower Hill · PRINCES
Mt Richmond · Bolwarra · Cashmore · Petrified Forest & Blowholes · Cape Bridgewater · Trewalla · Mt Chaucer 140m · Danger Point · Cape Sir William Grant · Lady Julia Percy Island · Port Fairy · Griffiths Island · Warrnambool · Logans Beach · Aringa

9 Cape Duquesne · Seals · Cape Bridgewater · Portland · Portland Bay · Crossley

CAPE NELSON STATE PARK · Cape Nelson

10 N

11

12 SOUTHERN OCEAN

13

GRAMPIANS & CENTRAL WEST p. 50

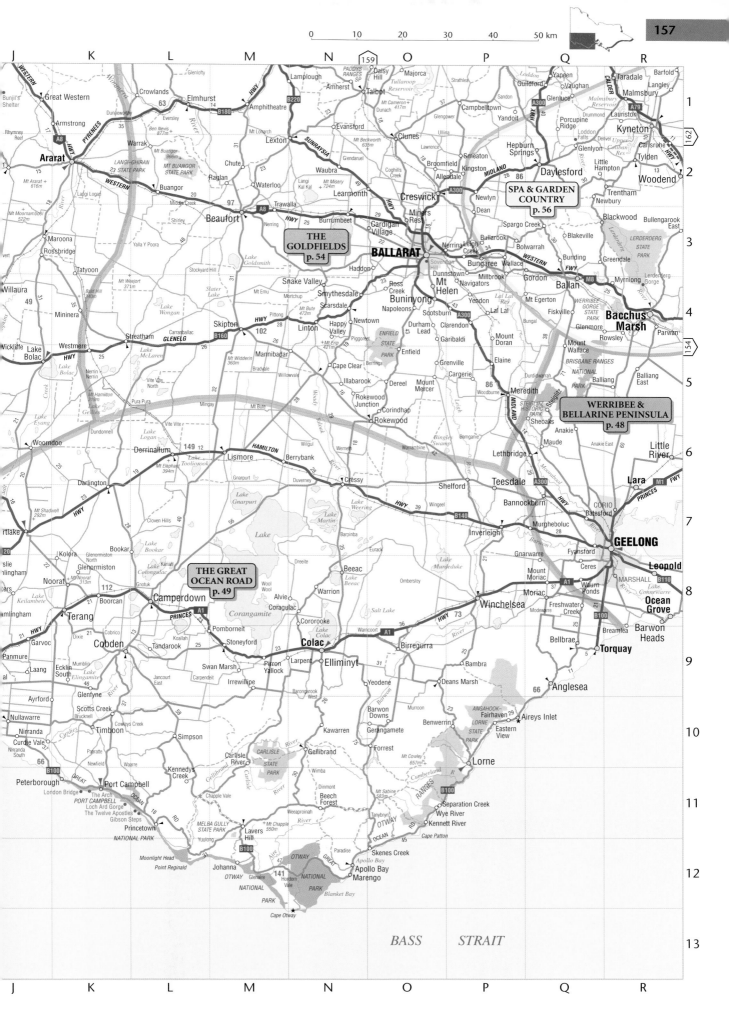

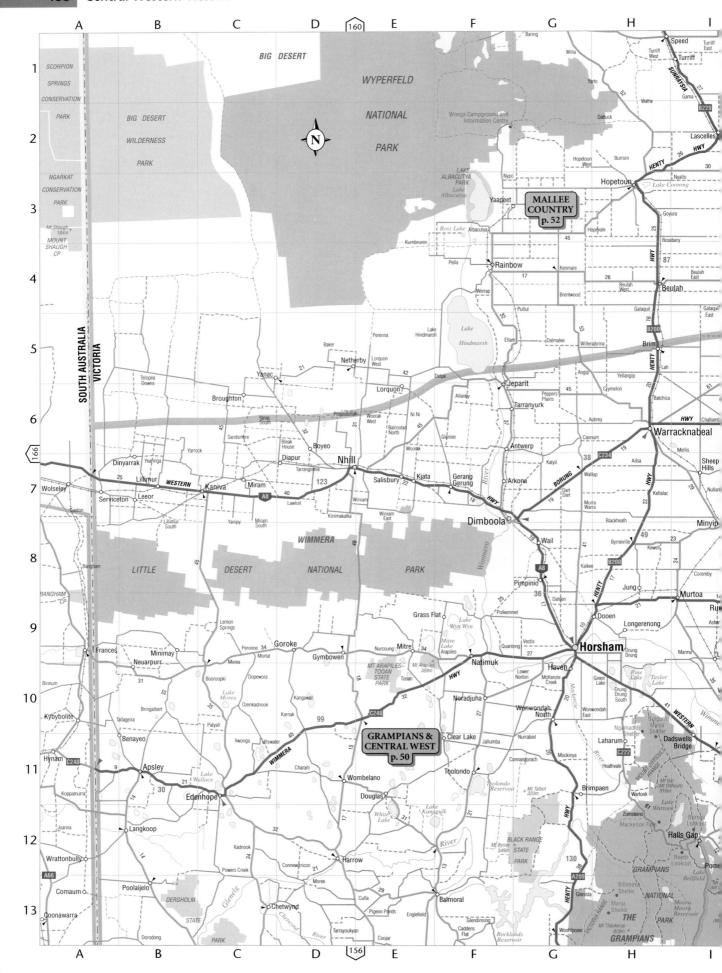

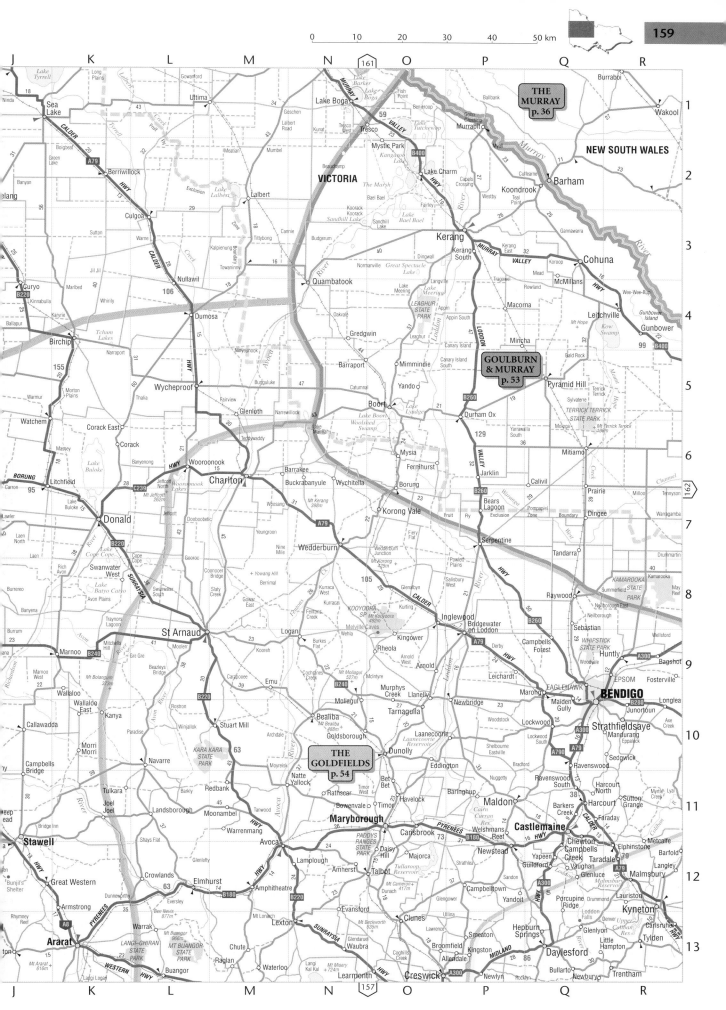

150

**NEW SOUTH WALES**

CHOWILLA REGIONAL RESERVE

Lock 6

Lake Littra

Lake Victoria

SILVER CITY HWY
79

Rufus River

Lock 7

Murray

Lindsay Point

Lock 8

Neds Corner

Lock 9

Kulnine

Kulnine East

**VICTORIA**

Lake Wallawalla

Lake Cullulleraine

Darling River

Fletcher Lake

Curlwaa

Wentworth

Dareton

Lock 10

Yelta

30

Merbein West

Merbein

Birdwoodton

Cabarita

Lake Gol Gol

Buronga

Gol Gol

**Mildura**

MALLEE

Trentham Cliffs

Nicholls Point

Billabong

Merbein South

Irymple

HWY

STURT 144

34

A20

Meringur North

24

13

Cullulleraine

13

Merrinee North

59

HWY

Koorlong

Cardross

Sunny Cliffs

17

20

Monak

Red Cliffs

Karadoc

Lindemans Karadoc Winery

STURT

80

Agricultural Check Point

Morkalla

Karween

Meringur

Werrimull

24

21

Karawinna

Merrinee

Pirlta

36

Benetook

Thurla

Yatpool

Iraak

17

30

Yarrara

Bambill

Tunart

Kurnwill

Bambill South

Tarrango

CALDER

Carwarp

Ginquam

Boonoonar

Nangiloc

Colignan

17

KEMENDOK NP

MURRAY–KULKYNE PARK

**SUNSET COUNTRY**

Rocket Lake

35

Nowingi

HATTAH–KULKYNE

103

A79

NATIONAL

Lake Mournpall

Lake Lockie

PARK

Kulkyne

River

**MURRAY–SUNSET**

169

Meribah

**NATIONAL**

Fruit Fly Exclusion Zone Boundary

Hattah

Cramenton

34

MURR KULKY PARK

**PARK**

Trinita

26

HWY

Peebinga

PEEBINGA CP

Berrook

Wymlet

**MALLEE COUNTRY p. 52**

Kiamil

8

Boorongie North

MALLEE

Wagant

Boltons Bore

Koonda

Pink Lakes

Mt Gnarr 98m

Paignie

Galah

Tiega

Boorongie

Ouyen

31

Goongee

Pallarang

Kattyong

Timberoo

Boulka

Nunga

A79

Woorn

Sunset

Manya

Tyalla

Linga

HWY

Torrita

Walpeup

Timberoo South

Bronzewing

B220

Mulcra

Duddo

B12

140

Tutye

21

Boinka

20

Underbool

21

41

**MALLEE**

SUNRAYSIA

Agricultural Check Point

Pinnaroo

B57

Panitya

MALLEE

Cowangie

Danyo

19

Gunner

Dunt Peak

35

Gypsum

28

166

Ngallo

Murrayville

6

B12

24

Mt Observatory 93m

Dering

Tempy

66

Patchewollock

Baring

22

Speed

**BIG DESERT**

Willa

Turriff West

Turriff East

Turriff

HWY

27

SCORPION SPRINGS CONSERVATION PARK

**WYPERFELD**

Yarto

52

Gama

B220

**NATIONAL**

Wonga Campground and Information Centre

Dattuck

Wathe

Lascelles

BIG DESERT

WILDERNESS PARK

**PARK**

Hopetoun West

Burroin

HENTY HWY

26

NGARKAT CONSERVATION PARK

Nypo

LAKE ALBACUTYA PARK

Lake Albacutya

Hopetoun

Nyallo

Lake Coorong

30

158

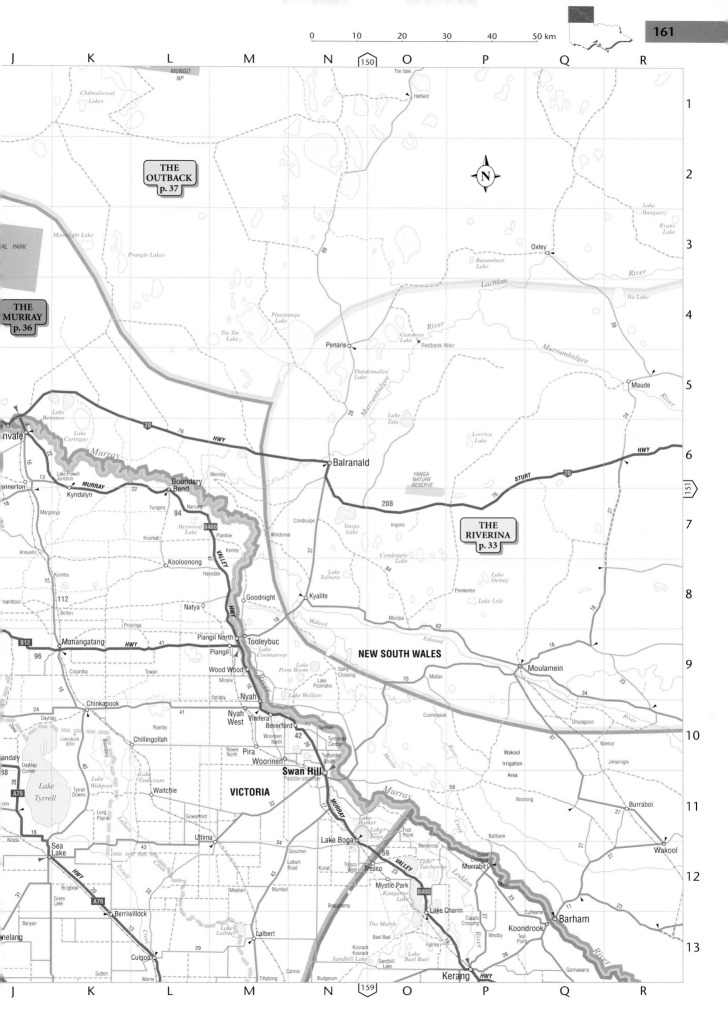

0  10  20  30  40  50 km

THE
OUTBACK
p. 37

THE
MURRAY
p. 36

THE
RIVERINA
p. 33

J  K  L  M  N  150  O  P  Q  R

1  2  3  4  5  6  151  7  8  9  10  11  12  13

MUNGO
NP

Chibnalwood
Lakes

The Vale

Hatfield

AL PARK

Moonlight Lake

Prungle Lakes

Lake
Bungarry

Ryans
Lake

Lachlan
River

Ita Lake

Pitarpunga
Lake

Tin Tin
Lake

Ganaway
Lake

Redbank Weir

Bunumburt
Lake

Oxley

Penarie

Murrumbidgee

River

Murrumbidgee

Maude

River

Lake
Benanee

Lake
Caringay

Murray

20  76  HWY

Lake
Tala

Loorica
Lake

STURT  HWY

20

nvale

3

22

16

13

Lake Powell
Junction

MURRAY

Kyndalyn

Margooya

Boundary
Bend

22

Weimby

Narrung

94

Balranald

208

YANGA
NATURE
RESERVE

76

24

27

annerton

18

Annuello

Koorkab

Kenley

B400
Heywood
Lake

Piambie

Yungera

VALLEY

47

Condoulpe

Yanga
Lake

Impimi

Condouple
Lake

84

Lake
Demaj

Lake Lyle

Perekerten

Koimbo

112

Kooloonong

Haysdale

Windomal

37

Lake
Talbetts

nnambool

Bolton

Natya

Goodnight

HWY

18

Kyalite

Wakool

Moolpa

62

Edward

18

Prooinga

Manangatang  HWY  41

Piangil North

Tooleybuc

18

70

Mallan

Moulamein

34

B12

96

16

Cocamba

Towan

Piangil

Wood Wood

Lake Coomaroop

Lake
Poon Boom

Stony
Crossing

23

Chinkapook

Daytrap
Corner

40

Ryanby

Miralie

Yarraby

Nyah

Spleeva

Lake Wollare

Cunninyeuk

River

Dhuragoon

Niemur

Chillingollah

Nowie
North

Pira

Nyah West

Vinifera

Beverford

42

Ferry

Tyntynder
Central

37

Jimaringle

Woorinen
North

29

Wood
Wood

andaly

Daytrap
Corner

28

A79

Lake
Tyrrell

Tyrrell
Downs

Lianiduck
93m

Lake
Wahpool

Lake
Timboram

Waitchie

Long
Plains

Gowanford

Woorinen

Tyntynder
South

Swan Hill
Paddle-steamer

17

MURRAY

Lake
Barker

Lake
Boga

Fish
Point

Benjeroop

Ballbank

Wakool
Irrigation
Area

Noorong

59

Burraboi

27

rrin

18

Ninda

Sea Lake

Ultima

34

Goschen

HWY

Lake Boga

Green
Crossing

27

27

Wakool

38

B12

A79

Labert

Tyrrell

Creek

43

Lalbert
Road

Kunat

Tresco
West

Tresco

23

59

VALLEY

Lake
Tutchewup

Murrabit

Green
Crossing

Culfearne

11

23

Barham

Koondrook

37

Bdigbeat

20

A79

Green
Lake

32

Meatian

Mumbel

Mystic Park

B400

Kangaroo
Lake

Beauchamp

Lake Charm

Capels
Crossing

Westby

Teal
Point

26

23

Banyan

Berriwillock

13

Lake
Lalbert

The Marsh

Bael Bael

Fairley

River

Loddon

nelang

Culgoa

Sutton

Warne

29

Tittybong

Cannie

Budgerum

Koorack
Koorack
Sandhill Lake

Lake
Bael Bael

Sandhill
Lake

26

Kerang  HWY

Gannawarra

River

NEW SOUTH WALES

VICTORIA

159

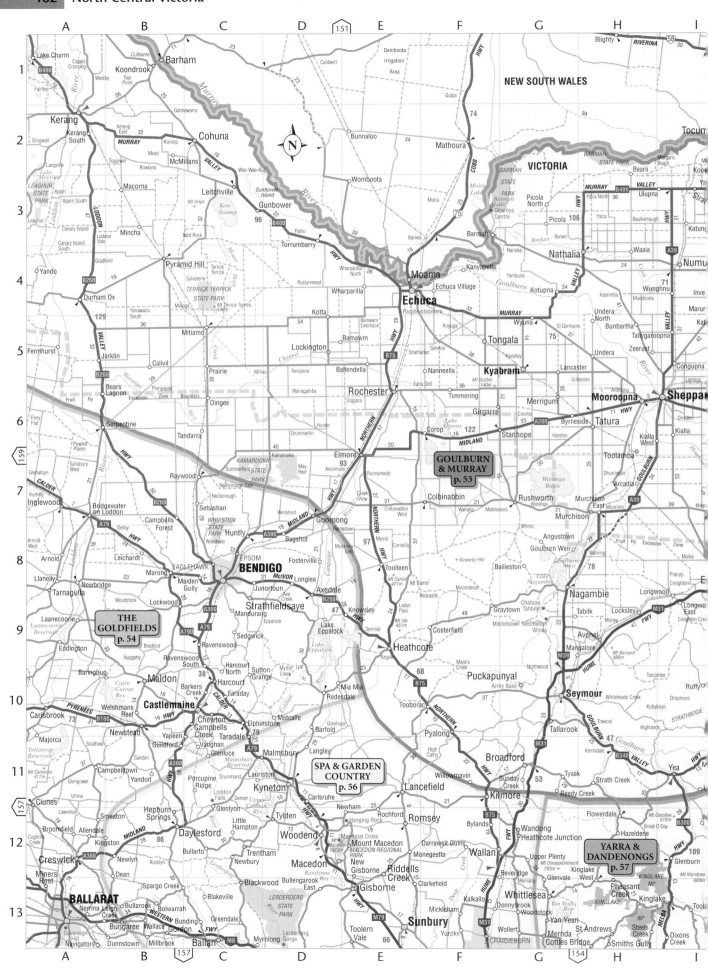

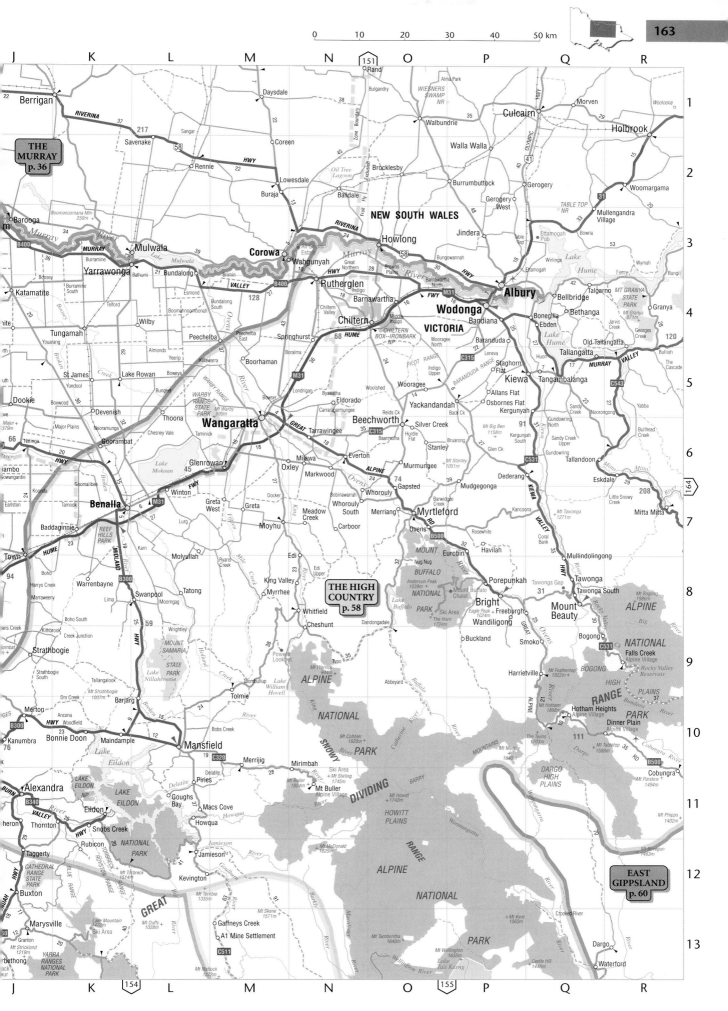

THE MURRAY p. 36

THE HIGH COUNTRY p. 58

EAST GIPPSLAND p. 60

RIVERIA

NSW
VICTORIA

Howlong
Jindera
Table Top
Ettamogah Pub
Bowna
Talmalmo
Jingellic
Murray
Ournie
Tooma

Albury
Wodonga
Bandiana
Bellbridge
Bethanga
Talgarno
Granya
MT GRANYA STATE PARK
MOUNT LAWSON STATE PARK
Burrowye
Guys Forest
Mt Alfred
Walwa
Welaregang
Tintaldra
Towong

Barnawartha
Chiltern
CHILTERN BOX-IRONBARK NP
HUME
Boneglla
Ebden
Lake Hume
Old Tallangatta
Tallangatta
Tallangatta East
MURRAY VALLEY
Bullioh
Darbyshire
Koetong
Shelley
Berringama
B400 HWY
Corryong
Towong Upper
Khancoban

Eldorado
Wooragee
Yackandandah
Beechworth
Silver Creek
Stanley
Kiewa
Tangambalanga
Allans Flat
Osbornes Flat
Kergunyah
Sandy Creek
Noorongong
Yabba
Lucyvale
WABBA WILDERNESS PARK
Cravensville
Biggara
Scammell's Spur Lookout

Everton
Markwood
Gapsted
Whorouly
Whorouly South
Carboor
Myrtleford
Merriang
Ovens
Eurobin
Havilah
Dederang
Tallandoon
Eskdale
Mitta Mitta
Dartmouth
Lake Dartmouth
Sassafras Gap
Mt Gibbo

MOUNT BUFFALO NATIONAL PARK
Porepunkah
Bright
Wandiligong
Freeburgh
Tawonga
Tawonga South
Mount Beauty
Bogong
ALPINE NATIONAL PARK
Mt Bogong 1986m
Falls Creek
Glen Wills
Sunnyside
Omeo
Benambra

Buckland
Smoko
Harrietville
Hotham Heights
Dinner Plain
BOGONG HIGH PLAINS
GREAT DIVIDING RANGE
Anglers Rest
Shannonvale
Hinnomunjie Bridge
Lake Omeo
Hinnomunjie
The Brothers

Cobungra
DARGO HIGH PLAINS
GREAT ALPINE RD
Omeo
Cassilis
Tongio
Tongio West
Swifts Creek

SNOWY RANGE NATIONAL PARK
HOWITT PLAINS
Dargo
Waterford
Castleburn
Cobbannah
Brookville
Doctors Flat
Ensay North
Ensay
Ensay South

Licola
AVON WILDERNESS PARK
MITCHELL RIVER NATIONAL PARK
Bullumwaal
Tambo Crossing
Buchan
Murrindal

Culloden
Stockdale
Glenaladale
Woodglen
Lindenow
Walpa
Lindenow South
Hillside
Fernbank
Briagolong
Clifton Creek
Wiseleigh
Mossiface
Bruthen
Nowa Nowa
Wairewa

Lucknow
Calulu
Wy Yung
East Bairnsdale
Nicholson
Johnsonville
Swan Reach
Colquhoun

Bairnsdale
PRINCES HWY
Metung
Kalimna
Nungurner
Lakes Entrance
Lake Tyers

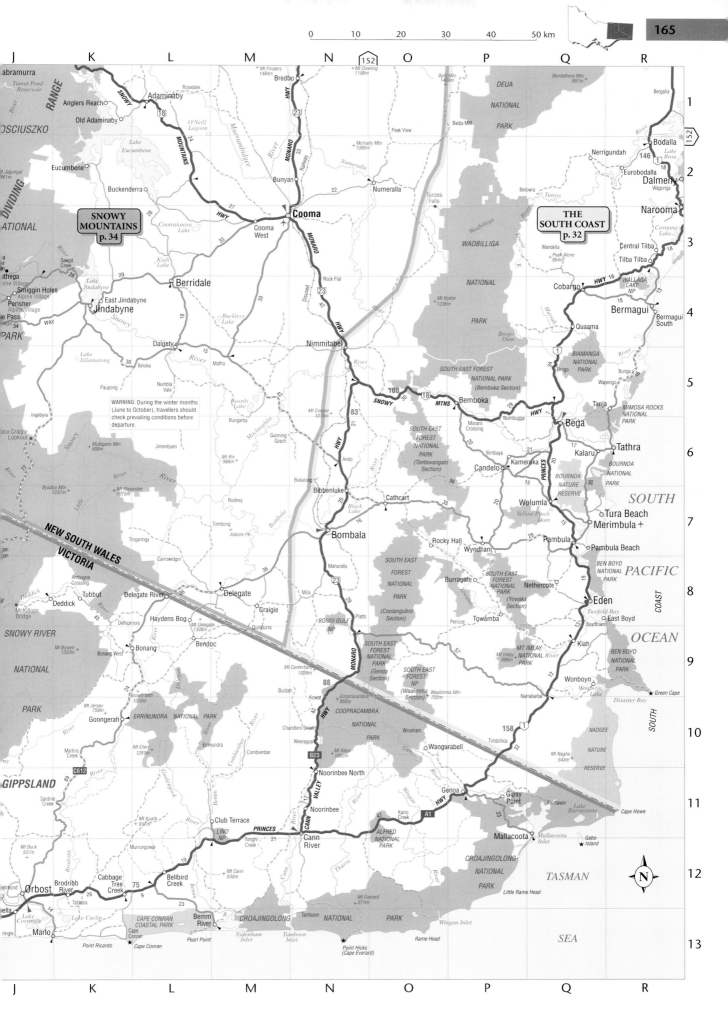

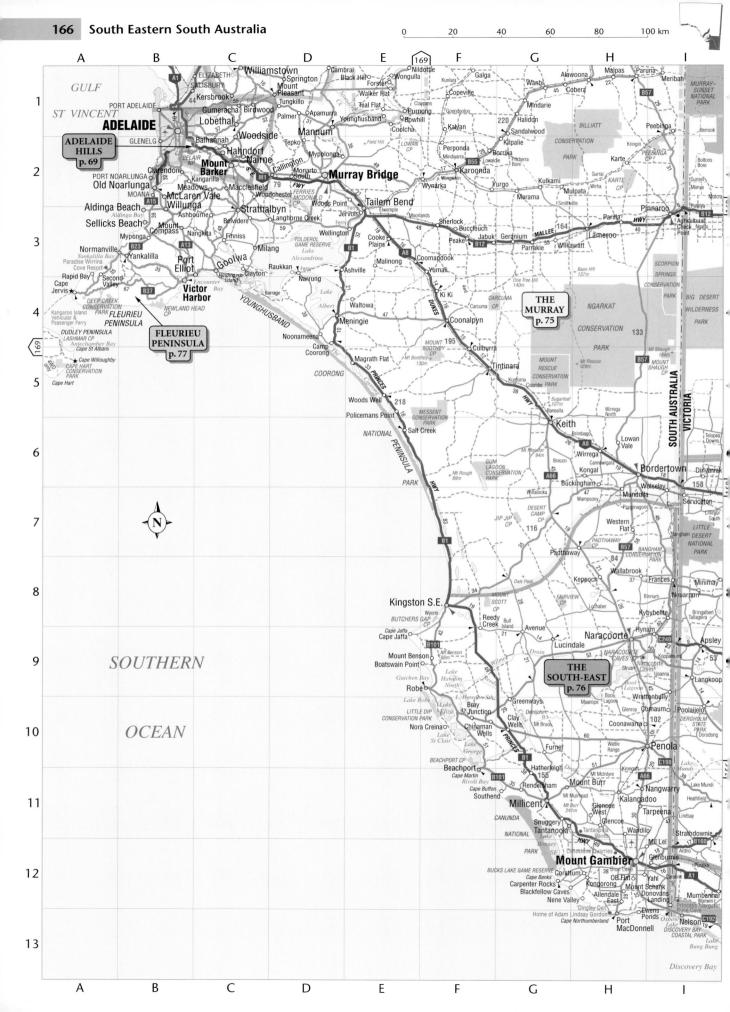

0   20   40   60   80   100 km

A   B   C   D   E   169   F   G   H   I

**GULF**
**ST VINCENT**

PORT ADELAIDE
**ADELAIDE**
GLENELG

ADELAIDE
HILLS
p. 69

PORT NOARLUNGA
Old Noarlunga
MOANA
Aldinga Beach
Sellicks Beach

Normanville
Yankalilla

Rapid Bay
Second
Valley
Cape
Jervis

FLEURIEU
PENINSULA
p. 77

SOUTHERN

OCEAN

ELIZABETH
SALISBURY
Williamstown
Kersbrook
Gumeracha
Lobethal
Birdwood
Springton
Mount
Pleasant
Tungkillo

Cambrai
Black Hill
Forster
Walker Flat
Teal Flat
Nildottie
Wongulla
Galga
Copeville
Kunlara
Alawoona
Wanbi
Cobera
Malpas
Paruna
Meribah

**MURRAY**
**BRIDGE**

**Mount Gambier**

*Discovery Bay*

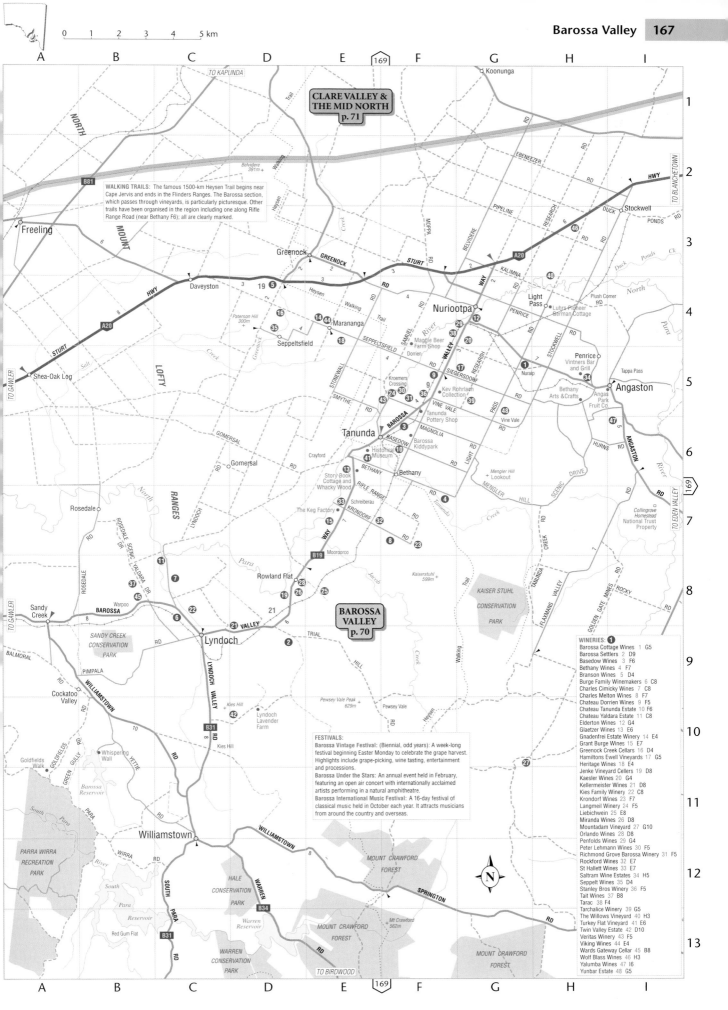

**WALKING TRAILS:** The famous 1500-km Heysen Trail begins near Cape Jervis and ends in the Flinders Ranges. The Barossa section, which passes through vineyards, is particularly picturesque. Other trails have been organised in the region including one along Rifle Range Road (near Bethany F6); all are clearly marked.

CLARE VALLEY & THE MID NORTH p. 71

BAROSSA VALLEY p. 70

**FESTIVALS:**
**Barossa Vintage Festival:** (Biennial, odd years): A week-long festival beginning Easter Monday to celebrate the grape harvest. Highlights include grape-picking, wine tasting, entertainment and processions.
**Barossa Under the Stars:** An annual event held in February, featuring an open air concert with internationally acclaimed artists performing in a natural amphitheatre.
**Barossa International Music Festival:** A 16-day festival of classical music held in October each year. It attracts musicians from around the country and overseas.

**WINERIES:**
Barossa Cottage Wines 1 G5
Barossa Settlers 2 D9
Basedow Wines 3 F6
Bethany Wines 4 F7
Branson Wines 5 D4
Burge Family Winemakers 6 C8
Charles Cimicky Wines 7 C8
Charles Melton Wines 8 F7
Chateau Dorrien Wines 9 F5
Chateau Tanunda Estate 10 F6
Chateau Yaldara Estate 11 C8
Elderton Wines 12 G4
Glaetzer Wines 13 E6
Gnadenfrei Estate Winery 14 E4
Grant Burge Wines 15 E7
Greenock Creek Cellars 16 D4
Hamiltons Ewell Vineyards 17 G5
Heritage Wines 18 E4
Jenke Vineyard Cellars 19 D8
Kaesler Wines 20 G4
Kellermeister Wines 21 D8
Kies Family Winery 22 C8
Krondorf Wines 23 F7
Langmeil Winery 24 F5
Liebichwein 25 E8
Miranda Wines 26 D8
Mountadam Vineyard 27 G10
Orlando Wines 28 D8
Penfolds Wines 29 G4
Peter Lehmann Wines 30 F5
Richmond Grove Barossa Winery 31 F5
Rockford Wines 32 E7
St Hallett Wines 33 E7
Saltram Wine Estates 34 H5
Seppelt Wines 35 D4
Stanley Bros Winery 36 F5
Tait Wines 37 B8
Tarac 38 F4
Tarchalice Winery 39 G5
The Willows Vineyard 40 H3
Turkey Flat Vineyard 41 E6
Twin Valley Estate 42 D10
Veritas Winery 43 F5
Viking Wines 44 E4
Wards Gateway Cellar 45 B8
Wolf Blass Wines 46 H3
Yalumba Wines 47 I6
Yunbar Estate 48 G5

GAWLER RANGES NP

PINKAWILLINIE CONSERVATION PARK

Lake Gilles

LAKE GILLES CONSERVATION PARK

KULLIPARU CONSERVATION PARK

COCATA CP

BARWELL CONSERVATION PARK

HAMBIDGE CONSERVATION PARK

CARAPPEE HILL CP

SHEOAK HILL CP

MIDDLECAMP HILLS CP

MIDDLEBACK RANGE

WHYALLA CONSERVATION PARK

MUNYAROO CONSERVATION PARK

LAKE NEWLAND CONSERVATION PARK

BASCOMBE WELL CONSERVATION PARK (4WD only)

HINCKS CONSERVATION PARK

RUDALL CP

YELDULKNIE CP

FRANKLIN HARBOR CONSERVATION PARK

EYRE PENINSULA & NULLARBOR p. 73

EYRE PENINSULA

GREAT AUSTRALIAN BIGHT

FLINDERS HWY

EYRE HWY

LINCOLN HWY

SPENCER GULF

COFFIN BAY NATIONAL PARK

COFFIN BAY PENINSULA

KELLIDIE BAY CP

LINCOLN NATIONAL PARK

SIR JOSEPH BANKS GROUP CONSERVATION PARK

THISTLE ISLAND

YORKE PENINSULA p. 72

YORKE PENINSULA

POINT PEARCE ABORIGINAL LAND GOOSE ISLAND CP

INVESTIGATOR STRAIT

KANGAROO ISLAND

KANGAROO ISLAND p. 78

SOUTHERN OCEAN

FLINDERS CHASE NATIONAL PARK

FLINDERS CHASE NP

WESTERN RIVER WILDERNESS PROTECTION AREA

RAVINE DES CASOARS WILDERNESS PROTECTION AREA

CAPE TORRENS WILDERNESS PROTECTION AREA

CAPE BOUGUER WILDERNESS PROTECTION AREA

CAPE GANTHEAUME WILDERNESS PROTECTION AREA

CAPE GANTHEAUME CP

**Towns and localities (selected):**
Cungena, Poochera, Minnipa, Yaninee, Pygery, Wudinna, Kyancutta, Koongawa, Warramboo, Lock, Warrow, Coulta, Edillilie, Koppio, Wanilla, Wangary, Coffin Bay, Port Lincoln, North Shields, Poonindie, Louth Bay, Tumby Bay, Lipson, Yallunda Flat, Cummins, Yeelanna, Cockaleechie, Ungarra, Butler Tanks, Port Neill, Wharminda, Arno Bay, Verran, Rudall, Cleve, Carpa, Cowell, Elbow Hill, Kielpa, Darke Peak, Caralue, Waddikee, Mangalo, Kimba, Buckleboo, Iron Knob, Iron Baron, Whyalla, Cowled Landing, Kapinnie, Mount Hope, Sheringa, Elliston, Bramfield, Talia, Colton, Port Kenny, Venus Bay, Chandada, Capietha, Kadina, Moonta, Wallaroo, Yorketown, Warooka, Minlaton, Port Victoria, Maitland, Brentwood, Marion Bay, Stenhouse Bay, Cape Borda, Rocky River, Vivonne Bay, Karatta, Parndana, Kingscote

**Selected features:**
Kaldoonera Hill 136m, Mt Granite 438m, Mt Yardea 425m, Mt Nott 433m, Mt Double 440m, Mt Sturt 427m, Pildappa Rock, Turtle Rock, Mt Wudinna 261m, Sapphire Flat, Ucontitchie Hill 170m, Mt Damper, Mt Wedge 247m, Kappawanta Hill 99m, Sheoak Hill 366m, Lake Hamilton, Lake Malata, Lake Greenly, Tod River Res, Mt Darke Peak 448m, Caralue Bluff 484m, Carple Puntha Hill 479m, Mt Geharty 277m, Granite Hill 252m, Mt Middleback 446m, Mt Whyalla SE 232m, Cooyerdoo Hill 269m, Burkitt Hill 254m, Rockwater Hill 97m, Peterlumbo Hill 391m, Sisters Hill 247m, Burrows Hill 253m, Mt Miccolo 362m, Myall Creek

Anxious Bay, Cape Finniss, Locks Well Beach, Drummond Point, Point Sir Isaac, Gallipoli Beach, Farm Beach, Avoid Bay, Point Whidbey, Point Avoid, Yangie Bay Lookout, Sleaford Mere, Sleaford Bay, Cape Tournefort, Whalers Way, West Point, Cape Carnot, Liguanea Island, Hopkins Island, Flinders Monument, Cape Donington, Boston Bay, Boston Island, Taylor Island, Albatross Island, Wedge Island, Gambier Islands, North Neptunes, South Neptunes, Reevesby Island, Roxby Island, Spilsby Island, Stickney Island

A1, B100, B91, B90, B89, B88, B86, B23, HWY

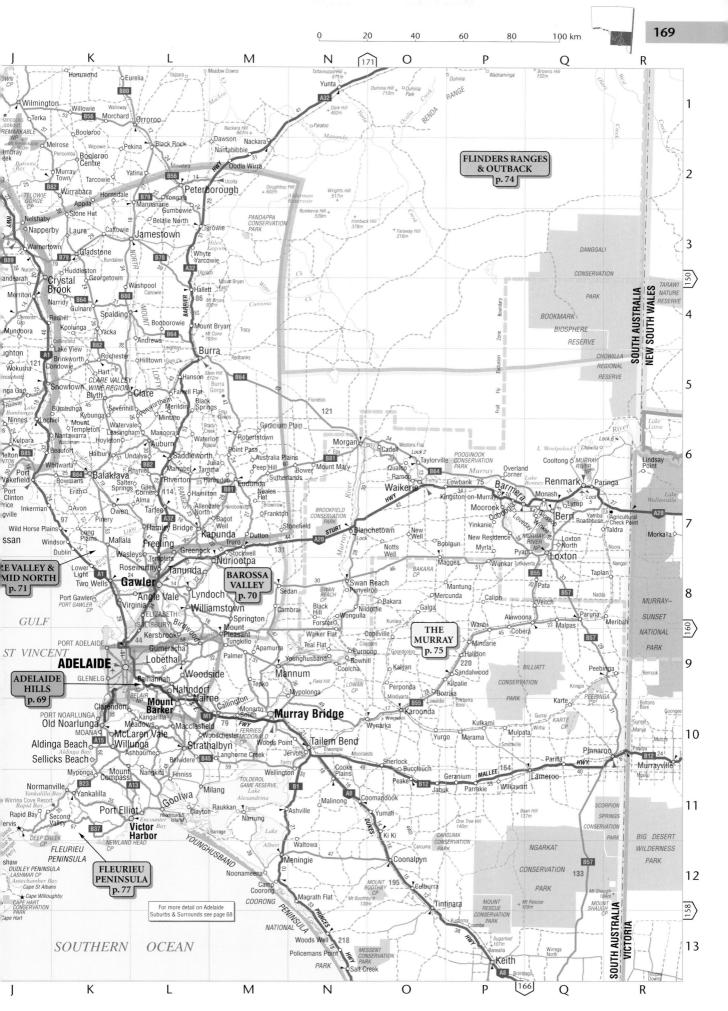

SOUTHERN OCEAN

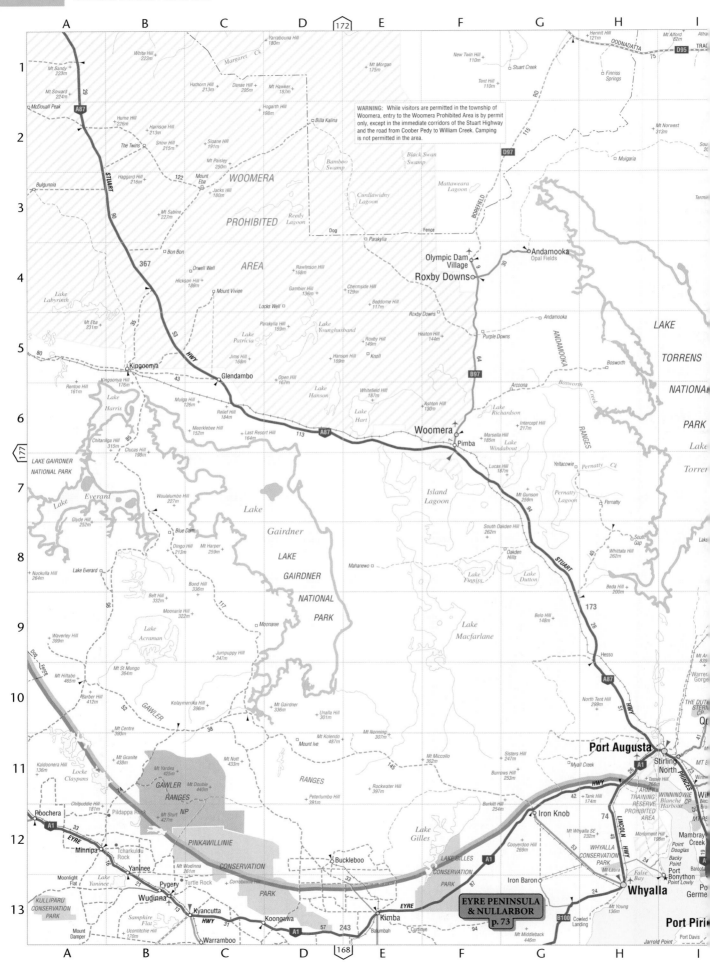

WARNING: While visitors are permitted in the township of Woomera, entry to the Woomera Prohibited Area is by permit only, except in the immediate corridors of the Stuart Highway and the road from Coober Pedy to William Creek. Camping is not permitted in the area.

EYRE PENINSULA & NULLARBOR p. 73

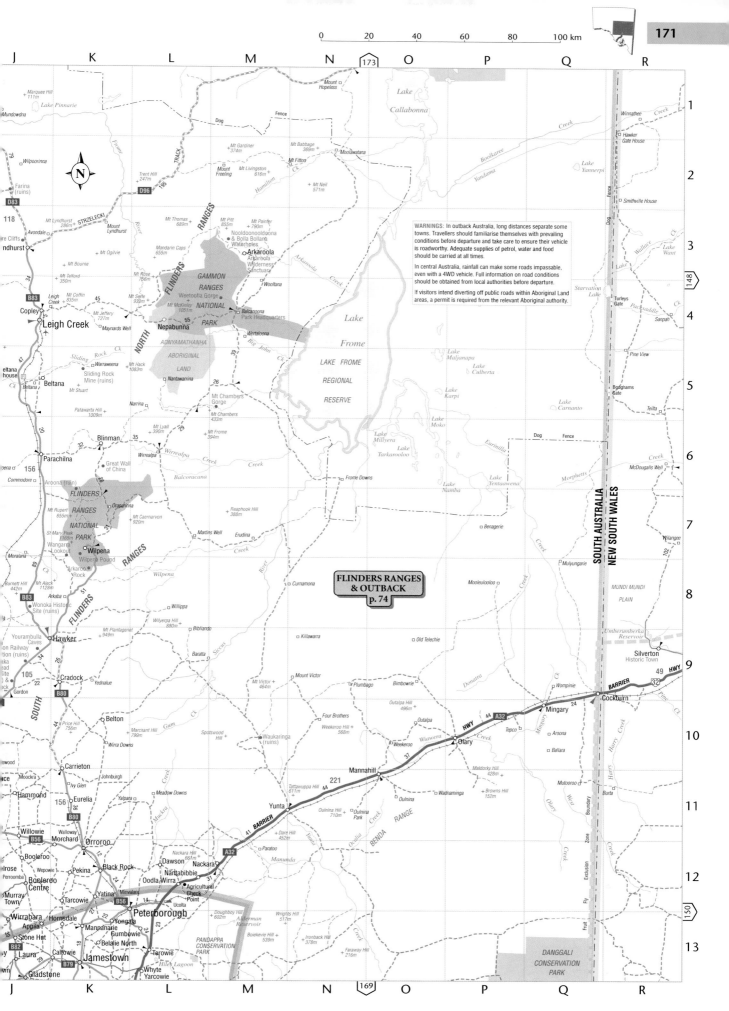

0   20   40   60   80   100 km

J K L M N 173 O P Q R

1

Lake Callabonna

Mount Hopeless

Winnathee Creek

Hawker Gate House

2

Marquee Hill 111m
Lake Pinnarie
Mundowdna
Dog
Fence

Mt Gardiner +374m
Mt Babbage 369m +
Mt Livingston 616m +
Mt Fittoo
Moolawatana

Bookaree Creek
Yandama

Lake Yannerpi

Smithville House

148

3

Farina (ruins)
D83
118
Avondale
re Cliffs
ndhurst

Mt Lyndhurst 286m +
STRZELECKI
Mount Lyndhurst
D96
Trent Hill +247m

Mt Thomas +689m
Mt Pitt 855m +
Mt Painter +790m +
Nooldoonooldoona & Bolla Bollana Waterholes
Mandarin Caps 655m
Arkaroola
Arkaroola Wilderness Sanctuary

Arkaroola Creek

WARNINGS: In outback Australia, long distances separate some towns. Travellers should familiarise themselves with prevailing conditions before departure and take care to ensure their vehicle is roadworthy. Adequate supplies of petrol, water and food should be carried at all times.

Lake Want

4

Copley
Leigh Creek
D83
Mt Coffin 835m +
Leigh Creek
45
Mt Ogilvie +
Mt Bourne +
Mt Telford 350m +
Mt Rose 756m +
Mt Serle 938m +
Mt McKinley 1051m
Weetootla Gorge
55
Balcanoona
Park Headquarters

FLINDERS RANGES
GAMMON RANGES
NATIONAL
Mt Jeffery 727m +
Nepabunna
Wooltana
Mt Neil 571m +

In central Australia, rainfall can make some roads impassable, even with a 4WD vehicle. Full information on road conditions should be obtained from local authorities before departure.

If visitors intend diverting off public roads within Aboriginal Land areas, a permit is required from the relevant Aboriginal authority.

Starvation Lake
Turleys Gate
Paddaple Ck
Sanpah
Pine View

5

eltana house
Beltana
B83
NORTH
47
Sliding Rock Ck
Warraweena
Sliding Rock Mine (ruins)
Mt Hack 1083m +
Nantawarrina
PARK
Wertaloona
ADNYAMATHANHA ABORIGINAL LAND
Big John Ck
39
26
Mt Chambers Gorge

LAKE FROME REGIONAL RESERVE

Lake Frome

Lake Maljanapa
Lake Culberta
Lake Karpi
Lake Carnanto
Lake Carmanto

Booghams Gate
Teilta

6

156
Parachilna
Beltana
Mt Stuart +
Narrina
Patawarta Hill 1009m +
Blinman
35
32
Wirrealpa
Wirrealpa Creek
Mt Lyall +390m
Mt Chambers 433m +
Mt Frome 394m +

Lake Moko
Lake Millyera
Lake Tarkarooloo

Dog Fence
Eurinilla Ck
Morphetts Ck
McDougalls Well

7

Commodore
Aroona (ruin)
Great Wall of China
Balcoracana Creek
FLINDERS RANGES NATIONAL PARK
Mt Rupert 655m +
Orapariinna
Mt Caernarvon 920m +
Reaphook Hill 388m +
Martins Well
Erudina

Frome Downs
Lake Namba
Lake Yentaawena
Benagerie

Mulyungarie
102
Milangee

8

Moralana
St Mary Peak 1165m +
Wangarla Lookout
Wilpena
Wilpena Pound
FLINDERS RANGES
Burnett Hill 442m +
Mt Aleck 1128m +
Arkaba
Arkaroo Rock
B83
Wonoka Historic Site (ruins)
51
Wilpena Creek
Wilpena River
Willippa
Wilyerpa Hill 880m +
Bibliando

Curnamona

FLINDERS RANGES & OUTBACK p. 74

Mooleulooloo

SOUTH AUSTRALIA NEW SOUTH WALES

MUNDI MUNDI PLAIN

9

Yourambulla Caves
on Railway tion (ruins)
aka ead site
k
Gordon
105
Hawker
34
Mt Plantagenet 949m +
Baratta
Killawarra
Old Telechie

Umberumberka Reservoir
Silverton Historic Town
49 HWY
BARRIER
32
Pine Ck

10

SOUTH
Cradock
22
B80
Yednalue
Belton
Price Hill 756m +
Marchant Hill 799m +
Mt Victor +464m
Mount Victor
Spotswood Hill +
Waukaringa (ruins)
Plumbago
Bimbowrie
Weekeroo Hill 568m +
Weekeroo
37
Four Brothers
Outalpa Hill 496m +
Outalpa
HWY
Olary
Wiawera
4A A32
Tepco
Mingary
24
Aroona
Ballara
Cockburn
Wompinie

11

Carrieton
Johnburgh
Ivy Glen
Moockra
Hammond
Eurelia
156
B80
Yalpara
Meadow Downs
Muckra Ck
Mannahill
221
Tattawuppa Hill 611m +
44
Yunta
Ouinina Hill 710m +
Ouinina Park
RANGE
BENDA
Okolia Ck
Oulnina
Wadnamina
Browns Hill 152m +
Mutooroo
Burta
Boundary
Zone
Harry West Ck
Olary

12

swood
Wilyerpa
Willowie
Morchard
B56
Orroroo
Booleroo Centre
Pekina
Black Rock
Dawson
Nackara
Narrtabibbie
Oodla Wirra
41
BARRIER
A32
Nackara Hill 661m +
Paratoo
Manunda
Dare Hill 452m +
Junta Ck
Exclusion

150

13

Irose
Perrooma
Murray Town
Wirrabara
Hornsdale
Appila
Stone Hut
B82
Laura
B79
Gladstone
Booleroo
Tarcowie
Yatina
Minvalara
B56
Peterborough
Yongala
Mannanarie
Gumbowie
Belalie North
Jamestown
Terowie
Whyte Yarcowie
Hansens Lagoon
Agricultural Check Point
Ucolta
14
Doughboy Hill 602m +
Alderman Hill
Wrights Hill 517m +
Boiekevie Hill 539m +
Ironback Hill 378m +
Faraway Hill 216m +
PANDAPPA CONSERVATION PARK
DANGGALI CONSERVATION PARK
Fruit Fly

J K L M N 169 O P Q R

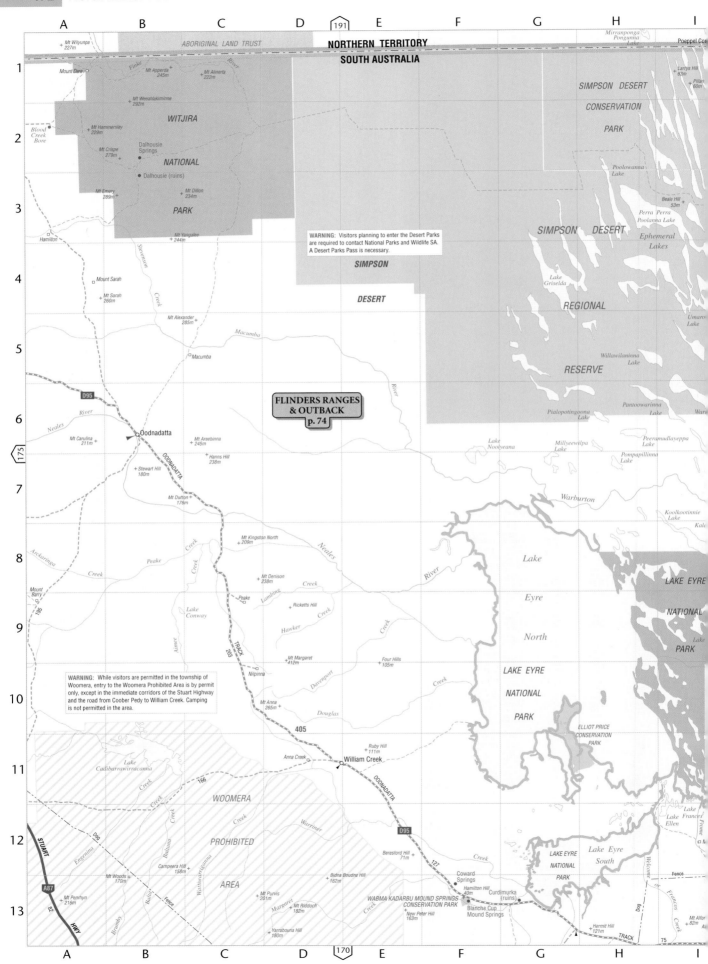

FLINDERS RANGES & OUTBACK p. 74

**WARNING:** Visitors planning to enter the Desert Parks are required to contact National Parks and Wildlife SA. A Desert Parks Pass is necessary.

**WARNING:** While visitors are permitted in the township of Woomera, entry to the Woomera Prohibited Area is by permit only, except in the immediate corridors of the Stuart Highway and the road from Coober Pedy to William Creek. Camping is not permitted in the area.

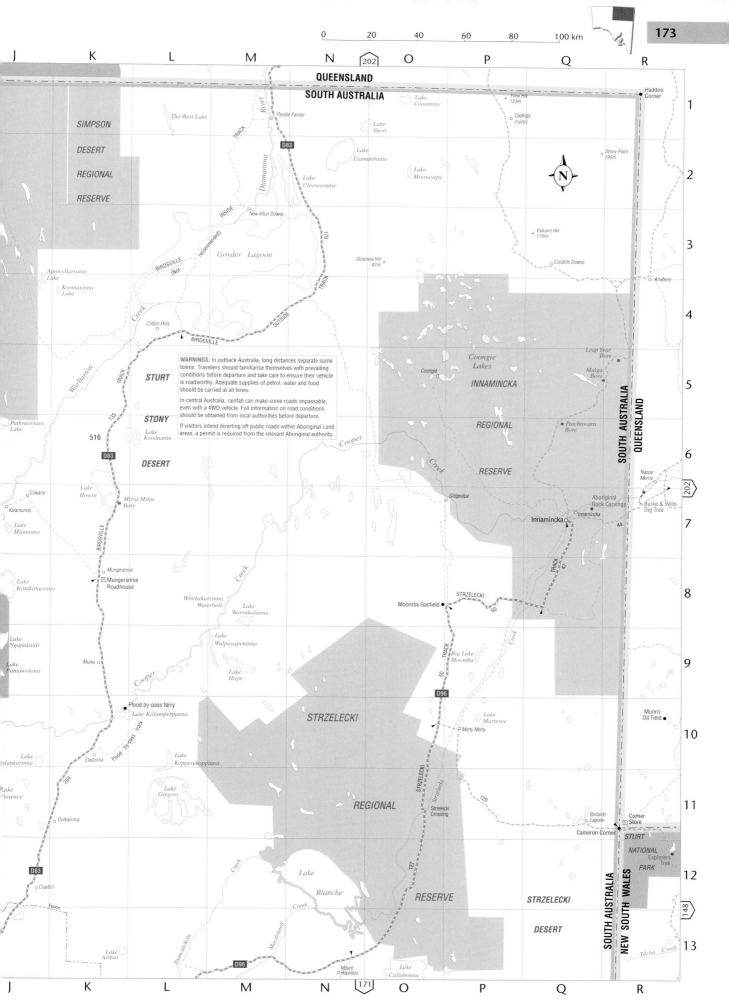

0   20   40   60   80   100 km

J   K   L   M   N   O   P   Q   R

QUEENSLAND
SOUTH AUSTRALIA

Haddon
Corner

SIMPSON

DESERT

REGIONAL

RESERVE

The West Lake

Lake
Cooninnie

Frew Hill
123m

Cadelga
(ruins)

River

TRACK

Pandie Pandie

D83

Lake
Short

Lake
Etamunbanie

Stony Point
195m

Lake
Uloowaranie

Lake
Moorayepe

Diamantina

INSIDE

(recommended)

New Alton Downs

179

Pulcara Hill
170m

BIRDSVILLE (Not

Goyder Lagoon

Dickinna Hill
87m

Cordillo Downs

Apawyilarranie
Lake

Koomarinna
Lake

TRACK

Arrabury

Creek

OUTSIDE

Clifton Hills

BIRDSVILLE

Coongie
Lakes

Leap Year
Bore

Mulga
Bore

Warburton

TRACK

STURT

133

STONY

516

D83

Lake
Koodnanie

INNAMINCKA

Cooper

REGIONAL

Patchawara
Bore

Pathraootara
Lake

DESERT

RESERVE

Nappa
Merrie

Cowarie

Lake
Howitt

Mirra Mitta
Bore

Creek

Gidgealpa

Aboriginal
Rock Carvings

Burke & Wills
Dig Tree

Kalamurina

Lake
Miamiana

Innamincka

Innamincka

4

BIRDSVILLE

WARNINGS: In outback Australia, long distances separate some
towns. Travellers should familiarise themselves with prevailing
conditions before departure and take care to ensure their vehicle
is roadworthy. Adequate supplies of petrol, water and food
should be carried at all times.

In central Australia, rainfall can make some roads impassable,
even with a 4WD vehicle. Full information on road conditions
should be obtained from local authorities before departure.

If visitors intend diverting off public roads within Aboriginal Land
areas, a permit is required from the relevant Aboriginal authority.

TRACK
47

Mungerannie

Mungerannie
Roadhouse

Creek

Winthekarrinna
Waterhole

Lake
Warrakalanna

STRZELECKI

Moomba Gasfield

60

Lake
Kittakittaooloo

Lake
Walpayapeninna

TRACK

Big Lake
Moomba

Creek

Lake
Ngapakaldi

Lake
Hope

50

Lake
Puntawolona

Cooper

D96

Flood by-pass ferry
Lake Killamperpunna

Munro
Oil Field

Lake
Murteree

Merty Merty

Flood   by-pass   track

204

Etadunna

Lake
alankarinna

Lake
Kopperekoppinna

STRZELECKI

127

STRZELECKI

Bollards
Lagoon

Corner
Store

Strzelecki
Crossing

120

Lake
Florence

Dulkaninna

REGIONAL

Cameron Corner

STURT

Lake
Gregory

NATIONAL

Explorers
Tree

PARK

D83

Clayton

127

RESERVE

STRZELECKI

SOUTH AUSTRALIA
NEW SOUTH WALES

148

Fence

Lake
Blanche

DESERT

Creek

Macdonnell

Toonumbyin

Lake
Arthur

D96

Mount
Hopeless

Lake
Callabonna

Tilcha Creek

SOUTH AUSTRALIA
QUEENSLAND

202

J   K   L   M   N   O   P   Q   R

202

171

148

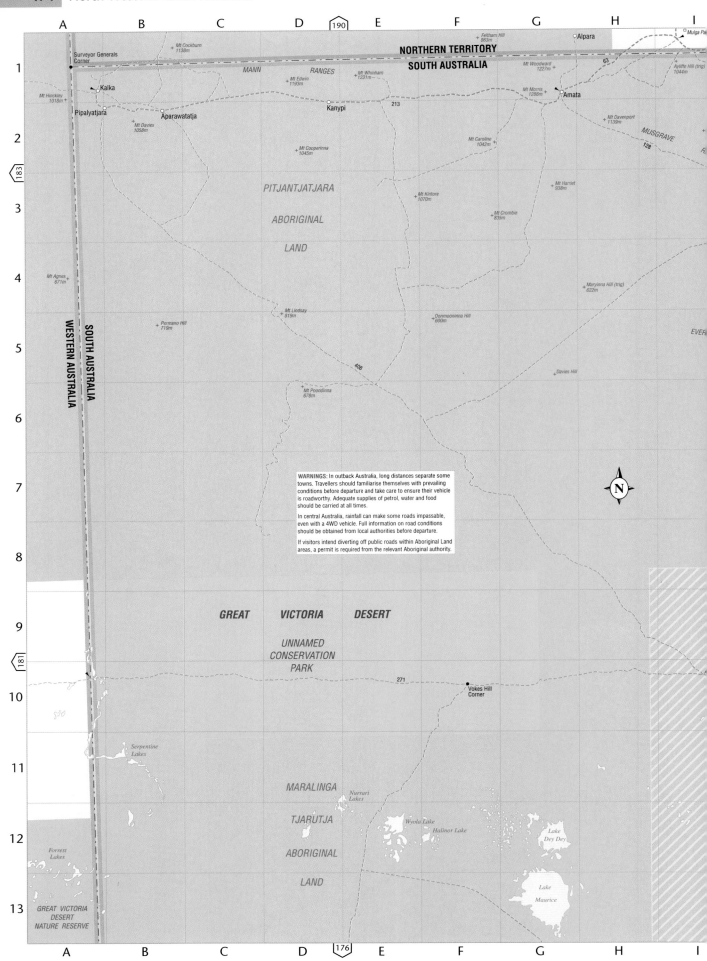

WARNINGS: In outback Australia, long distances separate some towns. Travellers should familiarise themselves with prevailing conditions before departure and take care to ensure their vehicle is roadworthy. Adequate supplies of petrol, water and food should be carried at all times.

In central Australia, rainfall can make some roads impassable, even with a 4WD vehicle. Full information on road conditions should be obtained from local authorities before departure.

If visitors intend diverting off public roads within Aboriginal Land areas, a permit is required from the relevant Aboriginal authority.

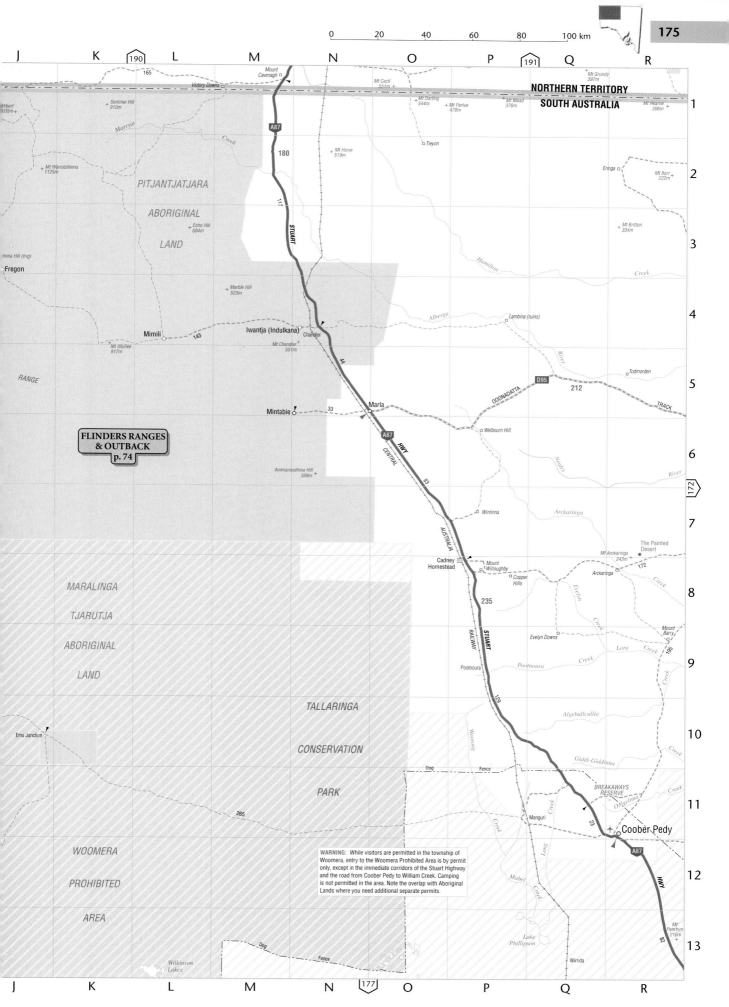

0   20   40   60   80   100 km

J   K   L   M   N   O   P   Q   R

190   191

165
Mount
Cavenagh
Victory Downs

NORTHERN TERRITORY
SOUTH AUSTRALIA

Mt Grundy
397m

1

Mt Cecil
551m
Mt Darling
544m
Mt Parlue
478m
Mt Mead
376m
Mt Hearne
306m

A87

Mt Cuthbert
1035m+

Sentinel Hill
910m

PITJANTJATJARA

180

Mt Howe
519m

Tieyon

Eringa
Mt Barr
222m

2

Marryat
Creek

117

Mt Warrabilinna
1125m

ABORIGINAL

STUART

Echo Hill
604m

Mt Britton
334m

3

Corinna Hill (trig)

LAND

Hamilton
Creek

Fregon

Marble Hill
523m

Alberga
Lambina (ruins)

River

4

Mimili
143
Iwantja (Indulkana)
Chandler

Todmorden

RANGE

Mt Illbillee
917m

Mt Chandler
551m

44

OODNADATTA

D95
212

TRACK

5

FLINDERS RANGES
& OUTBACK
p. 74

Mintabie
33
Marla

A87

Welborn Hill

Neales
River

6

Animaroodinna Hill
359m

CENTRAL

HWY

83

172

MARALINGA

Wintinna

Arckaringa

7

AUSTRALIA

Cadney
Homestead

Mount
Willoughby

Copper
Hills

Mt Arckaringa
243m

The Painted
Desert

172

Arckaringa
Creek

8

TJARUTJA

235

Evelyn

ABORIGINAL

RAILWAY

STUART

Evelyn Downs

Creek

Lora

Mount
Barry

195

9

LAND

Pootnoura

Pootnoura
Creek

Creek

Emu Junction

TALLARINGA

129

Algebullcullia

10

CONSERVATION

Giddi-Giddinna
Creek

Dog   Fence

BREAKAWAYS
RESERVE

Oodgelina
Creek

11

PARK

265

Manguri
Creek

23

Coober Pedy

WOOMERA

WARNING: While visitors are permitted in the township of
Woomera, entry to the Woomera Prohibited Area is by permit
only, except in the immediate corridors of the Stuart Highway
and the road from Coober Pedy to William Creek. Camping
is not permitted in the area. Note the overlap with Aboriginal
Lands where you need additional separate permits.

A87

12

PROHIBITED

Mabel
Creek

HWY

AREA

Lake
Phillipson

Mt Penrhyn
216m

82

13

Dog   Fence

Wilkinson
Lakes

Wirrida

J   K   L   M   N   O   P   Q   R

177

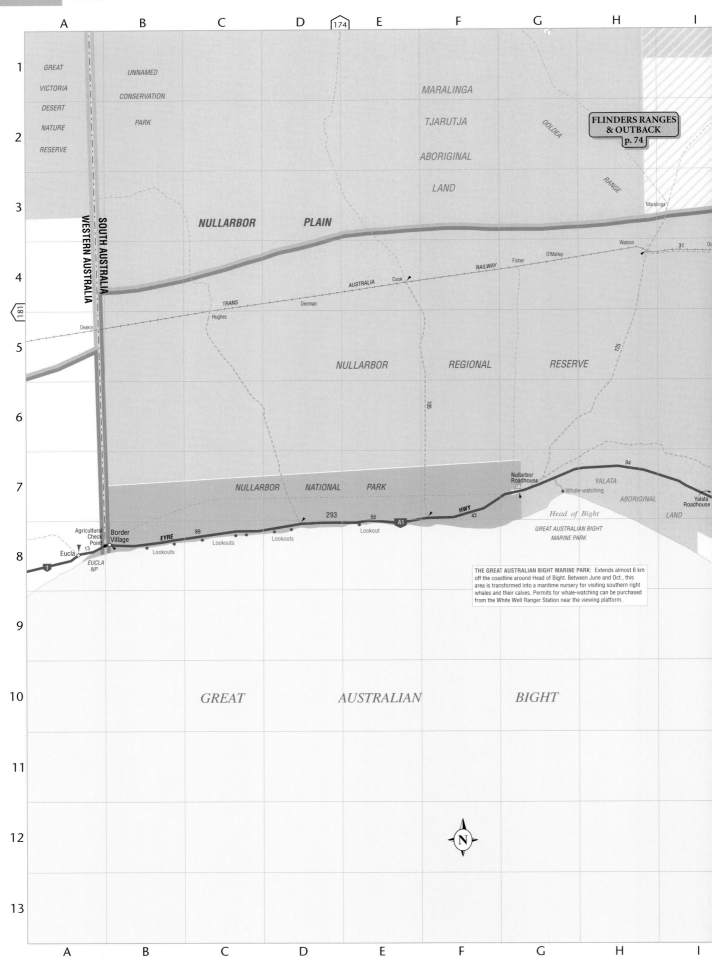

THE GREAT AUSTRALIAN BIGHT MARINE PARK: Extends almost 6 km off the coastline around Head of Bight. Between June and Oct., this area is transformed into a maritime nursery for visiting southern right whales and their calves. Permits for whale-watching can be purchased from the White Well Ranger Station near the viewing platform.

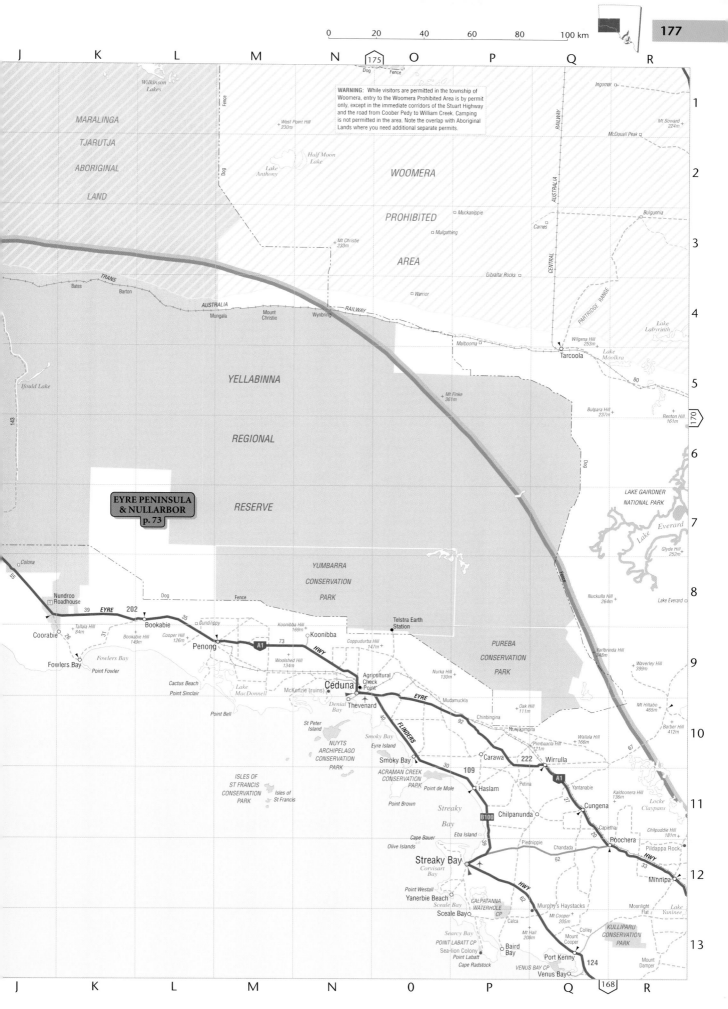

0   20   40   60   80   100 km

EYRE PENINSULA
& NULLARBOR
p. 73

WARNING: While visitors are permitted in the township of
Woomera, entry to the Woomera Prohibited Area is by permit
only, except in the immediate corridors of the Stuart Highway
and the road from Coober Pedy to William Creek. Camping
is not permitted in the area. Note the overlap with Aboriginal
Lands where you need additional separate permits.

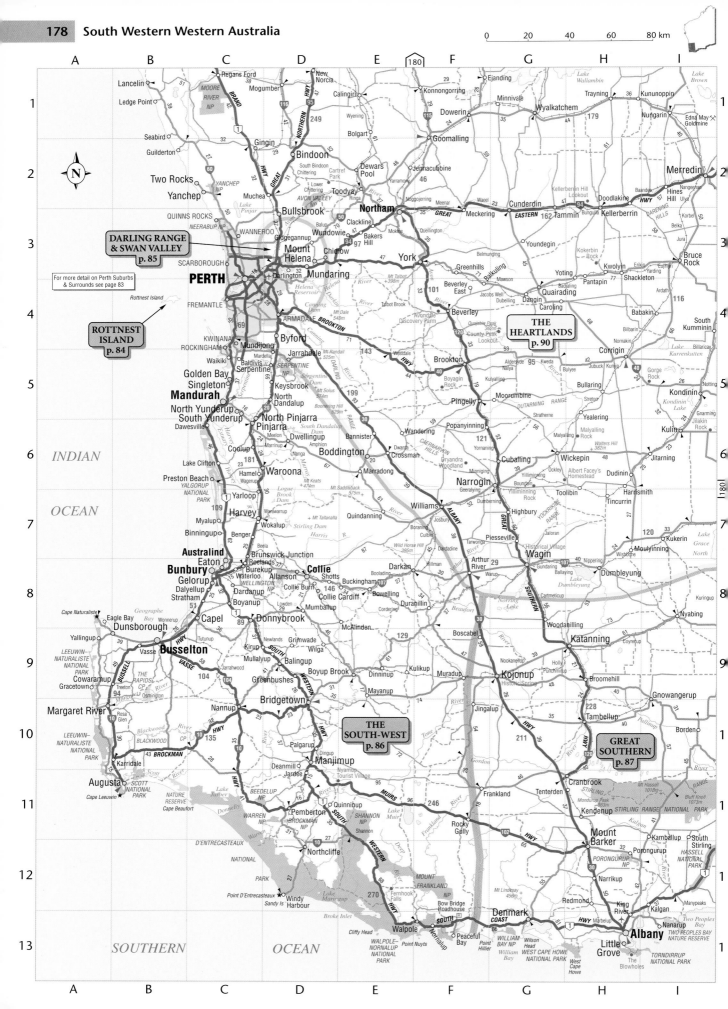

DARLING RANGE & SWAN VALLEY p. 85

For more detail on Perth Suburbs & Surrounds see page 83

ROTTNEST ISLAND p. 84

THE HEARTLANDS p. 90

THE SOUTH-WEST p. 86

GREAT SOUTHERN p. 87

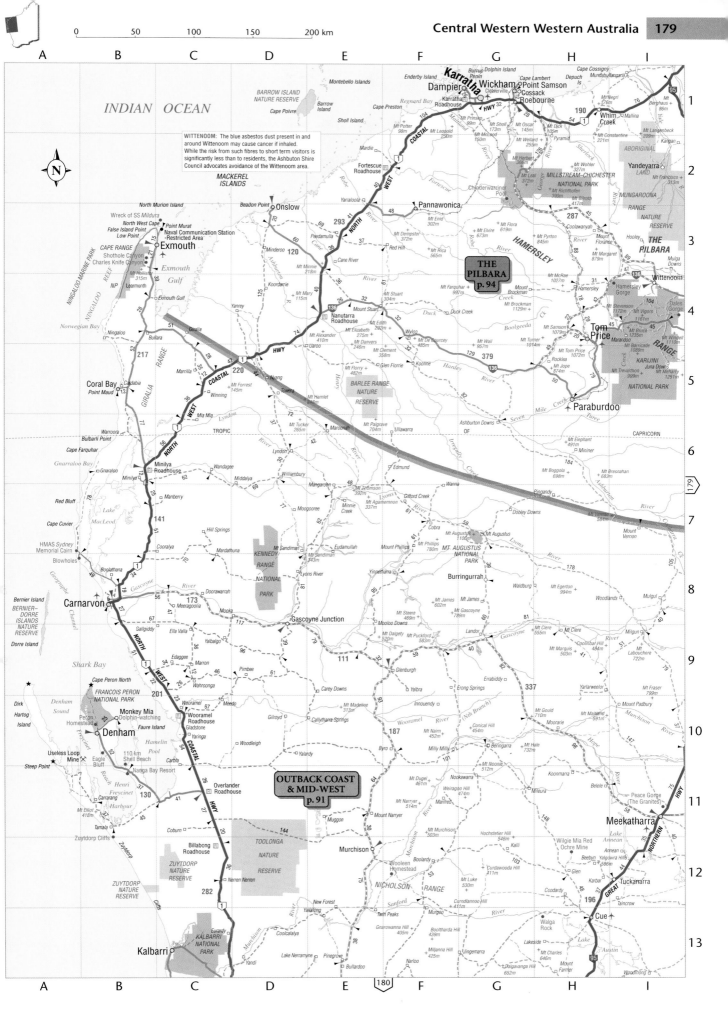

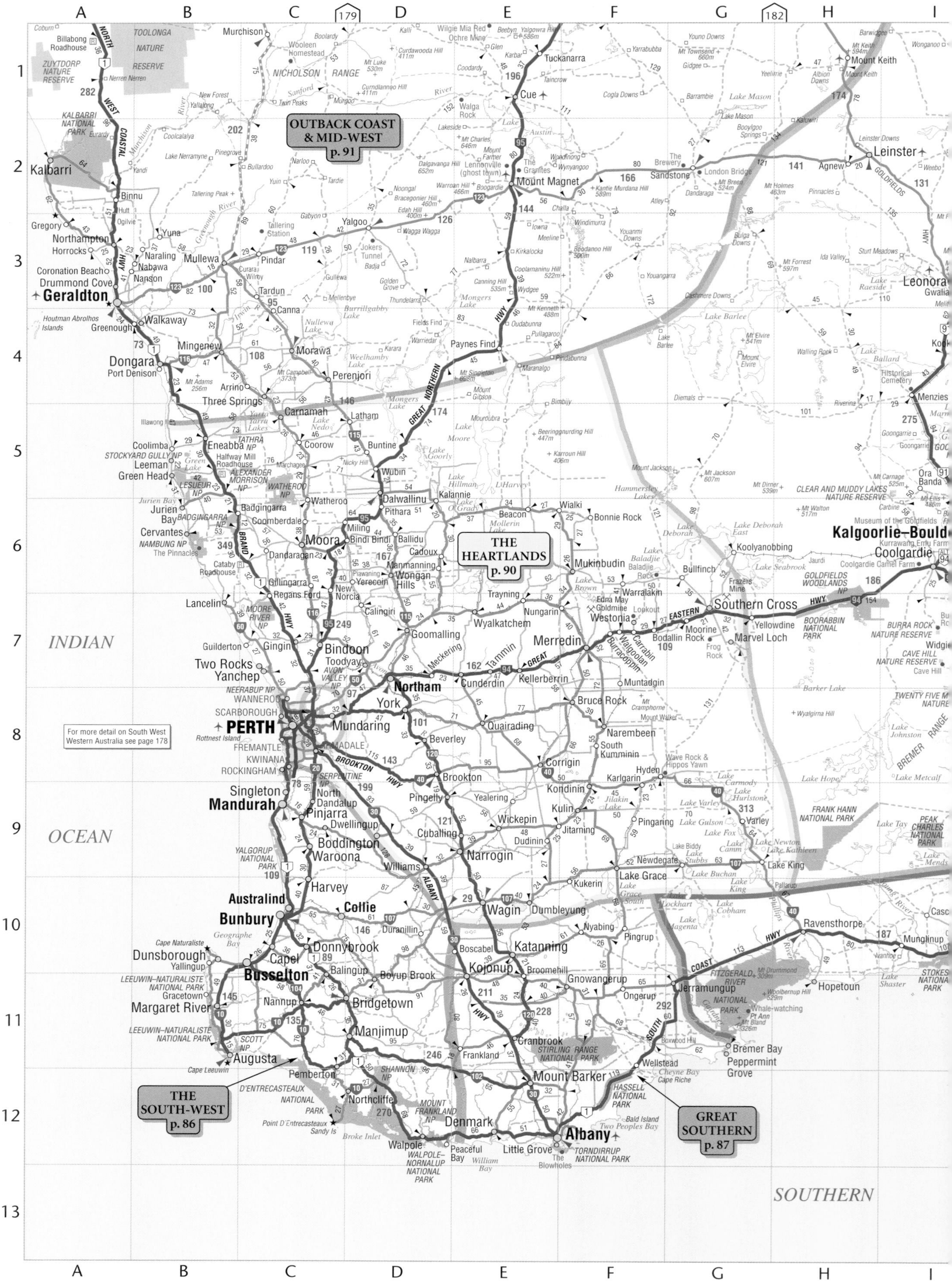

A B 179 C D E F G 182 H I

1
2
3
4
5
6
7
8
9
10
11
12
13

**OUTBACK COAST & MID-WEST**
p. 91

**THE HEARTLANDS**
p. 90

**THE SOUTH-WEST**
p. 86

**GREAT SOUTHERN**
p. 87

For more detail on South West
Western Australia see page 178

INDIAN

OCEAN

SOUTHERN

Kalbarri
KALBARRI NATIONAL PARK
ZUYTDORP NATURE RESERVE
TOOLONGA NATURE RESERVE
Murchison
Billabong Roadhouse
Coburn
Nerren Nerren
Binnu
Gregory
Northampton
Horrocks
Coronation Beach
Drummond Cove
**Geraldton**
Greenough
Walkaway
Dongara
Port Denison
Three Springs
Arrino
Mingenew
Morawa
Perenjori
Carnamah
Coorow
Latham
Buntine
Eneabba
Coolimba
Leeman
Green Head
Jurien Bay
Cervantes
The Pinnacles
Badgingarra
Watheroo
Dalwallinu
Pithara
Kalannie
Beacon
Bonnie Rock
Mukinbudin
Moora
Dandaragan
Gillingarra
Regans Ford
Lancelin
Guilderton
Gingin
Two Rocks
Yanchep
Wanneroo
Scarborough
**PERTH**
Fremantle
Kwinana
Rockingham
Singleton
**Mandurah**
North Dandalup
Pinjarra
Dwellingup
Boddington
Waroona
Harvey
Australind
**Bunbury**
Collie
Donnybrook
Capel
**Busselton**
Dunsborough
Yallingup
Gracetown
Margaret River
Augusta
Nannup
Balingup
Bridgetown
Boyup Brook
Manjimup
Pemberton
Northcliffe
Walpole
Denmark
**Albany**
Little Grove
Mount Barker
Frankland
Cranbrook
Kojonup
Katanning
Broomehill
Gnowangerup
Ongerup
Jerramungup
Bremer Bay
Peppermint Grove
Hopetoun
Ravensthorpe
Munglinup
Wellstead
Williams
Narrogin
Wagin
Dumbleyung
Nyabing
Pingrup
Lake Grace
Lake King
Newdegate
Varley
Kukerin
Wickepin
Cuballing
Dudinin
Jitarning
Kulin
Kondinin
Karlgarin
Hyden
Pingaring
Corrigin
Brookton
Pingelly
Beverley
York
Northam
Mundaring
Toodyay
Bindoon
Goomalling
Calingiri
Wongan Hills
Dowerin
Wyalkatchem
Trayning
Nungarin
Merredin
Kellerberrin
Tammin
Cunderdin
Meckering
Quairading
Bruce Rock
Narembeen
South Kumminin
Muntadgin
Westonia
Warralakin
Southern Cross
Marvel Loch
Yellowdine
Bodallin
Moorine Rock
**Kalgoorlie–Boulder**
Coolgardie
Koolyanobbing
Bullfinch
Menzies
Leonora
Gwalia
Leinster
Agnew
Sandstone
Mount Keith
Tuckanarra
Cue
Mount Magnet
Yalgoo
Paynes Find
Wubin
Pindar
Mullewa
Tardun
Canna
Yuna
Naraling
Nabawa
Nanson
Murchison

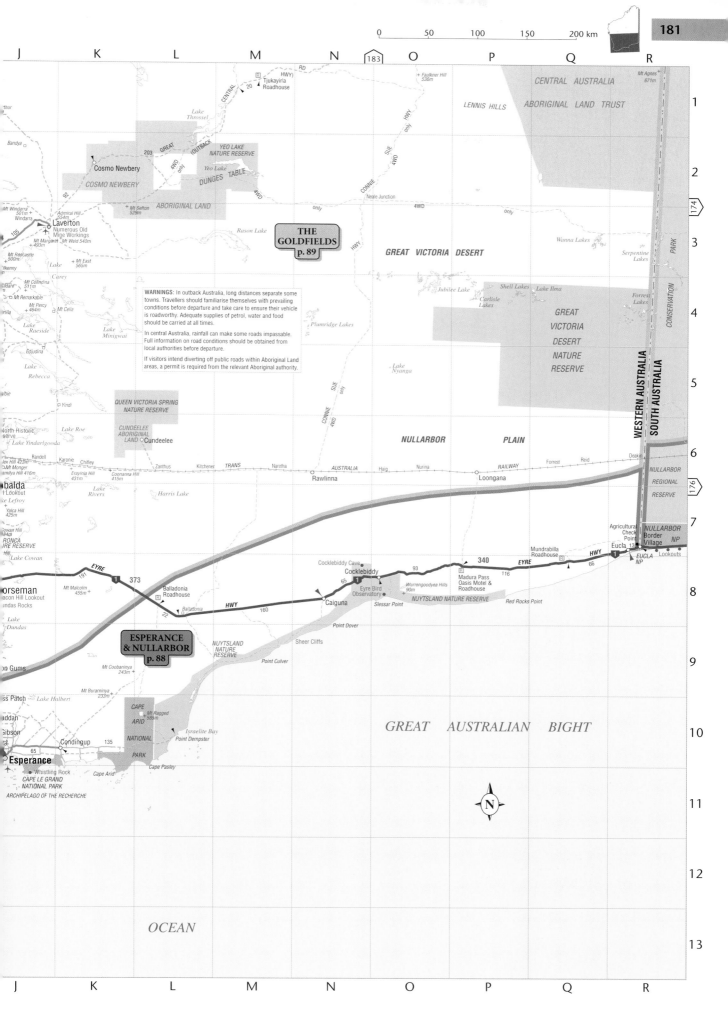

0    50    100    150    200 km

CENTRAL AUSTRALIA ABORIGINAL LAND TRUST

THE GOLDFIELDS p. 89

GREAT VICTORIA DESERT

**WARNINGS:** In outback Australia, long distances separate some towns. Travellers should familiarise themselves with prevailing conditions before departure and take care to ensure their vehicle is roadworthy. Adequate supplies of petrol, water and food should be carried at all times.

In central Australia, rainfall can make some roads impassable. Full information on road conditions should be obtained from local authorities before departure.

If visitors intend diverting off public roads within Aboriginal Land areas, a permit is required from the relevant Aboriginal authority.

GREAT VICTORIA DESERT NATURE RESERVE

QUEEN VICTORIA SPRING NATURE RESERVE

CUNDEELEE ABORIGINAL LAND

NULLARBOR PLAIN

WESTERN AUSTRALIA / SOUTH AUSTRALIA

NULLARBOR REGIONAL RESERVE

ESPERANCE & NULLARBOR p. 88

NUYTSLAND NATURE RESERVE

GREAT AUSTRALIAN BIGHT

CAPE LE GRAND NATIONAL PARK

ARCHIPELAGO OF THE RECHERCHE

OCEAN

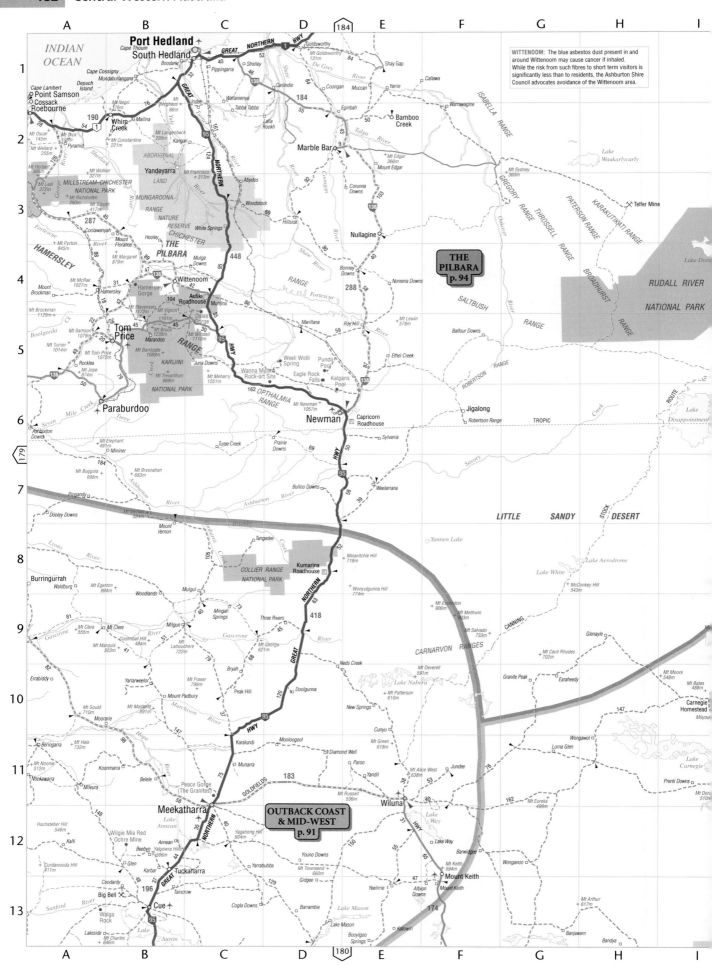

THE PILBARA p. 94

OUTBACK COAST & MID-WEST p. 91

**WITTENOOM:** The blue asbestos dust present in and around Wittenoom may cause cancer if inhaled. While the risk from such fibres to short term visitors is significantly less than to residents, the Ashburton Shire Council advocates avoidance of the Wittenoom area.

0 50 100 150 200 km

J K L M N O P Q R

185

1

Mt Cornish
363m +        + Mt Crown Head
                749m

Mt Romilly
353m +        + Mt Elliott
                418m

KEARNEY

Lake Gregory

Lake Jeavons

2

ABORIGINAL

Lake Dennis

Lake Lucas

Lake White

N

Percival Lakes

Tobin Lake

LAND

Lake Wills

Lake Hazlett

3

Lake
Auld

STOCK

WARNINGS: In outback Australia, long distances separate some
towns. Travellers should familiarise themselves with prevailing
conditions before departure and take care to ensure their vehicle
is roadworthy. Adequate supplies of petrol, water and food
should be carried at all times.

In central Australia, rainfall can make some roads impassable.
Full information on road conditions should be obtained from
local authorities before departure.

If visitors intend diverting off public roads within Aboriginal Land
areas, a permit is required from the relevant Aboriginal authority.

4

Lake
George

fred CANNING

ROUTE

Gary Junction

Lake
Mackay

Lake
Fawcett

KIWIRRKURRA
ABORIGINAL
LAND

Kiwirrkurra

Mt Webb
+ 532m

5

OF

CAPRICORN

NGAANYATJARRA

Mt Tietkens
+ 546m

Ininti

190

Kintore
Mt Leisler
+ 901m

6

Windy Corner

ABORIGINAL LAND

Lake Macdonald

GIBSON     DESERT

CENTRAL AUSTRALIA
ABORIGINAL LAND TRUST

7

Lake Cobb

Lake
Hopkins

WESTERN AUSTRALIA
NORTHERN TERRITORY

Mt Morley
+ 530m

Lake Cohen

McPhersons Pillar
+ 530m

Lake
Hancock

8

GIBSON DESERT

Lake
Newell

Lake
Christopher

Mt Taylor
+ 1001m

Kaltukatjara
(Docker River)

Lake Jones

MUNGILLI ABORIGINAL LAND

Charles Knob
+ 551m

NATURE RESERVE

Warakurna
16

Giles
Meteorological
Station

PETERMANN
RANGES

9

MUNGILLI
CLAYPAN
NATURE
RESERVE

Mt Lampe
497m +

HWY    Everard Junction

Mt Everard
+ 544m

Warakurna
Roadhouse    29

76

Mt William Lambert
517m +

452

UNBARREL

Mt Johnson
+ 534m

Mt Beadell
+ 530m

Notabilis Hill
468m +

215     336

105

10

Thryptomene Hill
439m +

Lake
Breaden

Mt Samuel
+ 619m

Jackie Junction

Bentley Hill
581m

Blackstone

RANGE

Mt Gosse
+ 885m

Surveyor
Generals
Corner

Mt Cockburn
+ 1138m

SUTHERLAND     RANGE

Boyd
Lagoon

BAKER

Mt Harvest
+ 558m

WARBURTON

Mt Talbot 623m +

Mt Rawlinson
603m +     670m

Mt Elvire
603m +

248

Mt Scott 668m +

Mt Aloysius
+ 1085m

55

Mt Hinckley
+ 1018m

Kalka

Aparawatatja

11

Mt Worsnop
+ 461m

Lake Gillen

NGAANYATJARRA

RANGE

Warburton
Roadhouse

Mt Eveline
631m +

Mt Palgrave
539m

Mt Eliza
646m +

BARROW    RANGE

Mt Cooper
+ 670m

Pipalyatjara

Mt Davies
+ 1058m

IDA    RANGE

ABORIGINAL LAND

THE
GOLDFIELDS
p. 89

RD

HWY

565

HWY)

209

SUE
4WD
only

CENTRAL AUSTRALIA

WESTERN AUSTRALIA
SOUTH AUSTRALIA

174

12

Wells

Calachini Hills
+ 543m

Empress
Spring

59

Tjukayirla
Roadhouse

CENTRAL

(OUTBACK

Faulkner Hill
+ 536m

Mt Agnes
671m +

Permiano Hill
719m

GREAT

20

Lake
Throssel

CONNIE

LENNIS HILLS     ABORIGINAL LAND TRUST

13

YEO LAKE
NATURE RESERVE

J K L M N O P Q R

INDIAN OCEAN

GREAT SANDY DESERT

THE PILBARA
p. 94

Cape Leveque · One Arm Point
Thomas Bay · Cygnet Bay · LOMBADINA ABORIGINAL RESERVE
Lombadina
Pender Bay
Beagle Bay · BEAGLE BAY ABORIGINAL RESERVE
Beagle Bay · Lake Paterson
Cape Baskerville · DAMPIER PENINSULA
Carnot Bay
Cape Bertholet · POINT COULOMB NATURE RESERVE · Country Downs · Fraser River
Coulomb Point
James Price Point
Cape Boileau
Waterbank · Roebuck Roadhouse · NORTHERN · 145 · 115
BROOME HWY
Cable Beach · 34
**Broome** · Roebuck Plains · Lake Eda · Taylors Lagoon · Yakka
Gantheaume Point · 30 · Ungani Lakes
Roebuck Bay
Thangoo
Cape Villaret · 4WD only
Gourdon Bay · 80
Cape Latouche Treville · GREAT
Port Smith
False Cape Bossut
La Grange Bay
Bidyadanga
Cape Bossut
Frazier Downs · 73
Admiral Bay
Cape Frezier
Cape Jaubert · Nita Downs
Desault Bay
Cape Missiessy · 286
Anna Plains · Mt Phire 90m
Beach · 103
Wallal Downs · Mandora · Mile · HWY
Eighty · 45 · Sandfire Roadhouse
94 · NORTHERN
281
De Grey · Pardoo Station · Pardoo Roadhouse
50
Goldsworthy
**Port Hedland**
Cape Thouin · South Hedland · 52 · Mt Goldsworthy 131m · 84 · Shay Gap
Boodarie · 40 · Strelley · De Grey River · Callawa
Cape Cossigny · Pippingarra · 46 · Coorigan · Muccan · Yarrie
Mundabullangana · 32 · 138 · Carlindie
Depuch Island
179 · 182

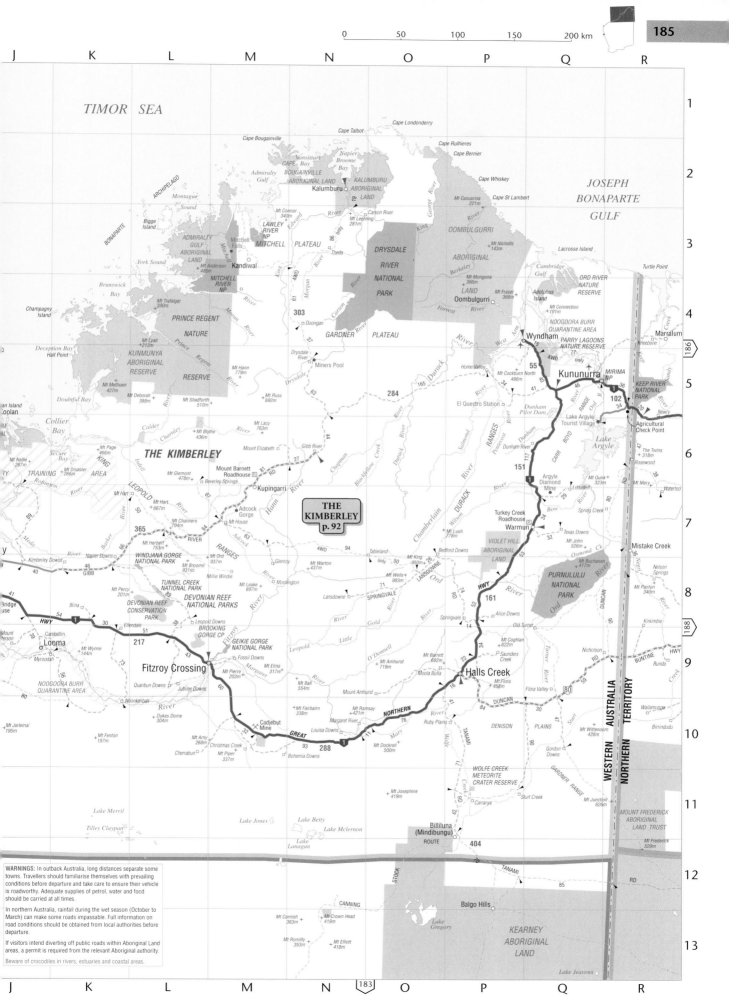

0    50    100    150    200 km

J   K   L   M   N   O   P   Q   R

TIMOR SEA

1

Cape Talbot
Cape Londonderry

Cape Bougainville

Cape Rulhieres
Cape Bernier

JOSEPH
BONAPARTE
GULF

2

Cape Whiskey
Cape St Lambert

Vansittart
Bay

Napier
Broome
Bay

CAPE
BOUGAINVILLE
ABORIGINAL LAND

KALUMBURU
ABORIGINAL
LAND

Admiralty
Gulf

Mt Casuarina
221m

Lacrosse Island

Kalumburu

Montague
Sound

ADMIRALTY
GULF
ABORIGINAL
LAND

LAWLEY
RIVER
NP

19
only

Mt Connor
340m

Carson River

86
only

Mt Learning
281m

George

Cambridge
Gulf

ORD RIVER
NATURE
RESERVE

Turtle Point

3

Bigge
Island

MITCHELL
RIVER
NP

MITCHELL

PLATEAU

Theda

Mt Nicholls
143m

ARCHIPELAGO

BONAPARTE

Mt Anderson
485m

Kandiwal

Mitchell
Falls

DRYSDALE
RIVER
NATIONAL
PARK

OOMBULGURRI

Mt Mongona
366m

Adolphus
Island

Mt Fraser
366m

Mt Connection
191m

NOOGOORA BURR
QUARANTINE
AREA

Marralum

York Sound

PRINCE REGENT

NATURE

61
4WD

303

GARDNER    PLATEAU

Carson

ABORIGINAL

LAND

Oombulgurri

West Arm

Kneebone

186

Brunswick
Bay

Mt Trafalgar
390m

Mt Lyall
+213m

Doongan

37

Forrest

River

Wyndham

15

PARRY LAGOONS
NATURE RESERVE

77
only

4WD

5

Deception Bay
Hall Point

KUNMUNYA
ABORIGINAL
RESERVE

RESERVE

Mt Hann
779m

Drysdale
River

Miners Pool

63

284

165

Home Valley

34

Mt Cockburn North
486m

55

41

Kununurra

46

MIRIMA
NP

36

KEEP RIVER
NATIONAL
PARK

5

Mt Methuen
427m

Mt Deborah
399m

Mt Shadforth
510m

Mt Russ
+692m

Calder

Mt Lacy
763m

Mt Elizabeth

Gibb River

44

81

El Questro Station

117

Dunham
Pilot Dam

Lake Argyle
Tourist Village

Dunham River

102

34

Agricultural
Check Point

20

Newry

Doubtful Bay

Collier
Bay

KING

TRAINING
AREA

Mt Page
466m

Secure
Bay

Mt Disaster
+266m

Mt Hart
+213m

THE KIMBERLEY

Charnley

Mt Blythe
436m

27

Mount Elizabeth

Chapman

RANGES

151

Argyle
Diamond
Mine

Lissadell

Spring Creek

The Twins
+318m

Rosewood

Mt Quirk
+323m

Mt Mary

Waterloo

6

Mt Nellie +
267m

Robinson

Mt Glemont
478m

Mount Barnett
Roadhouse

RD

Beverley Springs

Kupingarri

Hann

Blackfellow Creek

Durack

Wilson

CARR

BOYD

Bow

29

80

7

Mt Hart
+667m

50

Mt Chalmers
704m

67

64

Adcock

Mt House

63

4WD

94

Tableland

50

Mt Lush
778m

Turkey Creek
Roadhouse

Warmun

34

32

Texas Downs

Mt John
526m

Mt Buchanan
+417m

Osmond  Ck

Mistake Creek

Mt Panton
340m

7

LEOPOLD

365

Adcock
Gorge

Mt Herbert
753m

66

Mt Ord
937m

RIVER

Mt Broome
931m

Millie Windie

RANGES

Glenroy

Mt Warton
+437m

Mt King
950m+

only

Bedford Downs

Ord

VIOLET HILL
ABORIGINAL
LAND

53

PURNULULU
NATIONAL
PARK

DUNCAN

Nelson
Springs

8

RIVER

Mt Percy
+362m

Kimberley Downs

Napier Downs

40

46

GIBB

WINDJANA GORGE
NATIONAL PARK

TUNNEL CREEK
NATIONAL PARK

89

DEVONIAN REEF
CONSERVATION
PARK

DEVONIAN REEF
NATIONAL PARKS

Mt Leake
697m

Mortington

Lansdowne

71

River

LANSDOWNE

SPRINGVALE

Mt Wells +
983m

Springvale

HWY

161

Gold

RD

14

Alice Downs

Old Turner

95

Kirkimbie

188

Bridge
House

Medsa

89

HWY

54

30

Ellendale

51

Blina

38

BROOKING
GORGE CP

GEIKIE GORGE
NATIONAL PARK

Leopold Downs

Fossil Downs

Mt Pierre
203m+

Little

O'Donnell

River

Mt Amhurst
+719m

Mt Barrett
692m+

P Saunders
Creek

22

Mt Coghlan
+622m

34

Turner

Nicholson

River

RD

59

80

Buntine

Bunda

HWY

9

Loola

Mt Wynne
144m

217

43

Fitzroy Crossing

60

Quanbun Downs

Jubilee Downs

Mt Elma
317m+

Mt Ball
554m

Moola Bulla

Halls Creek

16

Mt Flora
458m

Flora Valley

Flora

DENISON

30

DUNCAN

84

PLAINS

Sturt

Mt Wittenoom
428m

Nicholson

Wallamunga

Birrindudu

WESTERN  AUSTRALIA

NORTHERN  TERRITORY

Camballin

Myroodah

56

73

Christmas Creek

32

GREAT

Louisa Downs

41

Ruby Plains

River

DUNCAN

Gordon
Downs

90

Mt Junction
626m

10

Mt Jarlemai
195m

Mt Fenton
187m

Dukes Dome
304m

Mt Amy
268m

Cherrabun

Mt Piper
337m

Bohemia Downs

93

288

NORTHERN

Margaret River

76

Mary

Mt Dockrell
500m

Walla

TANAMI

RD

42

Carranya

Sturt Creek

DENISON

GARDNER RANGE

STOCK

11

Lake Merril

Tilley Claypan

Lake Jones

Lake Betty

Lake Mclernon

Lake
Lanagan

Mt Josephine
419m

WOLFE CREEK
METEORITE
CRATER RESERVE

Billiluna
(Mindibungu)

ROUTE

404

TANAMI

MOUNT FREDERICK
ABORIGINAL
LAND TRUST

Mt Frederick
529m

RD

12

CANNING

Mt Carnish
363m

Mt Crown Head
419m

Lake
Gregory

85

Balgo Hills

KEARNEY
ABORIGINAL
LAND

RD

13

Mt Romilly
353m

Mt Elliott
418m

Lake Jeavons

J   K   L   M   N   183   O   P   Q   R

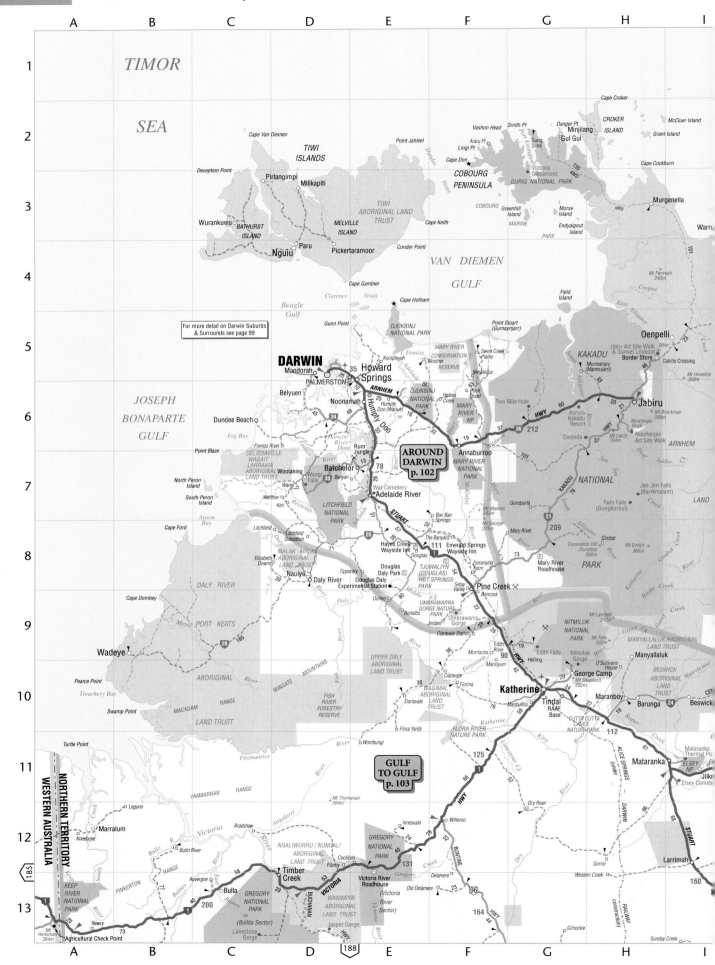

For more detail on Darwin Suburbs & Surrounds see page 99

AROUND DARWIN p. 102

GULF TO GULF p. 103

TIMOR

SEA

TIWI ISLANDS

Cape Van Diemen

Deception Point

Pirlangimpi

Milikapiti

TIWI ABORIGINAL LAND TRUST

Wurankuwu

BATHURST ISLAND

MELVILLE ISLAND

Nguiu

Paru

Pickertaramoor

Point Jahleel

Cape Keith

Conder Point

Cape Croker

CROKER ISLAND

McCluer Island

Vashon Head

Smith Pt

Danger Pt

Minjilang

Gul Gul

Grant Island

Araru Pt

Lingi Pt

Gurig Store

Port Essington

Victoria Settlement

Cape Cockburn

Cape Don

COBOURG PENINSULA

GURIG NATIONAL PARK

COBOURG MARINE PARK

Greenhill Island

Morse Island

Endyalgout Island

only

Murgenella

Warru

Cape Keith

VAN DIEMEN

GULF

Cape Gambier

Clarence Strait

Beagle Gulf

Cape Hotham

Gunn Point

Field Island

Mt Permain 240m

Cooper

East Alligator

Oenpelli

Ubirr Art Site Walk & Sunset Lookout

Border Store

Cahills Crossing

Mt Howship 368m

DARWIN

Mandorah

PALMERSTON

Howard Springs

Koolpinyah

DJUKBINJ NATIONAL PARK

L. Finniss

MARY RIVER CONSERVATION RESERVE

Woolner

Swim Creek Plains

Melaleuca

KAKADU

Munmarlary (Mammularri)

Jabiru

Mt Brockman 289m

Belyuen

Noonamah

Humpty Doo (Waruk)

Helens Creek

Point Stuart

MARY RIVER NP

Two Mile Hole

HWY

Aurora Kakadu Resort

Nourlangie Rock

Nourlangie Art Site Walk

ARNHEM

JOSEPH BONAPARTE GULF

Dundee Beach

Fog Bay

Darwin River Dam

Rum Jungle

Annaburroo

Cooinda

Mt Cahill 154m

Jim Jim Falls (Barrkmalam)

Point Blaze

Finniss River

Batchelor

War Cemetery

MARY RIVER NATIONAL PARK

McKinlay

NATIONAL

Twin Falls (Gungkurdul)

LAND

North Peron Island

DELISSAVILLE WAGAIT LARRAKIA ABORIGINAL LAND TRUST

Woolaning

Wang Falls

Banyan

Adelaide River

Ban Ban Springs

Goodparla

Mt Masson 243m

Mt George 275m

Mary River

KAKADU

Gimbat

ARNHEM

South Peron Island

Welltree

Keri

LITCHFIELD NATIONAL PARK

Mt Evelyn 365m

Coronation Hill (Guratba) 300m

Gimbat Creek

Cape Ford

Litchfield Outstation

Hayes Creek Wayside Inn

Douglas

STUART

Esmeralda Farm

Mary River Roadhouse

209

Anson Bay

MALAK MALAK ABORIGINAL LAND TRUST

Elizabeth Downs

Emerald Springs Wayside Inn

PARK

Nauiyu

Tipperary

Daly River

Douglas Daly Park

Douglas Daly Experimental Station

TJUWALIYN (DOUGLAS) HOT SPRINGS PARK

Pine Creek

Bonrook

Setay Valley

Birdie Creek

DALY RIVER

Cape Dombey

Ooloo

Daly

UMBRAWARRA GORGE NATURE PARK

Bonalbo

Jindare

River

Katherine Creek

PORT KEATS

Moyle River

Umbrawarra Gorge

Claravale Station

NITMILUK NATIONAL PARK

Mt Lambell 317m

MANYALLALUK ABORIGINAL LAND TRUST

Wadeye

185

ABORIGINAL

River

Ferguson

Claravale

Morrisons

Edith River

Edith Falls

Nitmiluk Gorge

Mt Felix 332m

O'Sullivans House

Manyallaluk

Grace Ck

Waterhouse

Pearce Point

Treachery Bay

Swamp Point

WINGATE

MOUNTAINS

UPPER DALY ABORIGINAL LAND TRUST

FISH RIVER FORESTRY RESERVE

WAGIMAN ABORIGINAL LAND TRUST

Dorisvale

Florina

Claravale

Helling

HWY

George Camp

Mt Shepherd 232m

Edith Gorge

Katherine

Maranboy

BESWICK ABORIGINAL LAND TRUST

Beswick

MACADAM

RANGE

LAND TRUST

Flora Yards

Manbulloo

Tindal RAAF Base

CUTTA CUTTA CAVES NATURE PARK

Roper

Barunga

CEN

Turtle Point

FLORA RIVER NATURE PARK

Katherine

King

Limestone Ck

112

Matarank Thermal Po

NORTHERN TERRITORY / WESTERN AUSTRALIA

Wombungi

Mataranka

ELSEY NP

Jilkr

Elsey Cemetery

Legune

YAMBARRAN

RANGE

Fitzmaurice

River

125

HWY

Dry River

DARWIN

Mt Thymanan 304m

Willeroo

ALICE SPRINGS

Marralum

Kneebone

Victoria

Bradshaw

R

Angolarri

Innesvale

GREGORY NATIONAL PARK

BUNTINE

STUART

Larrimah

160

Bullo River

Bullo

River

NGALIWURRU / NUNGALI ABORIGINAL LAND TRUST

Coolibah

Fitzroy

Victoria River Roadhouse (Victoria River Sector)

Old Delamere

Delamere

Gorrie

Western Creek

WESTERN AUSTRALIA

KEEP RIVER NATIONAL PARK

PINKERTON

RANGE

Baines

Auvergne

Bulla

GREGORY NATIONAL PARK

(Bullita Sector)

Timber Creek

BUCHANAN

VICTORIA

WANIMIYN ABORIGINAL LAND TRUST

Jasper Gorge

Gregory

Creek

96

HWY

Gilnockie

RAILWAY construction

Mt Hensman 384m

Newry

Agricultural Check Point

Limestone Gorge

Sunday Creek

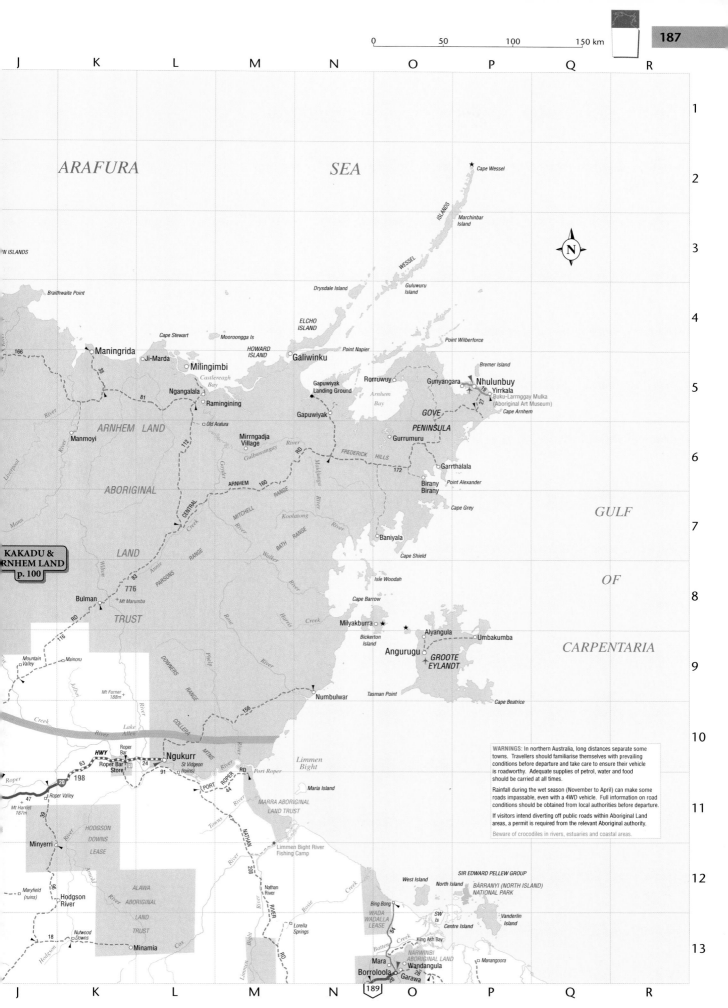

0    50    100    150 km

J    K    L    M    N    O    P    Q    R

1

ARAFURA          SEA

N ISLANDS

★ Cape Wessel

2

Marchinbar
Island

WESSEL

ISLANDS

N

3

Braithwaite Point

Drysdale Island

Guluwuru
Island

Point Wilberforce

4

166                    Cape Stewart        Mooroongga Is
Maningrida                        HOWARD
Ji-Marda          ISLAND
35                                                        Galiwinku        Point Napier        Bremer Island

ELCHO
ISLAND

5
Milingimbi                                                                Gunyangara    Nhulunbuy
81                                        Rorruwuy                                79    Yirrkala
Ngangalala        Castlereagh                Gapuwiyak                            Buku-Larrnggay Mulka
Bay                Landing Ground    Arnhem    27    (Aboriginal Art Museum)
Ramingining                                Bay                            Cape Arnhem
ARNHEM    LAND        112                                            GOVE
Old Arafura                                        PENINSULA
Manmoyi                                        Gapuwiyak
Mirrngadja                                Gurrumuru
Village        River
6
ABORIGINAL                    Gulbuwangay        FREDERICK    HILLS    Garrthalala
ARNHEM    160                        Mangungu        172        Point Alexander
Manyngu                                            Birany
Birany

CENTRAL        MITCHELL                Koolatong        Cape Grey        GULF

7
Creek        RANGE        BATH    RANGE    River    Baniyala
LAND        RANGE            Wollee        Cape Shield

KAKADU &        PARSONS        Isle Woodah        OF
ARNHEM LAND        776                                    Cape Barrow
p. 100        83    + Mt Marumba        Harris
Bulman        Wilton                Rose        Creek        Milyakburra ★        ★        CARPENTARIA
8
RD        116                                    Bickerton        Alyangula
TRUST                                    Island        Umbakumba
Mountain        Mainoru        Phelp            Angurugu    GROOTE
Valley                                        EYLANDT
9
Mt Furner        DOWNERS        River
188m +        RANGE                        Tasman Point        Cape Beatrice

Creek        COLLERA        Lake        Numbulwar
Allen        156
River        MTNS
10
HWY        Roper                Limmen                WARNINGS: In northern Australia, long distances separate some
Bar                Bight                towns. Travellers should familiarise themselves with prevailing
63        Roper Bar        24    Ngukurr        RD    Port Roper                conditions before departure and take care to ensure their vehicle
20    198        Store        91    St Vidgeon        PORT    44                is roadworthy. Adequate supplies of petrol, water and food
Roper        47        (ruins)        ROPER    Maria Island                should be carried at all times.
Roper Valley
11
Mt Harriet                        MARRA ABORIGINAL                Rainfall during the wet season (November to April) can make some
187m +        39                        LAND TRUST                roads impassable, even with a 4WD vehicle. Full information on road
Minyerri        HODGSON                Limmen Bight River                conditions should be obtained from local authorities before departure.
DOWNS                Fishing Camp
LEASE                                        If visitors intend diverting off public roads within Aboriginal Land
96                            NATHAN                areas, a permit is required from the relevant Aboriginal authority.
12
Maryfield        ALAWA                Nathan                SIR EDWARD PELLEW GROUP        Beware of crocodiles in rivers, estuaries and coastal areas.
(ruins)        ABORIGINAL        208    River        West Island        BARRANYI (NORTH ISLAND)
Hodgson        LAND        River        North Island    NATIONAL PARK
River        TRUST        RIVER        Rose        Bing Bong        SW    Centre Island    Vanderlin
18        Creek    WADA    Is        Island
Nutwood                                WADALLA        King Ash Bay
13
Downs        Minamia        Cox        Lorella        LEASE    54        NARWINBI
Springs                        ABORIGINAL
Hodgson                        Limmen        Batten    Creek    LAND    Manangoora
Mara    Wandangula
189        Borroloola    26    Garawa

J    K    L    M    N    O    P    Q    R

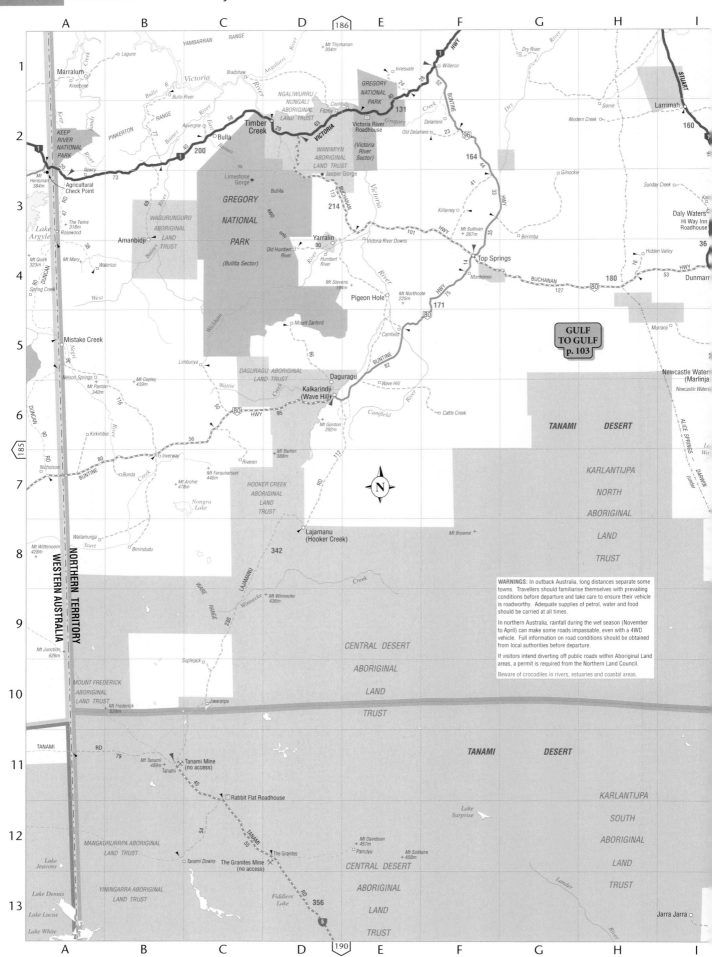

GULF
TO GULF
p. 103

**WARNINGS:** In outback Australia, long distances separate some towns. Travellers should familiarise themselves with prevailing conditions before departure and take care to ensure their vehicle is roadworthy. Adequate supplies of petrol, water and food should be carried at all times.

In northern Australia, rainfall during the wet season (November to April) can make some roads impassable, even with a 4WD vehicle. Full information on road conditions should be obtained from local authorities before departure.

If visitors intend diverting off public roads within Aboriginal Land areas, a permit is required from the Northern Land Council.

Beware of crocodiles in rivers, estuaries and coastal areas.

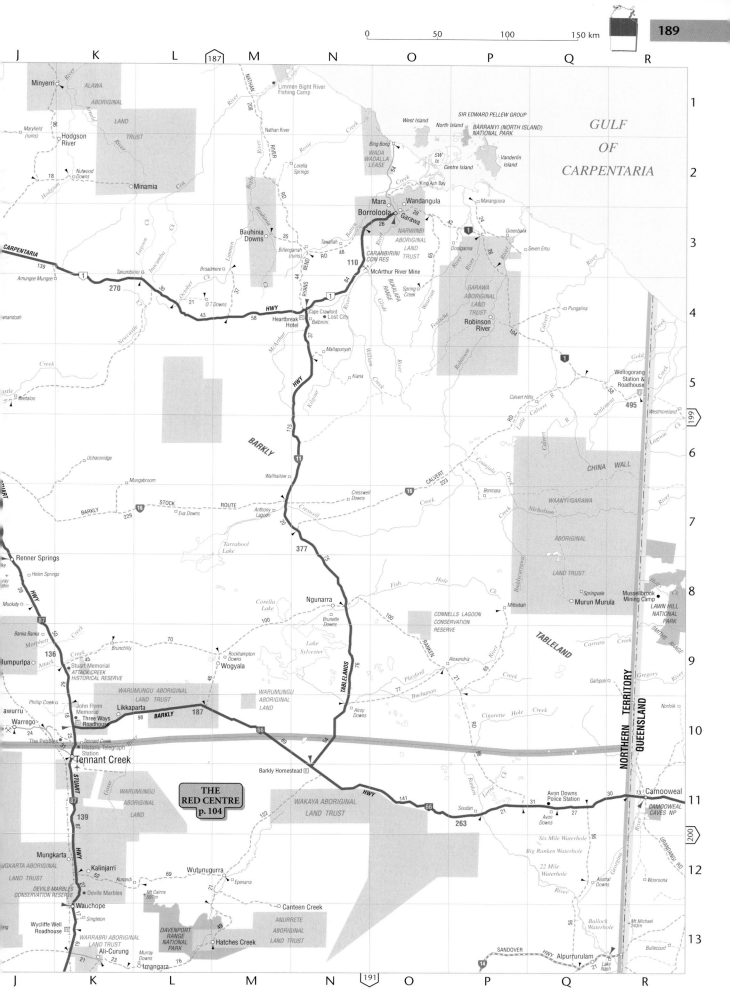

0   50   100   150 km

J K L M N O P Q R

GULF
OF
CARPENTARIA

1
2
3
4
5
6
7
8
9
10
11
12
13

SIR EDWARD PELLEW GROUP

BARRANYI (NORTH ISLAND)
NATIONAL PARK

West Island
North Island
Centre Island
Vanderlin
Island
SW
Is
King Ash Bay

Minyerri
ALAWA
ABORIGINAL
LAND
TRUST

Maryfield
(ruins)
Hodgson
River
96
Minamia
18
Nutwood
Downs
Cox

Bauhinia
Downs
35
Broadmere
O T Downs
37
21
43
58

Tanumbirini
30
October
Ck

Amungee Mungee
139
270

CARPENTARIA

Limmen Bight River
Fishing Camp

Lorella
Springs
Billengarrah
(ruins)

NATHAN
208
RIVER
Rosie
Batten

Tawallah
RYANS
BEND
RD
44
CapeCrawford
Heartbreak
Hotel
Lost City
Balbirini
37
Mallapunyah
Kiana
110
84
48

Mara
Borroloola
Garawa
Wandangula
28
26

Bing Bong
54
Manangoora
42
24
26
Greenbank
Doolgarina
Seven Emu

NARWINBI
ABORIGINAL
LAND
TRUST
CARANBIRINI
CON RES
McArthur River Mine
Spring
Creek
65
BUKALARA
RANGE
Glyde

GARAWA
ABORIGINAL
LAND
TRUST
Robinson
River
104

Wollogorang
Station &
Roadhouse
58
495
Westmoreland
199

Pungalina
Gold

Calvert Hills
Calvert
RD
Little Calvert R
Benmara
223
CALVERT
16

CHINA WALL

William
HWY
115
BARKLY
11
Wallhallow

Ucharonidge
Mungabroom
BARKLY
229
16
STOCK
ROUTE
Eva Downs
Anthony
Lagoon
20
377
75

Cresswell
Downs
Creswell
Ck
Calvert
RD
Nicholson
WAANYI/GARAWA

ABORIGINAL

LAND
TRUST
Springvale
Murun Murula
Mitiebah
Mussellbrook
Mining Camp
LAWN HILL
NATIONAL
PARK
SMITHS RANGE

Tarrabool
Lake
Corella
Lake
Lake
Sylvester

Ngunarra
100
Brunette
Downs
CONNELLS LAGOON
CONSERVATION
RESERVE

Fish
Hole
Ck
100

TABLELAND
Carrara
Creek
Gallipoli
Norfolk

Renner Springs
Helen Springs
Muckaty
39
HWY
87

Banka Banka
50
136
lumpurlpa
Brunchilly
70
45
Rockhampton
Downs
O T Downs
Wogyala
46
Morphett Ck
29

WARUMUNGU ABORIGINAL
LAND TRUST
WARUMUNGU
ABORIGINAL
LAND
Alroy
Downs
76
TABLELANDS
Playford
Buchanan
77
RANKEN
Alexandria
RD
65
Cigarette Hole Creek

Phillip Creek
John Flynn
Memorial
Three Ways
Roadhouse
Likkaparta
98
BARKLY
187
66
89
54

awurru
Warrego
24
18
The Pebbles
26
31
Tennant Creek
Historic Telegraph
Station
Stuart Memorial
ATTACK CREEK
HISTORICAL RESERVE

Barkly Homestead
HWY
141
66
263

Soudan
21
Avon
Downs
Avon Downs
Police Station
31
27
30
13 Camooweal

CAMOOWEAL
CAVES NP

THE
RED CENTRE
p. 104

WAKAYA ABORIGINAL
LAND TRUST
122

Mungkarta
Kalinjarri
52
Kurundi
69
Wutunugurra
Epenarra
21

NGKARTA ABORIGINAL
LAND TRUST
DEVILS MARBLES
CONSERVATION RESERVE
Devils Marbles
Mt Cairns
597m

Wauchope
Singleton
Wycliffe Well
Roadhouse
17

Canteen Creek

ANURRETE
ABORIGINAL
LAND TRUST

DAVENPORT
RANGE
NATIONAL
PARK
Hatches Creek
49

WARRABRI ABORIGINAL
LAND TRUST
Ali-Curung
21
Murray
Downs
23
1mangara
76

Six Mile Waterhole
Big Ranken Waterhole
22 Mile
Waterhole
56
Austral
Downs
Wooroona

56
Bullock
Waterhole
Mt Michael
243m
Bullecourt

SANDOVER
HWY
Alpururlam
Lake
Nash
21
14

NORTHERN TERRITORY
QUEENSLAND

STUART
HWY
87
139
87

STUART

200
URANDANGI RD

## ULURU–KATA TJUTA NATIONAL PARK

Uluṟu–Kata Tjuṯa National Park is renowned for its rock monolith, Uluṟu (Ayers Rock) and for Kata Tjuṯa (The Olgas), a group of towering dome-shaped rocks. This World Heritage-listed area is of vital cultural and religious significance to Anangu, the traditional owners of the area. Anangu hold freehold title to the park and lease it back to Parks Australia.

CULTURAL CENTRE: The Uluṟu–Kata Tjuṯa Cultural Centre, designed in the shape of two snakes, is located on the approach road to Uluṟu. Anangu hope that visitors will leave the centre with a new appreciation of their culture and land.

ULURU: Uluṟu rises majestically 348 metres above a wide, sandy flood plain. The rock is 9.4 kilometres in circumference. There are many walking tracks around the base of the monolith and various ranger-guided tours. Anangu prefer that visitors respect their culture and not climb Uluṟu.

KATA TJUTA: Kata Tjuṯa, 52 kilometres west of Uluṟu, is a collection of red domed rocks separated by deep canyons. The highest, Mt Olga, rises to 546 metres. Walking tracks lead to Olga Gorge and the Valley of the Winds.

ACCOMMODATION: Yulara, situated outside the national park, is the location of Ayers Rock Resort. Accommodation ranges from camping and budget accommodation to international-standard hotels.

WARNING: Visitors planning to travel along Larapinta Drive through Aboriginal Land require a permit. Check road conditions before departing; 4WD vehicle may be required.

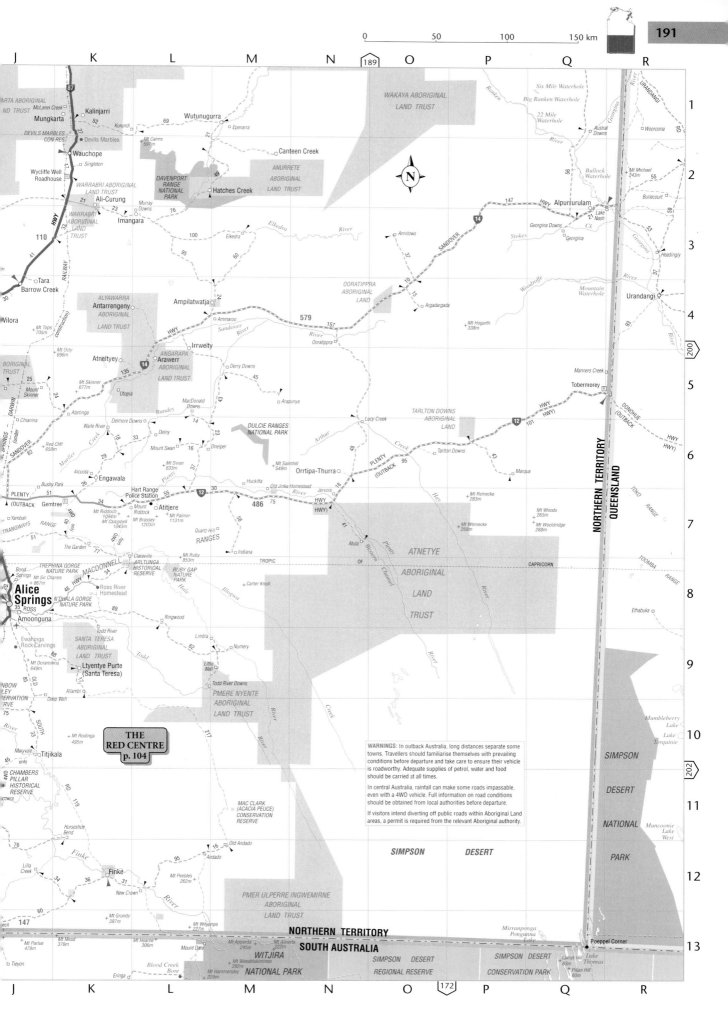

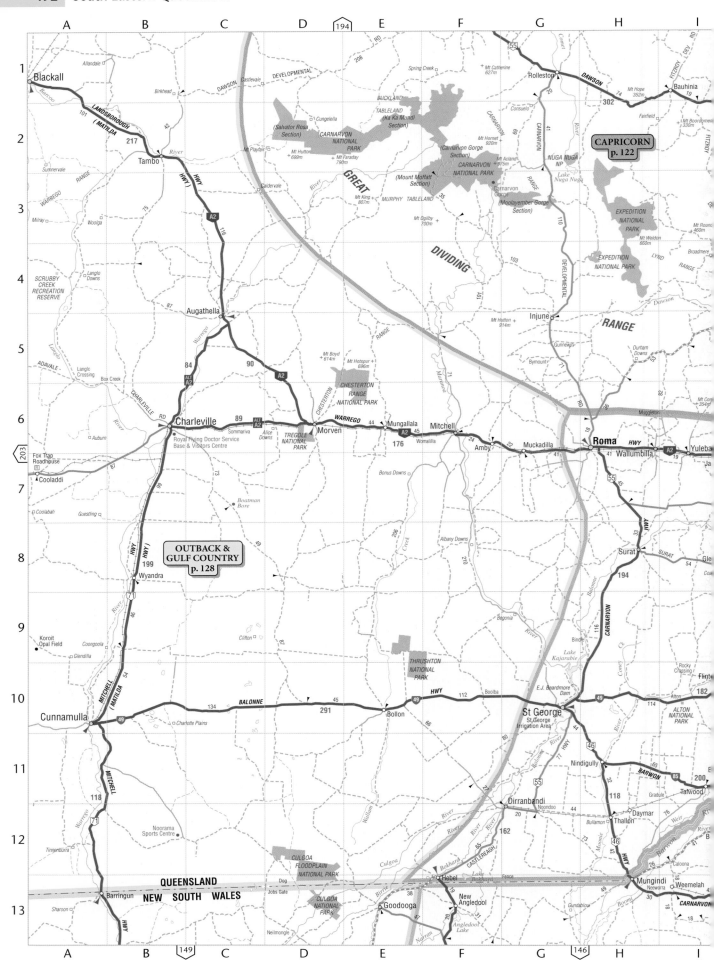

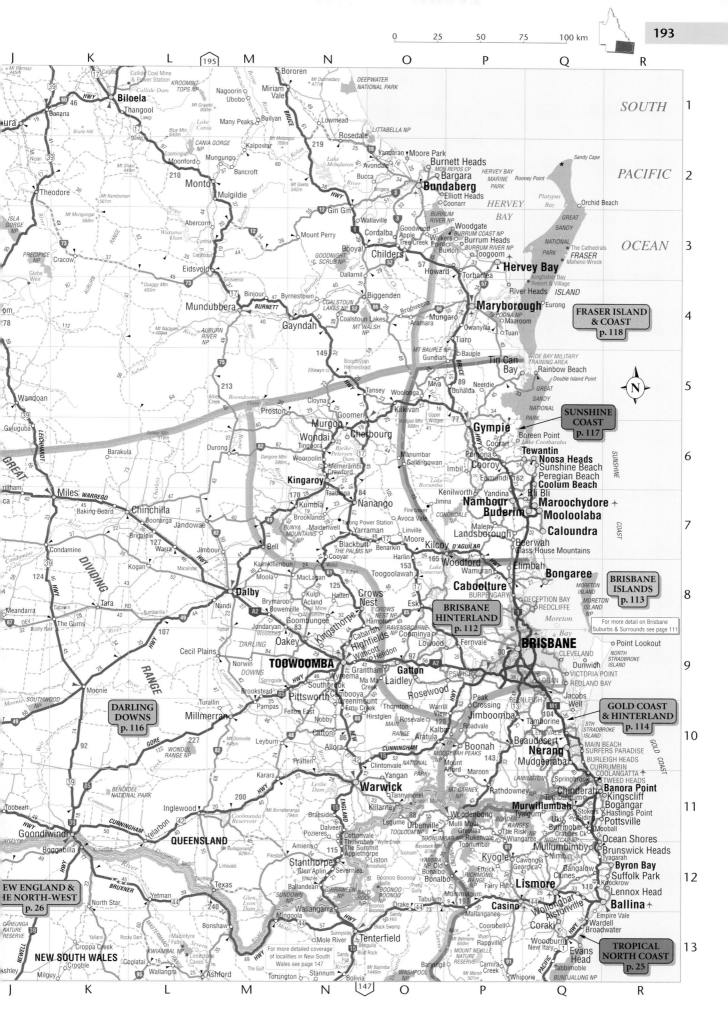

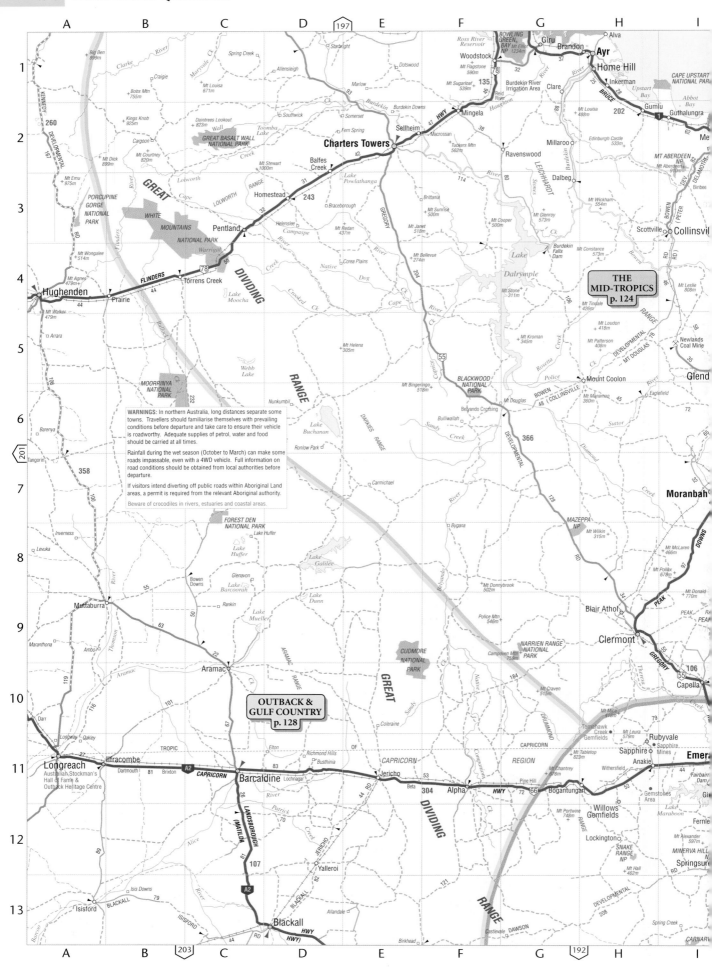

WARNINGS: In northern Australia, long distances separate some towns. Travellers should familiarise themselves with prevailing conditions before departure and take care to ensure their vehicle is roadworthy. Adequate supplies of petrol, water and food should be carried at all times.

Rainfall during the wet season (October to March) can make some roads impassable, even with a 4WD vehicle. Full information on road conditions should be obtained from local authorities before departure.

If visitors intend diverting off public roads within Aboriginal Land areas, a permit is required from the relevant Aboriginal authority.

Beware of crocodiles in rivers, estuaries and coastal areas.

THE MID-TROPICS p. 124

OUTBACK & GULF COUNTRY p. 128

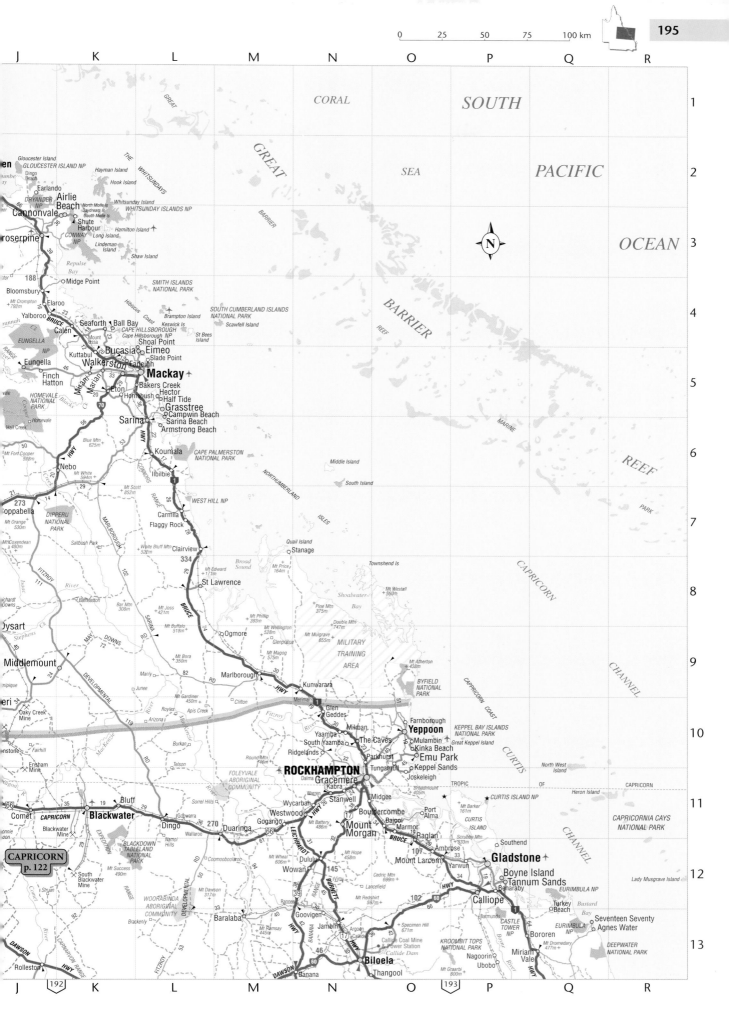

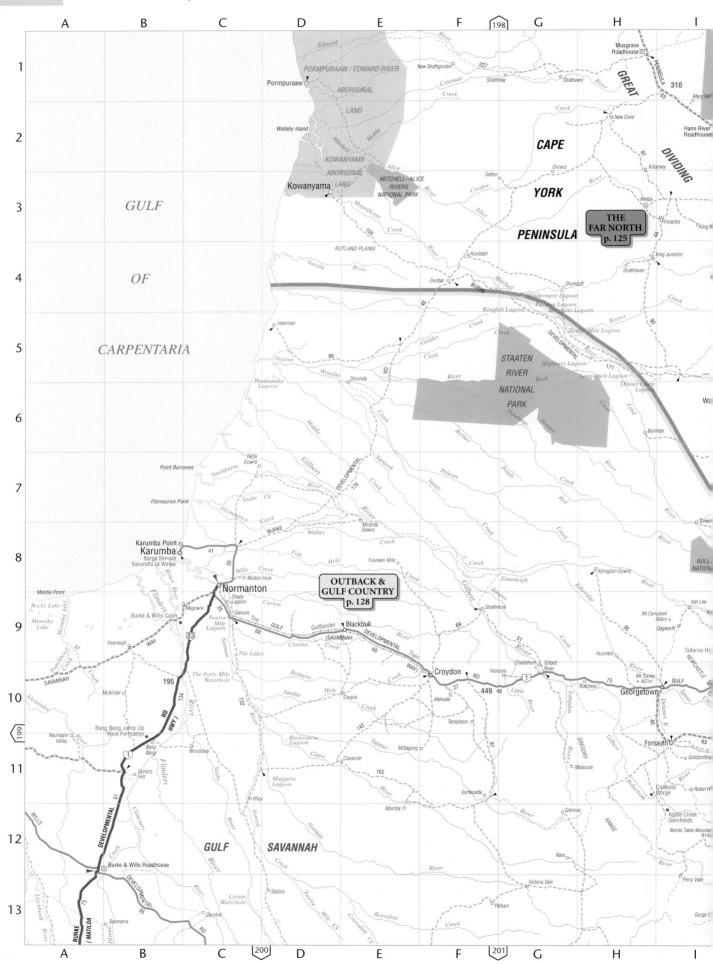

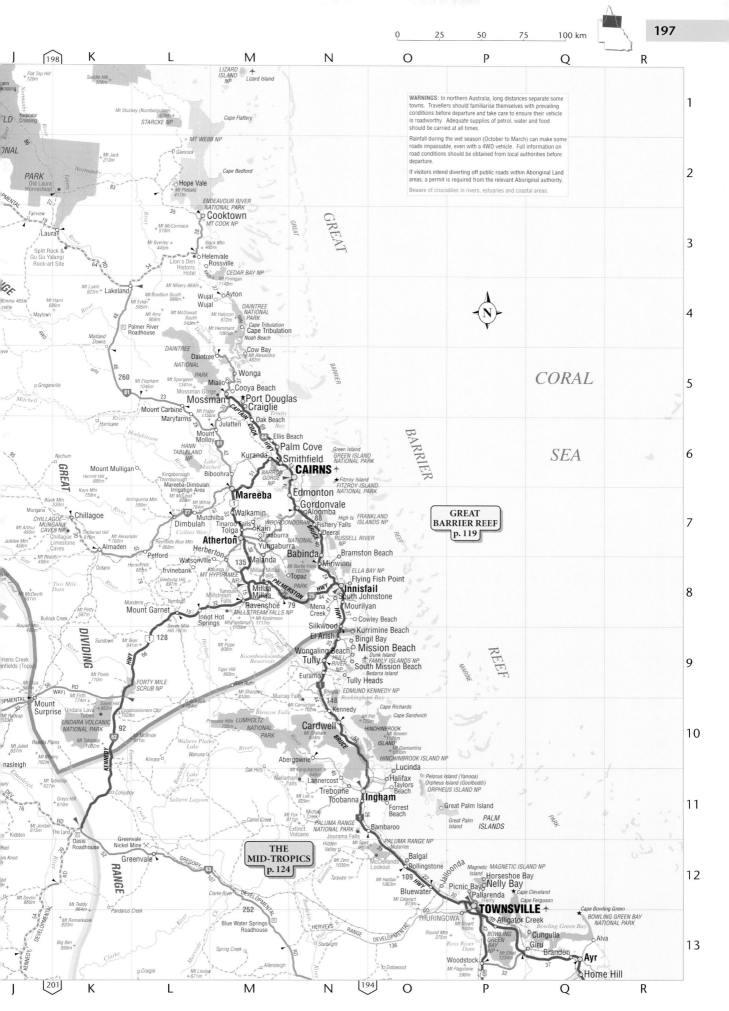

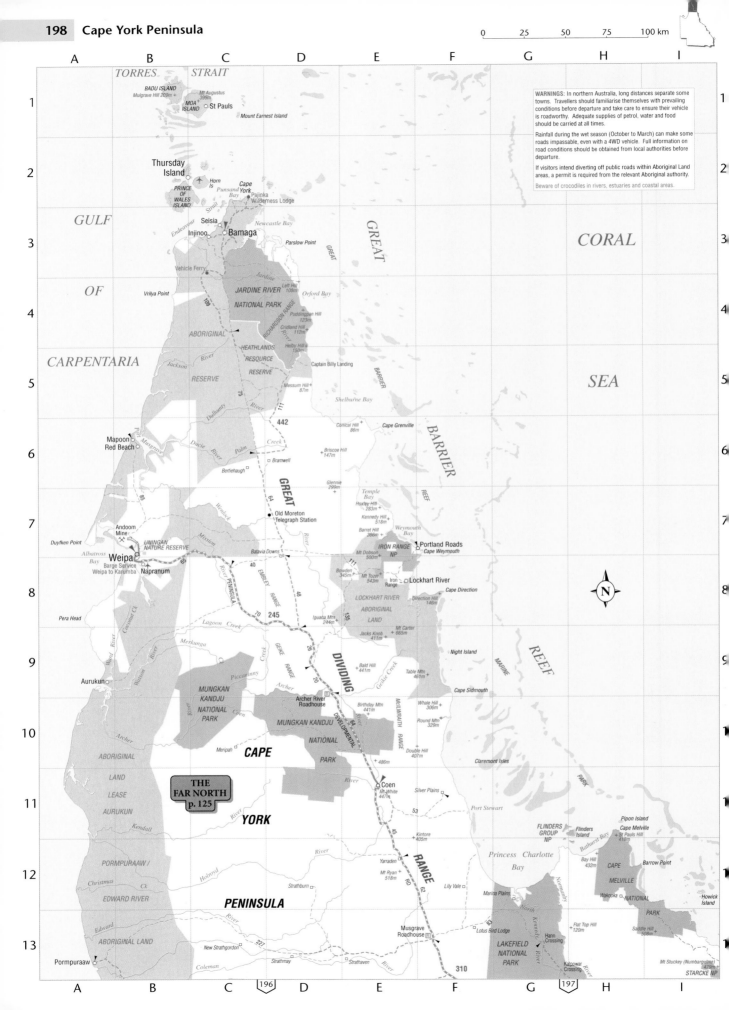

A    B    C    D    E    F    G    H    I

**WARNINGS:** In northern Australia, long distances separate some towns. Travellers should familiarise themselves with prevailing conditions before departure and take care to ensure their vehicle is roadworthy. Adequate supplies of petrol, water and food should be carried at all times.

Rainfall during the wet season (October to March) can make some roads impassable, even with a 4WD vehicle. Full information on road conditions should be obtained from local authorities before departure.

If visitors intend diverting off public roads within Aboriginal Land areas, a permit is required from the relevant Aboriginal authority.

Beware of crocodiles in rivers, estuaries and coastal areas.

TORRES   STRAIT

BADU ISLAND
Mulgrave Hill 209m +
MOA ISLAND
Mt Augustus 399m +
○ St Pauls
Mount Earnest Island

GULF

Thursday Island
Horn Is
Punsand Bay
Cape York
Pajinka
Wilderness Lodge

PRINCE OF WALES ISLAND

OF

Endeavour
Seisia
Injinoo
Bamaga
Newcastle Bay
Parslow Point

Vehicle Ferry

CARPENTARIA

Vrilya Point

JARDINE RIVER NATIONAL PARK
Jardine
Left Hill 108m +
Orford Bay
RICHARDSON RANGE
Puddingpan Hill 123m +
Gridand Hill 112m +
Helby Hill 150m +
HEATHLANDS RESOURCE RESERVE
Captain Billy Landing

ABORIGINAL
RESERVE

Jackson
River
Ducie River
Dulhunty
River
Palm
Creek
Messum Hill 87m +
Shelburne Bay

442

Conical Hill 86m +
Cape Grenville

Mapoon
Red Beach
Musgrave
Bramwell
Bertiehaugh
Briscoe Hill 147m +

BARRIER

GREAT
Glennie 299m +
Temple Bay
Huxley Hill 283m +
Kennedy Hill 518m +
Barret Hill 366m +

85

Old Moreton Telegraph Station

Wenlock
Weymouth Bay

Andoom Mine
Duyfken Point
Weipa
Barge Service
Weipa to Karumba
Napranum
UNINGAN NATURE RESERVE
Batavia Downs
Mt Dobson 500m +
IRON RANGE NP
Portland Roads
Cape Weymouth

Albatross Bay

PENINSULA

40

Pera Head

Coconut Ck
Mission
River
EMBLEY
RANGE
48
111
Bowden 345m +
Mt Tozer 543m +
Iron Range
Lockhart River
Cape Direction

70    245

Iguana Mtn 244m +
135
LOCKHART RIVER ABORIGINAL LAND
Direction Hill 146m +

Lagoon   Creek
Merkunga
Piccaninny
Archer
26
GENE
RANGE
20
Jacks Knob 411m +
Mt Carter 665m +
Night Island
Cape Sidmouth

Aurukun

Ward River
Winston River
Coen
Archer
MUNGKAN KANDJU NATIONAL PARK
DIVIDING
Bald Hill 441m +
Grassie Creek
Table Mtn 461m +

MARINE

REEF

MUNGKAN KANDJU NATIONAL PARK
Archer River Roadhouse
Birthday Mtn 441m +
Whale Hill 306m +
Round Mtn 329m +

Meripah

**CAPE**

Double Hill 407m +
Claremont Isles

ABORIGINAL
LAND
LEASE
AURUKUN

**THE FAR NORTH**
p. 125

River
Coen
Mt White 447m +
Silver Plains
Port Stewart

**YORK**

53
FLINDERS GROUP NP
Flinders Island
Pipon Island
Cape Melville
St Pauls Hill 438m +

Kendall
River
45
Kintore 405m +
Princess   Charlotte
Bay
Bay Hill 432m +
Barrow Point

**PENINSULA**

Yarraden
Mt Ryan 518m +
62
Lily Vale
Marina Plains
Wakooka
CAPE MELVILLE NATIONAL PARK
Howick Island

PORMPURAAW /
Christmas
Ck
EDWARD RIVER

Strathburn
Strathmay

83
Musgrave Roadhouse
Lotus Bird Lodge
Flat Top Hill 120m +
Saddle Hill 508m +

Edward
ABORIGINAL LAND
New Strathgordon
Strathmay
LAKEFIELD NATIONAL PARK
Hann Crossing
Kalpowar Crossing
Mt Stuckey (Numbargidne)
STARCKE NP

Pormpuraaw
Coleman
310

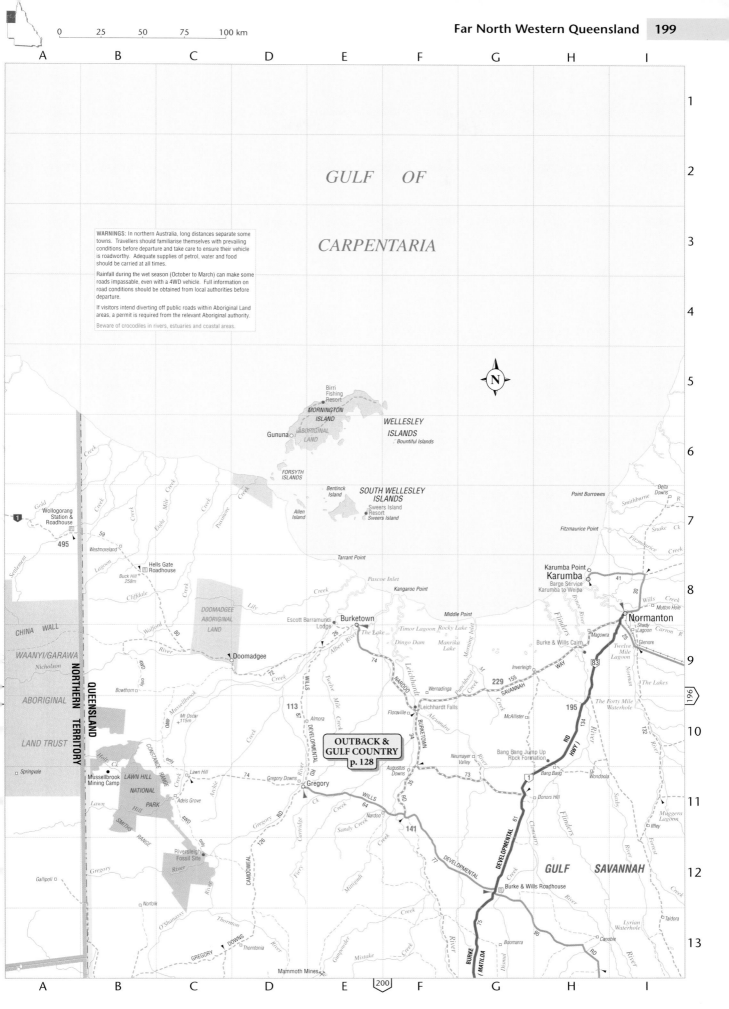

0  25  50  75  100 km

A B C D E F G H I

1

2

*GULF   OF*

3

*CARPENTARIA*

WARNINGS: In northern Australia, long distances separate some towns. Travellers should familiarise themselves with prevailing conditions before departure and take care to ensure their vehicle is roadworthy. Adequate supplies of petrol, water and food should be carried at all times.

Rainfall during the wet season (October to March) can make some roads impassable, even with a 4WD vehicle. Full information on road conditions should be obtained from local authorities before departure.

If visitors intend diverting off public roads within Aboriginal Land areas, a permit is required from the relevant Aboriginal authority.

Beware of crocodiles in rivers, estuaries and coastal areas.

4

N

5

Birri Fishing Resort

*MORNINGTON ISLAND*          *WELLESLEY ISLANDS*

Gununa   ABORIGINAL LAND          Bountiful Islands

6

*FORSYTH ISLANDS*

Bentinck Island     *SOUTH WELLESLEY ISLANDS*     Point Burrowes     Delta Dowris

Gold  Wollogorang Station & Roadhouse     Allen Island     Sweers Island Resort   Sweers Island     Fitzmaurice Point     Smithburne   R     Snake  Ck

495     59

7

Westmoreland     Tarrant Point     Karumba Point     41

Hells Gate Roadhouse     Pascoe Inlet     Kangaroo Point     Karumba     Barge Service Karumba to Weipa     30     Wills  Creek

Buck Hill 258m     80     Normanton     Mutton Hole

8

Cliffdale     Creek     Middle Point     Burke & Wills Cairn     Magowra     Shady Lagoon     Carron  R

CHINA  WALL     *DOOMADGEE ABORIGINAL LAND*     Escott Barramundi Lodge     Burketown     The Lake     Timor Lagoon  Rocky Lake     25     Glenore

WAANYI/GARAWA     Walford     26     Dingo Dam     Manrika Lake     83     Twelve Mile Lagoon

Nicholson     River     74     Leichhardt     Inverleigh     229  155  SAVANNAH     WAY     The Lakes

9

*ABORIGINAL*     Doomadgee     72     Wernadinga     McAllister     195     The Forty Mile Waterhole     132

*LAND TRUST*     Bowthorn     113     87     Almora     Floraville     Leichhardt Falls     Neumayer Valley     Bang Bang Jump Up Rock Formation     134     River

10

Springvale     Mt Oscar 115m     34     Augustus Downs     73     Bang Bang     Wondoola

Mussellbrook Mining Camp     *LAWN HILL*     Lawn Hill     74  Gregory Downs     Gregory     WILLS     64     141     Donors Hill     Muggera Lagoon

11

*NATIONAL PARK*     Adels Grove     126     Nardoo     Creek     Sandy Creek     77     61     Iffley

*SMITHS RANGE*     Riversleigh Fossil Site     OUTBACK & GULF COUNTRY p. 128     *GULF  SAVANNAH*

12

Gallipoli     Gregory     River     CAMOOWEAL     Burke & Wills Roadhouse     Lyrian Waterhole     Taldora

Norfolk     O'Shanassy     Thornton     75     95     Canobie     River

13

GREGORY  DOWNS     Thorntonia     River     Mistake     Boomarra     Dismal

Mammoth Mines

A B C D E F G H I

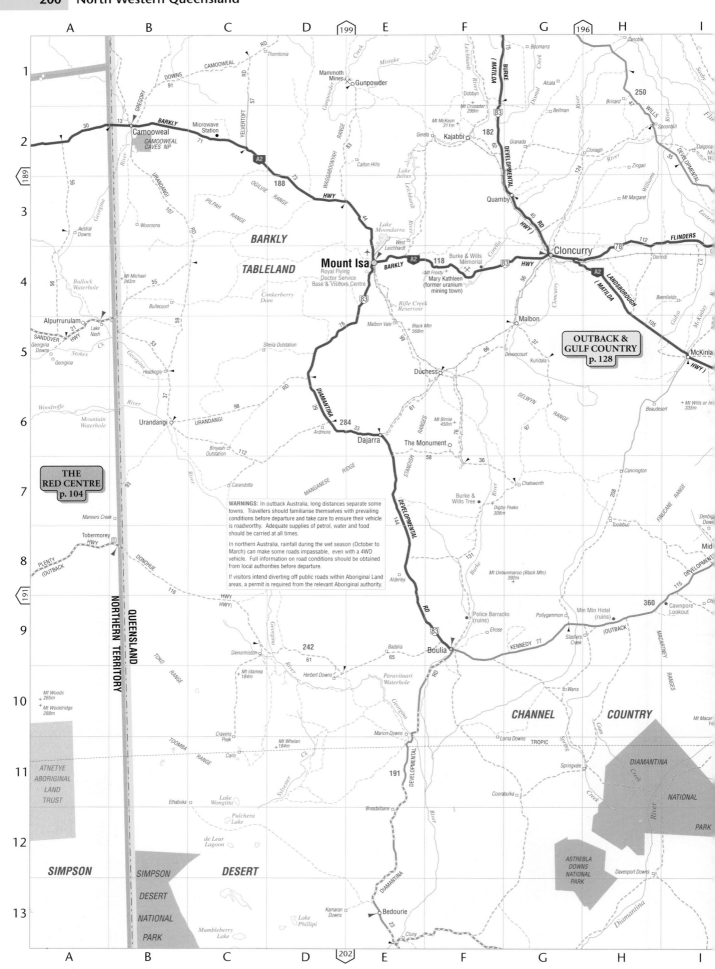

**OUTBACK & GULF COUNTRY** p. 128

**THE RED CENTRE** p. 104

**WARNINGS:** In outback Australia, long distances separate some towns. Travellers should familiarise themselves with prevailing conditions before departure and take care to ensure their vehicle is roadworthy. Adequate supplies of petrol, water and food should be carried at all times.

In northern Australia, rainfall during the wet season (October to March) can make some roads impassable, even with a 4WD vehicle. Full information on road conditions should be obtained from local authorities before departure.

If visitors intend diverting off public roads within Aboriginal Land areas, a permit is required from the relevant Aboriginal authority.

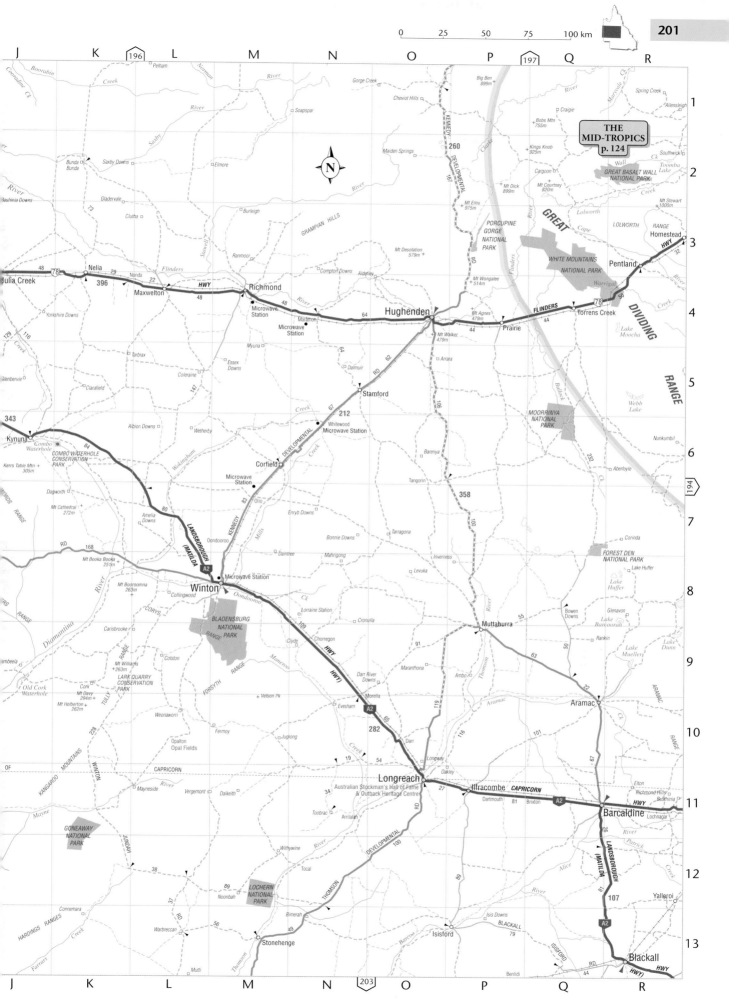

THE RED CENTRE p. 104

NORTHERN TERRITORY

QUEENSLAND

SIMPSON DESERT NATIONAL PARK

SIMPSON DESERT

Mumbleberry Lake

Lake Torquinie

Lake Phillipi

Kamaran Downs

Bedourie

DIAMANTINA

23

Cluny

Flood bypass track

Lake Machattie

Glengyle 56

191 RD 32

Bilpa Morea Claypan

Cacoory (ruins)

DEVELOPMENT 80

EYRE

Mt Lewis +100m

River

Durrie

Betoota

Shallow Lake

Moonda Lake

BIRDSVILLE 114 DEVELOPMENTAL 50 51

DIAMANTINA River 133

Monkira

DEVELOPMENTAL 400 82

92

Mt Collins +260m

Mooraberee

Currawilla 53

Lake Cuddapan 51

Astrebla Downs NP

Muncoonie Lake West

Birdsville

Queensland
SOUTH AUSTRALIA

Poeppel Corner

Mirranponga Pongunna Lake

Simpson Desert Conservation Park

Larrys Hill 63m   Pillan Hill 60m

Lake Thomas

The West Lake

Pandie Pandie

D83

Lake Short

Lake Etamunbanie

Lake Mooràyepe

Lake Cooninnie

Cadelga (ruins)

Frew Hill 123m

Stony Point 195m

Haddon Corner

Lake Yamma Yamma

Poolowanna Lake

Bealie Hill 53m

Perra Perra Poolanna Lake

Ephemeral Lakes

SIMPSON DESERT

SIMPSON DESERT REGIONAL RESERVE

Lake Griselda

Umaroona Lake

Willawilaninna Lake

Pantoowarinna Lake
Pialopotingoona Lake

Peeramudlayeppu Lake

Pompapillinna Lake

Apawyilarranie Lake

Koonarinna Lake

BIRDSVILLE (not recommended)

INSIDE

DIAMANTINA

TRACK

New Alton Downs

Goyder Lagoon

179

Dickinna Hill 87m

OUTSIDE

TRACK

Pulcara Hill 170m

Cordillo Downs

Arrabury

Cooks Outst...

Lake Pure

Lake Walk...

Clifton Hills

BIRDSVILLE

133 516

Creek

TRACK

STURT

STONY

DESERT

Lake Koodnanie

Coongie

Coongie Lakes

INNAMINCKA REGIONAL RESERVE

Leap Year Bore

Mulga Bore

Patchawara Bore

SOUTH AUSTRALIA

QUEENSLAND

Cooper

Pathraootara Lake

Lake Warrandirrinna

Cowarie

Kalamurina

Warburton

Koolkootinnie Lake

Kalamurra Lake

Lake Miamiana

Lake Howitt

Mirra Mitta Bore

BIRDSVILLE

Lake Kittakittaooloo

Mungeranie
Mungerannie Roadhouse

Gidgealpa

Creek

Innamincka

Aboriginal Rock Carvings

Nappa Merrie

Burke & Wills Dig Tree

44

TRACK 47

FLINDERS RANGES & OUTBACK p. 74

Winthekarrinna Waterhole

Lake Warrakalanna

Lake Walpayapeninna

Lake Hope

Moomba Gasfield

STRZELECKI 60

Creek

TRACK 50

STRZELECKI

Tickalara Oil Field

LAKE EYRE NATIONAL PARK

Lake Eyre North

Lake Ngapakaldi

Mulka

Lake Puntawolona

Creek

Cooper

Flood by-pass ferry

Lake Killamperpunna

Flood by pass track

Lake Palankarinna

Etadunna

Lake Florence

Lake Gregory

Lake Koppereekoppinna

Big Lake Moomba

Lake Marteree

Merty Merty

STRZELECKI REGIONAL RESERVE

STRZELECKI

120

Strzelecki Crossing

Cameron Corner

Munro Oil Field

Bollards Lagoon

Corner Store

Dog

STURT NATION...

ELLIOT PRICE CONSERVATION PARK

Dulkaninna

D83

Lake Eyre South

Lake Frances

Lake Ellen

Mulloorina

Lake Blanche

D96

STRZELECKI DESERT

Explorers Tree

WARNING: Visitors planning to enter Desert Parks are required to contact the National Parks and Wildlife SA. A Desert Pass is necessary.

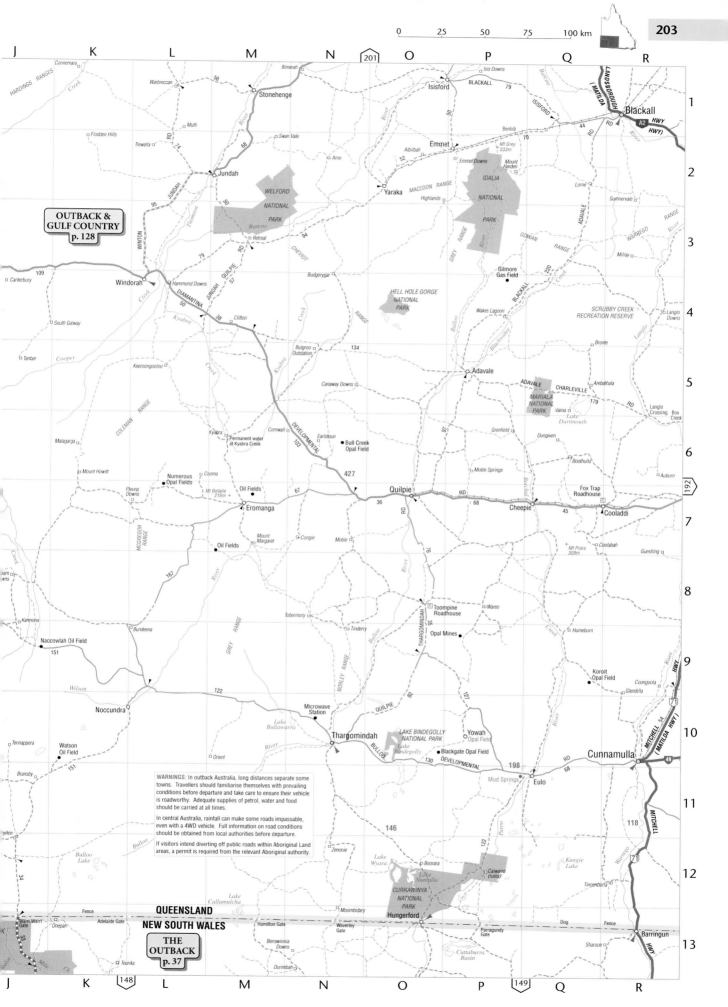

0   25   50   75   100 km

Connemara
HARDINGS RANGES
Creek
Warbreccan
Bimerah
Stonehenge
Mutti
Flodden Hills
Trewalla
Swan Vale
Isis Downs
BLACKALL   79
Isisford
Benlidi
LANDSBOROUGH (MATILDA
Blackall
HWY)
A2   HWY)
ISISFORD   RD
44   1

Jundah
Arno
Emmet
Albilbah
52
Emmet Downs
Mt Grey 533m
Mount Harden
70
ADAVALE RD
Lorne
RANGE   2

WINTON
95
JUNDAH   RD
OUTBACK & GULF COUNTRY p. 128
WELFORD NATIONAL PARK
Barcoo
Retreat
94
Yaraka
MACEDON RANGE
Highlands
IDALIA NATIONAL PARK
Sumnervale
WARREGO   River

Canterbury   109
Windorah
DIAMANTINA   Hammond Downs
QUILPIE   RD
79
57
CHEVIOT
Budgerygar
RANGE
HELL HOLE GORGE NATIONAL PARK
GREY RANGE
Wakes Lagoon
Gilmore Gas Field
GOWAN RANGE
220
BLACKALL
Milray
SCRUBBY CREEK RECREATION RESERVE
Langlo Downs   3

South Galway
50
Kyabra   38
Clifton
Creek
Bulgroo Outstation
134
Bullo
Blackwater
Bronte
Langlo
4

Tanbar
Cooper
Keeroongooloo
Kyabra   Creek
Canaway Downs
Adavale
ADAVALE
MARIALA NATIONAL PARK
CHARLEVILLE
179   RD
Ambathala
Langlo Crossing
Box Creek   5

Malagarga
COLEMAN RANGE
Kyabra   Cornwall
DEVELOPMENTAL
103
Earlstoun
Bull Creek Opal Field
91
Grenfield
Varna
Lake Dartmouth
Dungiven
Boothulla
Auburn   6

Mount Howitt
Numerous Opal Fields
Cooma
Mt Bellalie 216m +
Oil Fields
67
427
Quilpie   36   RD
68   Cheepie   45
Fox Trap Roadhouse
Cooladdi
192   7

Plevna Downs
Eromanga
Mount Margaret
Congie
Moble
76
Mt Prara 309m
Coolabah
Guestling   7

MCGREGOR RANGE
Oil Fields
167
River
GREY RANGE
Tobermory
Tinderry
THARGOMINDAH
Toompine Roadhouse
35
Opal Mines
Wareo
Humeburn   8

Karmona
Naccowlah Oil Field
151
122
Wilson
NORLEY RANGE
Bulloo   River
82
127
Koroit Opal Field
Coongoola
Glendilla
HWY
71   9

Noccundra
Watson Oil Field
Microwave Station
QUILPIE   RD
Lake Bindegolly NATIONAL PARK
Yowah Opal Field
Cunnamulla
MITCHELL   54
(MATILDA HWY)
49   10

Tennappera
151
Orient
Lake Bullawarra
River
Thargomindah
Lake Bindegolly
Blackgate Opal Field
BULLOO
DEVELOPMENTAL   130
198
68   RD
Eulo
Mud Springs   11

Bransby
WARNINGS: In outback Australia, long distances separate some towns. Travellers should familiarise themselves with prevailing conditions before departure and take care to ensure their vehicle is roadworthy.  Adequate supplies of petrol, water and food should be carried at all times.

In central Australia, rainfall can make some roads impassable, even with a 4WD vehicle.  Full information on road conditions should be obtained from local authorities before departure.

If visitors intend diverting off public roads within Aboriginal Land areas, a permit is required from the relevant Aboriginal authority.

146
Zenonie
122
Paroo
Kungie Lake
118
MITCHELL   11

yilco
Bulloo
Bulloo Lake
34
Lake Callamulcha
Zenonie
Lake Wyara
Boorara
Lake Numalla
Cairwarro (ruins)
Tinnenburra
71   12

Warri Warri Gate
Onepah
Fence
Adelaide Gate
39
QUEENSLAND
NEW SOUTH WALES
THE OUTBACK p. 37
Hamilton Gate
Berrawinnia Downs
Moombidary
Waverley Gate
CURRAWINYA NATIONAL PARK
Hungerford
Parragundy Gate
Dog   Fence
Sharoon
Barringun
HWY   13

Teurika
Ourimbah
Cuttaburra Basin

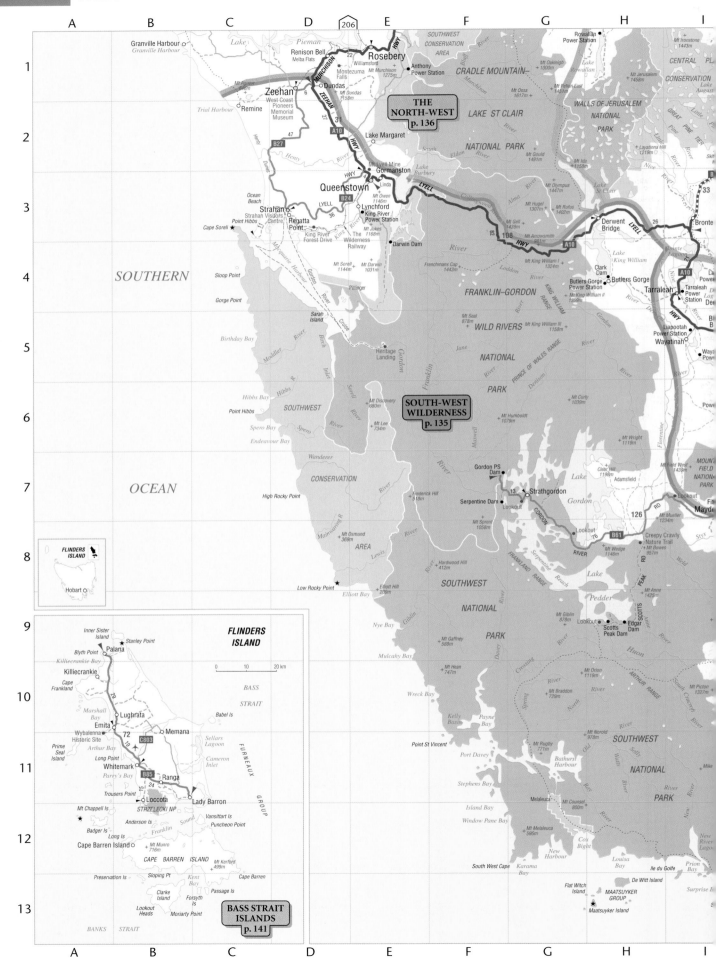

THE
NORTH-WEST
p. 136

SOUTH-WEST
WILDERNESS
p. 135

BASS STRAIT
ISLANDS
p. 141

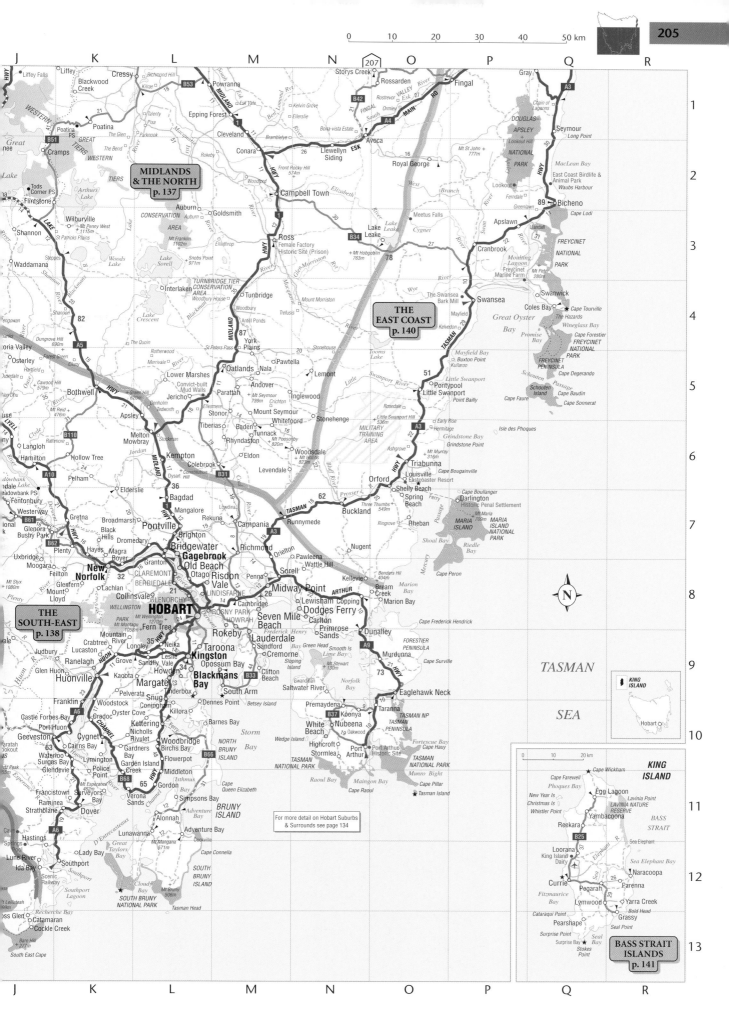

0  10   20   30   40   50 km

J    K    L    M    N    O    P    Q    R

1

Liffey Falls  Liffey
Blackwood
Creek  Cressy  Richmond Hill
Powranna  MIDLAND  Storys Creek  207
Rossarden  Fingal  Gray  A3
B53  South  Esk  B42  FINGAL  MAIN
Epping Forest  Ormley  Seymour  Long Point
Poatina  Pisa  Kelvin Grove  Ellersie  VALLEY  RD
Poatina
PS  The Glen  Parknook  Cleveland  Bona-vista Estate  A4  ESK  2
GREAT  WESTERN  The Bend  Bramblelye  Avoca  DOUGLAS-
APSLEY
Cramps  TIERS  Conara  Llewellyn
Siding  Royal George  Mt St John
777m  NATIONAL  MacLean Bay
Tods
Corner PS  Arthurs  WESTERN  Campbell Town  Front Rocky Hill
574m  West  PARK  East Coast Birdlife &
Animal Park
Flintstone  Lake  TIERS  Branch  Lookout  Waubs Harbour

MIDLANDS
& THE NORTH
p. 137

Wilburville  Mt Penny West
1115m  Auburn  Goldsmith  Meetus Falls  Swan  Ferndale  89  Bicheno
Shannon  St Patricks Plains  CONSERVATION
AREA  Auburn  Lake
Leake  Greenlaw  Apslawn  Cape Lodi  3
Waddamana  Mt Franklin
1102m  Ross  B34  Lake  78  Cygnet  Cranbrook  31  FREYCINET
Female Factory
Historic Site (Prison)  Leake  + Mt Hobgoblin
763m  River  Moulting
Lagoon  NATIONAL
Sleeps  Woods  Glen Morriston  Freycinet
Marine Farm  Swanwick  PARK
Dungrove Hill
690m  A5  Lake  Interlaken  TURNBRIDGE TIER
CONSERVATION
AREA  Tunbridge  Wye  The Swansea
Bark Mill  Swansea  Mt Peter
280m  Coles Bay  Cape Tourville  4
Osterley  Forest Green  Woodbury House  Woodbury  Mayfield  Great Oyster  The Hazards
Hartfield  The Quoin  Trefusis  Stonehouse  Mayfield Bay  Bay  Wineglass Bay
Jericho  St Peters Pass  87  York
Plains  Buxton Point  FREYCINET
Bothwell  Rotherwood  Antill Ponds  Kellevedon  Promise  Cape Forestier
Merrivale  Mt Seymour
739m  Crichton  Little Swanport Hill
536m  Bay  NATIONAL
Lower Marshes  Oatlands  Nala  Little Swanport
River  Early Rise  FREYCINET  PARK
Green Hill
620m  Jericho  Parattah  Andover  51  Little Swanport  Hermitage  PENINSULA  Cape Degerando
Apsley  Denholm
Tedworth  Stonor  14  Mount Seymour  Inglewood  Pontypool  Isle des Phoques  Schouten  Passage
Melton
Mowbray  Stockman  Tiberias  Baden  Whiteford  Stonehenge  A3  Point Bailly  Schouten
Island  Cape Baudin
Rathmore  Tunnack  Mt Ponsonby
820m  Rosedale  Cape Faure  Cape Sonnerat
Langloh  Kempton  Rhyndaston  Eldon  Woodsdale  Grindstone Bay
Hamilton  Colebrook  Levendale  + Mt Hobbs
822m  Bluff River  Ashgrove  Grindstone Point  6
Pelham  Constitution
Hill  B31  Mt Murray
316m  Cape Bougainville
Eldersile  36  Dysart  Prosser  Triabunna  Grindstone Point
Bagdad  Lowdina  Buckland  Louisville
Eastcoaster Resort  Cape Boullanger
Mangalore  62  Orford  Shelly Beach  Darlington
Historic Penal Settlement
Pontville  Rekuna  Campania  TASMAN  18  Runnymede  Spring  St Maria
Brighton  Campania  A3  Rheban  Ferry  MARIA  ISLAND
New  32  Richmond  Nugent  Ringrove  ISLAND  NATIONAL
Norfolk  Orielton  Pawleena  Riedle  PARK
Gagebrook  Otago  Penna  Wattle Hill  Shoal Bay  Bay
Old Beach  Sorell  Kellevie  Cape Peron

THE
EAST COAST
p. 140

Risdon
Vale  Midway Point  ARTHUR  Bream
Creek  Mercury  Cape Frederick Hendrick
Cambridge  26  Marion  Marion Bay
HOBART  Seven Mile
Beach  Lewisham  Copping  Bay
Dodges Ferry
THE
SOUTH-EAST
p. 138  Carlton  N

Taroona  Rokeby  Carlton  Primrose
Sands  Dunalley  FORESTIER
PENINSULA  TASMAN
Kingston  Lauderdale  Murdunna  SEA
Blackmans  Sandford  Cremorne  73  HWY  Eaglehawk Neck
Margate  Bay  Clifton
Beach  Sloping
Island  Premaydena  Koonya  Taranna  TASMAN NP
Tinderbox  South Arm  Green Head  B37  Nubeena  TASMAN
Dennes Point  Betsey Island  Smooth  White  19  Oakwood  PENINSULA
Killora  Lime Bay  Beach  Highcroft  Port
Arthur  Port Arthur
Historic Site
Barnes Bay  Norfolk  Stormlea  Cape Hauy
Woodbridge  Bay  Fortescue Bay
NORTH  Wedge Island  TASMAN
Franklin  BRUNY  Mt Stewart  NATIONAL
130m  Saltwater River  Gwandalan  PARK
Port Huon  Woodstock  ISLAND  Cape Pillar
Geeveston  Cygnet  Garden Island  Maingon Bay  Cape Raoul
Waterloo  Creek  Middleton  Raoul Bay  Tasman Island

KING
ISLAND

Hobart

TASMAN

SEA

0   10    20 km

KING
ISLAND

Cape Wickham
Phoques Bay  Cape Farewell  New Year Is
Christmas Is  Egg Lagoon  Lavinia Point
Whistler Point  LAVINIA NATURE
RESERVE
Reekara  Yambacoona  BASS
STRAIT
B25  Sea Elephant
Loorana
King Island
Dairy  Sea Elephant Bay
Currie  Naracoopa
Pegarah  Parenna
Fitzmaurice
Bay  Lymwood  Yarra Creek
Cataraqui Point  Pearshape  Bold Head
Grassy
Surprise Point  Seal Bay
Surprise Bay  Stokes
Point

BASS STRAIT
ISLANDS
p. 141

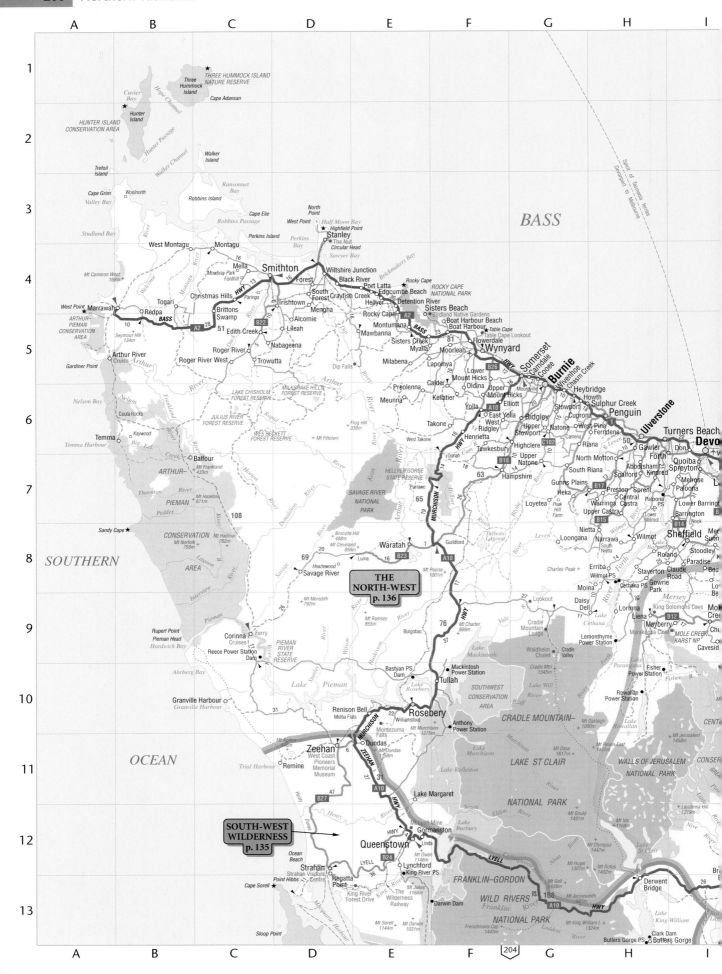

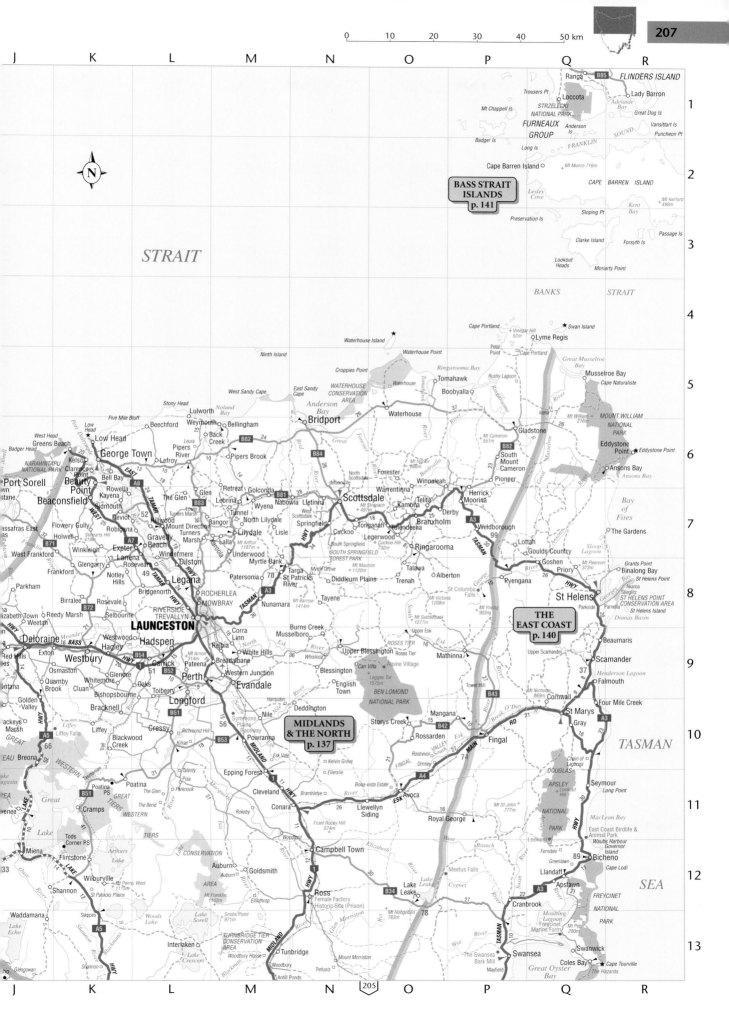

0  10  20  30  40  50 km

J K L M N O P Q R

FLINDERS ISLAND
Ranga
Trousers Pt
Loccota  Lady Barron
Adelaide
Bay
Mt Chappell Is  STRZELECKI  Great Dog Is
NATIONAL PARK
FURNEAUX  Anderson  Vansittart Is
GROUP  Is
Badger Is  Puncheon Pt
Long Is  SOUND
FRANKLIN

BASS STRAIT
ISLANDS
p. 141
Cape Barren Island  Mt Munro 716m  CAPE  BARREN  ISLAND

Lesley
Cove
Kent
Bay
Mt Kerford
499m
Preservation Is
Sloping Pt

Clarke Island  Forsyth Is  Passage Is

Lookout
Heads  Moriarty Point

BANKS  STRAIT

STRAIT

Waterhouse Island  Cape Portland  Vinegar Hill  Swan Island  Lyme Regis
52m
Ninth Island  Waterhouse Point  Petal  Cape Portland
Point
Croppies Point  Ringarooma Bay  Great Musselroe  Musselroe Bay
Bay  Cape Naturaliste
West Sandy Cape  East Sandy  WATERHOUSE  Waterhouse  Tomahawk  Rushy Lagoon
Cape  CONSERVATION  Boobyalla
Anderson  AREA  Mt William  MOUNT WILLIAM
Stony Head  Bay  Waterhouse  216m  NATIONAL
Lulworth  Noland  Mt Cameron  PARK
Five Mile Bluff  Bay  531m  Eddystone  Eddystone Point
Weymouth  Bellingham  Bridport  Gladstone  Point
West Head  Beechford  Back  Pioneer  South  Ansons Bay
Greens Beach  Low  Creek  Bred  Forester  Mount  Ansons Bay
Badger Head  Head  Pipers  Pipers Brook  Cameron
Kelso  Lefroy  River  North  Warrentinna  Herrick  Bay
George Town  Scottsdale  Telita  Moorina  of
NARAWNTAPU  Clarence  Rowella  Glen  Golconda  West  Kamona  Derby  Fires
NATIONAL  Point  Kayena  Lebrina  Scottsdale  Branxholm  The Gardens
PARK  Beauty  The Glen  Wyena  Springfield  Tonganah  Weldborough  Lottah
Port Sorell  Point  Deviot  Tunnel  Cuckoo  Tulendeena  Goshen  Goulds Country
Beaconsfield  Robigana  North Lilydale  Legerwood  Priory  Binalong Bay
Flowery Gully  Hillwood  Mount Direction  Lilydale  Ringarooma  Ryengana  St Helens Point
Holwell  Turners  Lisle  Talawa  Goshen  St Helens
West Frankford  Exeter  Marsh  Underwood  Alberton  Priory  Dianas Basin
Winkleigh  Lalla  Myrtle Bank  St Helens
Frankford  Glengarry  Rosevears  Patersonia  Trenah  Parkside
Parkham  Notley  Dilston  Targa  Diddleum Plains  Beaumaris
Birralee  Hills  Legana  St Patricks  Tayene  Scamander
Rosevale  Bridgenorth  River  Nunamara  St Marys  Falmouth
Reedy Marsh  Selbourne  ROCHERLEA  Cornwall  Four Mile Creek
Weetah  MOWBRAY  Burns Creek  St Marys  Gray
Deloraine  RIVERSIDE  Musselboro  Mangana  TASMAN
Westwood  TREVALLYN  Upper Blessington  Storys Creek  Fingal
Hagley  LAUNCESTON  Corra  Rossarden  Avoca
Exton  Hadspen  Linn  White Hills  Blessington  English  Mathinna
Westbury  Carrick  Breadalbane  Town  Royal George
Osmaston  Perth  Western Junction  Deddington  Bicheno
Whitemore  Evandale  Hampden  Llandaff
Longford  Nile  Apslawn
Bracknell  Cressy  Conara  Cranbrook
Campbell Town  Swansea
Ross  Coles Bay
Swanwick

MIDLANDS
& THE NORTH
p. 137

THE
EAST COAST
p. 140

TASMAN

SEA

205

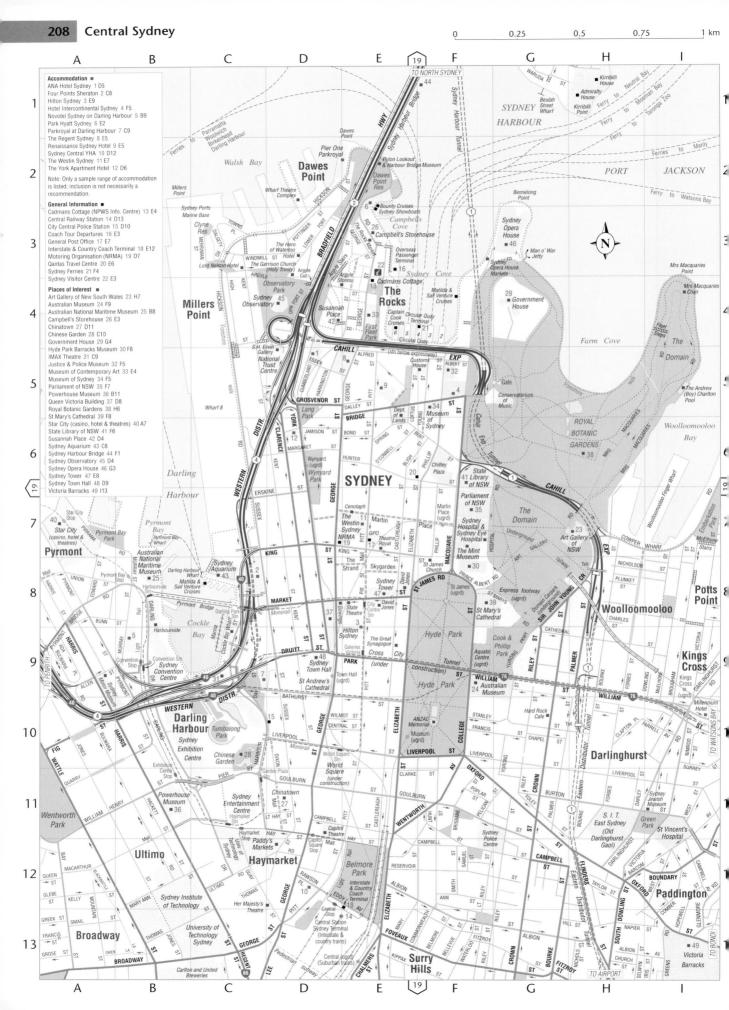

0    0.25    0.5    0.75    1 km

**Accommodation** ■
ANA Hotel Sydney 1 D5
Four Points Sheraton 2 C8
Hilton Sydney 3 E9
Hotel Intercontinental Sydney 4 F5
Novotel Sydney on Darling Harbour 5 B9
Park Hyatt Sydney 6 E2
Parkroyal at Darling Harbour 7 C9
The Regent Sydney 8 E5
Renaissance Sydney Hotel 9 E5
Sydney Central YHA 10 D12
The Westin Sydney 11 E7
The York Apartment Hotel 12 D6

Note: Only a sample range of accommodation
is listed; inclusion is not necessarily a
recommendation.

**General Information** ■
Cadmans Cottage (NPWS Info. Centre) 13 E4
Central Railway Station 14 D13
City Central Police Station 15 D10
Coach Tour Departures 16 E3
General Post Office 17 E7
Interstate & Country Coach Terminal 18 E12
Motoring Organisation (NRMA) 19 D7
Qantas Travel Centre 20 E6
Sydney Ferries 21 F4
Sydney Visitor Centre 22 E3

**Places of Interest** ■
Art Gallery of New South Wales 23 H7
Australian Museum 24 F9
Australian National Maritime Museum 25 B8
Campbell's Storehouse 26 E3
Chinatown 27 D11
Chinese Garden 28 C10
Government House 29 G4
Hyde Park Barracks Museum 30 F8
IMAX Theatre 31 C9
Justice & Police Museum 32 F5
Museum of Contemporary Art 33 E4
Museum of Sydney 34 F5
Parliament of NSW 35 F7
Powerhouse Museum 36 B11
Queen Victoria Building 37 D8
Royal Botanic Gardens 38 H6
St Mary's Cathedral 39 F8
Star City (casino, hotel & theatres) 40 A7
State Library of NSW 41 F6
Susannah Place 42 D6
Sydney Aquarium 43 C8
Sydney Harbour Bridge 44 F1
Sydney Observatory 45 D4
Sydney Opera House 46 G3
Sydney Tower 47 E8
Sydney Town Hall 48 D9
Victoria Barracks 49 I13

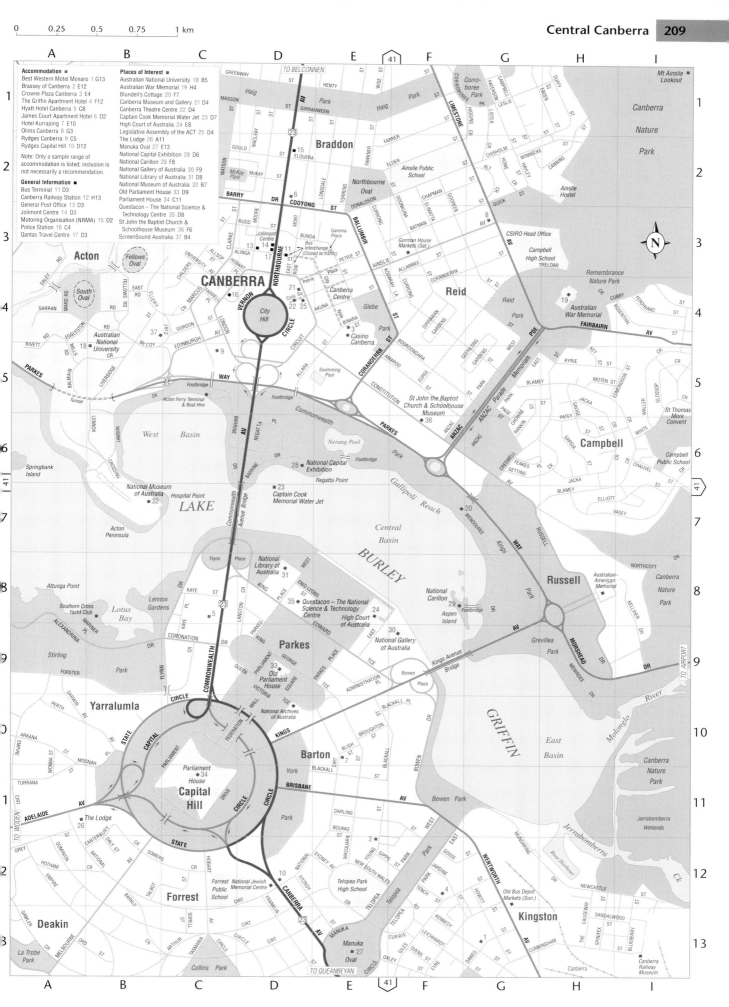

0    0.25    0.5    0.75    1 km

**Accommodation** ■
Best Western Motel Monaro 1 G13
Brassey of Canberra 2 E12
Crowne Plaza Canberra 3 E4
The Griffin Apartment Hotel 4 F12
Hyatt Hotel Canberra 5 C8
James Court Apartment Hotel 6 D2
Hotel Kurrajong 7 E10
Olims Canberra 8 G3
Rydges Canberra 9 C5
Rydges Capital Hill 10 D12

Note: Only a sample range of
accommodation is listed; inclusion is
not necessarily a recommendation.

**General Information** ■
Bus Terminal 11 D3
Canberra Railway Station 12 H13
General Post Office 13 D3
Jolimont Centre 14 D3
Motoring Organisation (NRMA) 15 D2
Police Station 16 C4
Qantas Travel Centre 17 D3

**Places of Interest** ■
Australian National University 18 B5
Australian War Memorial 19 H4
Blundell's Cottage 20 F7
Canberra Museum and Gallery 21 D4
Canberra Theatre Centre 22 D4
Captain Cook Memorial Water Jet 23 D7
High Court of Australia 24 E8
Legislative Assembly of the ACT 25 D4
The Lodge 26 A11
Manuka Oval 27 E13
National Capital Exhibition 28 D6
National Carillon 29 F8
National Gallery of Australia 30 F9
National Library of Australia 31 D8
National Museum of Australia 32 B7
Old Parliament House 33 D9
Parliament House 34 C11
Questacon – The National Science &
Technology Centre 35 D8
St John the Baptist Church &
Schoolhouse Museum 36 F6
ScreenSound Australia 37 B4

Grid references A–I across the top and bottom; 1–13 down the sides.

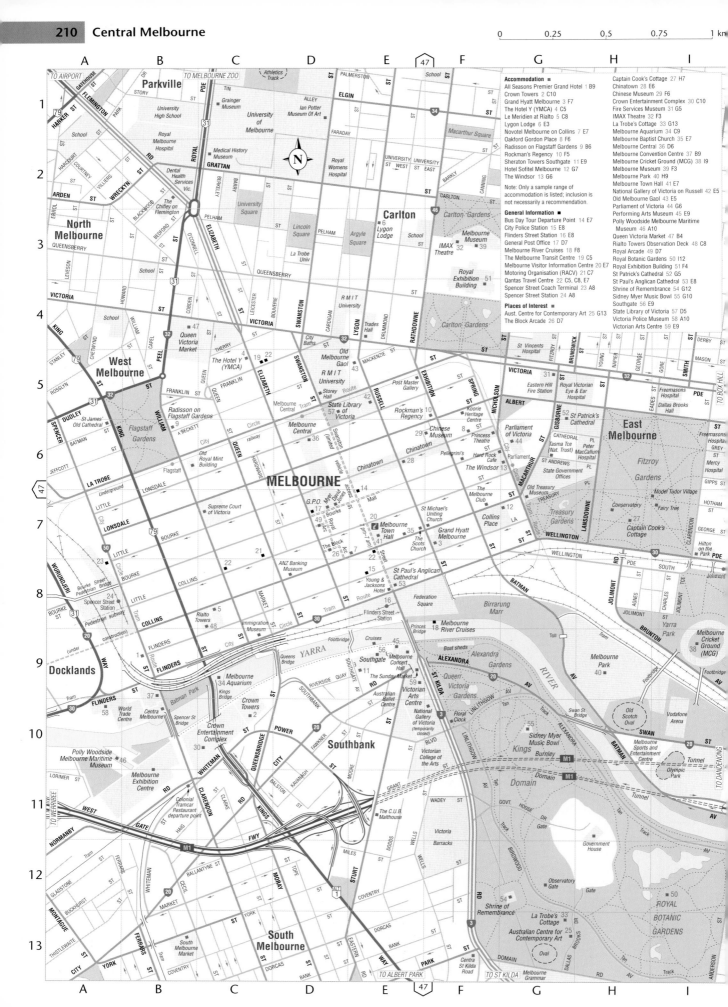

**Accommodation** ■
All Seasons Premier Grand Hotel 1 B9
Crown Towers 2 C10
Grand Hyatt Melbourne 3 F7
The Hotel Y (YMCA) 4 C5
Le Meridien at Rialto 5 C8
Lygon Lodge 6 E3
Novotel Melbourne on Collins 7 E7
Oakford Gordon Place 8 F6
Radisson on Flagstaff Gardens 9 B6
Rockman's Regency 10 F5
Sheraton Towers Southgate 11 E9
Hotel Sofitel Melbourne 12 G7
The Windsor 13 G6

Note: Only a sample range of accommodation is listed; inclusion is not necessarily a recommendation.

**General Information** ■
Bus Day Tour Departure Point 14 E7
City Police Station 15 E8
Flinders Street Station 16 E8
General Post Office 17 D7
Melbourne River Cruises 18 F8
The Melbourne Transit Centre 19 C5
Melbourne Visitor Information Centre 20 E7
Motoring Organisation (RACV) 21 C7
Qantas Travel Centre 22 C5, C8, E7
Spencer Street Coach Terminal 23 A8
Spencer Street Station 24 A8

**Places of Interest** ■
Aust. Centre for Contemporary Art 25 G13
The Block Arcade 26 D7

Captain Cook's Cottage 27 H7
Chinatown 28 E6
Chinese Museum 29 F6
Crown Entertainment Complex 30 C10
Fire Services Museum 31 G5
IMAX Theatre 32 F3
La Trobe's Cottage 33 G13
Melbourne Aquarium 34 C9
Melbourne Baptist Church 35 E7
Melbourne Central 36 D6
Melbourne Convention Centre 37 B9
Melbourne Cricket Ground (MCG) 38 I9
Melbourne Museum 39 F3
Melbourne Park 40 H9
Melbourne Town Hall 41 E7
National Gallery of Victoria on Russell 42 E5
Old Melbourne Gaol 43 E5
Parliament of Victoria 44 G6
Performing Arts Museum 45 E9
Polly Woodside Melbourne Maritime
   Museum 46 A10
Queen Victoria Market 47 B4
Rialto Towers Observation Deck 48 C8
Royal Arcade 49 D7
Royal Botanic Gardens 50 I12
Royal Exhibition Building 51 F4
St Patrick's Cathedral 52 G5
St Paul's Anglican Cathedral 53 E8
Shrine of Remembrance 54 G12
Sidney Myer Music Bowl 55 G10
Southgate 56 E9
State Library of Victoria 57 D5
Victoria Police Museum 58 A10
Victorian Arts Centre 59 E9

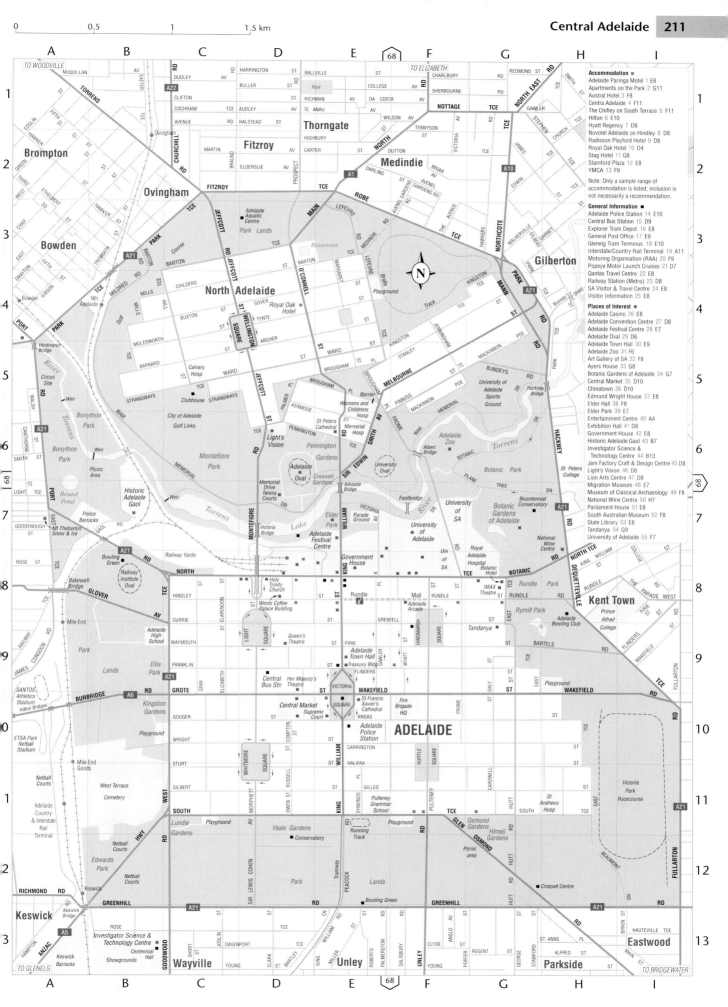

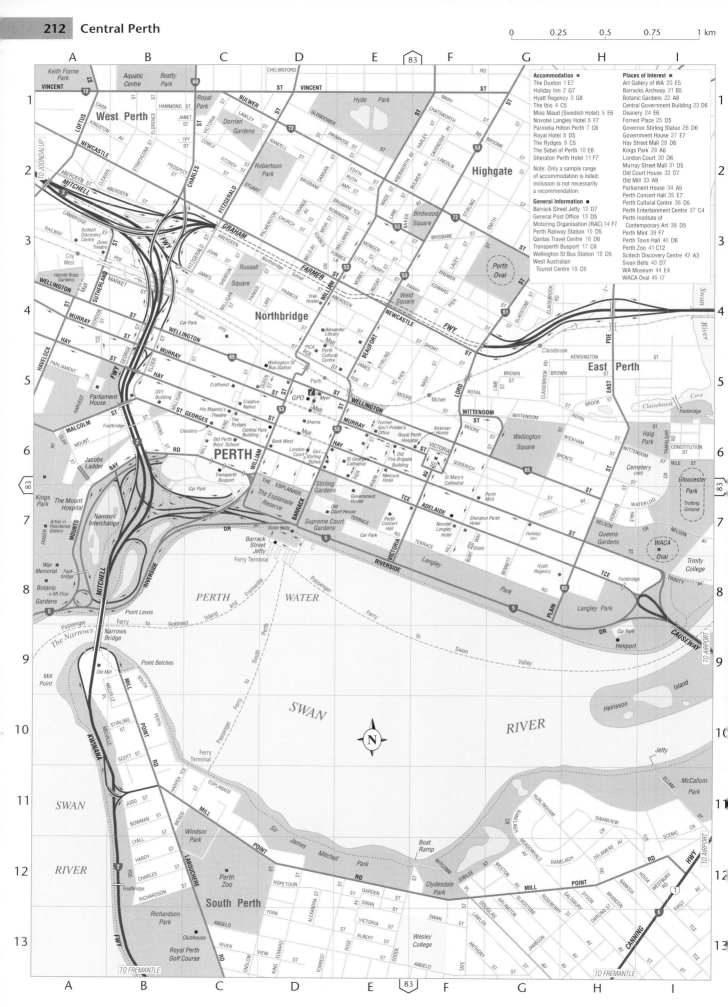

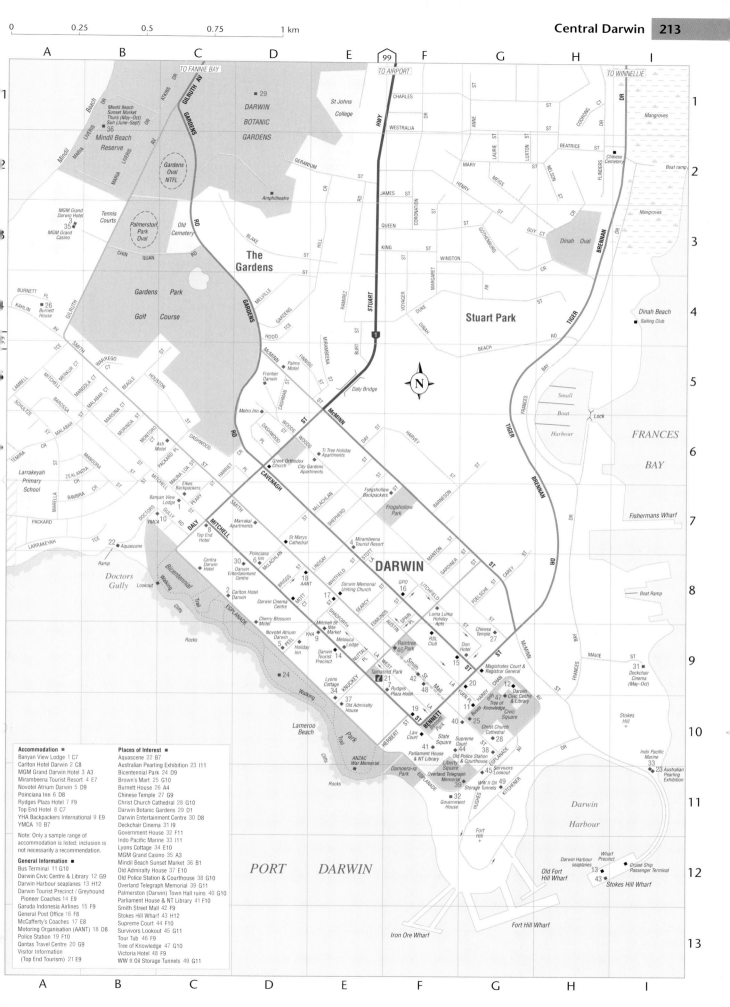

0     0.25     0.5     0.75     1 km

TO FANNIE BAY

DARWIN BOTANIC GARDENS

29

St Johns College

Mindil Beach Sunset Market Thurs (May–Oct) Sun (June–Sept)

36

Mindil Beach Reserve

MGM Grand Darwin Hotel
3
35
MGM Grand Casino

Tennis Courts

Palmerston Park Oval

Old Cemetery

Gardens Oval NTFL

Amphitheatre

GERANIUM

CHARLES ST

WESTRALIA

Chinese Cemetery

BEATRICE

Mangroves

Boat ramp

Mangroves

Dinah Oval

TO WINNELLIE

The Gardens

BLAKE

MELVILLE

Gardens Park Golf Course

HOOD TCE

GARDENS TCE

McMINN

Frontier Darwin

FINNISS

Palms Motel

MIRAMBEENA

JAMES ST

QUEEN

KING ST

WINSTON

Stuart Park

Dinah Beach Sailing Club

FRANCES BAY

Metro Inn

Daly Bridge

HARVEY

Small Boat Harbour

Lock

Larrakeyah Primary School

BURNETT PL

26
Burnett House

KAHLIN

Asti Motel

Elkes Backpackers

Greek Orthodox Church

City Gardens Apartments

Ti Tree Holiday Apartments

Frogshollow Backpackers

Frogshollow Park

Fishermans Wharf

Banyan View Lodge
1

YMCA
10

Marrakai Apartments

St Marys Cathedral

Mirambeena Tourist Resort
4

DARWIN

Boat Ramp

Aquascene
22

Ramp

Doctors Gully

Lookout

Centra Darwin Hotel

30

Darwin Entertainment Centre

Poinciana Inn
6

18
AANT

17

Darwin Memorial Uniting Church

GPO
16

Luma Luma Holiday Apts

Chinese Temple
27

Deckchair Cinema
31

Bicentennial Park

Carlton Hotel Darwin
2

Darwin Cinema Centre

Cherry Blossom Motel

Novotel Atrium Darwin
5

Holiday Inn

YHA
9

Mitchell St Nite Market

Melaleuca Lodge

Darwin Tourist Precinct

14

Raintree Park
46

21
7

RSL Club

Don Hotel

15

42

Don Hotel

Magistrates Court & Registrar General

Stokes Hill

Indo Pacific Marine
33
23
Australian Pearling Exhibition

Rocks

24

Lyons Cottage
34

Rydges Plaza Hotel

48

20

Bus

11

12
Darwin Civic Centre & Library
47
Tree of Knowledge

Civic Square

37
Old Admiralty House

19

25

40

Christ Church Cathedral
28

Deckchair Cinema (May–Oct)

Lameroo Beach

Law Court
41

State Square

Supreme Court
44

38
Old Police Station & Courthouse

45
Survivors Lookout

Stokes Hill

Indo Pacific Marine

Cliffs

ANZAC War Memorial

Damoera-ra Park

Parliament House & NT Library

Liberty Square

Overland Telegraph Memorial
39

49
WW II Oil Storage Tunnels

Darwin Harbour

Rocks

32
Government House

PORT DARWIN

Fort Hill

Darwin Harbour seaplanes

Old Fort Hill Wharf

Wharf Precinct

13

43
Stokes Hill Wharf

Cruise Ship Passenger Terminal

Iron Ore Wharf

Fort Hill Wharf

**Accommodation** ■
Banyan View Lodge 1 C7
Carlton Hotel Darwin 2 C8
MGM Grand Darwin Hotel 3 A3
Mirambeena Tourist Resort 4 E7
Novotel Atrium Darwin 5 D9
Poinciana Inn 6 D8
Rydges Plaza Hotel 7 F9
Top End Hotel 8 C7
YHA Backpackers International 9 E9
YMCA 10 B7

Note: Only a sample range of accommodation is listed; inclusion is not necessarily a recommendation.

**General Information** ■
Bus Terminal 11 G10
Darwin Civic Centre & Library 12 G9
Darwin Harbour seaplanes 13 H12
Darwin Tourist Precinct / Greyhound
  Pioneer Coaches 14 E9
Garuda Indonesia Airlines 15 F9
General Post Office 16 F8
McCafferty's Coaches 17 E8
Motoring Organisation (AANT) 18 D8
Police Station 19 F10
Qantas Travel Centre 20 G9
Visitor Information
  (Top End Tourism) 21 E9

**Places of Interest** ■
Aquascene 22 B7
Australian Pearling Exhibition 23 I11
Bicentennial Park 24 D9
Brown's Mart 25 G10
Burnett House 26 A4
Chinese Temple 27 G9
Christ Church Cathedral 28 G10
Darwin Botanic Gardens 29 D1
Darwin Entertainment Centre 30 D8
Deckchair Cinema 31 I9
Government House 32 F11
Indo Pacific Marine 33 I11
Lyons Cottage 34 E10
MGM Grand Casino 35 A3
Mindil Beach Sunset Market 36 B1
Old Admiralty House 37 E10
Old Police Station & Courthouse 38 G10
Overland Telegraph Memorial 39 G11
Palmerston (Darwin) Town Hall ruins 40 G10
Parliament House & NT Library 41 F10
Smith Street Mall 42 F9
Stokes Hill Wharf 43 H12
Supreme Court 44 F10
Survivors Lookout 45 G11
Tour Tub 46 F9
Tree of Knowledge 47 G10
Victoria Hotel 48 F9
WW II Oil Storage Tunnels 49 G11

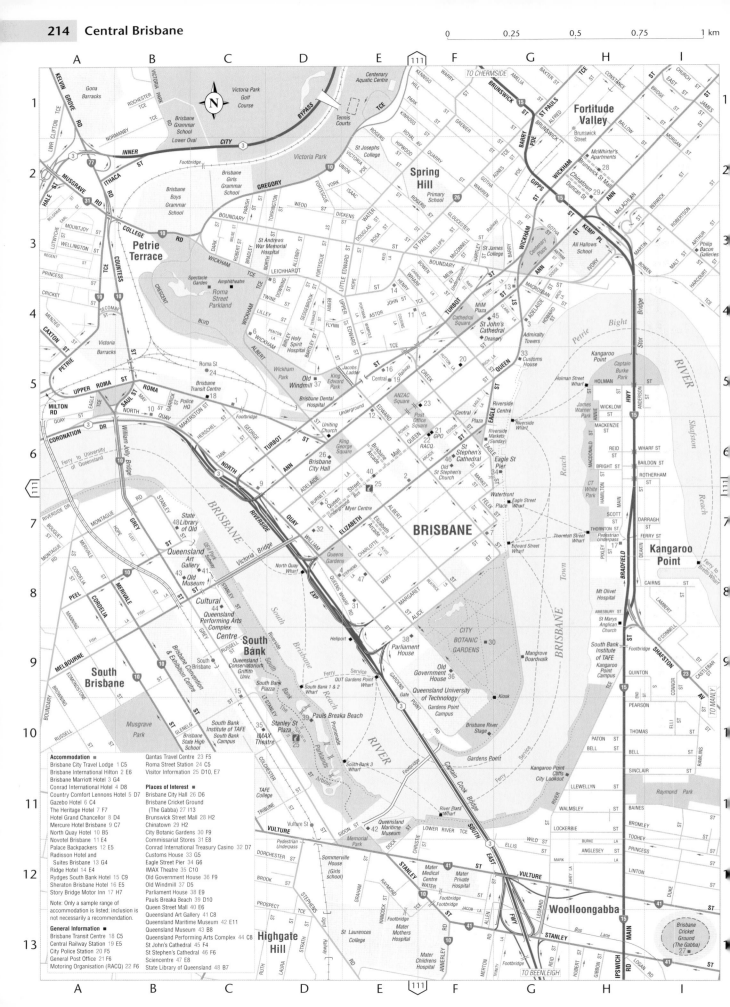

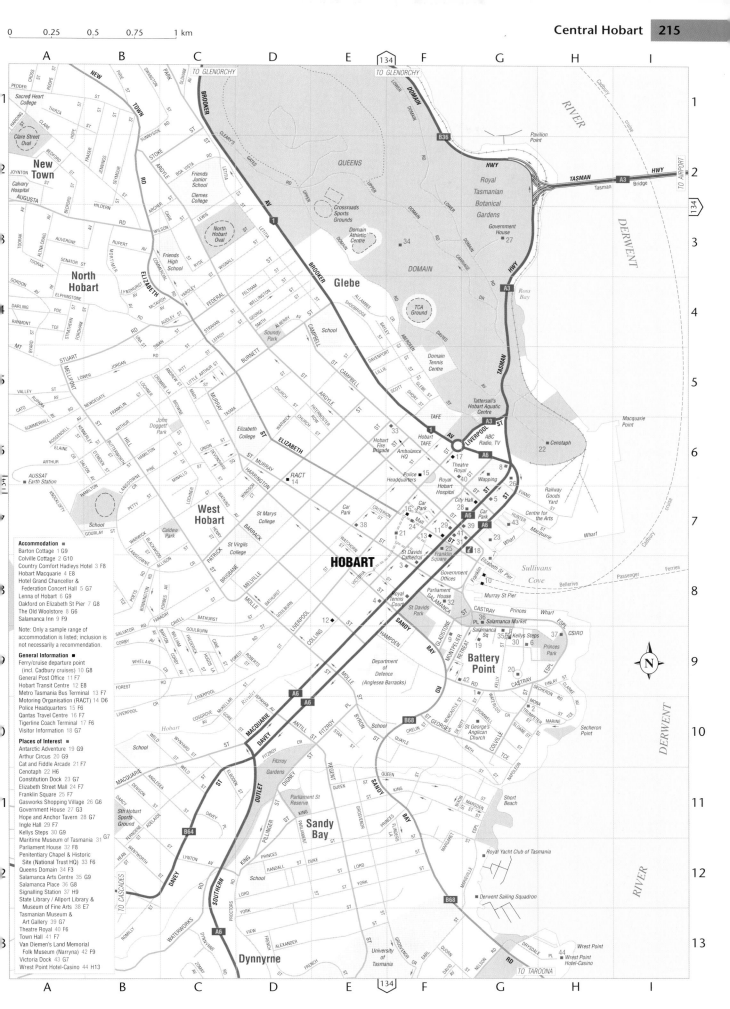

0   0.25   0.5   0.75   1 km

TO GLENORCHY

TO GLENORCHY

**New Town**

Sacred Heart College

Clare Street Oval

Calvary Hospital

AUGUSTA

**North Hobart**

North Hobart Oval

Friends Junior School

Clemes College

Friends High School

QUEENS

Crossroads Sports Grounds

Domain Athletic Centre

**Glebe**

Soundy Park

School

**DOMAIN**

Royal Tasmanian Botanical Gardens

Government House

RIVER

Pavilion Point

TASMAN   HWY

Tasman Bridge

TO AIRPORT

134

Ross Bay

TCA Ground

Domain Tennis Centre

**West Hobart**

John Doggett Park

Elizabeth College

St Marys College

St Virgils College

Caldew Park

School

AUSSAT Earth Station

Tattersall's Hobart Aquatic Centre

ABC Radio, TV

Hobart TAFE

Hobart Fire Brigade

Ambulance HQ

Police Headquarters

Car Park

**HOBART**

Hobart Hospital

Theatre Royal

City Hall

Wapping

Macquarie Point

Cenotaph

Railway Goods Yard

Centre for the Arts

Wharf

St Davids Cathedral

Franklin Square

Government Offices

Parliament House

St Davids Park

Royal Tennis Court

Salamanca Market

Elizabeth St Pier

Sullivans Cove

Bellerive

Passenger   Ferries

Murray St Pier

Castray

Princes   Wharf

**Battery Point**

Salamanca Sq

Kellys Steps

Princes Park

CSIRO

Secheron Point

Short Beach

St George's Anglican Church

**Sandy Bay**

Fitzroy Gardens

Parliament St Reserve

Sth Hobart Sports Ground

Department of Defence (Anglesea Barracks)

School

Queen

Royal Yacht Club of Tasmania

Derwent Sailing Squadron

RIVER

School

School

University of Tasmania

TO CASCADES

**Dynnyrne**

TO TAROONA

Wrest Point

Wrest Point Hotel-Casino

DERWENT

N

# INDEX OF PLACE NAMES

This index includes all towns, localities, roadhouses and national parks shown on the maps and mentioned in the text.

Place names are followed by a map page number and grid reference, and/or the text page number on which that place name occurs.

The alphabetical order followed in the index is that of 'word-by-word', where all entries under one word are grouped together. Where a place name consists of more than one word, the order is governed by the first and then the second word. For example:

Green Point
Greenbank
Greens Beach
Greenwood
Greg Greg
Gregory

Names beginning with Mc are indexed as Mac and those beginning with St are indexed as Saint.

The following abbreviations and contractions are used in the index:

ACT – Australian Capital
    Territory
JBT – Jervis Bay Territory
NSW – New South Wales
NT – Northern Territory
Qld – Queensland
SA – South Australia
Tas. – Tasmania
Vic. – Victoria
WA – Western Australia

Bundarra NSW 147 K7
Bundella NSW 146 H12
Bunding Vic. 157 Q3, 162 C13
Bundjalung National Park NSW 147 Q4, 193 Q13
Bundook NSW 145 N1, 147 M13
Bundure NSW 151 N10
Bunga NSW 152 G10, 165 R5
Bungal Vic. 157 P4
Bungarby NSW 152 E10, 165 M6
Bungaree Vic. 157 P3, 162 B13
Bungawalbin National Park NSW 147 P4
Bungeet Vic. 163 L5
Bungendore NSW 144 H12, 152 F5, 29
Bungil Vic. 163 R3, 164 E1
Bungle Bungle National Park see Purnululu National Park
Bungle Bungles WA 185 L6, 6, 92, 93
Bungonia NSW 144 I11, 152 G4
Bungowannah NSW 151 P13, 163 O3
Bungulla NSW 147 M4, 193 N13
Bungulla WA 178 H3
Bunguluke Vic. 159 M5
Bungunya Qld 146 G1, 192 I11
Bungwahl NSW 145 O3
Buninyong Vic. 157 O4, 54
Bunnaloo NSW 151 K12, 162 E2
Bunnan NSW 145 K1
Buntine WA 180 D5
Bunya Mountains National Park Qld 193 M7, 112
Bunyah NSW 145 O2
Bunyan NSW 152 E8, 165 N2
Bunyip Vic. 154 G6
Buraja NSW 151 O12, 163 M2
Burcher NSW 144 B7, 151 R5
Burekup WA 178 C8
Burgooney NSW 151 P4
Burke & Wills Roadhouse Qld 196 B12, 199 G12
Burkes Flat Vic. 159 N9
Burketown Qld 199 E8, 128
Burleigh Heads Qld 193 Q10
Burnett Heads Qld 193 O2
Burnie Tas. 206 G6, 136
Burns Creek Tas. 207 N9
Burnt Yards NSW 144 F7
Buronga NSW 150 D7, 160 G3
Burpengary Qld 111 B4, 193 P8
Burra SA 169 L5, 71
Burraboi NSW 151 J11, 159 R1, 161 R11
Burracoppin WA 180 F7
Burraga NSW 144 H8, 152 F1
Burragate NSW 152 F11, 165 P8
Burramine Vic. 163 K3
Burramine South Vic. 163 K4
Burrandana NSW 144 B13, 151 R11
Burrawang NSW 145 J10, 152 I3, 30
Burraway NSW 144 D1
Burrell Creek NSW 145 O1, 147 N13
Burren Junction NSW 146 E7
Burrereo Vic. 159 J8
Burrill Lake NSW 145 J13, 152 I6
Burringbar NSW 147 Q2, 193 Q11
Burringurrah WA 179 G8, 182 A8
Burrinjuck NSW 144 E11, 152 D4
Burroin Vic. 158 H2, 160 H13
Burrowa-Pine Mountain National Park Vic. 152 A8, 164 F2, 59
Burrowye Vic. 151 R13, 152 A8, 164 F1
Burrum Vic. 159 J9
Burrum Coast National Park Qld 193 P3
Burrum Heads Qld 193 P3, 118
Burrum River National Park Qld 193 P3
Burrumbeet Vic. 157 N3
Burrumbuttock NSW 151 P12, 163 P2
Bushfield Vic. 156 I9
Bushy Park Tas. 134 A1, 205 J7, 138
Bushy Park Vic. 155 M5
Busselton WA 178 B9, 180 C10, 86
Butchers Ridge Vic. 152 C12, 164 I9
Bute SA 169 J5
Butler Tanks SA 168 E6
Butlers Gorge Tas. 204 H4, 206 H13
Buxton NSW 145 J9, 152 I2
Buxton Qld 193 P3
Buxton Vic. 154 G1, 163 J12
Byabarra NSW 147 O12
Byaduk Vic. 156 F6
Byaduk North Vic 156 F6
Byawatha Vic. 163 N5
Byfield National Park Qld 195 O9
Byford WA 178 D4
Bylands Vic. 47 C1, 154 C1, 162 F12
Bylong NSW 144 I3
Bymount Qld 192 G5
Byrneside Vic. 162 G6

Byrnestown Qld 193 N4
Byrneville Vic. 158 H8
Byrock NSW 149 P7
Byron Bay NSW 147 R2, 193 R12, 25

Cabarita Vic. 150 D7, 160 G3
Cabarlah Qld 193 N9
Cabawin Qld 193 K8
Cabbage Tree Creek Vic. 165 K12
Cable Beach WA 92
Caboolture Qld 111 B3, 193 P8
Cabramatta NSW 19 B9
Cabramurra NSW 152 C8, 165 J1
Cactus Beach SA 177 L9, 73
Caddens Flat Vic. 156 F2, 158 F13
Cadell SA 169 O6
Cadney Homestead SA 175 P8
Cadoux WA 180 D6
Cahills Crossing NT 186 H5
Caiguna WA 181 N8
Cairns Qld 197 N6, 125, 127
Cairns Bay Tas. 205 K10
Calca SA 177 P13
Calder Tas. 206 F6
Caldwell NSW 151 J12, 162 D1
Calen Qld 195 K4
Calingiri WA 178 E1, 180 D7
Caliph SA 169 P8
Calivil Vic. 159 Q6, 162 B5
Callala Bay NSW 145 K11, 152 I4
Callawadda Vic. 159 J10
Calleen NSW 144 A7, 151 Q5
Callide Qld 193 K1, 195 N13
Callignee Vic. 155 K8
Callignee North Vic. 155 L8
Callington SA 68 I7, 166 D2, 169 M10
Calliope Qld 195 P12
Caloona NSW 146 F3, 192 I12
Caloundra Qld 193 Q7, 117
Caltowie SA 169 K3, 171 K13
Calulu Vic. 155 P4, 164 E13
Calvert Vic. 157 J3
Camballin WA 185 J9
Camberwell Vic. 47 C8
Cambewarra NSW 145 J11, 152 I4
Cambooya Qld 193 N9
Cambrai SA 166 D1, 169 M8
Cambridge Tas. 134 H4, 205 M8
Camdale Tas. 206 G5
Camden NSW 145 K8, 152 I1
Camena Tas. 206 G6
Cameron Corner Qld 148 A2, 202 H13
Camira Creek NSW 147 P4, 193 P13
Camooweal Qld 189 R11, 200 B2, 129
Camooweal Caves National Park Qld 189 R11, 200 B2
Camp Coorong SA 166 D4, 169 M12
Campania Tas. 134 H1, 205 M7
Campbell ACT 209 H6
Campbell Town Tas. 205 M2, 207 N12
Campbells Bridge Vic. 159 J11
Campbells Creek Vic. 159 Q12, 162 C10
Campbells Forest Vic. 159 Q9, 162 B7
Campbelltown NSW 145 K8
Campbelltown Vic. 157 P1, 159 P12, 162 A11
Camperdown Vic. 157 L8
Campwin Beach Qld 195 L5
Camurra NSW 146 H5
Canary Island Vic. 159 P4, 162 A3
Canary Island South Vic. 159 O5, 162 A3
Canbelego NSW 149 O10
Canberra ACT 41 G4, 144 G12, 152 E5, 209, 29, 39–41
Candelo NSW 152 G10, 165 P6
Cangai NSW 147 O5
Cania Gorge National Park Qld 193 L2
Caniambo Vic. 163 J6
Canimble NSW 144 E7
Cann River Vic. 152 E13, 165 N11
Canna WA 180 C4
Cannawigara SA 166 H6
Cannie Vic. 159 M3, 161 M13
Canning Stock Route WA 182 G9, 185 N12
Canning Vale WA 83 G13
Cannington WA 83 G10
Cannonvale Qld 195 K3
Cannum Vic. 158 G6
Canomodine NSW 144 F6
Canonba NSW 146 A12, 149 R9
Canowie SA 169 L4
Canowindra NSW 144 E7, 27
Canteen Creek NT 189 M13, 191 M2
Canunda National Park SA 166 G11, 76
Capalaba Qld 111 E9
Caparra NSW 147 N13
Cape Arid National Park WA 181 K10, 88
Cape Barren Island Tas. 204 B12, 207 Q2, 141
Cape Borda SA 168 F12, 78

Cape Bridgewater Vic. 156 C9, 49
Cape Byron NSW 147 R2, 25
Cape Clear Vic. 157 N5
Cape Conran Vic. 165 K13
Cape Crawford NT 189 N4
Cape du Couedic SA 168 F13, 78
Cape Gantheaume Conservation Park SA 168 H12
Cape Gantheaume Wilderness Protection Area SA 168 H13
Cape Hillsborough National Park Qld 195 K4, 124
Cape Jaffa SA 166 E9, 76
Cape Jervis SA 166 A4, 169 J11, 77
Cape Le Grand National Park WA 181 J11, 88
Cape Leveque WA 184 H6, 92
Cape Melville National Park Qld 198 H12
Cape Otway Vic. 157 N13, 49
Cape Palmerston National Park Qld 195 L6
Cape Paterson Vic. 154 G10
Cape Range National Park WA 179 B3, 91
Cape Schanck Vic. 61
Cape Tribulation Qld 197 M4, 125, 127
Cape Upstart National Park Qld 194 I1
Cape Vlamingh WA 178 B4, 84
Cape Woolamai Vic. 154 E9, 62
Cape York Peninsula Qld 196 G2, 198 C10, 2, 125, 126, 127
Capel WA 178 C8, 180 C10
Capella Qld 194 I10
Capels Crossing NSW 159 P2, 161 P13, 162 A1
Capertee NSW 144 I5
Capietha SA 168 A1, 177 Q11
Capricorn Region Qld 194 E11, 122–3
Capricorn Roadhouse WA 182 E6
Capricornia Cays National Park Qld 195 R11
Captain Billy Landing Qld 198 D5
Captains Flat NSW 144 H13, 152 F6
Carabost NSW 152 A6
Caragabal NSW 144 C8
Caralue SA 168 E4
Caramut Vic. 156 I6
Carapooee Vic. 159 M9
Carapook Vic. 156 D4
Carawa SA 177 P10
Carboor Vic. 163 N7, 164 A5
Carcoar NSW 144 G7
Carcuma SA 166 F4, 169 O12
Cardigan Village Vic. 157 O3
Cardinia Vic. 47 H13, 154 F6
Cardross Vic. 150 D7, 160 G4
Cardwell Qld 197 N10
Cargerie Vic. 157 P5
Cargo NSW 144 F6
Carinda NSW 146 A8
Carine WA 83 B4
Carisbrook Vic. 159 O11, 162 A10
Carlingford NSW 19 D6
Carlisle WA 83 G9
Carlisle River Vic. 157 M10
Carlsruhe Vic. 157 R2, 159 R13, 162 D11
Carlton Tas. 205 N8
Carlton Vic. 210 E3
Carmila Qld 195 L7
Carnamah WA 180 C5
Carnarvon WA 179 B8, 91
Carnarvon National Park Qld 192 D2, 194 I13, 122
Carnegie Homestead WA 182 I10
Caroda NSW 146 I7
Caroline SA 156 A6, 166 I12
Caroling WA 178 G4
Caroona NSW 146 I12
Carpa SA 168 F5
Carpendeit Vic. 157 L9
Carpenter Rocks SA 166 G12
Carrabin WA 180 F7
Carrajung Vic. 155 L8
Carrajung South Vic. 155 L8
Carranballac Vic. 157 L4
Carraragarmungee Vic. 163 N5
Carrathool NSW 151 M7
Carrick Tas. 207 L9, 137
Carrieton SA 171 K10
Carroll NSW 146 I10
Carroll Gap NSW 146 I10
Carron Vic. 159 J7
Carrow Brook NSW 145 L2
Carrowidgin NSW 152 D11, 165 L8
Cartmeticup WA 178 G8
Carwarp Vic. 150 D8, 160 G5
Cascade WA 180 I10
Cascade National Park NSW 147 O8
Cashmore Vic. 156 D9
Casino NSW 147 P3, 193 P12
Cassilis NSW 144 I1
Cassilis Vic. 152 A12, 164 F9
Castambul SA 68 E3

Casterton Vic. 156 C4, 50
Castle Forbes Bay Tas. 205 K10
Castle Hill NSW 19 C5
Castle Tower National Park Qld 195 P13
Castleburn Vic. 155 N3, 164 D11
Castlemaine Vic. 159 Q11, 162 C10, 54, 55
Casuarina NT 99 C5
Cataby Roadhouse WA 180 B6
Catamaran Tas. 205 J13
Cathcart NSW 152 F11, 165 O7
Cathedral Rock National Park NSW 147 N8
Catherine Hill Bay NSW 145 M5
Cathundral NSW 144 C1, 146 B13
Catumnal Vic. 159 N5
Caulfield Vic. 47 C8
Cavan NSW 144 F11, 152 D4
Caveat Vic. 162 I10
Cavendish Vic. 156 F4, 50
Caveside Tas. 206 I9
Cawongla NSW 147 P2, 193 Q12
Cecil Plains Qld 193 M9
Cedar Bay National Park Qld 197 M3
Cedar Party Creek NSW 147 N13
Ceduna SA 177 N9, 73
Cement Creek Vic. 154 G3
Central Castra Tas. 206 H7
Central Coast NSW 145 M7, 22
Central Tilba NSW 152 H9, 165 R3, 32
Ceratodus Qld 193 L3
Ceres NSW 144 D2
Ceres Vic. 157 Q8
Cervantes WA 180 B6
Cessnock NSW 145 M4, 20, 21
Chaelundi National Park NSW 147 N7
Chain of Ponds SA 68 F2, 69
Challambra Vic. 158 I6
Chambers Pillar Historical Reserve NT 191 J11, 105
Chambigne NSW 147 O6
Chandada SA 168 A1, 177 Q12
Chandler SA 175 N4
Chandlers Creek Vic. 152 E12, 165 M10
Channel Country Qld 200 G10
Chapple Vale Vic. 157 L11
Charam Vic. 158 D11
Charles Darwin National Park NT 99 C7
Charlestown NSW 145 M5
Charleville Qld 192 B6, 129
Charleyong NSW 144 I12, 152 G5
Charlotte Pass NSW 152 C9, 165 J4, 34
Charlton NSW 149 Q5
Charlton Vic. 159 M6
Charnwood ACT 41 D2
Charters Towers Qld 194 E2, 124
Chasm Creek Tas. 206 G6
Chatsbury NSW 144 I10, 152 G3
Chatswood NSW 19 G6
Chatsworth NSW 147 Q5
Chatsworth Vic. 156 I6
Cheepie Qld 203 Q7
Cheesemans Creek NSW 144 F5
Chelsea Vic. 47 D11
Cheltenham NSW 19 E5
Cherbourg Qld 193 N6
Chermside Qld 111 C7
Cheshunt Vic. 163 N9
Chesney Vale Vic. 163 L6
Chesterton Range National Park Qld 192 E6
Chetwynd Vic. 156 C2, 158 C13
Chewton Vic. 159 Q11, 162 C10
Chidlow WA 178 D3
Chifley ACT 41 E7
Chifley WA 181 K6
Childers Qld 193 O3, 123
Childers Vic. 154 I7
Chilla Well NT 190 E4
Chillagoe Qld 197 K7, 125, 126
Chillagoe-Mungana Caves National Park Qld 197 K7
Chillingham NSW 147 Q1
Chillingollah NSW 150 G13, 161 L10
Chilpanunda SA 177 Q11
Chiltern Vic. 151 P13, 163 O4, 164 A2, 59
Chiltern Box-Ironbark National Park Vic. 163 O4, 164 A2
Chiltern Valley Vic. 163 N4, 164 A2
Chinaman Wells SA 166 F10
Chinbingina SA 177 P10
Chinchilla Qld 193 K7, 116
Chinderah NSW 147 Q1, 193 Q11
Chinkapook Vic. 150 F10, 161 K10
Chipping Norton NSW 19 B9
Chisholm ACT 41 F8
Chittering WA 178 D2
Chorregon Qld 201 N9
Christmas Hills Tas. 206 C4
Chudleigh Tas. 206 I9
Church Point NSW 19 I2

Einasleigh Qld 197 J10
Ejanding WA 178 F1
El Arish Qld 197 N9
Elaine Vic. 157 P5
Elands NSW 147 N12
Elanora Heights NSW 19 I4
Elaroo Qld 195 J4
Elbow Hill SA 168 G5
Elcombe NSW 146 I6
Elderslie Tas. 205 K7
Eldon Tas. 205 M6
Eldorado Vic. 163 N5, 164 A3
Elimbah Qld 111 B3, 193 P8
Elizabeth SA 68 D1, 166 C1, 169 L8
Elizabeth Beach NSW 145 P2, 23
Elizabeth Town Tas. 207 J8
Ella Bay National Park Qld 197 N8
Ellalong NSW 145 L4
Ellam Vic. 150 D13, 158 F5
Ellenborough NSW 147 N12
Ellenbrook WA 83 I1
Ellendale Tas. 205 J7
Ellerslie Vic. 157 J8
Ellerston NSW 145 L1, 147 K13
Elliminyt Vic. 157 N9
Ellinbank Vic. 154 H7
Elliott NT 189 J6
Elliott Tas. 206 F6
Elliott Heads Qld 193 O2
Ellis Beach Qld 197 M6
Elliston SA 168 A5
Elmhurst Vic. 157 L1, 159 L12
Elmore Vic. 162 E6
Elong Elong NSW 144 F2
Elphinstone Vic. 159 R12, 162 C10
Elsey National Park NT 186 I11, 103
Elsinore NSW 149 L10
Elsmore NSW 147 K6
Eltham NSW 147 Q3
Elwomple SA 166 E3, 169 N10
Emerald Qld 194 I11, 122, 123
Emerald Vic. 47 H9, 154 F5, 57
Emerald Beach NSW 147 P7
Emerald Hill NSW 146 H10
Emerald Springs Wayside Inn NT 186 F8
Emita Tas. 204 B10, 141
Emmaville NSW 147 L5
Emmdale Roadhouse NSW 149 J10
Emmet Qld 203 P2
Empire Vale NSW 147 Q3, 193 Q12
Emu Vic. 159 M9
Emu Bay SA 168 H11, 78
Emu Creek Qld 193 N10
Emu Downs SA 169 M5
Emu Junction SA 175 J10
Emu Park Qld 195 O10, 123
Endeavour River National Park Qld 197 L2
Eneabba WA 180 B5
Enfield SA 68 D3
Enfield Vic. 157 O5
Engadine NSW 19 C13
Engawala NT 191 K6
Englefield Vic. 156 E2, 158 E13
English Town Tas. 207 N9
Enmore NSW 147 M9
Enngonia NSW 149 N2
Ensay Vic. 152 B12, 155 R1, 164 G10
Ensay North Vic. 155 R1, 164 G10
Ensay South Vic. 152 A13, 155 Q1, 164 G10
Entally House Tas. 137
Eppalock Vic. 159 R10, 162 D9
Epping Forest Tas. 205 M1, 207 M11
Epsom Vic. 159 R9, 162 C8
Erica Vic. 155 J5, 62, 63
Erigolia NSW 151 O6
Erikin WA 178 H3
Erith SA 169 K7
Erldunda NT 190 I11
Eromanga Qld 203 M7
Erriba Tas. 206 H8
Erringibba National Park Qld 193 J8
Errinundra Vic. 152 D12, 165 L10
Errinundra National Park Vic. 152 D12, 165 L10
Escotts Hole NSW 24
Esk Qld 193 O8
Eskdale Vic. 163 R6, 164 D4
Esmond Vic. 151 O13, 163 L4
Esperance WA 181 J10, 88
Essendon Vic. 47 B6
Eton Qld 195 K5
Ettamogah NSW 151 Q13, 163 P3, 164 C1
Ettrick NSW 147 P2, 193 P12
Euabalong NSW 151 P3
Euabalong West NSW 151 O3
Euchareena NSW 144 G4
Eucla WA 176 A8, 181 R7, 88
Eucla National Park WA 176 A8, 181 R8, 88

Eucumbene NSW 152 D8, 165 K2
Eudunda SA 169 M6
Eugowra NSW 144 E6
Eujinyn WA 178 I3
Eulo Qld 203 Q11, 129
Eumundi Qld 193 P6, 117
Eumungerie NSW 144 E1
Eungai Creek NSW 147 O10
Eungella NSW 147 P1
Eungella Qld 195 J5
Eungella National Park Qld 195 J4, 124
Eurack Vic. 157 O7
Euramo Qld 197 N9
Euratha NSW 151 P6
Eurelia SA 169 K1, 171 K11
Euri Qld 194 I2
Eurimbula National Park Qld 195 Q13, 122
Euroa Vic. 162 I8
Eurobin Vic. 163 P7, 164 B5
Eurobodalla NSW 152 G8, 165 R2
Eurobodalla National Park NSW 152 H8
Eurong Qld 193 Q4
Eurongilly NSW 144 C11, 152 A4
Euston NSW 150 F8, 161 J6
Eva Valley NT 186 H9
Evandale Tas. 207 M9, 137
Evans Head NSW 147 Q4, 193 Q13, 25
Evansford Vic. 157 N1, 159 N12
Everard Junction WA 183 L9
Eversley Vic. 157 L1, 159 L12
Everton Vic. 163 N6, 164 A4
Ewens Ponds SA 166 H13
Exeter Tas. 207 L7
Exford Vic. 157 R4
Exmouth WA 179 C3, 91
Expedition National Park Qld 192 H3
Exton Tas. 207 K9
Eyre Peninsula SA 168 C6, 73

Fairfield NSW 19 B8
Fairhaven Vic. 152 G13, 165 Q11
Fairhaven Vic. 157 P10
Fairholme NSW 144 B6, 151 R4
Fairley Vic. 159 O2, 161 O13, 162 A1
Fairview Vic. 159 M5
Fairy Dell Vic. 162 E6
Fairy Hill NSW 147 P3, 193 P12
Falls Creek NSW 145 K11, 152 I4
Falls Creek Vic. 163 R9, 164 D7, 58
Falmouth Tas. 207 Q9
Family Islands National Park Qld 197 O9
Faraday Vic. 159 Q11, 162 C10
Farleigh Qld 195 K5
Farnborough Qld 195 O10
Farnham NSW 144 G4
Farrell Flat SA 169 L5
Farrer NSW 41 F7
Fawkner Vic. 47 C5
Feilton Tas. 205 K8
Felton East Qld 193 N10
Fentonbury Tas. 205 J7
Fentons Creek Vic. 159 N8
Fern Tree Tas. 134 E6, 205 L9
Fernbank Vic. 155 O5, 164 E13
Ferndale NSW 151 P11
Ferndale WA 83 G11
Ferndene Tas. 206 H6
Fernihurst Vic. 159 O6, 162 A5
Fernlees Qld 194 I12
Ferntree Gully Vic. 47 G8
Fernvale Qld 193 P9
Fields Find WA 180 D4
Fiery Flat Vic. 159 O7, 162 A6
Fifield NSW 144 B4, 151 R2
Finch Hatton Qld 195 J5
Fine Flower Creek NSW 147 O5
Fingal NSW 147 Q1
Fingal Tas. 205 P1, 207 P10, 140
Finke NT 191 K10
Finke Gorge National Park NT 190 H9, 105
Finley NSW 151 M12, 162 I1
Finniss SA 68 F11, 166 C3, 169 L11
Fish Creek Vic. 154 I10
Fish Point Vic. 159 O1, 161 O11
Fisher ACT 41 E7
Fisher SA 176 G4
Fishery Falls Qld 197 N7
Fiskville Vic. 157 Q4
Fitzgerald Tas. 204 I7
Fitzgerald River National Park WA 180 G11
Fitzroy SA 211 D2
Fitzroy Crossing WA 185 M9, 93
Fitzroy Island Qld 197 N6, 119, 120
Fitzroy Island National Park Qld 197 N7, 120
Fitzroy River WA 185 M9, 93
Five Ways NSW 144 A2, 149 Q12
Flaggy Rock Qld 195 L7
Flamingo Beach Vic. 155 O7

Flaxton Qld 117
Fletcher Qld 147 L3, 193 N12
Fleurieu Peninsula SA 68 B12, 166 A4, 169 K12, 9, 77, 78
Flinders Vic. 154 D9
Flinders Chase National Park SA 168 F13, 78
Flinders Group National Park Qld 198 G11
Flinders Island Tas. 204 C9, 207 R1, 141
Flinders Ranges SA 171 K8, 3, 74
Flinders Ranges National Park SA 171 K7, 74
Flinton Qld 192 I10
Flintstone Tas. 205 J2, 207 K12
Flora River Nature Park NT 186 F10
Florida NSW 149 O10
Florieton SA 169 N5
Flowerdale Tas. 206 F5
Flowerdale Vic. 154 E1, 162 H12
Flowerpot Tas. 205 L10
Flowery Gully Tas. 207 K7
Flying Fish Point Qld 197 N8
Flynn Vic. 155 L7
Flynns Creek Vic. 155 K7
Foleyvale Aboriginal Community Qld 195 M11
Footscray Vic. 47 B7, 154 C4
Forbes NSW 144 D6
Fords Bridge NSW 149 M4
Fordwich NSW 145 L4
Forest Tas. 206 D4
Forest Den National Park Qld 194 C7, 201 Q7
Forest Hill NSW 144 B12, 151 R10, 152 A5
Forest Reefs NSW 144 G6
Forester Tas. 207 O6
Forestier Peninsula Tas. 205 O9
Forge Creek Vic. 155 P5
Forrest ACT 209 C12
Forrest Vic. 157 O10
Forrest WA 181 Q6
Forrest Beach Qld 197 O11
Forsayth Qld 196 I11
Forster SA 166 E1, 169 N8
Forster–Tuncurry NSW 144 P2, 145 P2, 23
Fortescue Roadhouse WA 179 F2
Forth Tas. 206 I7
Fortis Creek National Park NSW 147 O5
Fortitude Valley Qld 111 C8, 214 H1
Forty Mile Scrub National Park Qld 197 L9
Foster Vic. 155 J10, 62
Fosterville Vic. 159 R9, 162 D8
Four Mile Creek Tas. 207 Q10
Fowlers Bay SA 177 K9
Fox Ground NSW 145 K11
Fox Trap Roadhouse Qld 192 A7, 203 Q7
Framingham Vic. 157 J8
Framingham East Vic. 157 J8
Frampton NSW 144 C11, 152 B3
Frances SA 158 A9, 166 I8
Francistown Tas. 205 K11
Francois Peron National Park WA 179 B9, 91
Frank Hann National Park WA 180 H9
Frankford Tas. 207 K8
Frankland WA 178 F11, 180 E11
Frankland Islands National Park Qld 197 N7
Franklin Tas. 134 B9, 205 K10
Franklin–Gordon Wild Rivers National Park Tas. 204 F4, 206 F13, 13, 135
Franklin River Tas. 204 E6, 206 F13, 13, 135
Frankston Vic. 47 D13, 154 D6
Frankton SA 169 M7
Fraser Island Qld 193 Q3, 118
Frederickton NSW 147 O10
Freeburgh Vic. 163 Q8, 164 C6
Freeling SA 167 A3, 169 L7
Freemans Reach NSW 145 K7
Freemans Waterhole NSW 145 M5
Fregon SA 175 J3
Fremantle WA 83 A12, 178 C4, 180 C8, 5
French Island Vic. 154 E8, 61
French Island National Park Vic. 154 E8
Frenchs Forest NSW 19 G5
Frenchmans Cap Tas. 204 F4, 206 F13
Freshwater Creek Vic. 157 Q8
Freycinet National Park Tas. 205 Q4, 207 Q12
Freycinet Peninsula Tas. 205 Q5, 140
Frogmore NSW 144 F9, 152 D2
Fulham Vic. 155 M6
Fullerton NSW 144 H9, 152 F2
Furneaux Group Tas. 204 C11, 141
Furner SA 166 G10
Furracabad NSW 147 L6
Fyansford Vic. 157 Q7
Fyshwick ACT 41 H5

Gaffneys Creek Vic. 155 J2, 163 M13
Gagebrook Tas. 134 F2, 205 L7
Galah Vic. 160 G9
Galaquil Vic. 158 H4
Galaquil East Vic. 158 I4
Galga SA 166 F1, 169 O8

Galiwinku NT 187 M5
Gallangowan Qld 193 O6
Galong NSW 144 E10, 152 D3
Galston NSW 19 D3, 145 L7
Gama Vic. 158 I1, 160 I12
Gammon Ranges National Park SA 171 L4, 74
Ganmain NSW 144 A11, 151 Q9
Gannawarra Vic. 159 Q3, 161 Q13, 162 B2
Gapsted Vic. 163 O7, 164 A4
Gapuwiyak NT 187 N5
Garah NSW 146 G4, 192 I13
Garawa NT 187 O13, 189 O3
Garden Island Creek Tas. 134 D11, 205 K11
Gardens of Stone National Park NSW 144 I5
Gardners Bay Tas. 205 K10
Garema NSW 144 D7
Garfield Vic. 154 G6
Garibaldi Vic. 157 O4
Garigal National Park NSW 19 H4
Garland NSW 144 F7
Garra NSW 144 F5
Garrawilla NSW 146 G11
Garrthalala NT 187 O6
Garvoc Vic. 157 J9
Gary Junction WA 183 M4
Gascoyne Junction WA 179 D8
Gatton Qld 193 O9, 112
Gatum Vic. 156 F3
Gawler SA 169 L8, 70
Gawler Tas. 206 H6
Gawler Ranges National Park SA 168 C1, 170 B11
Gayndah Qld 193 N4, 123
Gazette Vic. 156 G6
Geelong Vic. 154 A6, 157 R7, 48
Geeralying WA 178 F7
Geeveston Tas. 134 A10, 205 K10
Geikie Gorge National Park WA 185 M9, 93
Gelantipy Vic. 152 C12, 164 I9
Gellibrand Vic. 157 N10
Gelliondale Vic. 155 L10
Gembrook Vic. 154 F5, 57
Gemtree NT 191 K7
Genoa Vic. 152 F13, 165 P11
Geographe Bay WA 91
George Camp NT 186 G10
George Town Tas. 207 K6
Georges River National Park NSW 19 C11
Georges Creek Vic. 163 R4, 164 D2
Georges Plains NSW 144 H6
Georgetown Qld 196 I10
Georgetown SA 169 K4
Georgica NSW 147 P2, 193 Q12
Geraldton WA 180 A3, 91
Gerang Gerung Vic. 158 F7
Gerangamete Vic. 157 O10
Geranium SA 166 G3, 169 P11
Geranium Plain SA 169 M6
Gerogery NSW 151 Q12, 163 P2
Gerogery West NSW 151 Q13, 163 P2
Gerringong NSW 145 K11
Geurie NSW 144 F3
Gibraltar Range National Park NSW 147 N5
Gibson WA 181 J10
Gibson Desert WA 183 N7
Gidgegannup WA 178 D3
Gidginbung NSW 144 B9, 151 R7, 152 A2
Giffard Vic. 155 N8
Gilbert River Qld 196 G10
Gilberton SA 211 G3
Giles Corner SA 169 L7
Gilgai NSW 147 K6
Gilgandra NSW 146 D13
Gilgooma NSW 146 D9
Gilgunnia NSW 149 N13, 151 N1
Gillenbah NSW 151 P9
Gilliat Qld 200 I4
Gillieston Vic. 162 G5
Gillingarra WA 180 C6
Gin Gin NSW 144 D1, 146 C13
Gin Gin Qld 193 N2, 122
Gindie Qld 194 I11
Gingin WA 178 C2, 180 C7, 90
Ginquam Vic. 160 G5
Gippsland Vic. 60, 62–3
Gippsland Lakes Vic. 155 Q5, 59, 60
Gipsy Point Vic. 152 G13, 165 P11
Girgarre Vic. 162 F6
Girilambone NSW 149 Q9
Girral NSW 144 A7, 151 Q5
Girraween National Park Qld 147 M3, 193 N12, 116
Girrawheen WA 83 D3
Giru Qld 194 G1, 197 Q13
Gisborne Vic. 154 B2, 162 E13
Gladfield Vic. 162 A4

Explore Australia Publishing Pty Ltd
12 Claremont Street
South Yarra, Victoria 3141, Australia

This edition published by Explore Australia
Publishing Pty Ltd, 2003

10 9 8 7 6 5 4 3 2 1

Printed in China by Everbest Printing Co. Ltd

*Publisher's Note:* Every effort has been made to ensure that the information in this book is accurate at the time of going to press. The publisher welcomes information and suggestions for correction or improvement. Email: explore@hardiegrant.com.au

*Disclaimers:* The publisher cannot accept responsibility for any errors or omissions. The representation on the maps of any road or track is not necessarily evidence of public right of way.

www.hardiegrant.com.au

## Acknowledgements

**Desktop publishing**
P.A.G.E Pty Ltd
J&M Typesetting

**Text**
This edition was produced with assistance from visitor information centres and local government offices around Australia. Full acknowledgements appear in *Explore Australia* (21st edition) published by Penguin Books Australia Ltd in 2002.

**Maps**
The publisher acknowledges the assistance to revise and check the maps from the various regional tourism associations, the Geographical Names Board and local government offices.

**Photography**
**Front cover:**
Green Island, Queensland (Auscape International/Jean-Paul Ferrero)
Twelve Apostles, Victoria (John Meier)
Wineglass Bay, Tasmania (Tourism Tasmania/Joe Shemesh)
Ballooning over Yarra Valley, Victoria (Andrew Chapman; hot air balloon courtesy of Global Ballooning)
Uluru, Northern Territory (John Meier)
Sydney Opera House, New South Wales (Explore Australia Publishing/Nick Rains)

**Back cover:**
The road to Mount Wilson, New South Wales (Australian Scenics)

**Title page:**
Beach at Palm Cove, Queensland (John Meier)

**Contents page:**
Rainbow Valley, Northern Territory (Jeff Drewitz)

**Capital city features:**
**Sydney** Stock Photos (David Scaletti); Stock Photos (Lance Nelson); **Canberra** Explore Australia Publishing (J. P. & E. S. Baker); **Melbourne** Stock Photos (Roger du Buisson); Stock Photos (Roger du Buisson); **Adelaide** Explore Australia Publishing (J. P. & E. S. Baker); **Perth** Explore Australia Publishing (Nick Rains); **Darwin** Auscape (Tim Acker); **Brisbane** Tourism Queensland; John Meier; **Hobart** Geoff Murray

**Other images:**
ANT Photo Library (Kelvin Aitken, Jutta Hosel, C. & S. Pollitt, Klaus Uhlenhut); Auscape International (John Cancalosi, Jean-Paul Ferrero, Jeff & Sandra Foote, Brett Gregory, Jean-Marc La Roque, David Parer & Elizabeth Parer-Cooke, Glenn Tempest); Australian National Botanic Gardens (M. Crisp, Murray Fagg, D. Greig, R. Hotchkiss); Australian Picture Library (Robin Bickford, Roy Bisson, Jon Carnemolla, Craig Lamotte, Lightstorm, Ian Lloyd, Leo Meier, Nick Rains, Redferns, Steve Vidler, Gerry Whitmont); J. P. & E. S. Baker; Explore Australia Publishing (J. P. & E. S. Baker, Ricky Eaves, Chris Groenhout, Graeme & Margaret Herald, John Krutop, Gary Lewis, Heidi Marfurt, Don Skirrow, Ken Stepnell, John & Jan Tait); Andrew Gregory; Murray Jones; Alex Julius; Lochman Transparencies (Bill Belson, Jiri Lochman, Peter & Margy Nicholas, Col Roberts, Dennis Sarson, Alex Steffe, Len Stewart, Geoff Taylor); John McLeish; McWilliams Wines; Jonathan Marks; Ted Mead; John Meier; Geoff Murray; Queensland Museum (Museum of Tropical North Queensland); Nick Rains; Christo Reid; Don Skirrow; Robin Smith; South Australian Tourism Commission; Sovereign Hill, Ballarat; Sport The Library; Stock Photos (Kelvin Aitken, Bill Bachman, Mike Brahman, Diana Calder, Bette Devine, Excitations, Ted Grambeau, Mark Newton, Otto Rogge, David Simmonds, Stocktake, James Walshe); Steve Strike; Tandanya; Tourism New South Wales; Tourism Queensland; Tourism Queensland (Susan Wright); Tourism Tasmania (Geoff Apostolidis, Richard Bennett, Dennis Harding, Ray Joyce, Steve Lovegrove, Geoff Murray, Gary Myros, Nick Osborne, Joe Shemesh, Peter Whyte); Tourism Victoria; Trezise Bush Guide Service

# USEFUL INFORMATION

## TOURIST BUREAUS

**New South Wales**
New South Wales Visitor Information
Line
13 20 77
www.visitnsw.com.au

Sydney Visitor Centre The Rocks
106 George St
The Rocks
(02) 9255 1788
www.sydneyvisitorcentre.com

**Canberra**
Canberra Visitors Centre
330 Northbourne Ave
Dickson
(02) 6205 0044
www.canberratourism.com.au

**Victoria**
Victorian Tourism Information Service
13 28 42
www.visitvictoria.com

Melbourne Visitor Information Centre
Melbourne Town Hall
Cnr Swanston and Little Collins sts
Melbourne
(03) 9658 9658
www.melbourne.vic.gov.au

**South Australia**
South Australian Visitor and Travel Centre
1 King William St
Adelaide
(08) 8303 2033, 1300 655 276
www.visit.adelaide.on.net
www.tourism.sa.gov.au

**Western Australia**
Western Australian Visitors Centre
Cnr Forrest Pl. and Wellington St
Perth
(08) 9483 1111, 1300 361 351
www.perthwa.com
www.westernaustralia.net

**Northern Territory**
Tourism Top End
Cnr Mitchell and Knuckey sts
Darwin
(08) 8936 2499
www.ntholidays.com

Central Australian Tourism Industry
Association
60 Gregory Tce
Alice Springs
(08) 8952 5800
www.centralaustraliantourism.com

**Queensland**
Brisbane Visitor Information Centre
Queen Street Mall
Brisbane
(07) 3006 6290
www.brisbanetourism.com.au
www.queensland-holidays.com.au

**Tasmania**
Tasmanian Travel Information Centre
Cnr Elizabeth and Davey sts
Hobart
(03) 6230 8233
www.discovertasmania.com.au

## ABORIGINAL LAND AUTHORITIES
Aboriginal land is privately owned. In some parts of Australia, Commonwealth and State laws do not permit people to enter Aboriginal land unless they have been issued with a permit. The relevant land councils, to whom applications for permits and any inquiries must be directed, are:

**Northern Territory**
Central Lands Council
31–33 Stuart Hwy
Alice Springs 0871
(08) 8951 6211
www.clc.org.au

Northern Lands Council
9 Rowlings St
Casuarina 0810
(08) 8920 5100
www.nlc.org.au

Tiwi Land Council
(Melville and Bathurst islands)
Unit 5, 3 Bishop St
Stuart Park 0820
(08) 8981 4898

Ngaanyatjarra Council
(including Great Central Road)
Shop 6, 58 Head St
Alice Springs 0871
(08) 8950 1711

**Queensland**
Queensland Aboriginal Coordination
Council
17 Aclin St
(PO Box 6512)
Cairns 4870
(07) 4031 2623

**South Australia**
Anangu Pitjantjatjara Yankunytjatjara
Land Council
PMB 227 Umuwa
via Alice Springs NT 0872
(08) 8954 8111

**Western Australia**
197 St Georges Tce
Aboriginal Lands Trust Level 1,
(PO Box 7770 Cloister Square) Perth 6850
(08) 9235 8000
www.dia.wa.gov.au

## TIME ZONES
Australia has four time zones:

- Eastern Standard Time (EST), in Queensland, Australian Capital Territory, New South Wales, Victoria and Tasmania. (Note: Broken Hill in central western New South Wales operates on CST, half an hour behind the rest of New South Wales.)

- Central Standard Time (CST is half an hour behind EST), in South Australia and Northern Territory.

- Western Standard Time (WST is two hours behind EST), in Western Australia.

- Central Western Time (CWT is 45 minutes ahead of WST), a local time zone operating from 3 km east of Caiguna in Western Australia to the South Australian border.

Daylight saving is adopted by some States in summer. In New South Wales, Victoria, Tasmania, Australian Capital Territory and South Australia, clocks are put forward 1 hour at the beginning of summer (the last Sunday in October, except in Tasmania, where the clocks are adjusted on the first Sunday in October). Northern Territory, Western Australia and Queensland do not have daylight saving.

**EMERGENCY**     **POLICE, AMBULANCE & FIRE BRIGADE, DIAL 000**

# Accident Action – Feel Confident with St John First Aid

It is reassuring to know that you have the simple skills to preserve life if, at any moment, you are confronted with an emergency.

## Priorities at an Accident Site

In dealing with the casualties of an accident, the St John DRABC Action Plan remains the first priority. However, an accident brings in other factors that have to be considered. The following guidelines will help:

### Hazards:

- Make sure everyone at accident site is protected, by safely parking your car and putting hazard lights on
- Light up a night accident scene with headlights
- Assess scene for other dangers and remove if possible
- Move casualty from danger if this is more appropriate (e.g. if there is a fire).

### Assessment:

Make a rapid assessment of:
- How many casualties
- Severity of injuries
- Any dangerous circumstances to report
- Whether anyone is trapped

Ensure all occupants of cars are accounted for.

### Help:

- Call 000 for an ambulance and police
- Consider need to call other services (e.g. fire brigade, electricity authority).

**Follow the remainder of the St John DRABC Action Plan to manage casualties.**

## St John DRABC Action Plan

This Action Plan is a vital aid to the first aider in assessing whether the casualty has any life-threatening conditions and if any immediate first aid is necessary.

**D - check for Danger**
- to you
- to others
- to casualty

**R - check Response**
- is casualty conscious?
- is casualty unconscious? If not responsive, turn casualty into the recovery position and **ring 000 for an ambulance.**

**A - check Airway**
- is airway clear of objects?
- is airway open?

**B - check for Breathing**
- is chest rising and falling?
- can you hear casualty's breathing?
- can you feel the breath on your cheek?

**C - check for signs of Circulation**
- can you see any movement including swallowing or breathing?
- can you see any obvious signs of life?
- can you feel a pulse?

**In any life-threatening situation, ring 000 for an ambulance. If possible, ask someone to do this for you so that you can stay with the casualty.**

# Learn St John First Aid